WRECKCHASING 101

A Guide To Finding

Aircraft Crash Sites

Nicholas A. Veronico

Ed Davies

A. Kevin Grantham

Robert A. Kropp

Enrico Massagli

Donald B. McComb

Michael B. McComb

Thomas Wm. McGarry

Walt Wentz

STANCE & SPEED

Dedicated to the pilots, air crews, and the families whose loved ones perished.
May their crash sites be found so that their sacrifices may be remembered.

To the memory of Thomas Wm. McGarry, coauthor and a great friend.

Published by Stance & Speed

www.stanceandspeed.com

This book is an update of two previously published books: *Wreckchasing: A Guide to Finding Aircraft Crash Sites* (1993, 1995, and 1997—Pacific Aero Press—www.pacaeropress.com); and *Wreckchasing 2: Commercial Aircraft Crashes & Crash Sites* (World Transport Press, 1996).

ISBN-10 0-9830-6064-9
ISBN-13 978-0-9830-6064-2

On the Front Cover:
Upper right: The tail of F2H-4 Banshee sits in the Saratoga Gap where it crashed on Feb. 22, 1959. Notice that the tail has been marked with a large 'X' to show that this aircraft has been located.
(Nicholas A. Veronico)

Main Photo: An unidentified F4U Corsair sits in an East Coast swamp near the end of World War II.
(Vought)

On the Back Cover:
At the site of actress Carole Lombard's DC-3 crash, a pair of gold/bronze pilot's wings were found. The wings show the air carrier's name and had the number "79" on the reverse. (David L. McCurry)

This Grumman F3F was recovered from the bottom of the Pacific Ocean near San Diego. As the F3F was lowered to the dock to be righted so it could sit on its landing gear, Navy personnel reached into the cockpit and removed the pencil used by the aircraft's pilot, then-First Lt. Robert E. Galer. Compare the cockpit photo of the F3F shortly after recovery to the shot of the restored aircraft's instrument panel.
(U.S. Navy and Nicholas A. Veronico)

Following the crash of N88942 in Union City, Calif., Transocean Air Lines sent a number of workers to help with the accident investigation and clean-up. From left to right: Transocean employees William "Bill" Dell, Wendell Davies, Mike Lewis, and an unidentified worker. (William Dell Collection)

Compass image by Lee Klancher

CONTENTS

Acknowledgments

This guide to finding aircraft wrecks came about more as a hobby than anything else. The lasting friendships generated by this common interest, however, have become irreplaceable.

A number of people are owed a debt of gratitude for their assistance in providing access to wreck sites and research materials. Thanks to: Kelly and Ian Abbott; Violet Andrada; Pat and Keith Armes; Brian Baum; Michael A. Bodisco, the Bureau of Alcohol, Tobacco and Firearms; John M. Campbell; Vickie and Ciro Buonocore of *In Flight USA*; Patrick Congdon—Midpeninsula Regional Open Space District; Veralyn Davids; William and Sally Dell; Pauline and Bruce Drum; retired Maj. John Elliott, USMC, Aviation Branch, U.S. Naval Historical Center, Washington, D.C.; Gary Fong, *San Francisco Chronicle*; Sally Gersbach; Betty and Wayne McPherson Gomes; Don Gridley; Stephen L. Griffin; Clint Groves; Todd Hackbarth; John Harjo; Bob Hofford; Earl Holmquist; Bill Hough; Nancy and Keith Hurt; Clay Jansson; Jerry Knight; Chris Kopel; Gary Larkins; Tillie and William T. Larkins; J.R. Lyons; Vickie and David McCurry; Michael H. Marlow; Kris Martinsen; Roy D. Meyers; Ken Miller; Murray Moore; Tom Northrop; Arthur Pearcy; Milo Peltzer; Taigh Ramey; Eleanor Rose; Jim Rowan; Dr. Lee Schaller; Christopher Schiess; John Shackleton and Anne McMillin, Public Affairs

Office, NAS Moffett Field; Greg Stone and Harrison Rued and many of the members of the Redwood Empire Aviation Historical Society; Ron Strong; Brian Sullivan; Bob Swanson; Arue Szura; Scott Thompson; Sig Unander; Heidi Van Zant; Betty S. Veronico; Pamela Veronico; Karen and Armand Veronico; Tony Veronico; John Wegg, *Airways* Magazine; John T. Wible; Jay Wisler; and Linda Zupcic.

The BCPA chapter started with a conversation between Dick Krug, Joel Harris and six photographic slides. Research materials and guidance were provided by Reg McGovern, Ray Brooks, John Escobar of the Midpeninsula Regional Open Space District, Mitch Postel of the San Mateo County Historical Society, Ken Fisher, Bob Swanson, and Roy Meyers. Since our visit, Christopher O'Donnell has worked tirelessly to obtain permission to place an interpretive plaque to the passengers and crew of *Resolution*. He succeeded in 2009. Nice work! The *Philippine Clipper* article benefitted from the knowledge of Bo Hiatt, Gary Urdahl, Elgin Long, Donna and Larry Struck, Gordon Werne, and Lila Lee of the Mendocino County Historical Society.

A note of appreciation for their assistance to: the NTSB; the National Technical Information Service; General Microfilm; the FAA; Bryce Canyon National Park; USGS; Bettman Archives; Donald Simonis and the Bureau of Land Management; George R. Perkins and the U.S. Forest Service; retired TWA captain Arthur E. Kelly; Accident Investigation Branch, Farnborough, England; Mr. R.A.R. Wilson of the Historical Aviation Service; retired 707 captains Peter J. Howard, Peter J. McKeown, and Eric Pritchard; Dick Wallin; Jon Proctor; Craig Fuller; Robb Hill; Dr. Dana X. Kerola; Jeff S. Johnson; JD Scroggins; Doug Scroggins; Scott Featherstone; William Walldock and Embry Riddle Aeronautical University; Harvey Gardner of Page Steel; James Thompson; Robert J. Serling; G. Pat Macha; Terry Geary of Wreckfinders; and Robert Brackett.

Nicholas A. Veronico
Ed Davies
A. Kevin Grantham
Robert A. Kropp
Enrico Massagli
Donald B. McComb
Michael B. McComb
Thomas Wm. McGarry
Walt Wentz

Preface

Aviation holds a certain intrigue in people's minds. Everyone has heard the stories of airplane wrecks. They are like the tales of sunken ships. Wreckchasing provides the thrill of discovery mixed with the romance of flight.

This book is the tool the authors never had. Trial and error, dead ends, and hours of picking other peoples' brains led us to the wrecks described within these pages. Of course, there is nothing better than stepping out of your car and walking 50 feet to an aircraft wreck, but for most of them, that is not the case.

The authors have confined their searches primarily to military aircraft and airliners that crashed prior to 1971. In our experience, almost all civilian aircraft wrecks have been removed, either by their owners or their insurance companies. Military aircraft that crashed in the 1940s and 1950s went down in areas that were inaccessible at the time.

With urban expansion and the logging of our forests, roads now crisscross these once remote areas. But, unless one is specifically looking for a crash site, anyone traveling down these roads would not even see wreckage of a plane lurking nearby.

In almost all military wrecks from the 1940s, the Army Air Forces or the Navy visited the site, removed the remains of the crew, and recovered or destroyed the bombsights, avionics, and radio gear. Rarely was the armament removed or the site cleared of wreckage. Thus the motivation and interest in searching for military aircraft wrecks, as there is a much better chance of finding aircraft remnants at the crash site.

Today, airliners are the most majestic birds in the sky. When one crashes, it is a tragedy. Despite the loss of life, many early airliner accidents led to positive changes in our air traffic control system and improved airliner designs.

Locating a crash site can be a challenging and moving experience. The sight of a former airliner broken into hundreds of small pieces can be overwhelming. Crash sites are extremely fascinating and one can spend hours exploring and mapping a location.

Crashes profiled in this book range from controlled flight into terrain, to mid-air collisions, to airliners that have been forced out of the sky by mother nature. All airliner crashes are not catastrophes, as evidenced by *The DC-3 That Crashed And Flew Again* (see page 105) and Appendix IV, *DC-3 Crashes In The United States*. It is hoped that this listing of DC-3 incidents will save wreckchasers from working long and hard at researching a crash, only to be disappointed at the outcome. The listing of piston, turbo-prop, and jet crashes has been narrowed down to sites where wreckage may still remain. Also included are aircraft that have crashed into bodies of water.

In the list of aircraft wrecks at the back of the book, some are given with the longitude and latitude. Note that these numbers are a starting point, somewhat general in nature, but they are the known crash points. The reader must undertake further research, as outlined in Part I, to find an exact location.

The authors have also included a number of stories of aircraft wrecks that readers of this book can locate easily. We suggest that you consider using one of these sites as a starting point for your first search. Also included are stories of aircraft recovered by the military and by professional aircraft salvage companies. Many aircraft restorers use components from these wrecks for patterns to replace parts too worn or unavailable from any other source.

Follow the steps presented, ask questions, and complete your research. Use common sense and be prepared for the hike (wreckchasing an aircraft crash site is truly 90 percent research and 10 percent hiking). An interesting adventure in an often-overlooked facet of aviation awaits.

Part I:

Introduction to Wreckchasing

Locating Wrecks

Since the dawn of time, man has envied the bird. Even before the Wright brothers took wing at Kitty Hawk in 1903, humans have been obsessed with flight. The airplane was first a curiosity, only for the brave; then a military weapon; later a pleasure craft; and most recently, a way to shrink the Earth. Air travel has brought Americans to within four hours flying time of Europe, and only a day's flying time to Australia or the Great Pyramids of Egypt.

However, as the old adage says: What goes up must come down. Aircraft fly without incident more than 99.9 percent of the time. It is that .01 percent that intrigues everyone. When an airplane crashes, it is headline news, and television reporters love aircraft crashes. A non-fatal crash of a single-engine Piper or Cessna will be shown on every news channel promotion during the evening in an attempt to get you to watch that station's late-night newscast. Some crashes have garnered almost as much airtime as the sports report.

For the wreckchasing enthusiast, the older the wreck, the better the chances of its remaining where it crashed. With the exception of general aviation airplanes, aircraft wrecks prior to 1960 are usually right where they landed.

This TBF is a graphic display of just how fine the line between life and death is. This Avenger missed a Hawaiian mountaintop by only 50 feet. (Gary Larkins)

Military Aircraft Wreckchasing

What is the first step to finding a military aircraft crash site? There are two ways to begin your search. One way is to find someone who has been involved, either as an eyewitness—an on-scene police officer or firefighter, a volunteer aiding in the rescue effort, or just a local who ventured to the site within months after the crash occurred. If you do not know any of these people, how do you find them? By doing your homework (see below).

The second way is to obtain a "crash locator" list. Almost 500 known aircraft wrecks are listed in Appendix I (see page 261), which contains wreck site coordinates combined from two such lists. Of course, many aircraft out there are not on the list, but this is a good starting point if you have not met someone who has first-hand knowledge of an aircraft crash site.

Wreck locator lists usually provide an aircraft type, location by longitude and latitude and/or the nearest topographical landmark, date of accident, and any remarks such as aircraft condition and whether it is marked (typically with a large orange "X"). These "exact locations" are provided for aerial search teams looking for recently lost aircraft. If wreckage is spotted, it can be checked against known wrecks so that valuable search team efforts are not wasted hiking to a 40-year-old, previously recorded site.

Doing Your Homework

Even if you have been told the "exact location" of a wreck or know an eyewitness, head to a public or college/university library to begin your search. If you do not have an aircraft crash you are already researching, decide on what era you want to cover. The period from the start of World War II through the end of the Korean War, 1942 to 1953, will be the most fruitful.

Begin with a local newspaper published in the area of a crash. Back copies will be available in a bound format, on microfilm, and today many newspaper archives are available on the Internet. Microfilm is best as you can quickly scan each day and then move on; plus, at most libraries, for a small fee, you can get a hard copy of any particular day. Note that if an aircraft crashed on the other side of the country and was carrying any hometown crew, it will be reported in the local paper. If you are looking for a wreck from the wreck locator and know the date, your newspaper search will be brief, but the information invaluable.

The newspaper will give you a number of key bits of information: the date of the accident (very important for obtaining official reports and records); the type of aircraft; who was involved—those souls on the airplane; and, most importantly for your search, the names of the local people and safety agencies who participated in the rescue or the crash investigation, as well as the condition of the wreck. Be sure to scan the following two weeks or so to find out if the wreckage was removed.

Most of all, the newspaper reports will often describe, in understandable terms, where the wreckage is located. Directions from the newspaper usually read, "The wreckage of the P-38 is one-quarter mile southeast of the Vista Point of Redwood Road in the trees bordering the Johnson Ranch … ," while the location of aircraft wreckage from an official report is, "crash occurred at 39°04'N latitude, 123°17'W longitude." This area could encompass up to five square miles, thus the importance of finding an account of the crash in the newspaper.

Five Killed in Crash of Bomber Near San Mateo

A four-motored army bomber crashed last night at Native Son's Park, on the King Mountain road, San Mateo county, carrying to death its five occupants.

Hamilton Field public relations officers said late last night the plane was on a combat training mission from Boise, Idaho, to Oakland.

The plane crashed in a heavy drizzle and burst into flames.

The bodies were recovered by sheriff's deputies. Names of the dead were withheld pending notification of next of kin.

The plane earlier had been reported missing. It had not issued a report since leaving its clearance post not far from its California destination, a Fourth Air Force public relations officer said.

One of the many tragic wartime aircraft crashes that appeared in the San Francisco Chronicle *on December 25, 1943. This tidbit of information is the beginning of a wreckchase. (Ed Davies Collection)*

Interviewing the Participants

Once you have learned the identity of the aircraft you are searching for and the names of those who participated in the crash's original investigation, you are ready to move forward. Taking the names reported in the paper, contact the newspaper to see if the reporter who wrote the story or the photographer are still in the area. The reporter will know the exact location and may have insights and details of the aftermath of the crash—some of which may not have made it into print.

The newspaper may have a photo archive or library that holds the negatives from the crash, or the photographer may have them. The reporter, photographer, newspaper archivist, and librarian are excellent people to interview.

After the reporter and photographer, start with the phone book or an Internet people search. You will be amazed at how many "old-timers" are still around. Most of them have excellent memories, and the sight and story of a plane crash are not likely to be forgotten. Also, many kids were taken to crash sites, so look for the eyewitness' next-of-kin.

While researching the crash of a British Commonwealth Pacific Airlines Douglas DC-6 on October 29, 1953, which killed 19, we found

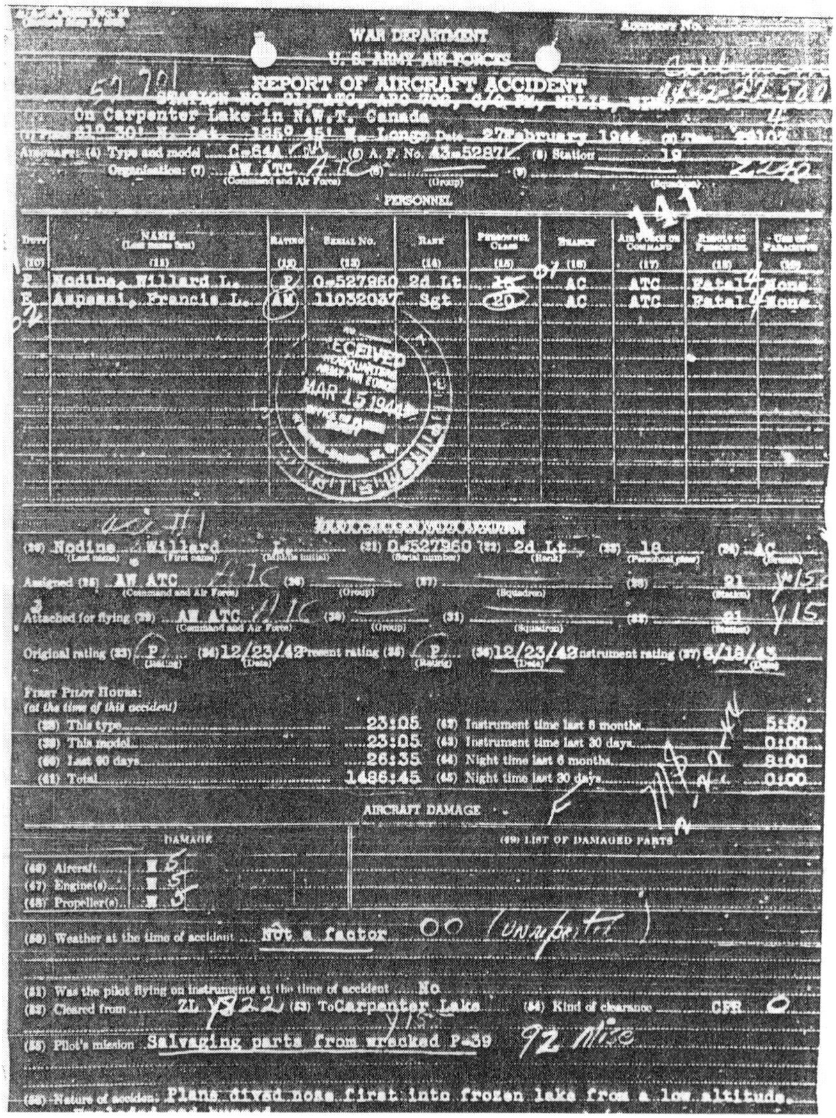

WAR DEPARTMENT
U. S. ARMY AIR FORCES
REPORT OF AIRCRAFT ACCIDENT
On Carpenter Lake in N.W.T. Canada
Date 27 February 1944
Aircraft: Type and model C-64A; A. F. No. 43-52871; Station 19
Organization: AW ATC

PERSONNEL

Duty	Name	Rating	Serial No.	Rank	Personnel Class	Branch	Air Force or Command	Result to Personnel	Use of Parachute
P	Nodine, Willard L.	P	O-527960	2d Lt		AC	ATC	Fatal	None
E	Ampssai, Francis L.	AM	11032037	Sgt	20	AC	ATC	Fatal	None

RECEIVED MAR 15 1944

Nodine Willard L. O-527960 2d Lt 18 AC
Assigned AW ATC
Attached for flying AW ATC
Original rating P 12/23/42 Present rating P 12/23/42 Instrument rating 6/18/43

First Pilot Hours: (at the time of this accident)
This type 23:05 — Instrument time last 6 months 5:50
This model 23:05 — Instrument time last 30 days 0:00
Last 90 days 26:35 — Night time last 6 months 8:00
Total 1486:45 — Night time last 30 days 0:00

AIRCRAFT DAMAGE
Aircraft; Engine(s); Propeller(s)

Weather at the time of accident Not a factor
Was the pilot flying on instruments at the time of accident No
Cleared from ZL To Carpenter Lake — Kind of clearance CFR
Pilot's mission Salvaging parts from wrecked P-39
Nature of accident: Plane dived nose first into frozen lake from a low altitude.

Typical Army Air Forces crash report. Page one gives the rough statistics, such as aircraft type, crew names, weather and flight plan.

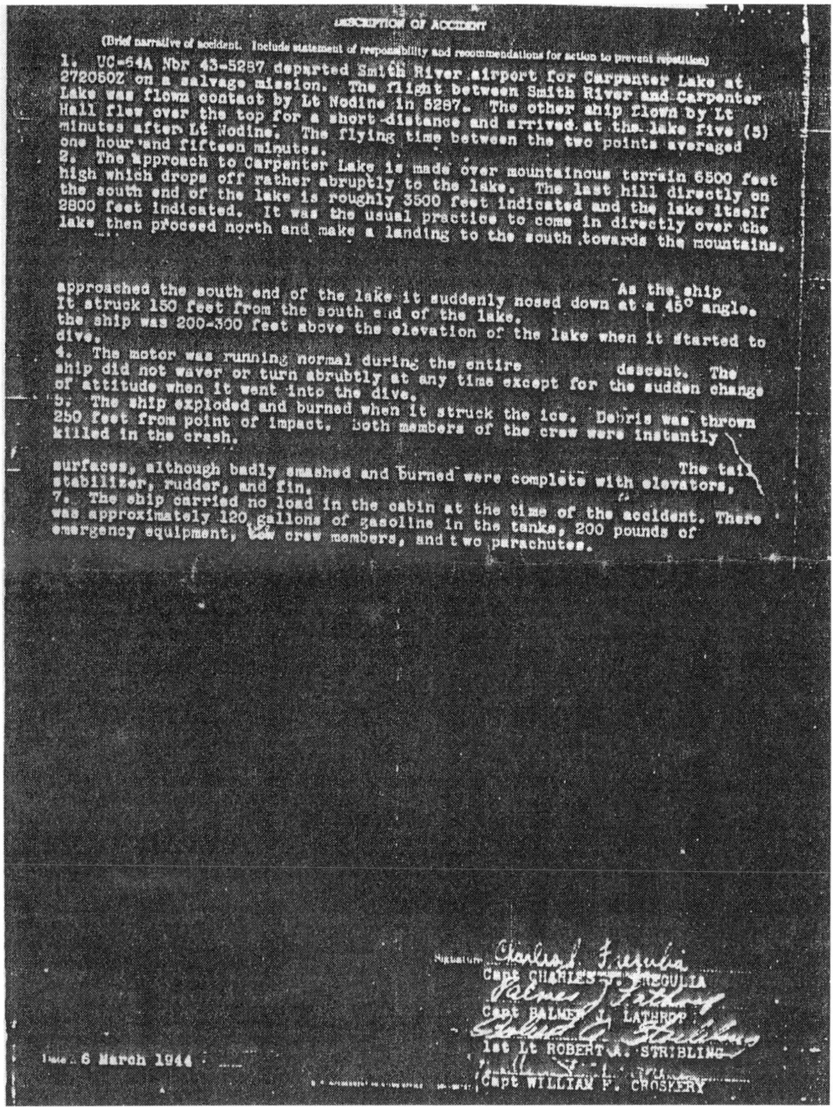
DESCRIPTION OF ACCIDENT

(Brief narrative of accident. Include statement of responsibility and recommendations for action to prevent repetition)

1. UC-64A Nbr 43-5287 departed Smith River airport for Carpenter Lake at 272050Z on a salvage mission. The flight between Smith River and Carpenter Lake was flown contact by Lt Nodine in 5287. The other ship flown by Lt Hall flew over the top for a short distance and arrived at the lake five (5) minutes after Lt Nodine. The flying time between the two points averaged one hour and fifteen minutes.

2. The approach to Carpenter Lake is made over mountainous terrain 6500 feet high which drops off rather abruptly to the lake. The last hill directly on the south end of the lake is roughly 3500 feet indicated and the lake itself 2800 feet indicated. It was the usual practice to come in directly over the lake then proceed north and make a landing to the south towards the mountains.

As the ship approached the south end of the lake it suddenly nosed down at a 45° angle. It struck 150 feet from the south end of the lake. the ship was 200-300 feet above the elevation of the lake when it started to dive.

4. The motor was running normal during the entire descent. The ship did not waver or turn abrubtly at any time except for the sudden change of attitude when it went into the dive.

5. The ship exploded and burned when it struck the ice. Debris was thrown 250 feet from point of impact. Both members of the crew were instantly killed in the crash.

The tail surfaces, although badly smashed and burned were complete with elevators, stabilizer, rudder, and fin.

7. The ship carried no load in the cabin at the time of the accident. There was approximately 120 gallons of gasoline in the tanks, 200 pounds of emergency equipment, crew members, and two parachutes.

Date 6 March 1944

Signature Capt CHARLES [illegible] FREGULIA
Capt BALMER J. LATHROP
1st Lt ROBERT A. STRIBLING
Capt WILLIAM F. CROSKERY

Page two is a narrative of the crash signed by the reviewing officers.
(Gary Larkins Collection)

that the response to the crash involved many agencies within the County of San Mateo, south of San Francisco, California. The county sheriff was involved, along with a number of local police and fire agencies, as well as the American Red Cross. While looking for this wreck, we used the newspaper account and cross-referenced it in our search of the telephone directory, which revealed the names of a number of police and fire officials and Red Cross volunteers, as well as the dentist who identified the bodies during the post-mortem examinations.

As we contacted each person, each remembered the wreck and was able to provide us with the location, the easiest way to get to it, and what geographical landmarks to look for, as well as many unreported details. The first-hand accounts of the crash scene were unbelievably interesting.

The turret cover from a Grumman 150-CE upper gun turret on a TBM/TBF torpedo bomber rests on a Hawaiian hillside. (Gary Larkins)

The county historical society and the city historian are two excellent sources of information as well. If they cannot help, they can always provide you with names of locals who might have been involved, or the name of the landowner—past and present—of the property where the crash occurred.

If the crash involved a fatality, check the records at the county coroner's office. The pilots' and passengers' death certificates will be held either with the coroner or at the county's Hall of Records. The coroner's records will provide you with the name of the pilot and the others involved, location of crash, time of death, and next of kin. Again, the records are filed by date.

Many of the people you contact will be very helpful; others will be negative. While searching for a 1943 bomber wreck, a gentleman—who we later found out had never been to the site—told us, "Hippies went in there and took out all the aluminum and sold it for scrap in the 1970s." It just wasn't so.

First of all, there probably was not a road near the crash site until the 1980s, and the site was so far from the nearest town that it would have been uneconomical for anyone to remove the aluminum. You've got to weed through the naysayers and BSers.

Documentation of an Aircraft Crash

At this stage you have settled on a crash and probably know the aircraft type and date of the crash. The following government agencies can provide the remaining pieces of the puzzle or add some very interesting supporting documentation to your aircraft crash research.

The crash reports for Air Force aircraft are held at the Air Force Inspection and Safety Center. Again, you will need the date, location, and the aircraft type, plus the serial number—if available. It is an Air Force policy to censor all reports before they are distributed to the public to protect the confidentiality of the crash investigators' opinions; however, the censor marks do not interfere with the location information. Forward your requests for military aircraft crash reports to:

Department of the Air Force
Headquarters Air Force Inspection & Safety Center
Kirtland Air Force Base, N.M. 87117

Please note that the above-mentioned agencies require that your request be in writing, either snail mail or email. They do not have the staff to process telephone requests.

After at 30 minutes of digging and pulling, Patrick Congdon retrieved this generator motor from an F2H-4 Banshee. It was too heavy to carry out and was returned to the hole. (Nicholas A. Veronico)

Engine, cowling, and prop at the crash site of a Grumman F6F-5N Hellcat night fighter at Kahoolwe, Hawaii. (Gary Larkins)

If you are looking for one specific type of aircraft, there are two ways to research a particular type. Each aircraft in the U.S. Navy or Air Force inventory is assigned a serial number and a corresponding record card that details the aircraft's assignments. Once you have settled on a particular type of aircraft, determine the serial number range assigned to that model.

Most hobby shops carry a large selection of books that detail this information, or you can obtain a copy of *U.S. Military Aircraft Designations and Serials Since 1909* compiled by John M. Andrade (ISBN 0-904597-21-0). This book was published by Midland Counties Publications, and although out of print, many used copies are available from second-hand aviation book sellers.

To order individual aircraft record cards by serial number, forward your request to:

U.S. Navy Aircraft
Department of the Navy
Naval Historical Center
805 Kidder Breese Street SE
Washington, D.C. 20374-5060

U.S. Air Force Aircraft
United States Air Force
Historical Research Center
USAFHRC/HD
Maxwell Air Force
Base, Ala. 36112-

To order aircraft record cards on microfilm, consult Appendices V, *U.S. Navy Pilot History Cards of Aircraft Accidents,* and VI, *Obtaining U.S. Air Force Aircraft History Cards.*

If your interest is primarily U.S. Navy aircraft, you really are in luck. The Navy maintains a set of microfilm reels detailing aircraft accidents and incidents by aircraft type and date. The reels, known as Pilot History Cards of Aircraft Accidents, are $30 each, but well worth it. See Appendix V.

Heading to the Wreck Site

Before heading to a site, determine who owns the land where the aircraft crashed. If the land is privately owned, contact the owner and obtain permission to venture onto the property. If possible, have the owner accompany you to avoid any problems. Otherwise, obtain written permission from the owner and carry the document with you.

If the aircraft wreck is on public lands, which many are, check with the local governing authority. Determine the times and conditions of land use, locations and conditions of roads nearest your destination, and whether any locked gates or barricades will restrict your entry. Do not carry firearms unless you've checked the governing authority's policy. Note that these policies often differ and do change. Depending upon the difficulty of your trek, you may be required, often on government lands, to obtain a hiking permit. This is for your safety, and is not something to avoid.

Obtain a topographical map of the area you intend to search and carry it with you. Having the map handy will keep you from getting lost and will aid you in subsequent trips. (See Appendix VII, *Obtaining USGS Topo Maps.*)

Once you have selected a day to visit the site, gather your research and plan your route. You should never go alone, so invite a couple of friends to join you. Of course if you don't find the wreck on the first day, they may become your ex-friends.

You'll need your USGS topographical map; a compass; good shoes; a pack with food and water; a lightweight jacket for traveling through brush; eye protection, such as sunglasses or safety glasses; cell phone; and a camera, flash, and plenty of battery and memory. Also consider taking toilet paper, sunscreen, and insect repellent. This list of supplies should not have to be mentioned, as most people devoted enough to go looking for a wreck have the common sense to think of these things beforehand. Have a good time but remember, safety comes first.

Also, leave a hiking plan with someone and an estimated time off the trail. When you're back to your car, give this person call and let them know of your adventure and your safe return.

Eureka! You've Found It

When you locate the wreckage, take a minute to focus on what is in front of you—a point of impact, a debris field, lots of scattered metal, and most of all, the exact spot where an aircrew made the ultimate sacrifice. A brief recap of the flight and remembrance of the crew is in order. Some people will fly flags over the site in honor of the crews as well.

Consider sketching the wreckage, making notes as to the terrain, and where the wings, fuselage, engines and other large pieces are located.

Do some of your own "accident investigation." Are there trees that have been topped? Did the airplane strike those trees during its descent before crashing? Are there major parts—such as wings or an elevator—some distance from the point of impact? Did the aircraft suffer a structural failure, or did it enter a high-speed dive and shed those pieces on its way to the ground?

You will always be able to discern the wings, tail, and any other large intact pieces. But what of the thousands of smaller pieces? Look for part numbers stamped on the formers and other components, data plates, numbers painted on the surfaces, overhaul tags, and so on.

If you turn a piece of metal over and it reveals a painted surface, turn it back, face down, after you have studied it. This will help preserve it for those who will follow. It is amazing how quickly the paint will fade when exposed to the elements.

Locate the point of impact. Check the surface for interesting parts, then kneel down and sift through the first two to three inches of topsoil, where many interesting aircraft parts may be found. In the past, searches of the topsoil have revealed parachute "D" rings, seatbelts, instruments, coins, shoes, Mae West life vests, ammunition shell brass, playing cards, canvas snaps, belt buckles, watches, wings and other insignia, and hundreds of miscellaneous items.

Souvenirs

Souvenirs may only be taken if the landowner permits it. If the wreck is on public land, always check with the local administrators as to their policy on aircraft parts removal. Many aircraft crash sites on public land fall under the jurisdiction's antiquities laws. Ignorance of the policies does not grant one the right to plunder an historic site. Basically, any crash more than 50 years old falls under these rules.

When you travel to a crash site, you may be pretty pumped up. Going in, an hour's walk can seem like 20 minutes if the route is downhill, but coming out may be more difficult. If the landowner has given permission to remove souvenirs and it's a long walk out, take only what you can carry, preferably in a small backpack.

Also, you never know when you'll find a loose propeller that needs a home. The wreck you find today may yield many parts that can be used as

Every wreckchaser dreams of finding a crash site like this F4U Corsair sitting in a swamp. Unfortunately, most wreckchases result in finding much smaller subassemblies like the star and bar insignia from the waist of B-17F 42-5318, which crashed 10 miles east of Covelo, California. (Vought Aircraft, Ed Davies)

patterns in aircraft restorations. If you do find a rare aircraft, contact your local aviation museum and ask if they need any parts or know of anyone looking for parts.

Before removing anything consider where it will end up. If you take it, most museums will not want it as the piece's removal from the site without proper archaeological documentation removes any provenance that part may have had. If you remove something, will it end up in your garage and eventually be discarded? Instead of taking a piece of the wreckage, consider taking pictures and memories; these are the best things to remove from a wreck site.

Placing Memorials

The term "memorial" scares most operators of public lands. Think more in terms of an "interpretive plaque"—something that educates the public, yet calls attention to the sacrifices made by those who perished in the aircraft crash.

Although the cost will typically have to come out of your pocket, placing an interpretive plaque is worth the effort. You will feel a personal satisfaction after you have researched a crash, visited the site, and paid tribute to those who lost their lives.

Contact the landowner regarding a suitable location. Many public lands will allow a small plaque at the site. You may be able to install a more elaborate tribute,—which may incorporate pieces of the aircraft,—at the local headquarters or city/town museum.

Recovering Armament: Don't

During World War II, thousands of aircraft flew daily on stateside training missions. If an aircraft went down, the primary focus was to rescue the survivors, remove any of the crew who might have perished, and then secure the bombsight and avionics. Most World War II crashes were in pretty remote areas, and the military had no interest in lugging out the heavy armament. Many of these wrecks have yielded internal parts for machine guns and cannons, but rarely a whole one. If you do find one, be sure to have your picture taken with it.

The law is very specific about citizens owning machine guns, even old, rusted, or bent ones. The Department of the Treasury's Bureau of

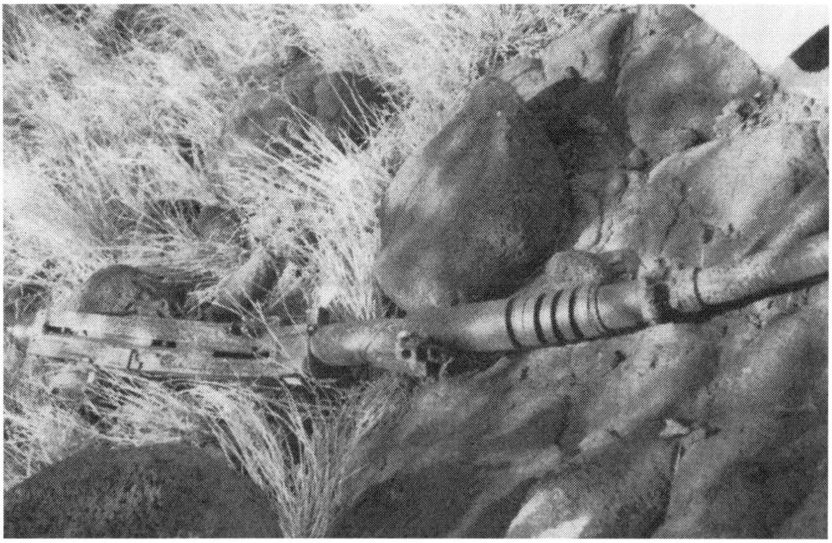

This 20mm cannon makes a tempting souvenir, but the jail time that would accompany its removal is not worth it. (Gary Larkins)

Alcohol, Tobacco, Firearms and Explosives (ATF) puts out an informative booklet entitled (Your Guide to) *Federal Firearms Regulations*. You can download a copy at www.atf.gov, and many gun shops also stock copies.

In a nutshell, the guide states that you may not possess or transport any machine gun that was not registered in accordance with the 1968 National Firearms Act (NFA). (Weapons, such as machine guns, are referred to as NFA firearms.) Basically, if your gun was on a hillside in 1968, it does not qualify for NFA status and must be donated to a museum or destroyed.

Because it came from an aircraft crash, you may save it from destruction by proving its historical significance. Your best bet is to photograph the weapon, leave it where you found it, and to contact the bureau. The bureau can arrange for you to show them where the weapon is located and donate it to a museum.

In rare circumstances, an unserviceable aircraft cannon or machine gun can be registered as a "Curio or Relic" through the bureau's Firearms Technology Branch, Room B230, Bureau of ATF, Washington, D.C. 20226. If this is the route you plan to take, photograph the weapon intended for recovery at the site. Photograph it from all sides to show that the weapon is indeed unserviceable. Leave the weapon at the site until you can obtain a ruling or are able to donate the weapon to an approved museum.

Remember: recovering, transporting, or possessing a non-NFA machine gun, its frame, or receiver is illegal. If convicted of possession of such a weapon, you may be subject to imprisonment and a $10,000 fine—no matter how good your intentions. Consult your local, state, and federal laws before recovering any automatic weapons.

Photography at the Site

Take a camera with you, but avoid expensive, fragile, or sensitive equipment. A digital point-and-shoot is fine, but a rugged digital SLR camera with a 28-85mm zoom lens is best. If your wreck is in the hills or in a forested area, adjust the ASA to 400 or more and use the flash. This will light the wreck, as well as fill in the faces of your companions.

Heading Home

No matter where the wreck is, inevitably, someone wants to bring back some choice piece, which usually weighs 200 pounds. Here's a good rule to follow when wreckchasing: "Only bring back what you can comfortably carry." Thus photos and memories are highly recommended.

Too many times people have tried to carry out something heavy, gotten tired, and then they left the souvenir miles from the wreck. This misplaced piece could be the rare part that is missing in the restoration of a potentially flyable aircraft, but there's no way to interpret the part when it is so far removed from the wreck site.

After you have had your fill, gather everyone together and police the area. Do not leave any litter, paper, garbage, or food wrappings. Restore the site to the way you found it to preserve the site for those who will follow and remember to turn painted surfaces down, away from the elements.

Removing the Entire Wreck

Not satisfied with just a few photos? How about the entire airplane? If the wreck you have located looks like it could be rebuilt, you will need to acquire title to the aircraft, as well as the landowner's permission, before removing it. For a military wreck, sometimes a letter and set of photographs describing the condition of the aircraft will get the ball rolling toward a clear title.

If the National Museum of the United States Air Force, at Wright-Patterson Air Force Base, Ohio, or the National Museum of Naval Aviation in Pensacola, Florida, does not have an interest in the aircraft and it has not been deemed historically significant, a release can be issued in a few weeks, at least for Air Force aircraft. But according to a Naval Air Systems Command public affairs officer, wreckchasers must obtain U.S. Navy permission before recovering an aircraft. The Navy reasons that "many of these aircraft went down with crew members on board and these aircraft are considered grave sites."

One of the first groups involved with the historical research of a Naval aircraft crash site is the Navy Bureau of Personnel's Office of Decedent Affairs, which will review records of the crash and the ultimate fate of the crew.

By law, the Navy never abandons equipment, including aircraft, without a formal act of abandonment, and the mere passage of time or lack of recovery effort by the Navy does not constitute legal abandonment.

The National Historical Preservation Act of 1966 is also a factor in exploring and salvaging aircraft. The law may require the Navy to preserve a crash site if the site is deemed of historical value.

Before taking any action on a U.S. Navy or Marine Corps aircraft, visit www.history.navy.mil and look at its Underwater Archaeology Branch pages. Here you'll find such publications as:

- *Policy Fact Sheet on Sunken Naval Vessels and Naval Aircraft*
- *New Protection for Sunken Military Vessels and Aircraft*
- *Archaeological Research Permits*
- *The Sunken Military Craft Act*

As for civilian aircraft, you will need to contact the FAA to find out the name of the last registered owner. In the case of a crash, the title of the wreckage may have been transferred to an insurance company.

Civilian or military, your best bet is to consult an aviation attorney before removing any aircraft.

Researching an Airliner Crash from Start to Finish

Decades after an airliner has crashed, its final resting place is an interesting sight. Everyone knows what an airliner looks like at the gate or lifting off headed for some exotic destination, but seeing the destruction of a crashed airliner first-hand is truly a remarkable sight. What was once a passenger-carrying aircraft becomes tons of twisted metal, usually lying scattered over a wide area. Some parts are recognizable, while others are mysterious lumps of metal, plastic, and fabric. All were once part of a flying airliner.

Locating a commercial aircraft crash site requires more research than any other type of aircraft crash. Many times the entire wreck site

Top: A sister ship to N88942, N90915 taxies at the company's home base of Oakland, California. N88942 was en route from Walker Air Force Base, Roswell, New Mexico, to Guam, with a single stop at Oakland. Thirty maintenance personnel from the 509th Bomb Wing and a crew of five, including Transocean's Chief Pilot Harvey W. Rogers, perished in the March 20, 1953 crash. (William T. Larkins)

Below: N88942 as no airplane should look. Transocean mechanic William "Bill" Dell took this photo shortly after the crash. The field was part of Andrada's Dairy near the intersection of Whipple and Alguire Roads in Alvarado, California. (William Dell)

has been swept clean, whether by a government safety organization, an insurance company, or the landowner. Thus, finding pieces of an actual aircraft are much like drilling for oil—sometimes you come up with a dry well. The intrigue is in locating the exact site, documenting your search, and hopefully finding an airliner's final resting place.

Choosing Your Site

In this volume, readers will visit the locations of a number of commercial aircraft crash sites, among them are the site of British Commonwealth Pacific Airlines' DC-6 *Resolution* (VH-BPE, manufacturer's serial number, or msn 43125), and Pan Am's Martin M-130 *Philippine Clipper*. Both crash sites hold substantial amounts of wreckage, partly due to their inaccessibility and the inhospitable terrain. The sites were chosen first on their geographic location: the BCPA DC-6 was a day trip for those wreckchasers living in the San Francisco Bay Area, while the *Philippine Clipper* was an overnighter. The second consideration was also of a geographic nature—researching the crash would require visits to local libraries, museums, and the conducting of interviews with any witnesses. For financial considerations these destinations needed to be close to home. The third consideration was the aircraft's type. The M-130 was a rare bird while the BCPA DC-6 was the ultimate in early 1950's air travel. Both represented types that are now extinct in passenger carrying service—the M-130 crash having the only known surviving parts of the type.

When looking for a crash site to explore, first try to choose an aircraft type you are interested in. If you have no interest in a particular type, then why go? Researching a crash takes time and patience, so it helps if the aircraft type holds your interest. Review Appendices II, III, and IV for a listing of commercial aircraft that have crashed. Use this as a starting point for your search.

Beginning Your Search

Ninety percent of the effort required to find a crash site is expended doing research. Careful planning will yield positive results and spare you from a pointless hike.

The following outline provides the recommended search path for locating a commercial aircraft crash site.

1. Decide on the type of aircraft to search for.

2. Prepare a worksheet. See Appendix IX: *Wreckchasing Worksheet.*

3. Obtain documentation. Begin with the aircraft's accident report.

4. Obtain newspaper or TV reports of the crash.

5. Obtain a topographical map of the crash site.

6. Interview the participants.

7. Locate the crash Site. Plan your trip.

8. Visit the crash site.

9. Make your research available to others.

Taking the First Step

Upon deciding on the specific aircraft crash site to investigate, prepare a worksheet. Fill in the make/model, registration or serial number at the time of the crash, any previous registrations, the manufacturer's serial number, and the plane's date of delivery to its first operator. Check whether it was a civilian airliner and note the airline name, or if military, fill in the branch of service and assigned unit. Some of this information is available in the appendices of this book, or it can be located in a number of reference books (See Bibliography/Suggested Reading). Next note the location of the wreck, and if you have a more specific idea of where the plane went down, list the 7.5 minute quadrangle map on which the site is located (See Appendix VII, *Obtaining USGS Topo Maps*).

The Internet newspaper archive or local library is your next destination. Commercial aircraft crashes receive huge amounts of attention from the press. Nothing sells papers or hooks TV viewers into tuning to the late news like a crash headline or sound bite. Start with the microfilm section and begin with the newspaper published closest to the crash site. Your search should begin with the edition following the crash. On the worksheet note the name of the newspaper and the pages where you find related articles. Copies of these pages should be added to your file. Take time to look through each day's newspaper for the next two weeks to one month. See if there is any mention of wreckage removal. Depending on your library, also check the *Los Angeles Times, New York Times*, or the major market daily in your area. These papers usually cover all aviation disasters.

The newspaper will usually provide you with a location of the crash, the names of emergency personnel who responded to the scene, and the names of local residents who witnessed the crash. A check of the local phone book will yield interesting results. Many of the names mentioned in the newspaper will still be residents of the local or surrounding area, sometimes more than 40 years after a crash. Note these names on the worksheet. Show their current addresses if you are able to locate anyone.

Transocean employees examine the wreckage of N88942 in an Alvarado barley field. William "Bill" Dell crouches down. (William Dell)

Fill in the location or the directions to the crash site given by the newspaper. Depending on the area and vintage of the crash, the newspaper may report something like, "A road had to be cut to the crash site in XYZ canyon." This is important information that can be transferred to a topo map to help pinpoint the location.

For this example we will research the crash of Transocean Air Lines C-54G-10-DO N88942, msn 36076. The C-54 was the military version of the DC-4 airliner and was 93 feet, 10 inches long, with a wingspan of 117 feet, 6 inches. The aircraft had a maximum speed of 280 knots at 23,000 feet. C-54G-10-DO is the 'G' model C-54, modification block 10, constructed by Douglas at Santa Monica, California.

Starting with the worksheet, fill in the above information; Make/Model C-54G-10-DO; Registration/Serial N88942; Operator Transocean Air Lines; Crash Date March 20, 1953.

If you desire, the civil history of this aircraft could be obtained by sending the aircraft type, registration number, and msn to:

Federal Aviation Administration
P.O. Box 25504
Oklahoma City, OK 73125-0504

If you are searching for a civil aircraft and know its identity, you can obtain crash reports from the National Transportation Safety Board. The date and location of the crash will be required. If you know the aircraft's serial number and civil registration, also enclose that information in your request. Write to:

National Transportation Safety Board
800 Independence Ave. S.W.
Washington, D.C. 20594

CIVIL AERONAUTICS BOARD
ACCIDENT INVESTIGATION REPORT

Adopted: October 9, 1953 Released: October 14, 1953

TRANSOCEAN AIR LINES, ALVARADO, CALIFORNIA, MARCH 20, 1953

The Accident

A Douglas DC-4 aircraft, N 88942, owned and operated by Transocean Air Lines, crashed in a field near Alvarado, California, at approximately 1838 1/ March 20, 1953. All of the 35 occupants including the crew of five were killed. The aircraft was demolished.

History of the Flight

Transocean Air Lines' Flight 942 of March 20, 1953, departed Roswell, New Mexico, at 1211 for Oakland, California. On board were 30 military passengers and a crew consisting of Captain H. E. Hum, First Officer F. W. Patchett, Chief Pilot H. W. Rodgers and Stewardesses V. Sandridge and L. Chapman. The flight was for the purpose of transporting military personnel in accordance with the company's contract with the United States Department of Defense. Prior to departure a DVFR (Defense Visual Flight Rules) flight plan was filed with ARTC (Air Route Traffic Control), indicating a flight to be flown at an altitude of at least 500 feet on top of clouds via Red Airway 88 to Albuquerque, New Mexico; Green Airway 4 to Palmdale, California; Blue Airway 14 and Amber Airway 1 to Bakersfield, California; Amber Airway 1 to Fresno, California; and Blue Airway 10 to Oakland, California. There was sufficient fuel on board for 10 hours and the flying time to Oakland was estimated to be six hours and 35 minutes. According to the company's records the gross weight of the aircraft at the time of takeoff was 63,817 pounds, which was within the allowable gross weight of 73,000 pounds; the load was properly distributed.

After departing Roswell the flight progressed in a routine manner and at 1451, when in the vicinity of Winslow, Arizona, the DVFR flight plan was changed to IFR (Instrument Flight Rules), still at least 500 feet on top of clouds.

At 1732 the flight reported that it was over Fresno, California, at 1730, that it was cruising at 8,000 feet (at least 500 feet on top of clouds), estimating Los Banos, California, at 1740 and requested further clearance. At 1744 Flight 942 called the Fresno radio communications station and asked that the requested clearance be expedited, stating that it was now at 7,000 feet, at least 500 feet on top. At 1747, the following clearance was issued the flight: "ARTC clears Transocean 942 to the Newark radio beacon, maintain 8,000, contact Oakland Approach Control after passing Evergreen, no delay expected, report reaching 8,000." Approaching Evergreen at 1809, the flight was

1/ All times referred to herein are based on the 24-hour clock and are Mountain Standard until the aircraft reached Fresno, California, and from this point on the times are Pacific Standard.

55562

The Civil Aeronautics Board issued its final report on the crash on October 14, 1953. On the day of the crash, the plane was being flown by a very experienced crew—possibly one of Transocean's best. The plane was low time, having flown only 5,976 total hours. Although undetermined, the report lists one possible cause for the crash as "the accumulation of ice on the surfaces of the aircraft in sufficient magnitude to have caused loss of control . . ." (Arue Szura Collection)

If these records can be located in storage, you will receive a microfiche copy of the history of N88942. Another route is to look up the aircraft history in books such as A.B. "Tony" Eastwood and John Roach's *Piston Engine Airliner Production List* (See Bibliography/ Suggested Reading). Presented by aircraft type in msn order, this book provides a summary of the FAA information—without the wait. *Piston Engine Airliner Production List* shows that N88942 was delivered to the U.S. Army Air Forces on October 9, 1945, as serial number 45-0623. The plane was then leased by the Army Air Force to Pan American World Airways sometime in 1946. (The FAA records would provide the exact date, as the books are sometimes vague on detailed points like this.) Pan Am christened the plane *Clipper Bostonian*. In 1951, the Air Force leased the plane to Transocean Air Lines. The carrier used the plane exclusively for Military Air Transport Service (MATS) contract flights. Within two years the plane had crashed on approach to the Oakland Airport on March 20, 1953, in the town of Alvarado, California.

Note that many universities, Embry-Riddle for example, have posted airliner crash reports on their websites for use by students. These are typically free downloads. In addition, a number of commercial vendors are now offering accident and crash reports for a fee. The nice thing about paying the fee is that the reports arrive very quickly and are usually of high quality. A quick Internet search will show you what's available.

Enter the following information on the worksheet: The town of Alvarado is located on the Newark, California quadrangle USGS map; The Civil Aeronautics Board (CAB) adopted its finding of the crash on October 9, 1953, and published the report on October 14, 1953, and the report number is 1-0016.

Now that the top half of the worksheet has been completed, the next step is to review the newspaper. Three major papers were published within a 50 mile radius of the crash site. They are the *San Francisco Chronicle, Oakland Tribune*, and the San Jose *Mercury News*.

Headlines read: "Wing Ice May Have Caused DC-4 Crash That Killed 35," *San Francisco Chronicle*; "35 Die In Eastbay Plane Disaster, Oakland-Bound DC-4 Jammed With Air Force Men, Falls and Burns In Barley Field Near Alvarado," *Oakland Tribune*. The *San Francisco Chronicle* coverage was good, but for a wreckchaser, the information in the *Oakland Tribune* was a gold mine.

The Flight, the Crash, and the Newspaper Accounts

Operating as Transocean Air Lines' Flight 942, N88942 left Walker Air Force Base, Roswell, New Mexico, at 12:11 pm MST, en route to Oakland, with a final destination of Guam. All 30 passengers were maintenance personnel from the 509th Bomb Wing—noted for dropping the atomic bombs on Japan. The flight was crewed by five. They were

Harvey W. Rogers, 41, pilot, who was Transocean's chief pilot; Herman E. Hum, 41, also a Transocean captain flying as the relief pilot; Fred W. Patchett, 37, Co-pilot; Velma Sandridge, 27, and Lucile M. Chapman, no age available, flew as stewardesses.

The flight reported passing over Winslow, Arizona, at 2:51 pm MST, where it refiled for an Instrument Flight Rules (IFR) flight plan. At 5:32 pm PST, Transocean Flight 942 checked in over Fresno, California, flying at 8,000 feet. Shortly thereafter, the flight was cleared into the Bay Area, first to report over Evergreen (near San Jose), then to contact Oakland Approach Control at the Newark radio beacon (fan marker and compass locator). Arriving at 6:09 pm over Evergreen, the flight was cleared to Newark, remaining at 8,000 feet. Less than a minute later, Flight 942 requested 7,000 feet but was denied due to traffic.

It was a drab spring day inside the Bay. The CAB report states that the weather was "Measured ceiling 1,300 feet broken, 1,800 feet overcast, light rain, fog, visibility two and one-half miles, wind south-southwest 17 miles per hour, altimeter setting 30.09." Not real bad flying weather—not the best either—but nothing weather-wise that should have given a large four-engine airliner or its highly skilled crew any problems.

At 6:19 the flight reported over the Newark radio beacon and was instructed to hold. Eight minutes passed before Oakland Approach Control cleared the flight to descend in the holding pattern and to cross the Newark radio beacon at 3,500 feet, reporting at each 1,000 foot level of descent, and then to make a straight-in approach to land. The flight reported beginning its descent from 8,000 feet at 6:30, and six minutes later stated that it had crossed the Newark radio beacon inbound for landing. That was the last transmission from the flight.

"At approximately 6:38, the aircraft crashed in a barley field. Impact and fire destroyed the aircraft. There were no survivors," the CAB report states. "Investigation revealed that the aircraft crashed in a large flat field located three miles from the Newark compass locator on a magnetic bearing of 323 degrees, and one and one-half miles northeast of the town of Alvarado, California. The surrounding terrain consisted of flat farmland on which were a few scattered houses, fences, and trees. The elevation of the field is approximately 17 feet above sea level.

"The aircraft first struck the ground on its right wing tip and with the wing in a near vertical position, then cartwheeled, and disintegrated. Wreckage was scattered over an area approximately 800 feet long and 300 feet wide. Due to impact forces and the resultant fire, the aircraft broke into numerous small pieces, many of which were destroyed by fire with only two large sections of the aircraft remaining after the crash. These were the fuselage center section with a portion of the left wing attached, which was found lying inverted approximately 634 feet from the point of first impact, and the rear section of the fuselage, including empennage,

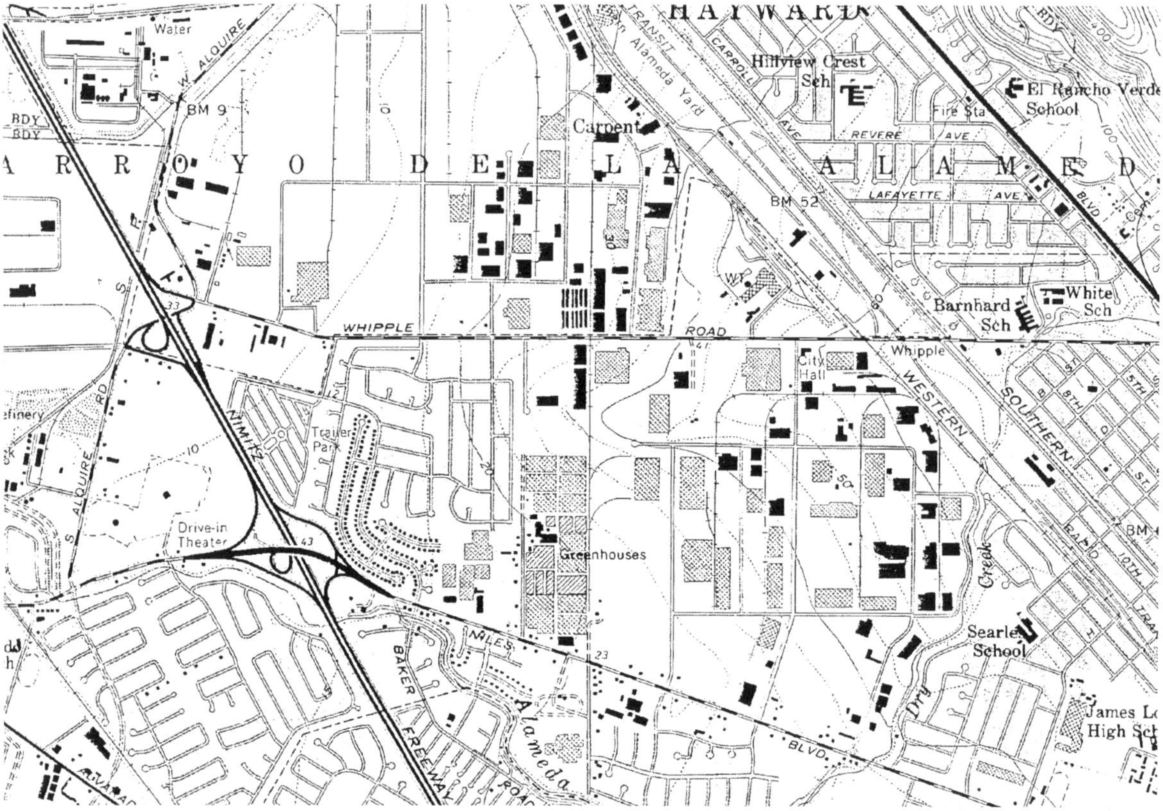

U.S.G.S. topo map showing Hayward and the Alvarado and Decoto districts. N88942 crashed off Whipple Road near what today is Highway 880. The crash location is highlighted by an arrow. (Courtesy U.S. Geological Survey)

from approximately Station 660 rearward to the tail cone, which was also lying nearby."

On Page 5 of the March 21, 1953, edition of the *Oakland Tribune*, witness William Silva, a resident of Whipple Road, reported finding "pieces of ice up to eight inches long and three inches thick with smooth rounded inner sides." This ice was presumed to have come from the leading edge of the C-54's wing. (Although the cause of the crash has never been determined, icing was suspected as a major factor. The CAB report said, "One pilot, who was holding over Newark at 8,000 feet approximately 35 minutes after the accident occurred, reported encountering severe icing conditions and mild turbulence with ice approximately three inches in diameter accumulating on antenna masts. He said that the ice began to melt when the 4,500-foot level was reached in the descent.") The paper also reported that Silva's house was southwest of the crash site. Silva and another witness, Henry Gomes, gave first-hand eyewitness accounts of the crash to the newspaper. Each wrote a column. Other witnesses named in the paper were Robert Lemos and Mrs. Edith Whipple. William Silva's wife, Wilma, was also listed.

The *Tribune* gave the location of the crash as "a fourth of a mile northeast of the intersection of Alguire Road and Whipple Road on the ranch operated by Frank and Rick Andrada."

Adding to the Worksheet, Interviewing the Participants

From the information in the CAB report and the newspapers, names of the witnesses and a location of the wreck have been learned. After entering this information on the worksheet, start with the local phone book or an Internet people search. Gomes, Lemos, and Whipple were not listed. Calls to others with the same last names could yield family members or next of kin, but that step was skipped after the Silva family was located. They had moved from their home near the crash site, but continued to work and raise a family in the community.

William Silva provided more clues to where the wreck site was, contrasting the area in 1953—before Interstate 880 was built—to the area today. In a phone interview, Silva said, "We lived where Walmart is now and the accident happened across the freeway, maybe a quarter of a mile away. The crash was on the east side of the freeway [which began construction

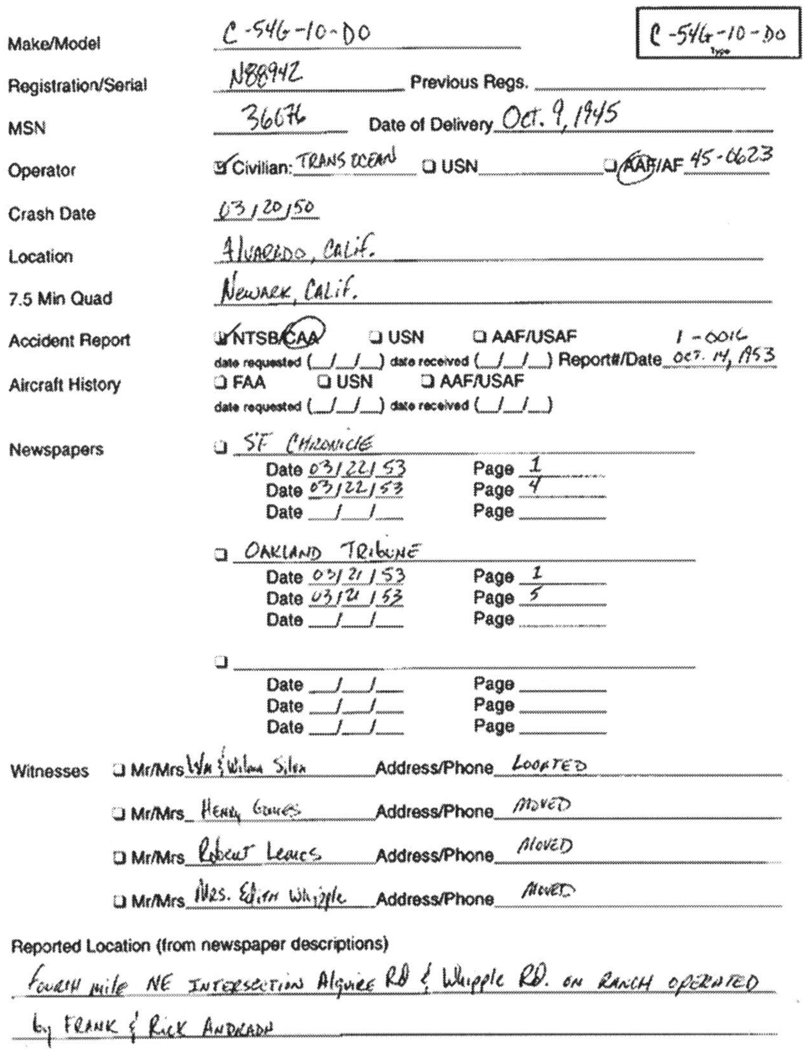
Make/Model C-54G-10-DO — C-54G-10-DO (type)
Registration/Serial N88942 Previous Regs.
MSN 36076 Date of Delivery Oct. 9, 1945
Operator ☑ Civilian: TRANS OCEAN ☐ USN ☐ AAF/AF 45-0623
Crash Date 03/20/50
Location Alvarado, Calif.
7.5 Min Quad Newark, Calif.
Accident Report ☑ NTSB/CAA ☐ USN ☐ AAF/USAF 1-0016
date requested (_/_/_) date received (_/_/_) Report#/Date Oct. 14, 1953
Aircraft History ☐ FAA ☐ USN ☐ AAF/USAF
date requested (_/_/_) date received (_/_/_)
Newspapers ☐ SF Chronicle
Date 03/22/53 Page 1
Date 03/22/53 Page 4
Date _/_/_ Page
☐ Oakland Tribune
Date 03/21/53 Page 1
Date 03/21/53 Page 5
Date _/_/_ Page
☐
Date _/_/_ Page
Date _/_/_ Page
Date _/_/_ Page
Witnesses ☐ Mr/Mrs Wm & Wilma Silva Address/Phone Located
☐ Mr/Mrs Henry Gomes Address/Phone Moved
☐ Mr/Mrs Robert Lemos Address/Phone Moved
☐ Mr/Mrs Mrs. Edith Whipple Address/Phone Moved
Reported Location (from newspaper descriptions)
Fourth mile NE intersection Alquire Rd & Whipple Rd. on ranch operated by Frank & Rick Andrade

A completed worksheet for the investigation into the crash site of Transocean's C-54G N88942 helps the wreckchaser gather information in an organized manner.

three years later in 1956-57]. We were in the house just before dinner. We heard this roar, the plane passing overhead. I looked outside and saw the plane going over our house and it was tilted to the left. The left wing hit the ground and then it burst into flame. I ran across the street [Whipple Road] to this field and tried to find somebody alive, to no avail. The plane disintegrated when it hit. When I came back I found some pieces of ice, like they came off the wing, which I reported at the inquest."

The location shown in the newspaper stated that the plane crashed on a ranch run by Frank and Rick Andrada, known as Andrada's Dairy. A review of the local phone book showed a listing for H. Rick Andrada. Unfortunately, he passed away in 1987. He was survived by his wife, Violet Andrada. She said, "The ranch was on the corner of Whipple and Alguire. It covered a large area and had a dairy. At the time of the crash, they had just plowed and planted barley. It had been raining something terrible. My brother-in-law and Henry [Rick] took care of the ranch." She mentioned that her husband and brother-in-law leased the ranch from a gentleman named Wiegman who lived in Alvarado.

Mrs. Andrada said that after the crash, "Billy Silva [William, mentioned above] grabbed my hand and we jumped out there in the field to see who we could save. The wreckage was on the property, I imagine, about four months. Some of the plane's motors were in the ground six feet deep. The military dug them out and removed everything. They had a regular guard walking back and forth with guns over their shoulders. Anyone who was coming into the ranch to visit us was under surveillance. They had to show identification before the soldiers would let them in. The Army watched every little thing, they didn't miss a trick.

"Henry wrote a letter to every mother who wrote a letter to him. He told them that they had a minister, Catholic, Protestant, Jewish, right there at the site giving them the last rites. A lot of the parents wrote and Henry kept those letters for years and years."

Finding the Crash Site

Having developed information from the newspapers and eyewitnesses, a street map was consulted to find the corner of Alguire and Whipple. How hard could it be to locate a point one-quarter mile northeast of the intersection of Alguire and Whipple? Whipple is a major street, it even has an off-ramp from Highway 880. The map showed an Alguire Parkway, but it was nowhere near and did not intersect Whipple Road. Now what?

Some original photos of the crash site would be helpful. Someone who was there and took photos would be even better. Author Arue Szura, who wrote *Folded Wings: A History of Transocean Air Lines*, was asked to help locate someone who participated in this dark chapter of the carrier's history. Szura pointed the search towards William F. "Bill" Dell, who was a

N88942's crash site then and now.

Top: Following the crash, Transocean sent a number of workers to help with the accident investigation and clean-up. From left to right: Transocean employees William "Bill" Dell, Wendell Davies, Mike Lewis, and an unidentified worker. (William Dell Collection)

Bottom: The crash site is still a plowed field to this day, although it was up for sale when this photo was taken. Arrows indicate a geographic feature used as a reference point when locating the crash site. Compare the two photos and notice how little has changed in the ensuing 50-plus years.
(Nicholas A. Veronico)

Transocean mechanic at the time and was assigned to help investigate the crash and comb through the wreckage. Dell's insights and photographs helped locate the crash site.

While plotting the gathered information onto the topo map, it was noticed that what is today Dyer Road was formerly S. Alguire Road, and today's Industrial Blvd. was once W. Alguire Road. Due to the cost of topo maps, consider photocopying or placing a sheet of tracing paper over the map before plotting any information. That will keep your map fresh and you can mark all over a copy if you need to.

Using all of the information garnered from the newspapers, CAB reports, and the eyewitness accounts, a likely crash location was plotted.

Today the area around the crash site has been built up as an industrial park. The crash location is to the rear of this lot. Wiegman Avenue is named after the man who owned the property in the 1950s. (Nicholas A. Veronico)

Upon arrival at the site, the photographs received from Dell were matched to the surrounding terrain. We had found it. Unfortunately, there was no wreckage left. However, it had been an interesting search.

If you would like to visit this location, take Highway 880 and exit at Whipple Rd. Drive east one-quarter mile to Wiegman (the street was named after the landowner). Turn left, pass the building on the right and stop at the vacant lot on the right. Walk back about 100 yards and look towards the hills. Match the photographs on these pages to the hills behind you. You are standing at the crash site.

The land is currently up for sale. Hopefully, once new owners have settled in, a plaque to honor the memories of those who perished can be placed at, or near the site.

Start your own wreckchasing adventure by following the steps outlined here. You will have an adventure to remember.

Military Aircraft Wreckchasing

Following the instructions shown above, let's locate McDonnell F2H-4 Banshee, Bureau Number 127614. This aircraft was found on the wreck locator (See Appendix I: *Military Aircraft Wrecks by State*) at 37°17'N 122°07'W, crash date February 22, 1959.

On March 22, 1945, the U.S. Navy contracted with McDonnell Aircraft Corp. of St. Louis, for two XF2D-1 prototype aircraft, a larger, improved version of the FH-1 Phantom. The first flight of an XF2D-1 Banshee was on January 11, 1947. The first Banshees became operational

Photographer Clay Jansson only shot two Banshees during his career, and one of them was Bureau Number 127614. Here are two views of F2H-4, Bureau Number 127614, at Marine Corps Air Station Kaneohe, Hawaii, in March 1956. Less than two years later the aircraft crashed north of the town of Saratoga, California. (Clay Jansson)

A left wing panel that was not "recovered by Skyline Boulevard," as reported by the San Mateo Times. *(Nicholas A. Veronico)*

in March 1949 with VF-171, and the type became affectionately known to its crews as the "Banjo."

Exactly 150 F2H-4s were built, and the last was delivered on September 24, 1953. A total of 892 F2H Banshees of all types were constructed. The F2H-4 was the Navy's standard carrier-based, all-weather air superiority fighter until 1959, and the last Banshees in the Naval Reserve were phased out in 1961 at NAS Oakland, California.

Obtain the Newspaper Account

On a foggy February 22, 1959, Lt. (j.g.) James F. Wyley, 26, crashed F2H-4 Banshee 127614 in Stevens Creek, north of the town of Saratoga, California. *The San Mateo Times* reported that both wings were torn away as the aircraft passed through trees near Skyline Boulevard and that the

Looking down on the final resting place of 127614 from the middle of the hill. The left wing panel is to the rear of the photographer, while the engines and canopy are at the bottom of the ravine. (Ron Strong)

The tail section of 127614 displays the Civil Air Patrol's orange "X" on the tail to inform over-flying pilots that this crash as been located. This orange "X" is referred to as "marked" on many crash locator lists. (Nicholas A. Veronico)

Navy Probes Plane Crash

Navy officials today started an investigation into the crash of a jet fighter plane near fog-shrouded Skyline boulevard just south of the San Mateo county line in which the pilot was killed.

The twin-jet Banshee, piloted by Lt. (j.g.) James F. Wyley, 26, of San Diego, swooped low over the highway late yesterday and slashed a swath through high trees along the Skyline. Both wings were torn from the fuselage by the trees.

The airplane's wings were recovered near Skyline boulevard, one only 100 yards from the road.

The jet's speed rocketed the fuselage a mile further on, into wild Stevens Creek canyon north of Saratoga. The charred jet and the body of the pilot was found by Santa Clara county deputy sheriffs who searched for five hours after the plane crashed.

Naval officials said Wyley was in one of two jets flying from North Island Naval Air station in San Diego to Alameda Naval Air station. The pilot of the other plane, identified only as Ensign L. L. Marshall, said he saw the other plane go down in the fog and rain and immediately radioed Moffett Field Naval Air station.

Lt. Wyley is survived by a wife living in Coronado.

The February 23, 1959 edition of the San Mateo Times *included coverage of the previous day's crash. Aside from the pilot's name, home field, and destination, a rough location is given, which is enough to begin the research for this wreckchase.*
Ed Davies Collection

wings were recovered about 100 yards east of Skyline (today, the left wing rests about 20 feet above the tail). The one-wing fuselage carried Lt. Wyley about one mile from the Skyline impact point down into Stevens Creek Canyon, where the aircraft struck the northeastern side.

Lt. Wyley was in a flight of two Airborne Early Warning Squadron Eleven (VAW-11) aircraft flying from NAS North Island, San Diego, California, to Alameda Naval Air Station, near Oakland. Ensign L.L. Marshall was Lt. Wyley's wingman on the flight.

Newspaper accounts reported that Ens. Marshall watched Lt. Wyley's aircraft descend into "the fog and rain." He immediately radioed a rough location of the missing aircraft to nearby Naval Air Station Moffett Field. Banshee 127614 and Lt. Wyley's body were found after a five-hour search by Santa Clara County deputy sheriffs.

Obtain the USGS Map

Upon locating the coordinates on the USGS map, we found that the aircraft now rests in the Saratoga Gap Open Space Preserve administered by the Midpeninsula Regional Open Space District. A call to the district's office put us in touch with Ranger Patrick Congdon, who was very knowledgeable and familiar with the site. With Ranger Congdon's assistance and the Open Space District's permission, we traveled to the site to discover most of the aircraft *in situ*, although extremely broken up.

Specifications

Length: 48 feet, 2 inches
Wingspan: 45 feet with tip tanks
Height: 14 feet, 6 inches
Crew: One pilot
Armament: Four 20mm cannons plus two hard points capable of carrying one 500-lb. bomb each
Weight (empty): 13,183 lbs.
Weight (max.): 28,500 lbs.
Max. Speed: 527 mph at sea level
Cruise Speed: 501 mph
Range: 1,716 miles
Service Ceiling: 46,500 feet
Engines: Two Westinghouse J34-WE-38, developing 3,600 static thrust each.
F2H-4 Bureau Nos: 126351/126353, 127547/127693

The Aircraft History Card

The information contained on the aircraft's history card, which was obtained from the U.S. Navy, shows that Bureau Number 127614 was constructed at McDonnell Aircraft Corp.'s St. Louis, Mo., assembly line.

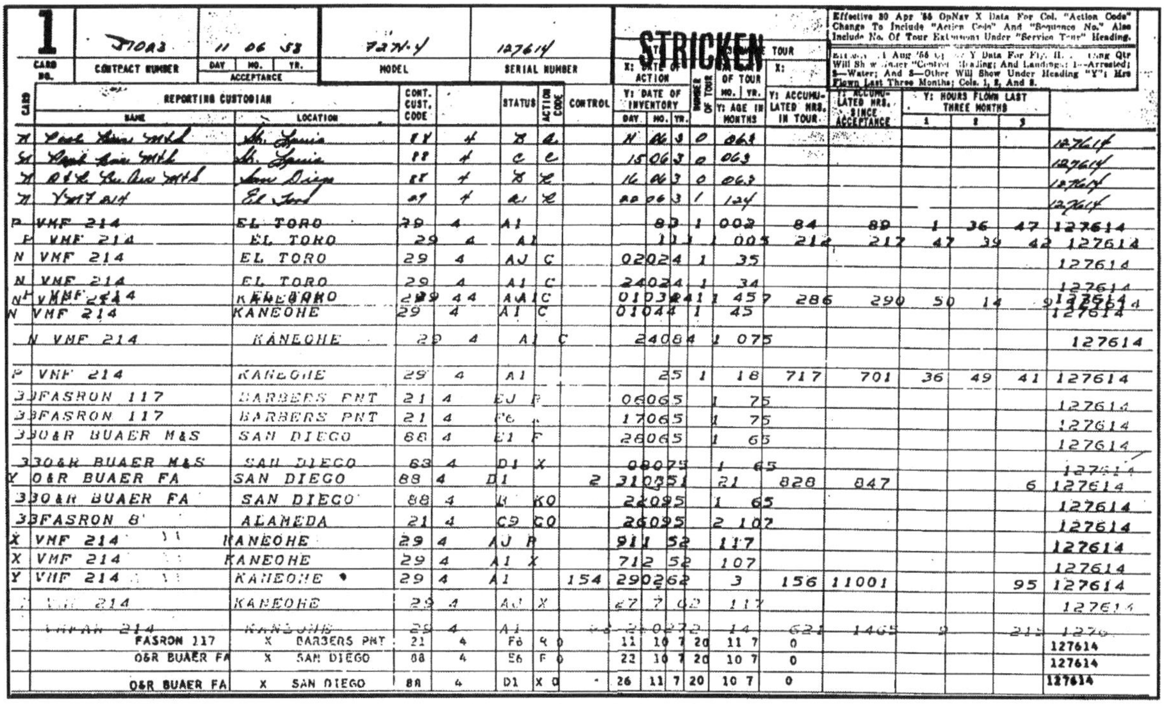

Card	Reporting Custodian Name	Location	Cont. Cust. Code		Status	Action Code	Control	Date of Inventory	No. of Tour	Age in Months	Accumulated Hrs. in Tour	Accumulated Hrs. Since Acceptance	Hours Flown Last Three Months 1	2	3	Serial
P	VMF 214	EL TORO	29	4	A1			83	1	002	84	89	1	36	47	127614
N	VMF 214	EL TORO	29	4	AJ	C		02024	1	35						127614
N	VMF 214	KANEOHE	29	4	A1	C		01044	1	45						127614
N	VMF 214	KANEOHE	29	4	A1	C		24084	1	075						127614
P	VMF 214	KANEOHE	29	4	A1			25	1	18	717	701	36	49	41	127614
3	FASRON 117	BARBERS PNT	21	4	EJ	R		06065	1	75						127614
3	FASRON 117	BARBERS PNT	21	4	F6			17065	1	75						127614
3	O&R BUAER M&S	SAN DIEGO	88	4	E1	F		26065	1	65						127614
Y	O&R BUAER FA	SAN DIEGO	88	4	D1		2	310751		21	828	847			6	127614
3	O&R BUAER FA	SAN DIEGO	88	4		KO		22095	1	65						127614
3	FASRON 8	ALAMEDA	21	4	C9	CO		26095	2	107						127614
X	VMF 214	KANEOHE	29	4	AJ	R		911 52		117						127614
X	VMF 214	KANEOHE	29	4	A1	X		712 52		107						127614
Y	VMF 214	KANEOHE	29	4	A1		154	290262		3	156	11001			95	127614
	FASRON 117	X BARBERS PNT	21	4	F6	R 0		11 10 7	20	11 7	0					127614
	O&R BUAER FA	X SAN DIEGO	88	4	E6	F 0		22 10 7	20	10 7	0					127614
	O&R BUAER FA	X SAN DIEGO	88	4	D1	X 0		26 11 7	20	10 7	0					127614

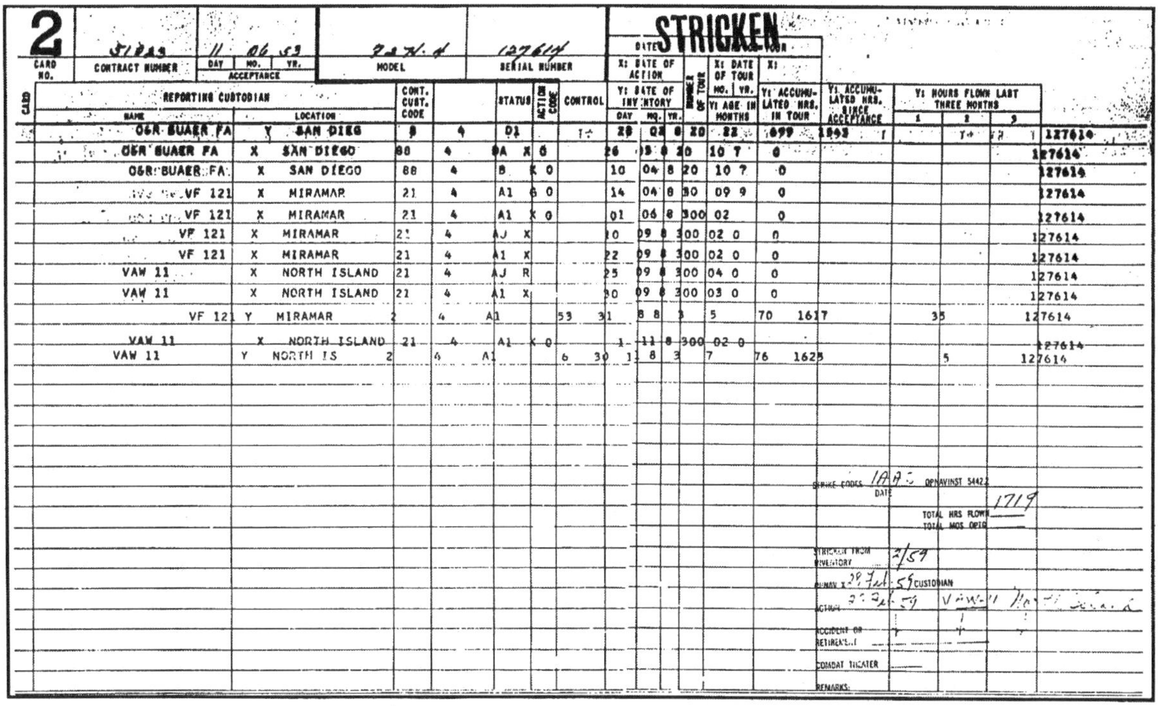

Card	Reporting Custodian Name	Location	Cont. Cust. Code		Status	Action Code	Control	Date of Inventory	No. of Tour	Age in Months	Accumulated Hrs. in Tour	Accumulated Hrs. Since Acceptance	Hours Flown Last Three Months 1	2	3	Serial
	O&R BUAER FA	Y SAN DIEG	8	4	D1			28 02 8	20	22	699	1593				127614
	O&R BUAER FA	X SAN DIEGO	88	4	A	X 0		26 03 8	20	10 7	0					127614
	O&R BUAER FA	X SAN DIEGO	88	4	B	K 0		10 04 8	20	10 7	0					127614
	VF 121	X MIRAMAR	21	4	A1	6 0		14 04 8	30	09 9	0					127614
	VF 121	X MIRAMAR	21	4	A1	X 0		01 06 8	300	02	0					127614
	VF 121	X MIRAMAR	21	4	AJ	X		10 09 8	300	02 0	0					127614
	VF 121	X MIRAMAR	21	4	A1	X		22 09 8	300	02 0	0					127614
	VAW 11	X NORTH ISLAND	21	4	AJ	R		25 09 8	300	04 0	0					127614
	VAW 11	X NORTH ISLAND	21	4	A1	X		30 09 8	300	03 0	0					127614
	VF 121	Y MIRAMAR	2	4	A1		53	31 8 8	3	5	70	1617		35		127614
	VAW 11	X NORTH ISLAND	21	4	A1	K 0		1 11 8	300	02 0						127614
	VAW 11	Y NORTH IS	2	4	A1		6	30 11 8	3	7	76	1625		5		127614

Strike codes 1AA; OPNAVINST 5442.2; Total hrs flown 1719; Stricken from inventory 2/59; Custodian VAW-11

Record cards for F2H-4 Buno. 127614 show the contract number the aircraft was acquired under, the date of acceptance by the Navy (November 11, 1953), and its first squadron assignment to the famous VMF-214 Blacksheep squadron on June 22, 1953. The second page shows its most recent squadron assignments, while the 'strike block' shows that the aircraft had flown 1,719 hours during its career. (U.S. Navy via Nicholas A. Veronico)

The aircraft's operational history is as follows:

11/06/53 Accepted by the U.S. Navy, St. Louis, Mo.
06/22/53 Delivered to VMF-214, MCAS El Toro, Calif.
03/01/54 Deployed to MCAS Kaneohe, Hawaii, with VMF-214
06/06/55 Assigned to FASRON-117, NAS Barbers Point, Hawaii
06/28/55 Flown to NAS North Island, San Diego, Calif., for overhaul
09/26/55 Assigned to FASRON-8, NAS Alameda, Calif.
11/09/55 Assigned to VMF-214, MCAS Kaneohe
10/11/57 Transferred to FASRON-117, NAS Barbers Point
10/22/57 Flown to NAS North Island, San Diego, for overhaul
04/14/58 Assigned to VF-121, NAS Miramar, Calif.
09/25/58 Assigned to VAW-11, NAS North Island, San Diego
02/22/59 Crashed, Fatal, Stevens Creek Canyon, Calif.
02/28/59 Stricken from Navy records with 1,719 hours total time

Key to Navy terms:
VAW - Navy Airborne Early Warning Squadron
VF - Navy Fighter Squadron
VMF - Marine Corps Fighter Squadron
FASRON - Fleet Aircraft Service Squadron

Part II:

Wreckchasing Reports from the Field

LOS ANGELES
TRIMOTOR

Chapter 1

Overdue from Kingman: The Crash of Fokker F-10A NC279E

Nicholas A. Veronico

The Fokker F-10A differed slightly from the F-10 model shown opposite. Fokker F-10A NC279E was lost on its delivery flight from the East Coast while en route to its final destination of Alhambra, California. The early airliner's remains rest in a remote canyon near Southern California's Lake Arrowhead. (Western Airlines via Veronico Collection)

A new standard of luxury in air travel was introduced in April 1928 when Western Air Express began service with the 10-passenger Fokker F-10 Trimotor. The air carrier had been granted $180,000 in 1927 by the Daniel Guggenheim Fund for the Promotion of Aeronautics to promote commercial air travel. This money was used to purchase three Fokker F- 10s for use on "The Model Airway," a route between Los Angeles and San Francisco/Oakland. Eventually Western Air Express would operate a fleet of five F-10s and 20 F-10As.

Powered by three 450-horsepower Pratt & Whitney Wasp radial engines, the F-10A could carry 12 passengers 765 miles at a cruising speed of 123 mph. Huge by the standards of the day, the F-10A had a wing span of 79 feet, 2 inches, a fuselage length of 50 feet, 7 inches, and weighed in at 13,100 pounds. For passengers, in-flight meals, operable windows for fresh air, and a rear cabin restroom increased the comfort level while airborne. For the flight crew, the cockpit boasted an instrument panel with lights for night flights and brakes for the main landing gear. Fokker eventually built 65 F-10s and 59 of the slightly larger F-10As. Western Air Express flew the F-10A until December 1935, when the last four of the type were sold from the fleet.

Fokker F-10A, NC279E, manufacturer's serial number (msn) 1011, was delivered to Western Air Express on February 2, 1929. It met an

The fuselage and engines of NC279E came to rest inverted after the wing separated from the fuselage in flight. Notice the fabric-covered fuselage, an engine, and main landing gear wheel. At the time the crash site was so remote, it took two weeks to find the plane wreck. (Veronico Collection)

untimely end just over one year later on February 23, 1930. While flying from Kingman, Arizona, to Alhambra, California, NC279E crashed eight miles northeast of Lake Arrowhead, California, during a severe snowstorm. Time of the crash was fixed at about 2:30 pm PST. Timc of the crash was determined by checking the wristwatches of the crew—one stopped at 2:25 and a second at 2:27. The clock in the instrument panel continued to tick until stopping at 2:45. The cabin of the airliner was void of passengers and only the crew of three, including Western Air Express pilot James E. Doles, co-pilot A.W. Bieher, and steward John Slaton, were killed in the crash.

Investigators at the time surmised that pilot Doles flew from Kingman to the eastern side of the San Bernardino Mountains where he encountered a snowstorm. While threading his way across the mountain range in the storm, Doles made the decision to turn back in an attempt to retrace his path to Kingman. He never made it.

From the damaged treetops in the area, investigators guessed that Doles must have been blown down into the treetops by a fierce gust of wind that weakened the wing's structure. Shortly after contact with the trees, the wing separated from the fuselage, fluttering to the ground. This sent the fuselage in a 45-degree dive through the trees, where it impacted the ground. The location of the fuselage's resting point was described as "an inaccessible canyon about eight miles northeast of Lake Arrowhead ... halfway between Hokum Creek and Luna Mountain ... and one mile from Mill Creek."

Wing Located; Where's the Fuselage?

Pat Macha lends scale to the Fokker F-10A's remains. The F-10A was powered by three 450-horsepower Pratt & Whitney Wasp engines, and could cruise at 123 mph for 765 miles. Twelve passengers were accommodated within the airliner's 50-foot, 7-inch fuselage. If this fuselage was recovered for restoration purposes, wings would have to be built from the original drawings. (G. Pat Macha)

After the snowstorm cleared, the first sign of the wreckage was seen six days after the crash by Mrs. Juanita Eloise Burns. Burns had spent five days flying over the area in her 90-horsepower Travelair biplane looking for the wreckage. On the day the wreckage was discovered, she was riding as an observer with Dudley Steele, a pilot for Richfield Oil Company. Burns spotted the wreckage in a canyon, and the pair returned to report their findings.

The next morning at 2:00 am, a search party was formed to hike into the site. Burns and Steele led the way, accompanied by Western Air Express's Fred Goodcell and deputy sheriffs Ernest Shay and Ed Mitchell. The search party tracked over pine- and spruce-studded ridges through a maze of canyons until dawn. As the sun rose over the tops in the east, Western Air Express pilot Monte Shelton circled over the wreckage to guide the searchers to the wing.

Upon locating the wing, they found it to be intact except for a few torn and missing pieces of fabric and a number of small holes in the leading edge. The wing tip was unscathed, putting to rest theories at the time that the plane's wing had struck a canyon wall, cartwheeling it into the ground. Although the wing had been located, no sign of the fuselage or the plane's three engines could be seen nearby.

Searchers fanned out in all directions, and two hours later volunteer searchers Lester Bugg, a Lake Arrowhead stone mason, and John Dexter, owner of the Squirrel Inn, signaled that they had discovered the engines, fuselage, and the remaining wing section. The fuselage had accordioned upon impact. The three engines were torn from their mounts and turned the wing into a twisted, broken mess. The bodies of the three crewmen were packed out and flown to Southern California's Alhambra Airport. From there the bodies were sent to their respective families for burial. After the crash investigation, the wreck was left on the mountain in what was considered a remote area in 1923.

The Crash Site Today

Due to the fabric-covered steel tube construction of the Fokker F-10A, there is no salvage value to the wreck site. However, the historical value is significant. Wreck authority G. Pat Macha is currently seeking a museum or interested parties who would like to recover the aircraft and begin the restoration process. Macha said, "The site is drivable with another hour or so walk up the mountain to reach the site. From the main highway, it is a long drive on dirt roads to get there. That's the primary hassle. The wreck is approachable only from the desert side of the mountain."

The Fokker F-10A's empennage rests in the brush. (G. Pat Macha)

Pat Macha with the twisted remains of the Fokker. To the right of the photo is the center engine. (G. Pat Macha)

The F-10A sat relatively untouched until the 1950s when a fire went through the area. This damaged the site further, but the plane still is considered worth recovering. Since the fire, the growth one would expect has not come back. Low scrub brush has returned, and although you must obtain permission, the trek to the site is considered worthwhile. Macha visited the site in the fall when the days were becoming short. He described the site, saying, "There is a big piece of fuselage with the vertical and horizontal tails still attached. The landing gears are there. The F-10A, besides having a tail wheel, had little skids. A skid was there. The wing had a heavy tubular metal frame with a wooden spar. There are wing ribs scattered about. The props are gone, but there are tons of engine parts and cowlings. We did not find any personal effects.

"That F-10 was a big bird, so it's pretty impressive from that standpoint. The wreck is interesting from the early technology standpoint, that type of construction. We have one rib section and one wing strut, a cylinder head, and a three-blade prop hub—all of which we would donate to any museum who recovers the aircraft.

"If somebody wanted to make an effort to recover the aircraft, it would not be that tough helicopter-wise."

The restoration and recovery of this early example of our commercial aviation heritage needs to be undertaken by an experienced, well-financed organization.

Chapter 2

The Fate of the Philippine Clipper

Ed Davies, Enrico Massagli, Nicholas A. Veronico

When Pan American issued its specifications for the successor to the Sikorsky S-42 Flying Boat, the company was making aviation history. The airline needed a larger aircraft to service its expanding Pacific routes—an airplane that could carry enough passengers, cargo, mail and fuel to make the 2,400-mile journey to the Hawaiian Islands economically feasible.

Pan American Airways' Martin M-130 Philippine Clipper *in flight over Alameda, California in the late 1930s. (Pacific Aerial Surveys courtesy Gordon Werne)*

The new design also needed to be able to fly the route with the style and luxury that travelers of the 1930s demanded. Pan American's concept heralded the dawn of a new era in aviation and opened up new corners of the globe to air travel.

Pan American's specifications resulted in the largest aircraft of its day, the Martin M-130. With a wingspan of 130 feet and a length of 90 feet, 10 inches, the M-130 could sleep 18 to 30 passengers in berths. Passengers also enjoyed a lounge and air-conditioned passenger cabins.

With a crew of seven men, the M-130 weighed almost 26 tons and carried 4,000 gallons of fuel. The airliner's four Pratt & Whitney R-1830s propelled her through the skies at a cruising speed of 130 mph.

Pan American agreed to buy three aircraft from Martin at a reported cost of $430,000 each. The *China Clipper* was the first of the type to fly in December 1934, only seven years after Charles Lindbergh had soloed

Philippine Clipper's *sister ship* China Clipper *in camouflage paint during World War II.* Philippine Clipper *was similarly marked when it crashed at the end of a flight from Hawaii to San Francisco. (Veronico Collection)*

across the Atlantic. The name later came to be used, interchangeably, to describe both the Martin M-130 and the later Boeing B-314's flights from the West Coast to the Orient.

In November 1935, the *Philippine Clipper*, registered NC14715, was delivered to Pan American, followed three months later by the last of the Martin M-130s, the *Hawaii Clipper*.

Whenever a "Clipper" aircraft would leave for the Pacific, it was accompanied by much media fanfare. The *Philippine Clipper* began service on the San Francisco to Manila run on November 22, 1935, and later pioneered the way to New Zealand and Hong Kong. She kept up the Pan American tradition of first class service, while leading the way across the Pacific as war clouds darkened in her path.

War Breaks Out, The End is Near

The *Philippine Clipper* left Wake Island (located west of the International Date Line) on December 8, 1941, at 7:00 am for a scheduled flight to Guam. Ten minutes later, Wake Island radio ordered her to return immediately. Pearl Harbor, the Philippines, and Midway Island were under Japanese attack. Because of the confusion created by these actions, no one at Wake was exactly sure what the next move for the *Philippine Clipper* should be.

At 11:30 am Wake Island time, a flight of 36 Imperial Japanese navy twin-engine Mitsubishi "Betty" bombers from Kwajalein flew in at wave-top altitude and attacked the island. The Wake Island Airfield and its U.S. Marine Corps Fighter Squadron suffered heavy damage from the Japanese attack.

The *Philippine Clipper* took between 20 and sixty 7.7mm machine gun hits during a strafing pass. Somehow, none of the bullets did critical damage, and the airliner was still fit to fly. Mechanics stripped the aircraft's interior of all non-essential weight, and late that afternoon the Clipper lifted off from the island's lagoon with a crew of eight, 22 Pan American employees, five passengers from the Guam flight, three Army officers, and one enlisted soldier. Without the aid of radio navigation, she flew through the night to Midway Island to take on fuel. At first light, she continued toward her home base at Pearl City, Hawaii.

Within months of the United States' official declaration of war with Japan, the U.S. Navy conscripted the Pan American flying boat fleet and their crews as part of the Naval Air Transport Service. This meant that the Pan American crews were officially active duty members of the U.S. Naval Reserve. Later in 1942, the Pan American crews were returned to civilian status. The operation of the Clippers, which remained Navy property, was then contracted back to Pan American.

The most sought-after of the Pan American Clippers were the Boeing B-314s. Their range and cargo capacity made them ideal for carrying VIPs and high-priority cargo across both the Atlantic and the Pacific routes. The Martin M-130s, on the other hand, did not have the range or the capacity of the newer Boeing 314s and the Navy relegated these aircraft to ferry flights between Hawaii and California.

The brilliant silver and orange prewar paint schemes of the *China Clipper* and the *Philippine Clipper* were quickly replaced with a crudely applied coat of non-specular blue/gray paint with large rectangular American Flags on the forward sections of their fuselages. Their distinguishing marks were the civilian registration numbers, the *China Clipper* had its name painted on its bow, and a wound stripe adorned the bow of the *Philippine Clipper* for having survived the attack on Wake Island.

The only other Martin M-130 built, the *Hawaii Clipper*, crashed at sea on July 28, 1938, somewhere between Guam and Manila. No trace of that aircraft was ever found.

The Final Flight

The *Philippine Clipper's* military service during 1942 had been uncomplicated, and January 1943 had started out even less eventful. On January 20, the *Philippine Clipper* sat tied to her pier at Pearl City, Hawaii.

For nearly a week, a series of arctic storms had been making the weather over the California coast very treacherous. The immediate forecast was so poor that the local Pan American operations manager had sent the crews back to their hotels with no realistic expectation of when the next flight to California might leave.

Around noon that day, Rear Adm. Robert H. English ordered Pan American to make the *Philippine Clipper* ready for immediate departure, which required the Clipper's crew to be rounded up. No documented reason can be found as to why Adm. English insisted on leaving on such short notice. Likewise, there is no explanation about his lack of concern over the weather in California.

It has been speculated that the admiral had scheduled a very high-priority meeting at the Mare Island Naval Shipyard near Vallejo, California, a major U.S. submarine base, on Thursday morning, January 21, 1943. Supposedly, the urgency of this meeting was created because of Japanese advancements in anti-submarine warfare equipment. U.S. submarine losses in the Pacific were growing, and the Navy was desperate for some form of electronic countermeasures.

Adm. English was a submarine veteran. After serving in the North Atlantic in World War I, Adm. English rose through the peacetime Navy to become the commandant of the Pacific Fleet Submarine Force.

The names and ranks of the U.S. Navy officers accompanying him on this California trip also lend credence to the theory of how important his meeting was: Capt. Robert Holmes, submarine commanding officer; Cdr. John J. Crane, submarine commanding officer; Cdr. William G. Meyers, submarine commanding officer; Lt. Cdr. George R. Stone, submarine executive officer; Lt. Cdr. John O. Coll, submarine gunnery officer; Reserve Capt. Donald C. Godwin, a science professor; Cdr. Francis L. Black, staff attaché to COMPAC, San Diego; and Capt. Robert E. Thomas, a Navy civil engineer.

Also on the passenger manifest was Navy nurse, Lt. j.g. Edna Morrow. Lt. Morrow was not on Adm. English's staff but had been waiting for a space-available seat to return to the continental U.S. because she was suffering from terminal cancer. In the ultimate of ironies, she knew that she was going home to die.

Designated Flight V-1104, the Pan American crew consisted of Capt. Robert M. Elzey, 36; Orvan K. Judd, 23, first officer; John R. Maynard, 28, second officer and navigator; George H. Abel, 26, third officer and pilot; Leo A. Mackota, 32, first engineer; John J. Eage, senior second engineer; Clarence P. Thompson, first radio officer; George W. Angus, second radio officer; and John G. Hill, 33, steward.

In all, 19 souls left Pearl City at 5:30 pm PWT (Pacific War Time) January 20, 1943. The *Philippine Clipper's* intended destination was San Francisco Bay. In her tanks was sufficient fuel for 24.2 hours of flying.

One of the two Pratt & Whitney R-1830 radial engines remains at the wreck site. Souvenir hunters have removed a number of cylinders from this engine. (Nicholas A. Veronico)

Her estimated time of arrival in San Francisco was 10:18 am PWT, January 21, 1943. These calculations gave her a seven-hour flight reserve.

The Pan American flight watch office at Treasure Island received a radio-telegraph (Morse code) message from Flight V-1104 at 5:35 am PWT, giving its arrival time as 6:35 am It seems that they had picked up a significant tailwind and were arriving three-and-one-half hours early.

Satisfactory radio-telephone (voice) communications were established at 6:16 am, and at 6:18 am, Flight V-1104 again revised its ETA to 7:10 am. The establishment of radio-telephone communications is significant because the type of transmitter used was limited to short ranges.

At 6:22 am, Treasure Island advised Flight V-1104 that the current weather conditions precluded a night landing and suggested San Diego as an alternate: "We feel that San Diego is the only possibility, unless it would be possible to hold until after daylight. Landing conditions are such you could not land before daylight."

Receiving no reply, Treasure Island radio asked again: "How do you feel about San Diego? Impossible to land here before daylight."

Flight V-1104 replied: "Roger ... Thank you."

Confused by this answer, the Treasure Island radio operator then asked: "Will you give us what you might intend to do as quickly as you have decided? Standing by."

Donna Struck stands next to the largest piece of the Philippine Clipper *wreck, the partially covered tail section. (Nicholas A. Veronico)*

Based on the National Transportation Safety Board's transcript of the radio transmissions between the *Philippine Clipper* and Treasure Island, there never was a straight answer from the Clipper as to exactly what Capt. Elzey intended to do.

The most common weather problem encountered on San Francisco Bay was fog. During such periods, the Clippers had a secondary base at Clear Lake, a large fresh water lake located approximately 100 miles northeast of San Francisco and about 40 miles inland from the coast. But the problem that morning was much worse than local fog. The storm was of such a magnitude that the approach to Clear Lake, which was situated between two large mountains, was obscured. Clear Lake was strictly a visual flight rules (VFR) alternative.

The *Philippine Clipper* was a true flying boat. That meant that she was unable to operate from hard runways that may have been available just to the north of the storm, which was traveling in a southeast direction. San Diego was probably the only realistic alternative for the *Philippine Clipper*.

One major consideration, however, was that the end result of their flying to San Diego would have meant either an unpleasant overnight train ride for the admiral and his staff or remaining overnight in San Diego, with the intention of flying back to San Francisco the next day.

Even so, there was no guarantee that the weather would clear sufficiently for a flight to San Francisco on January 22 or even January 23.

Apparently, two other alternatives were considered, both supported by the flight profile and subsequent radio transmissions. The first alternative, originally suggested by Treasure Island radio, was to have the aircraft loiter in the San Francisco Bay Area and re-evaluate the landing conditions after daylight. The second alternative called for the pilot to fly out over the ocean, then slowly sink below the overcast in an effort to find the straits of the Golden Gate and gain entrance to San Francisco Bay.

Which of the two they were trying to implement is a matter of speculation. Based on the fact that they were flying north in the opposite direction, it is probably safe to say they were not planning an immediate trip to San Diego.

The next radio communication came at 6:50 am, when Treasure Island notified Flight V-1104 that its position was approximately 43 nautical miles west-southwest of San Francisco. Flight V-1104 acknowledged.

The next position report from the *Philippine Clipper* said that the aircraft was passing over the Farallon Islands, about 25 nautical miles due west of San Francisco. There is no known documentation of how Treasure Island or the *Philippine Clipper's* navigator fixed its position in either case.

The *Philippine Clipper* radioed Treasure Island this message at 7:15 am: "Been over the area, but now taking a course due west."

Treasure Island seemed surprised at the change of course and asked: "You are taking a course due west to sea. Is that correct?" The Clipper responded, "That's correct."

Treasure Island then asked about flying conditions. Flight V-1104 answered: "Flying conditions very poor. Require a change of altitude to 7,000 feet."

The final transmission between Flight V-1104 and Treasure Island took place at 7:20 am The *Philippine Clipper* radioed: "We are not interested in setting up on Oakland yet. We would like to have a fix, please, so would you arrange that? Go ahead."

No further transmissions between the *Philippine Clipper* and any other station transpired after that call.

Approximately nine minutes later, the *Philippine Clipper*, Flight V-1104, impacted the side of a mountain at the 2,600-foot level, flying due north, approximately 140 miles north of its last position fix.

The NTSB report explained the situation: "Because the westerly magnetic heading of 270 degrees, which when corrected for the variation of 18 degrees east, would result in a true heading of 288 degrees. This, together with the extremely strong south-southwest wind, estimated by the U.S. Weather Bureau to have been between 60 and 80 mph at an altitude of 3,000 to 7,000 feet, would make it quite evident that he was actually proceeding on a track closer to 35 degrees."

The NTSB report also states that Capt. Elzey, who had accumulated nearly 5,000 hours of command flying time, was not only unaware of his position and heading but also his altitude. In short, he was officially lost.

The final seconds of Flight V-1104 were witnessed by several residents around the small town of Boonville, California. At approximately 7:30 am, Mrs. Charles Wallach was surveying the rise of a creek near her home when the Clipper burst through the overcast. She was only able to observe the navigation lights for a few seconds and then listen to the howl of the engines at full throttle, which faded to a low rumble.

Wallach was the local air raid warden, and she attempted to call the sheriff's office to report the incident. The storm, however, had brought down the telephone lines, and the circuit was dead. The telephone remained out of service until January 25.

The failure of the Clipper to respond to the radio must not have worried the personnel at Treasure Island, for the normal routine for receiving the flight progressed on schedule. Pan American sent the receiving launch to the north end of San Francisco Bay to wait, while the radio operator continued to send "blind" messages to the flight.

Overdue from Hawaii

The Civil Aeronautics Administration and the Western Sea Frontier Command were notified of the loss of radio communications at 10:00 am, and a subdued air search was initiated. At 6:00 pm, Navy officials were finally satisfied that Flight V-1104 could no longer be airborne and initiated a full-scale search, which eventually stretched from Eureka in the north to Monterey, south of the San Francisco Bay area, and 225 miles out to sea.

The first local newspaper accounts of the search appeared on Saturday, January 23. The coverage was brief and only noted that the Navy was looking for a "large transport seaplane with 19 persons aboard."

On Sunday, January 24, the press released the names and photographs of the missing crew and passengers. By January 25, everyone's nerves were growing thin. The search was being conducted based on the last radio transmissions, which led everyone to believe that the Clipper had been relatively close to San Francisco and heading out to sea. Thousands of man-hours were being expended, and nothing had been found, not even an oil slick.

The two top Pan American executives at Treasure Island, chief pilot Joe Barrows and Western Divisional Manager Jack Tilton, headed up a team of experienced pilots that included Ken N. Beer, the chief pilot in

charge of training. They began to formulate a "what if" theory about the Clipper's loss.

From years of flying the Alaskan bush for Pan American, Barrows knew the unpredictability of arctic storms, and from the numerous times he had run-ins with the Navy over operating procedures, he and Tilton believed that Capt. Elzey had probably been flying under a great amount of stress.

Their common assumption was that Adm. English knew full well what the weather on San Francisco Bay was like when they left Hawaii and that he had forced them to leave anyway. Since he had displayed such a disregard for the advice of the Pan American crew then, he may have

James "Bo" Hiatt holds the original memorial plaque at the top of the ridge above the wreck site. Three minutes before impact, the Philippine Clipper *passed over Hiatt's childhood home as he waited for the school bus. (Nicholas A. Veronico)*

had the same disregard for Capt. Elzey's advice when they arrived in San Francisco.

The radio transmissions did seem to indicate that they had chosen not to loiter near Oakland until daylight. That being the case, they felt that Capt. Elzey probably chose the option to "scud run," to fly just below the overcast to get the admiral to his meeting.

Barrows, Tilton, and Beer concluded that the navigator may not have realized that the hurricane force winds aloft, which had brought them into San Francisco three-and one-half hours early, were now pushing them north and east over land. When Capt. Elzey was told that they were safely out at sea, they were actually some 20 miles inland.

Record-setting pilot Elgin Long, left, surveys an oil cooler and propeller blade from the Philippine Clipper *held by "Bo" Hiatt. (Ed Davies)*

The Philippine Clipper *debris field includes one of the wing-to-sponson struts in the upper right of the photo as well as the parts to two engines in the lower left. (Nicholas A. Veronico)*

From the crux of the available information, their theory seems correct. The *Philippine Clipper* had broken out of the overcast directly over the Wallach farm, and upon realizing their predicament, the pilot gave the aircraft full climb power. Flying in broken visibility, the northerly course took them into Bell Valley, a box canyon. It appears that the pilot even tried to turn with the terrain. Unfortunately, the mountain's slope at the top of the valley exceeded the Clipper's climb rate.

The *Philippine Clipper* missed clearing the crest only by about 200 vertical feet, impacting the hill in a nose-down attitude and catching fire. The steady rains and soaked underbrush quickly extinguished any secondary fires.

Once Mrs. Wallach was able to get her phone call through to the proper authorities, the Navy dispatched a Martin PBM Mariner from NAS Alameda, situated on at the center of San Francisco Bay, but it was unable to fly low enough to positively identify the wreckage. A Lockheed Electra 10A, flown by Lt. Cdr. Henry J. Hollenbeck, was sent to inspect the crash site from the air, and just five minutes before sunset, he pinpointed the Clipper's remains. Ten days after its loss, the *Philippine Clipper* was found.

Lowell "Ed" Wilcox and his wife placed this memorial marker at the Ukiah Airport, the closest public gathering place to the Philippine Clipper *crash site. The marker was subsequently moved to the Hiller Aviation Museum in San Carlos, California, which has an excellent display of Pan Am Clipper memorabilia. (Betty S. Veronico)*

Early the next morning, a U.S. Army detachment moved in and formed an armed perimeter around the wreckage. The soldiers were under direct orders to shoot anyone caught inside the perimeter without proper credentials. Until Adm. English's briefcase could be located, the military was taking no chances of its falling into the wrong hands. Days later, after the military had pulled out, several boys located the briefcase in the branches of a tall oak tree.

The final flight of the Philippine Clipper officially ended in tragedy due to the actions of Capt. Elzey, specifically "not having fixed his position at the time of entering San Francisco Bay, or anytime thereafter." It is interesting to note that this judgment was based on a report that never documents whether the *Philippine Clipper* actually flew over San Francisco Bay.

Consider that at 6:50 am (PWT) Treasure Island fixed the *Philippine Clipper's* position as 43 nautical miles west-southwest of San Francisco, then the Clipper's next report stated that it was 25 miles due west of San Francisco. The fact that it crashed more than 100 miles north of San Francisco 35 minutes later seems to document sufficient probability that Flight V-1104 never did fly over San Francisco Bay.

Whether or not Adm. English played any part in Capt. Elzey's actions is purely speculation. The general feeling among the Pan American pilots was that Robert McNair Elzey was a very professional and capable pilot, and the flight profile he flew was totally out of character for him. Radio transmissions in the final hour were out of keeping with the crisp and to-the-point exchanges that were the hallmark expected of Clipper captains. At best, the reports are a compilation of open-ended conversations that implied confusion and indecision.

The Crash Site

"Sure, I remember. I was just a boy," longtime Boonville resident James "Bo" Hiatt said, recalling the day of the *Philippine Clipper* crash. "We were living in Yorkville at the time, and I was waiting for the school bus. It was just before 7:30 am. It was raining, and my mother heard an airplane approaching and called me and my sister out to see it fly over. I could see the lights as it passed overhead. Airplanes were a pretty rare sight in those days."

Hiatt had been to the crash site of the *Philippine Clipper* a number of times in his youth. He knew the landowner, and he made arrangements to venture to the crash site for a closer look. (Because the crash site is on private property, prior permission must be obtained before traveling to the site.)

Standing at the top of the hill and looking around, the first thought to come to mind is, "If they had only been 200 feet higher and 200 feet to the right, they would have made it." If they could have cleared this canyon, they would have had ample room to climb up to a safe altitude. From there, the terrain slopes downward into the Ukiah Valley.

Even though the crash happened more than 60 years ago, there is an eerie feeling to be at the scene where 19 people lost their lives. The canyon is quiet, and the colors of summer—reds, greens and browns—make a beautiful picture. In the distance to the west, the blue Pacific Ocean can be seen framed by white clouds in the valleys below.

There are no paths, so a path had to be cut on our way down to the site. Hiatt and Gary Urdahl, a local logger, led the way down into the valley. The first 75 feet of the descent into the canyon is perfect deer or rattlesnake terrain, with large rocks, waist-high brush, and weeds. No wreckage was spotted at first.

At about the 100-foot level, 8-to-10-foot-tall trees replaced the brush and walking became easier. Navigating down the ravine under the trees, Hiatt pointed out the point of impact. It is a depression with telltale

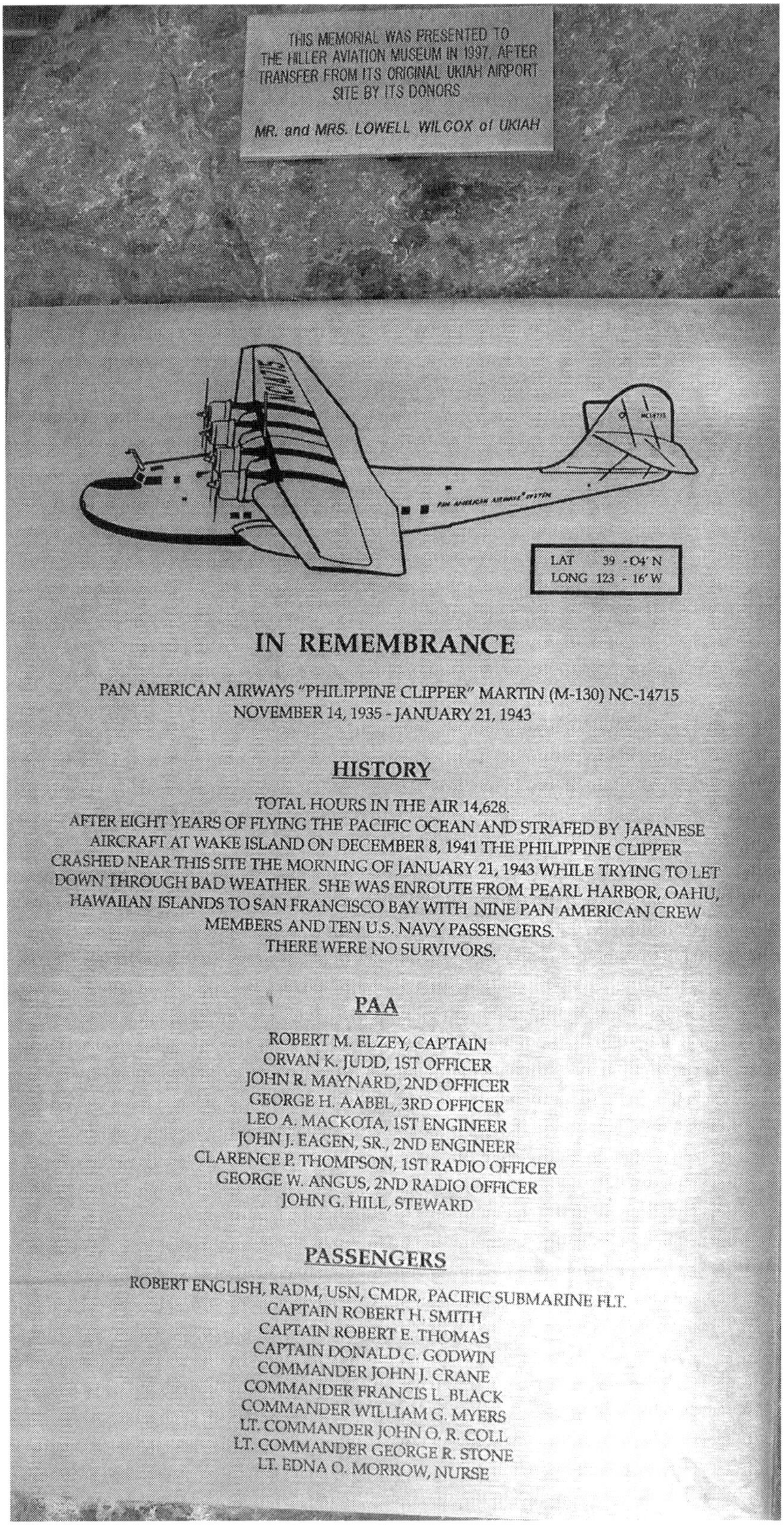
THIS MEMORIAL WAS PRESENTED TO
THE HILLER AVIATION MUSEUM IN 1997, AFTER
TRANSFER FROM ITS ORIGINAL UKIAH AIRPORT
SITE BY ITS DONORS
MR. and MRS. LOWELL WILCOX of UKIAH
LAT 39 - 04' N
LONG 123 - 16' W
IN REMEMBRANCE
PAN AMERICAN AIRWAYS "PHILIPPINE CLIPPER" MARTIN (M-130) NC-14715
NOVEMBER 14, 1935 - JANUARY 21, 1943
HISTORY
TOTAL HOURS IN THE AIR 14,628.
AFTER EIGHT YEARS OF FLYING THE PACIFIC OCEAN AND STRAFED BY JAPANESE
AIRCRAFT AT WAKE ISLAND ON DECEMBER 8, 1941 THE PHILIPPINE CLIPPER
CRASHED NEAR THIS SITE THE MORNING OF JANUARY 21, 1943 WHILE TRYING TO LET
DOWN THROUGH BAD WEATHER. SHE WAS ENROUTE FROM PEARL HARBOR, OAHU,
HAWAIIAN ISLANDS TO SAN FRANCISCO BAY WITH NINE PAN AMERICAN CREW
MEMBERS AND TEN U.S. NAVY PASSENGERS.
THERE WERE NO SURVIVORS.
PAA
ROBERT M. ELZEY, CAPTAIN
ORVAN K. JUDD, 1ST OFFICER
JOHN R. MAYNARD, 2ND OFFICER
GEORGE H. AABEL, 3RD OFFICER
LEO A. MACKOTA, 1ST ENGINEER
JOHN J. EAGEN, SR., 2ND ENGINEER
CLARENCE P. THOMPSON, 1ST RADIO OFFICER
GEORGE W. ANGUS, 2ND RADIO OFFICER
JOHN G. HILL, STEWARD
PASSENGERS
ROBERT ENGLISH, RADM, USN, CMDR, PACIFIC SUBMARINE FLT.
CAPTAIN ROBERT H. SMITH
CAPTAIN ROBERT E. THOMAS
CAPTAIN DONALD C. GODWIN
COMMANDER JOHN J. CRANE
COMMANDER FRANCIS L. BLACK
COMMANDER WILLIAM G. MYERS
LT. COMMANDER JOHN O. R. COLL
LT. COMMANDER GEORGE R. STONE
LT. EDNA O. MORROW, NURSE

traces of molten aluminum strewn in a six-foot-diameter circle. There is not much to see at the point of impact, so we moved on down.

Another 30 feet down, the tail cone and horizontal stabilizer came into view. This large piece has what appears to be an inspection hatch or bulkhead large enough to walk through. Small pieces of corrugated skin and a set of cowl flaps are visible, sticking straight up as if a flag to mark the final resting place of one of the buried Pratt & Whitney R-1830s.

Descending another 30 feet around a small bend is a large area strewn with wreckage. Huge portions of the fuselage and the strut from the wing to the "water wing" are immediately recognizable. This area is massive, stretching a good 300 feet down the gully and 200 feet out into the underbrush. One of the R-1830s is visible even after having had a few cylinders cut from it over the years. About 10 feet down from the engine is the propeller spider and shaft, all three blades neatly hacksawed off by earlier souvenir hunters.

Our group sifted through the large debris field for recognizable artifacts. A seat, a window frame from a cockpit window, an engine intake manifold, and many other easily recognizable aircraft parts were found.

Returning to the point of impact, we began to dig—not deep, mostly moving the top three to five inches of soil. At about two inches in depth, five feet out from the estimated point of impact, many snaps from a canvas cover came to the surface. Then a shout of amazement as an officer's coat button was found only three inches down, then another coat button, and another—then a plastic shirt button from just below the point of impact.

This was followed later by one of the most unusual finds, a 1938 Buffalo Nickel. Shortly thereafter, a 1938 penny came to the surface. Many other small pieces of history were recovered, from more snaps to belts or cargo belt buckles to broken pieces of dishes.

Except for the area where the surface digging took place, the site remained the same. The next good rain erased our footprints and hopefully will yield more artifacts from the *Philippine Clipper.*

Since our trip to the Philippine Clipper, Lowell "Ed" Wilcox had started a *Philippine Clipper* Museum at the FAA Flight Standards District Office at Ukiah Airport. The display was removed and a memorial plaque that had been placed on the ridge above the crash site has been moved to the Hiller Aviation Museum in San Carlos, California. The Hiller Museum houses an excellent display of the once proud Martin Clipper fleet.

The other two M-130s were lost. The *Hawaii Clipper* disappeared without a trace over the Pacific in 1938, and the *China Clipper* crashed in Trinidad in 1945 with 23 lives lost.

Chapter 3

P-63 Kingcobra Lost on Training Mission

Walt Wentz

On September 1, 1944, the end of the war was in sight. The once mighty Japanese military machine was being forced back to its home islands, and the Northwest Pacific had become an armed camp during four years of war.

On the Portland, Oregon, Army Air Base, the sky that autumn day was overcast, but visibility was listed as "unlimited." A flight of the 432nd Bomb Wing, Fighter Reconnaissance Training Unit, was taking off on a training mission to intercept a fictitious enemy aircraft.

Five Bell P-63 Kingcobras snarled down the runway and lifted off into the gray dawn at 7:10 am. Sleek, streamlined, and a pleasure to fly, these fighters did not have enough high-altitude maneuverability to challenge the Mitsubishi Zero, but the rugged Kingcobra was ideally suited for stateside training of young fighter pilots.

Leading the formation of five as they flew off to the southwest was Lt. L.A. Chiles. His wingman was 2nd Lt. Ernest N. Dorazio of Blairsville, Pennsylvania, a student pilot with almost 300 hours of flying time, including 44 hours in the P-63.

His Kingcobra, serial number 42-69137, had 320 hours flight time. It was getting a little weary, its wings slightly buckled from the rough handling by the dozens of student pilots.

U.S. Army Air Force Bell P-63 Kingcobra in flight. Second Lieutenant Ernest N. Dorazio perished in a similar aircraft when he struck a ridge 30 miles east of Portland, Oregon. (Walt Wentz Collection)

Page one of the Army Air Force's aircraft accident report on the crash of P-63A 42-69137. (Sig Unander Collection)

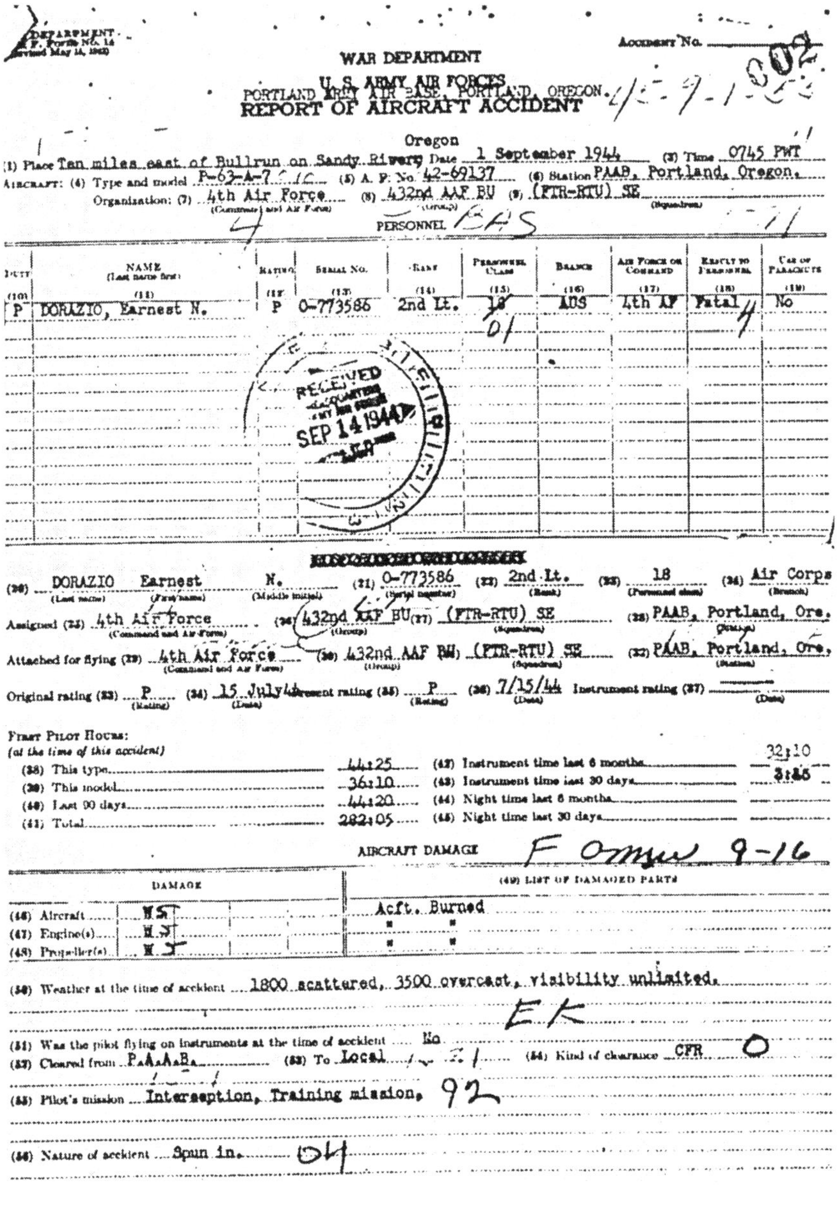

DEPARTMENT
A. F. Form NO. 14
Revised May 14, 1943

Accident No. 1-5-9-1-002

WAR DEPARTMENT
U. S. ARMY AIR FORCES
PORTLAND ARMY AIR BASE, PORTLAND, OREGON.
REPORT OF AIRCRAFT ACCIDENT

(1) Place Ten miles east of Bullrun on Sandy River, Oregon Date 1 September 1944 (2) Time 0745 PWT
Aircraft: (4) Type and model P-63-A-7 (5) A. F. No. 42-69137 (6) Station PAAB, Portland, Oregon.
Organization: (7) 4th Air Force (Command and Air Force) (8) 432nd AAF BU (Group) (9) (FTR-RTU) SE (Squadron)

PERSONNEL

Duty (10)	Name (Last name first) (11)	Rating (12)	Serial No. (13)	Rank (14)	Personnel Class (15)	Branch (16)	Air Force or Command (17)	Result to Personnel (18)	Use of Parachute (19)
P	DORAZIO, Earnest N.	P	0-773586	2nd Lt.	18 01	AUS	4th AF	Fatal 4	No

RECEIVED SEP 14 1944

[redacted]

(20) DORAZIO (Last name) Earnest (First name) N. (Middle initial) (21) 0-773586 (Serial number) (22) 2nd Lt. (Rank) (23) 18 (Personnel class) (24) Air Corps (Branch)
Assigned (25) 4th Air Force (Command and Air Force) (26) 432nd AAF BU (Group) (27) (FTR-RTU) SE (Squadron) (28) PAAB, Portland, Ore. (Station)
Attached for flying (29) 4th Air Force (Command and Air Force) (30) 432nd AAF BU (Group) (31) (FTR-RTU) SE (Squadron) (32) PAAB, Portland, Ore. (Station)
Original rating (33) P (Rating) (34) 15 July 44 (Date) Present rating (35) P (Rating) (36) 7/15/44 (Date) Instrument rating (37) —— (Date)

First Pilot Hours:
(at the time of this accident)

(38) This type	44:25	(42) Instrument time last 6 months	32:10
(39) This model	36:10	(43) Instrument time last 30 days	3:15
(40) Last 90 days	44:20	(44) Night time last 6 months	
(41) Total	282:05	(45) Night time last 30 days	

AIRCRAFT DAMAGE F Omsu 9-16

Damage		(49) List of Damaged Parts
(46) Aircraft	W.S.T.	Acft. Burned
(47) Engine(s)	W.S.T.	" "
(48) Propeller(s)	W.S.T.	" "

(50) Weather at the time of accident 1800 scattered, 3500 overcast, visibility unlimited. EK
(51) Was the pilot flying on instruments at the time of accident No
(52) Cleared from P.A.A.B. (53) To Local (54) Kind of clearance CFR O
(55) Pilot's mission Interception, Training mission. 92
(56) Nature of accident Spun in. 04

After making the "interception" at 10,000 feet, the formation turned east of the Bull Run Reservoir above the Sandy River as Lt. Chiles called the Portland Army Air Base for a vector home. The flight started a gradual descent into broken clouds at 8,500 feet.

"Some clouds have rocks in them," Lt. Dorazio's instructors had told him repeatedly. "In clouds, don't trust your senses—trust the instruments." Solid words of advice. Lt. Dorazio had a little more than 30 hours of instrument flight time.

The cloud layer was getting thicker. Looking for a way through, the flight descended into what looked, in the early morning dimness, like a large hole in the cloud. It wasn't. It was a thicker cloud.

Instantly, the pilots lost visual contact with each other, and the formation broke up in the mist. Several tense minutes passed as they descended, each man alone in the swirling grayness, earth and sky invisible, trying to "trust the instruments."

One plane came out of the clouds in a steep dive. As the pilot saw a ridge rushing up at him, he yanked back on the controls and his aircraft swooped back up into the mist, leaving him with the memory of that terrifying sight and distracting him from the instruments for a crucial instant. Was he climbing? Was he turning? In the gray disorienting void, his senses did not tell him.

When he came out of the clouds again, he had one wing down in a spin. As his flying mates watched, Lt. Dorazio's Kingcobra struck the ridge and exploded in a ball of fire.

At least Lt. Dorazio's family could take his body home for burial. His Kingcobra was bluntly written off as "aircraft burned." There was a war to finish, and the wreck was back in the hills, surrounded by second-growth timber, far from any road and impractical to salvage.

Greater events erased the memories of one student pilot's death. As the war receded into the past, Kingcobra 42-69137 lay forgotten on its timbered ridge, and the young trees grew up around the scars of the crash. The few P-63s that survived the war were scrapped and melted down to make aluminum pots and pans.

The Kingcobra Crash Site

Logger Kenny Valentine saw 42-69137 around 1981. It was still identifiable. The young trees that had sprouted around the crash site were now almost four decades old, and the seedlings had become valuable timber.

The Mount Hood National Forest, having jurisdiction over the Bull Run Watershed where the P-63 lay, had arranged logging sales in the area. As the area around the Kingcobra was logged, fallen trees were dragged back and forth over the wreck. It was reduced to scraps, and fragments of torn aluminum were scattered widely over the stump-speckled hillside.

The logging boss carried away the fighter's Allison engine. One of the .50-caliber wing guns was removed by a young logger, taken home, and then tossed into his backyard, where it lay around for a few years before being hauled to the dump. Other loggers had picked through the remains looking for anything of interest to them, and some had cut off bits for souvenirs.

After the final load of logs was hauled away, smashed electronic boxes, landing gear, tatters of aluminum skin, and hundreds of tiny parts and fragments buried in the rutted soil or tangled in the blackberries were all that remained. However, vague rumors of an old airplane crash somewhere in the Bull Run Watershed still circulated.

By 1988, Sig Unander, a native of Cornelius, Oregon, had heard those rumors. Unander was born 30 years too late to have had a chance to fly the warbirds that fascinate him. He carefully collects newspaper articles about old air crashes, listens to the rumors, then he studies and cross-references the stories. If one sounds like it might pay off, he begins by interviewing elderly outdoorsmen and witnesses.

Unander continues to venture into the rugged backcountry in an attempt to discover those few wrecks that have not been destroyed by military authorities or vandals. His purpose is to pinpoint the sites for historical purposes, to memorialize the now-forgotten aircrews, and to salvage usable parts needed in the restorations of the few surviving World War II aircraft.

The rumors of the Bull Run wreck sounded interesting. In several expeditions to the watershed, he spent a lot of time slogging around on steep, brushy hillsides without finding any trace of an aircraft. In the spring of 1989, Unander spoke to Bruce Rigby, a timber sales officer of the Columbia Gorge District of the Mount Hood National Forest, and Rigby's curiosity was aroused.

Rigby, a longtime World War II aircraft enthusiast, had himself found a P-38 Lightning wreck in the watershed years before. He began asking around among the old loggers and other woodsmen he knew.

Valentine told Rigby that he had seen an old wreck on Sandy Ridge when he helped log the site in 1981. Valentine took Rigby to the site, and then Rigby guided Unander to the shredded wreck.

When he first saw it, Valentine had been told it was a Bell P-39 Airacobra, the predecessor to the P-63 Kingcobra. But, by then, the scattering of aluminum debris gave no hint as to its origin.

As Unander and two friends began to work the site, Rigby and Valentine stopped by to check on their progress, then stayed to help dig. There is something fascinating about old warplane crash sites—an evocation of the grim days of the war, the ever-present hope that a usable part might be found, and the recreation of a doomed aircraft's last moments.

Unander and his friends slowly explored the wreck site with shovels and a metal detector, recovering both burned rubbish and shiny, new-looking components still bearing their original paint and military part numbers. One of those numbers prompted Unander, on a hunch, to telephone Dan Chvatal, an aircraft historian and collector in the Midwest.

Chvatal, the owner-restorer of two P-63s, consulted his old technical manuals and confirmed Unander's hunch. This was a P-63 Kingcobra, the successor of the P-39.

Now the mystery of how the aircraft got to Sandy Ridge and who was at the controls remained to be solved. Scanning the wartime issues of *The Sandy Post*, a local newspaper, Unander came across a front page story

that ran on September 7, 1944, describing the fatal crash of a Lt. Dorazio. The information was passed on to the Air Force.

About two months later, the Air Force sent an official copy of the War Department's report that described Lt. Dorazio's fatal crash. The aircraft serial number on the crash report matched the tail number found on the wreck.

The spot where the Kingcobra had struck was marked with a wing spar, a twisted propeller blade, and a surprisingly small patch of burned forest duff. The Kingcobra wreck yielded one main landing gear assembly and many airframe parts that will be used in the restoration of one of Chvatal's P-63s.

The remaining scattered wreckage was simply the bones of a once-beautiful aircraft, a memorial marking some long-lost history. Lt. Dorazio gave his life for his country as surely as if he had met a German or Japanese bullet. Yet, because he never went to war, he and his aircraft were forgotten until their story was brought back to light.

During the war years, student pilot errors, treacherous weather, or accidents brought down more than 300 military aircraft in the Pacific Northwest. Many have never been found. They lie hidden under the dense canopy of evergreen forests, entombed in ice on mountain peaks, and half-buried on the sea floor or on the silty bottoms of lakes and rivers.

Occasionally one is discovered, and a few of its parts may go to a restoration of one of the World War II aircraft that survive today. Other aircraft are out there, just waiting to be found.

Sig Unander is pictured at the crash site of P-63A 42-69137 in the Bull Run Watershed, 30 miles east of Portland, Oregon. Wreckage in the foreground is the aircraft's vertical stabilizer and part of the aircraft's tail. (Walt Wentz Collection)

Chapter 4

Memorial for a Corsair Pilot

A. Kevin Grantham

The center section of the wrecked Corsair could yield a number of parts that might serve as patterns in an FG-1A restoration.
(A. Kevin Grantham)

On March 15, 1944, Goodyear FG-1A Corsair, Bureau Number 13380, sat on the ramp at the Simmons Knot Airport, North Carolina. The Pratt & Whitney R-2800-8 radial engine was rumbling with its customary confidence. Meanwhile in the cockpit, Marine 2nd Lt. Edward J. Riordan was completing his cockpit checks before a night familiarization training flight.

Riordan had accumulated a total of 355.3 flying hours, 48 of those in the Corsair. Bureau Number 13380 had 128.5 hours on the airframe, while the engine had 143.8 hours running time. The plane was assigned to VMF-324, Marine Air Group 34, 3rd Marine Air Wing.

Unknown to anyone on the Simmons Knot ramp, disaster was soon to strike. Cpl. Donald S. Keefer was the plane captain for 13380 (which carried the training code 182A on the fuselage), and on March 16, 1944, he recounted the events of the previous evening:

"Plane Fox 182-A, of which I was plane captain, was scheduled for a night familiarization flight at 2200. On or about 2130, I made an inspection of the plane and found it satisfactory for flight.

"I was warming the plane up when Lt. Riordan came out to the plane. He also made an inspection of the plane and accepted it for flight. At his signal, I removed the chocks and guided him out to the taxi strip

The remains of the FG-1A's mighty R-2800-8 radial engine. (A. Kevin Grantham)

near Runway 22. Lt. Riordan moved out on the runway and prepared for takeoff.

"During takeoff, the engine of the plane was running smoothly, and as the plane was taking off, I was watching the tail light, which soon disappeared from sight. I started to turn and to continue on with my work when, suddenly, a burst of flames seemed to appear from the top of the trees.

"Upon investigation, this proved to be plane Fox 182-A piloted by Lt. Riordan. Plane Fox 182-A was flown by Lt. Riordan on the previous flight, and he did not note any defects that should be remedied before the next hop."

Note how the engine casting was sheared during impact. (A. Kevin Grantham)

Left to right: David Comer, Regan Register, and A. Kevin Grantham display some of the artifacts recovered from the crash of Goodyear FG-1A Buno. 13380. (A. Kevin Grantham)

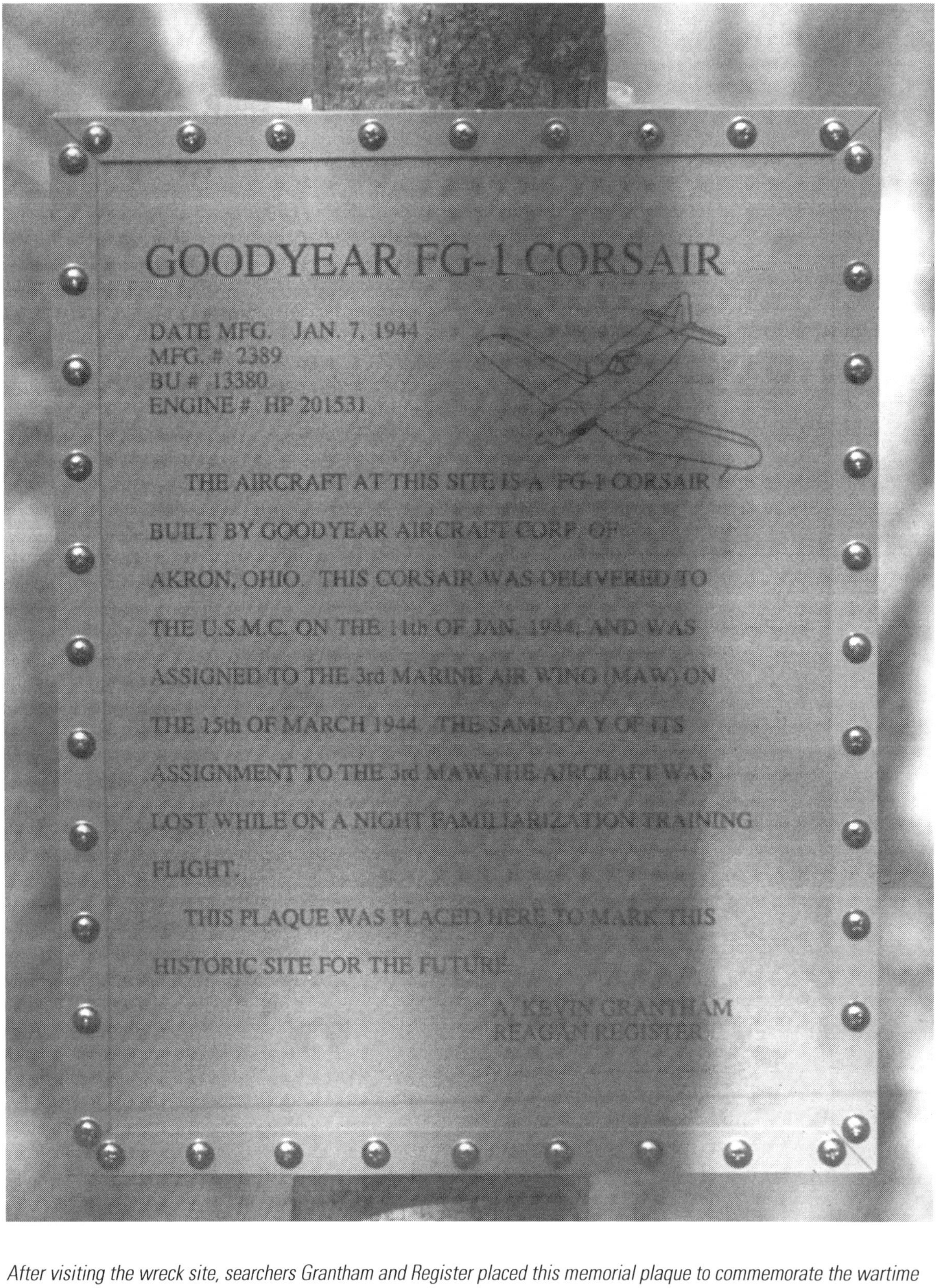

After visiting the wreck site, searchers Grantham and Register placed this memorial plaque to commemorate the wartime training loss and to explain the large chunks of metal to hikers who stumble onto the site. (A. Kevin Grantham)

The manufacturer's data plate was found among the wreckage.
(A. Kevin Grantham)

Another witness to the accident was 2nd Lt. William E. Lawhon: "I saw Lt. Riordan's plane take off normally and watched his plane clear the trees at the end of the runway. Then I took my eyes off the ship for an instant, and as I looked for it again, I observed a tremendous explosion a short distance beyond where I had last seen his lights."

The destruction of the Corsair was investigated by the Marines. However, due to the pressure of war and training requirements, only the pilot's body was removed along with a few salvageable bits and pieces. A report was made, and the incident was forgotten.

Forgotten, that is, until the author and some friends rediscovered the wreckage of the FG-1A in the Croatan National Forest near New Bern, North Carolina, during August 1987. The remains of the aircraft had been basically untouched since the accident investigation and comprised a considerable amount of wreckage.

Since that time, the author and Regan Register have coordinated two visits to this site with the Forestry Service in order to document as much of the plane as possible. They have also documented the wreck with a plaque for anyone who might discover the site in the future.

Chapter 5

B-24 Training Flight Ends Tragically on Arizona Mountainside

Robert A. Kropp

TB-24J 42-50890, similar to the aircraft shown here, crashed in northern Arizona during a wartime training mission. (U.S. Air Force Museum)

A burned and mangled BC-348 aircraft receiver, its variable capacitor still tuned to its final frequency, lies wedged between boulders on a remote Arizona mountain peak.

Rocks bear scars where four huge Hamilton-Standard propellers hit them at open throttle and then stopped; the spider gears of one propeller hub are twisted and broken in testament to the brute force of impact.

Less than 200 feet away from the impact site, control cables clang against a section of aluminum aircraft skin. Flung from the airframe during the impact, this section still contains a fragile dome light with its glass lens and 24-volt light bulb still intact. The boulder-strewn mountain peak is littered with 18 tons of airplane parts.

The crew of this B-24 Liberator probably never knew what happened on that fateful night of September 15, 1944, when their heavy bomber flew headlong into Kachina Peak of the San Francisco Peaks, just north of Flagstaff, Arizona.

Designated a TB-24J, she was built by Ford at the company's Willow Run, Michigan factory, and carried the Army Air Forces serial number 42-50890. A training ship assigned to the Army Air Forces Western Flying Training Center (AAFWFTC), the Liberator was stationed with the 3007th Army Air Forces Base Unit at Kirtland Field (now Kirtland Air Force Base), New Mexico.

Unlike the war-wearies usually assigned training duties, this Liberator was somewhat of an oddity. As a trainer, this Liberator was a "new" ship. The airframe had accumulated a total time of 645.40 hours since it rolled off the assembly line.

Two of her Pratt & Whitney R-1830s were original. The number two engine was the newest replacement, with 295.40 hours; number three had 334:30. This Liberator sported a bare metal finish and was painted only with the national insignia, aircraft numbers, and anti-glare black paint on the inside of the nacelles and in front of the pilot's windscreen.

Second Lt. Warren E. Crowther from Topeka, Kansas, was assigned to fly the Liberator on a navigation training mission from Bakersfield, California, back to Kirtland on that fateful Friday morning in September 1944. The New Mexico-based crew was going home.

Lt. Crowther's crew included student pilots Ray Shipley, Austin, Texas; Clyce H. McCelvey, Vernon, Texas; Charles W. McDonald, Oklahoma City, Oklahoma; and Patrick Pertuset, Portsmouth, Ohio; along with engineer James R. Hartzog, Silver Creek, Mississippi; radio operator John A. Franke Jr., Inglewood, California; and student engineer Hugh H. Brown, Gastonia, North Carolina. No doubt each man on board had made plans for the weekend—movies to catch in town, parties at the officers' or enlisted men's clubs, or perhaps Saturday night dates.

Debris field of TB-24J, 42-50890, atop Kachina Peak. The fuselage section and bomb bays are recognizable. (Robert A. Kropp Collection)

On the darkened airfield, the flight engineer walked around the bomber with a flashlight for a visual check, while the other crewmembers climbed aboard. The pilot and co-pilot began their preflight check. Ignition switches on. Throttles cracked one-third open. Booster pump on. Starters: "ACCEL" switch up; then "MESH."

Lt. Crowther started the number three engine first, then numbers four and two, and finally number one. As his co-pilot monitored engine oil and hydraulic pressures, the pilot taxied the heavy bomber toward the run-up area. Batteries were switched to generators; radio sets were turned on. The cold bomber was coming alive.

Turning the bomber downwind, Lt. Crowther called for a run-up check—superchargers set and locked, wing flaps 20 degrees, auxiliary hydraulic pump and power unit off, and cowl flaps closed.

After the tower cleared the Liberator for takeoff, Lt. Crowther released the brakes and turned the bomber into the active runway—trim tabs set for takeoff, propellers set at "high rpm," fuel mixtures "auto rich." The pilot opened the throttles, and the mighty Liberator began its takeoff roll.

The Liberator lifted off the tarmac at 12:48 am. As it began its gradual climb into the dark morning sky, the co-pilot lifted the landing gear, which folded into place with an assuring "clunk."

This may have been a familiar type of mission for someone like Lt. Crowther. Having earned his pilot wings just nine months earlier, he had racked up 512 hours in Liberators, 90 hours alone in the previous month. One-fifth of his total time in B-24s involved night flying, and he had spent more than 15 hours in the left seat of Liberators on nighttime training flights in August.

While the pilot may have been very familiar with the B-24, he had limited instrument flying experience—just over four hours total time, with half of that accumulated in the previous 30 days.

Lt. Crowther gently banked the plane and set a course, following a familiar route out of California and across Arizona. When he reached his desired cruising altitude, the pilot reduced power and trimmed the aircraft for level flight. The crew coupled their oxygen masks to airflow regulators and plugged their heated flight suits into rheostats at their respective stations.

To this point, their actions were routine. The crew settled back and prepared to accumulate their air hours and training time. At 3:02 am, the bomber reported in over Ash Fork, Arizona, which was experiencing a light storm with clouds broken to overcast at 6,000 feet. Occasional showers were reported by a weather officer at a neighboring Army airfield at Winslow, Arizona.

But the radio signal received at Ash Fork was the last message from TB-24J, 42-50890. Approximately 15 minutes later the airplane crashed against the west slope of the San Francisco Peaks, at an elevation of 12,500 feet.

The heavy bomber missed clearing the peak by less than 500 feet. The positioning of the wreckage indicates the Liberator may have clipped a wingtip on a pine tree, cartwheeled into the boulders, and exploded on impact.

A fairly intact outer wingtip is the largest section of wreckage. The landing gear is still tucked up into a wheel well in a portion of the massive Davis wing.

More than 60 years after the crash, military officials are still vague about the exact cause. The accident report is stored on microfilm records at the Air Force Inspection and Safety Center. The report, completed September 23, 1944, states the cause of the accident simply as, "Collision in full flight with object other than aircraft. Airplane collided with mountain while in full flight." Accident investigators determined the scene of the crash was 15 miles off course on the north side of the airway.

In Section 19 of the report, the condition of each crew member is marked "Fatal." Under the column "Use of Parachute," investigators wrote simply "None" eight times.

On September 19, 1944, Lt. Harry E. Campbell, wrote, "Investigation of the wreckage revealed no signs of engine malfunction. All four engines were delivering power at time of contact with the ground."

The Liberator was written off as a "complete wreck" and soon forgotten. With wartime aircrew training continuing at a hectic pace, mishaps such as this one occurred all too often. Portions of the accident report are still listed as "Restricted" information, especially specific information placing blame on the accident or forensic information.

Why did the Liberator stray so far off course? Did a pitot tube ice up and affect instruments, fooling the crew into believing they were higher than they actually were in an airspace well-known for tall mountains? Did a moment's carelessness claim the lives of eight men?

What was the rest of the crew doing when the heavy bomber struck the mountainside? Did the pilot see the mountain looming toward him and, at the last minute, heave on the controls and try to pull up? What did each man think in his final milliseconds of life?

No one, not even the military, can answer these questions. But, when you're standing at 12,000 feet on a craggy mountain with your lungs straining from the thin air and your legs aching from the arduous uphill climb, the mind wanders. The mental picture of a solid, heavy bomber traveling invincibly at 175 mph is quickly dispelled by glancing out over the twisted graveyard of aluminum in front of you. In a battle between airplane and mountain, the mountain always wins.

Vincent P. Murone, chief of the Reports Branch, said portions of the report are not releasable and have been redacted. "These portions

Some of the pieces of 42-50890 that are strewn on Kachina Peak. (Robert A. Kropp Collection)

contain the opinions and conclusions of the safety investigator as to the cause or recommendations for mishap prevention purposes," he said.

"Investigators are promised that their opinions and recommendations will be kept confidential as privileged safety information to encourage free and frank expressions of ideas. No time limit is placed on the promise of confidentiality; therefore, to ensure the continued confidence of current safety investigators in the safety privilege, we do not release opinions and recommendations even from these old safety reports."

Each year, thousands of people spend countless recreation hours in the shadow of the San Francisco Peaks, located about 10 miles north of Flagstaff. The mountains are a popular ski attraction during the winter and offer cool relief from the blistering triple-digit summer temperatures of the Phoenix metropolitan area. Despite the popularity of this mountain chain, the wreckage of the Liberator lies generally undisturbed because of its inaccessibility.

The "old-timers" in Flagstaff who do know about the Liberator wreck at the top of the mountain often refer to it as "the B-17." They are partially correct—there is a B-17 wreck on the mountaintop, but it is on another side. The confusion is easily understood considering the unusual circumstances. Less than one week after the Liberator crashed, a B-17G, which was on a training mission from Kingman Army Air Base, suddenly caught fire in flight and plummeted into Bear Jaw Canyon. All on board the B-17 were killed.

A memorial plaque for the Liberator and her crew has been placed at a ski lodge at the base of Humphreys Peak Trail. The memorial was erected in November 1988 by Mesa, Arizona, resident Richard Johnson and a local Boy Scout troop. The plaque reads:

"In the early morning hours of September 15, 1944, a U.S. Army Air Forces B-24 bomber on a night training mission crashed into the San Francisco Peaks, killing all eight crewmen. This memorial is dedicated to those young American airmen … For the cause of freedom, they gave up their lives."

The best way to get to the wreckage is to take the Humphreys Peak Trail, nothing more than a little path through the densely wooded forest. A little less than two hours into the hike, the trail makes a sharp turn at a small clearing in the trees. The steep trail continues to the crest of the peak, an additional two miles. Off to the left is a massive, boulder-strewn rockslide. To get to the wreckage, leave the trail and carefully proceed across the rockslide and continue up to the top of the mountain.

The horizontal stabilizer is recognizable in the debris. (Robert A. Kropp Collection)

The last mile up to the crash site is the most difficult because of the steep grade and the boulders, many of which are loose. Extreme caution should be exercised when on the rockslide, as a misplaced step could result in severe injury.

The remains of a Pratt & Whitney radial engine will be found about a half-hour after crossing the rock slide. The powerplant, which broke free of the wreckage, separated mid-crankcase, and cartwheeled down the mountain, can be found propped up against a large fallen tree. The crankcase still contains trace amounts of oil, despite having been stopped while in full flight by propellers hitting rocks and trees and the passage of more than a half-century.

The actual crash site is less than a half-hour from this engine. Hikers will know they are getting close when they start seeing small pieces of aluminum.

The main wreckage is strewn over several hundred feet, much of it imbedded in the rocks. The force of the impact triggered a rockslide; the explosive sounds of the impact and the rumbling boulders must have reverberated down the quiet canyon on the morning of the incident.

A trip to the remote crash site is best done during June and July. Snow can still be found on the ground at the crash site in June. Despite triple-digit temperatures in the Phoenix metropolitan area less than three hours away, temperatures on the rocky peak can drop to the mid-40s at night. Appropriate dress is strongly recommended. The hike should be avoided in mid-to-late August because of Arizona's monsoons. Recently, two hikers were struck by lightning while climbing Humphrey's Peak Trail, one fatally.

The author has personally seen sudden storms roll in unexpectedly while visiting the crash site in August, and the aluminum-littered landscape draws lightning like a magnet is drawn to steel. A pair of thick leather gloves, sturdy hiking boots, and extra drinking water should be considered mandatory items for making this trek; the gloves are necessary, not only for sorting through the razor-sharp pieces of aircraft wreckage, but for protecting one's hands on the rock slide. Some of the terrain is traversed on all fours.

Reverence and consideration should be exercised when visiting any aircraft crash site. While this Liberator remains fairly untouched by the masses over the years, some souvenir hunters have damaged parts that could have been utilized in a Liberator restoration. A section of wing has been needlessly split by someone wielding an axe, when access could have been gained by simply moving some large rocks and crawling into an opening near a fuel cell cavity. Access panels have been bent open with pieces of engine mount, when an extra few minutes with a Phillips screwdriver or a Dzus tool would have kept the panel itself intact. One souvenir hunter, intent on taking a propeller blade, used a hacksaw to remove the blade at the shank.

Another souvenir hunter must have spent hours disassembling a propeller hub and carefully placed the hardware removed from the unit in a tin can. The conscientious souvenir hunter went so far as to wrap the exposed gears with a piece of plastic and carefully placed rocks over the gears, still covered with 1944-vintage lubricants, to keep out debris and moisture.

Several propellers, albeit bent and damaged, have remained at the crash site for more than 35 years. Each year, another "mysteriously" disappears.

The Liberator's flight deck disintegrated upon impact. Small items—panel switches, pieces of instruments, twisted rudder pedals, wires, tubing, and oxygen regulators—are all that remain of the cockpit.

Pieces of thick Plexiglas and heavy chunks of casting are all that remain of the nose turret. Not a trace can be found of the Martin 250CE upper turret; usually the armor plate and the ring gear can be discerned even after an explosive impact and fire.

Some who have visited the crash site have speculated that the top turret was removed on this training bomber to free up more room to accommodate the student pilots in the typically crowded Liberator flight deck. Others have suggested the Martin could have broken free from the airframe during the impact and may have cartwheeled for several miles down the rugged rockslide. The latter seems improbable, as many heavy sections of armor plate and exhaust turbochargers remain in the immediate impact area.

A damaged but fairly intact Consolidated tail turret remained at the crash site for more than 40 years. The turret—still containing the seat, gun mounts, gun feed motor drives, ring gear, and many internal parts—was last seen at the site in the summer of 1991. It is hoped that those who remove items from these historic crash sites are doing so to aid other aircraft restorations or out of personal interest in warbirds and not for scrap purposes.

No armament or ammunition can be found among the wreckage. It is doubtful that the airplane carried any weapons during its final navigation training assignment.

While the military removed the remains of the perished crew from the crash site just days after the 1944 incident, some personal artifacts still remain in the wreckage. A shearling-lined, high-altitude flying boot was discovered a few years ago, in addition to several pairs of shoes, headsets, shirts, pants, pieces of flying jackets, and burned parachutes.

A damaged pair of sterling silver pilot wings were uncovered in the humus where the cockpit section impacted and burned, as was a dog tag belonging to Pvt. Brown. The dog tag was returned to Brown's family during the brief but emotion-filled ceremony of the memorial plaque

dedication, and the other personal artifacts were returned to the earth not far from the site.

One of the outer wing panels is still clearly marked "2-50890." If you want to move it for a photograph, it takes at least two people to turn the wing over. Don't try to do it alone—it's too heavy and the rock base is unstable. When you're through photographing the wing and the numbers, turn it back over again to protect it from the sun, rain and snow.

The crash site is located in the Coconino National Forest. The forest service discourages the removal of items from the area.

Remains of prop hub assembly of 42-50890. (Robert A. Kropp Collection)

Chapter 6

The Mystery of TWA Flight Three: Actress Carole Lombard Perishes in Crash

Donald B. McComb Jr. and Michael McComb

DC-3 NC1946 took actress Carole Lombard and twenty-one others to their deaths on January 16, 1942. The tail section rests inverted on a ledge on Mt. Potosi. (UPI/Bettmann)

On January 16, 1942, at 7:07 pm PST, a Transcontinental & Western Air (TWA) DC-3, NC1946, took off from the Las Vegas Western Airlines Terminal with 19 passengers and a crew of three for what should have been a routine flight to Burbank, California. Twenty minutes later, the DC-3 was a mass of flaming wreckage on the steep slopes of Mt. Potosi, 35 miles southwest of Las Vegas. The passenger list included 15 Army Air Corps servicemen, the wife of an Army Air Corps pilot, and notably actress Carole Lombard, her mother Bessie Peters, and Otto Winkler, Metro Goldwyn Mayer's (MGM) press agent for Lombard. The crew consisted of Captain Wayne Williams, First Officer Morgan A. Gillette, and Hostess Alice Getz.

This accident had most of the makings of a 1940s Hollywood movie. It included one of the most famous actresses of the time, traveling on a government mission. She carried thousands of dollars worth of expensive jewelry. An internationally famous violinist was bumped from the aircraft at Albuquerque and later suspected of being an enemy agent and saboteur who caused the crash. An FBI investigation of the accident was conducted by no less than J. Edgar Hoover himself, with the results of the investigation followed closely by the White House.

Clark Gable, center, leaves his Las Vegas hotel as plans for the funeral of his wife Carole Lombard are completed. With Gable are Howard J. Mannix, left, general manager and vice president of Metro Goldwyn Mayer studios, and friend Al Menasco. (UPI/Bettmann)

The story begins on the morning of January 12, 1942. The United States had been at war with Japan and Germany for less than a month. In Hollywood, a call for action went out. Clark Gable was picked to head the Hollywood Victory Committee. Wanting to do her part to help with the war effort, Gable's wife, Carole Lombard, volunteered to go on a fund-raising drive to sell war bonds for the Treasury Department. Lombard's goal was to raise $500,000 on a round-trip rail journey from Los Angeles to Indianapolis, Indiana, in her home state. Departure was set for the morning of the January 12 and she was to return to Los Angeles' Union Station eight days later.

Accompanied by her mother and press agent Winkler, the trio departed Union Station as scheduled. Making several fund-raising stops along the way, they arrived in Indianapolis on January 15. In a one-day flurry of appearances, Lombard gave speeches, signed autographs, and managed to exceed the Treasury Department's goal considerably. She raised a total of $2,107,513 for the war effort. Now at the end of what had been a very long day, Lombard was tired. She was not looking forward to

Soldiers prepare to lower the bodies of those killed in the crash. (UPI/Bettmann)

the long trip home with the additional fund-raising stops that had been added. She wanted to fly home. Her mother, who had never flown before, was against this idea. Winkler also attempted to talk Lombard out of flying by saying that she could get more rest on the train. Lombard was adamant, "I'll sleep on the plane, and we'll be home tomorrow." At around 1:00 am, she finally decided to let the matter rest on the flip of a coin: Heads for the train, tails the plane. The coin landed tails up.

After calling the airport, they discovered three cancellations on TWA Flight 3, inbound from New York, and due to depart Indianapolis at 4:00 am. Several stops later, the flight would arrive at the Los Angeles area's Burbank Airport some 17 hours after leaving Indianapolis. When they arrived at the airport another debate took place between mother and daughter about flying home. Lombard's mother, Mrs. Peters, was a strong believer in the occult, mainly astrology and numerology. Consulting her astrology charts, she pointed out that it was now January 16, and that the number 16 was a sign of impending accident or death. In addition, there were, according to Peters, "too many threes" involved in this trip.

The sheer rock face of Mt. Potosi is almost 90 degrees at the point of impact. (UPI/Bettmann)

They were a party of three, they were booked on Flight 3, a DC-3, and Lombard was 33 years old. Peters believed that "the number three is an unlucky number." In addition, Peters' personal astrologer had warned her to stay off airplanes in 1942.

At 3:16 am, the TWA DC-3 taxied up to the terminal at Indianapolis Airport. The DC-3-362, serial number 3295, NC1946, was delivered new to TWA in March 1941. After refueling, the passengers boarded and Flight 3 departed westbound into the predawn darkness.

Flight 3 next stopped at Wichita, Kansas, where several passengers deplaned, and a few others boarded. Among them was Joseph Szigeti, an internationally recognized concert violinist. Szigeti had fled Hungary to escape the war in Europe. He was heading to California to take part in the Irving Berlin film "Holiday Inn," in which Bing Crosby introduced the famous song "White Christmas."

After departing Wichita, Flight 3 headed for Albuquerque, New Mexico, the last scheduled stop before Burbank. Prior to the flight's arrival, TWA agents in Albuquerque received orders from the War Department

Close-up of one of the DC-3's engines on Mt. Potosi, near Las Vegas. (Michael B. McComb)

stating that 12 members of the Army Air Corps with priority tickets had to be given seats on Flight 3. According to records, five of the westbound passengers would have to be bumped from the flight. When Flight 3 landed, TWA Station Agent Ed Knudson informed the passengers of the situation. This was not well received. The Lombard party was asked to give up their seats. Winkler and Peters agreed, however Lombard, nearly home, was not about to be stopped. She told the TWA agent that she had been on a government mission, and that he would have to bump someone else. Because Lombard retained her seat, the other two members of her party were not bumped, and decided to continue on to California.

The only other civilian to retain a seat on Flight 3 was Mrs. Lois Hamilton, wife of an Air Corps pilot. Among the passengers deplaned at Albuquerque was violinist Szigeti. Also at Albuquerque, a crew change took place, with Williams, Gillette and Getz boarding. Before the flight could leave Albuquerque, one other problem had to be solved.

The Army Air Corps pilots and enlisted men had a lot of heavy luggage, duffel bags, parachutes, etc. This made the DC-3 heavier than allowed by federal regulations. In order for the flight to be legal, TWA agent Knudson made some "adjustments" to the figures in the paperwork. According to government records, Knudson counted four of the passengers as weighing 150 pounds each. In addition, he asked Lombard, Peters, and Hamilton their actual weight. Using these new figures, the aircraft was now "legal" for flight, but in actuality still weighed more then the Civil Aeronautics Administration (CAA) rules allowed.

Michael B. McComb poses with one of the DC-3's engines near the point of impact. (Michael B. McComb)

One of the landing gear with exposed oleo embedded in the rocks of Mt. Potosi. (Michael B. McComb)

At the time Captain Williams took command of Flight 3 on the afternoon of January 16, 1942, he had more than 12,000 hours of flight time. However, he had less than a perfect record as a pilot. In June 1929, he went to work for American Airways (predecessor to American Airlines). Late in 1931, Williams applied for a job with TWA, but was turned down because of word in the industry that he took unnecessary risks with company equipment and cargo. Nevertheless, shortly after the interview, TWA hired Williams as a night mail pilot. Within two years, he was fired, after being charged with damaging equipment, carelessness, and insubordination.

Williams was terminated because the official at TWA who had originally hired him changed his mind. Citing constant violations of air safety rules, the fall 1933 memo concluded, "I do not care to be responsible for his flying with passengers."

Aerial view of Mt. Potosi showing the rugged terrain and the valley beyond. The DC-3 impacted the face of Mt. Potosi near the radio towers shown at right. (Michael B. McComb)

Less than 60 days later, Captain Williams was rehired after the National Labor Relations Board ruled that his rights had been violated and that he should be reinstated, but as an airmail pilot only. During the next nine years Captain Williams' record showed no major complaint or disregard for the rules.

Departing Albuquerque

Now more than three hours behind schedule, Flight 3 finally departed. Because of strong headwinds that had been predicted for the route, Captain Williams decided to make two additional stops for fuel, at Winslow, Arizona, and Boulder City, Nevada.

Shortly after takeoff the crew of Flight 3 decided that they could save time by changing their flight plan. Captain Williams transmitted a request to TWA flight operations in Burbank. After recalculating fuel consumption Williams decided not to stop at Winslow for fuel. However, because the flight was behind schedule, they would be arriving after dark at Boulder City Airport, which had no landing lights. Captain Williams requested permission to land at Las Vegas. These changes were granted at 4:38 pm PST.

At 6:36 pm PST, Flight 3 taxied up to Las Vegas' Western Airlines Terminal building, located at what is now Nellis Air Force Base—this was an era when most airlines had their own airports. For this reason, the TWA station manager drove over from the company's airport at Boulder City to meet the flight. While the passengers went inside to grab a sandwich and something to drink, the DC-3 was fueled with 225 gallons of gasoline, and oil was added to the engines. A few minutes before 7:00 pm, the passengers boarded the DC-3 for the last leg of the trip.

Author Michael B. McComb prepares to head to the DC-3's crash site. (Michael B. McComb)

At 7:07 pm, NC1946 departed Las Vegas and turned towards the southwest. Captain Williams radioed back to the airport that they had "cleared the field" and were proceeding on course.

What happened at 7:23 pm is known. How it happened is not as clear. Climbing through 8,000 feet at over 150 miles per hour, the left wing of the DC-3 clipped a rocky ledge, cartwheeling the aircraft into the face of a cliff. With a thunderous explosion, hundreds of gallons of aviation gasoline detonated, scattering wreckage, bodies, and luggage down the face of the cliff. Most of the debris came to rest at the bottom of a ravine. Had Captain Williams been 550 feet higher he would have missed the top of Mt. Potosi with 15 feet to spare.

Accident Investigation

How did this happen? To this day no one really knows. Because this accident took the life of Carole Lombard, a personal friend of President Roosevelt, and because this accident occurred during wartime under less-than-clear circumstances, federal investigations on several levels were begun. The Civil Aeronautics Board (CAB) launched a conventional aircraft investigation into the crash. The Federal Bureau of Investigation (FBI) looked into the possible criminal aspects of the accident to determine if the aircraft had been sabotaged. This investigation was headed up by none

Artificial horizon instrument face from DC-3 N1946. (Michael B. McComb)

other than FBI Director J. Edgar Hoover. In addition, a Congressional probe reviewed the circumstances surrounding the accident.

One of the first things the FBI did was examine the aircraft wreckage for evidence of bomb damage. None was found. Another area scrutinized was the background of the passengers who had departed the aircraft at prior stops. One person who came under the FBI scrutiny was violinist Joseph Szigeti. Having come to the United States from Hungary, and having left the aircraft in New Mexico, he was immediately suspected of being a saboteur. For months the FBI probed into his past. Long after the investigation was closed, the FBI continued to read his mail. In the end, Szigeti was cleared.

CAB investigators noted errors in the flight plan filed by the co-pilot. This document still had all of the altitude settings and coordinates for the takeoff from Boulder City. The altitude filed was for a cruising altitude of 8,000 feet. This seems low, even for a flight out of Boulder City, as the mountains to the southwest reach upwards of 6,000 feet. However, with the route nearly 20 miles further north, the flight path crosses more into the heart of the Charleston range where there are several peaks greater than 8,000 feet in height.

Another contributing factor may have been the fact that since the bombing of Pearl Harbor, the beacon system had been blacked out

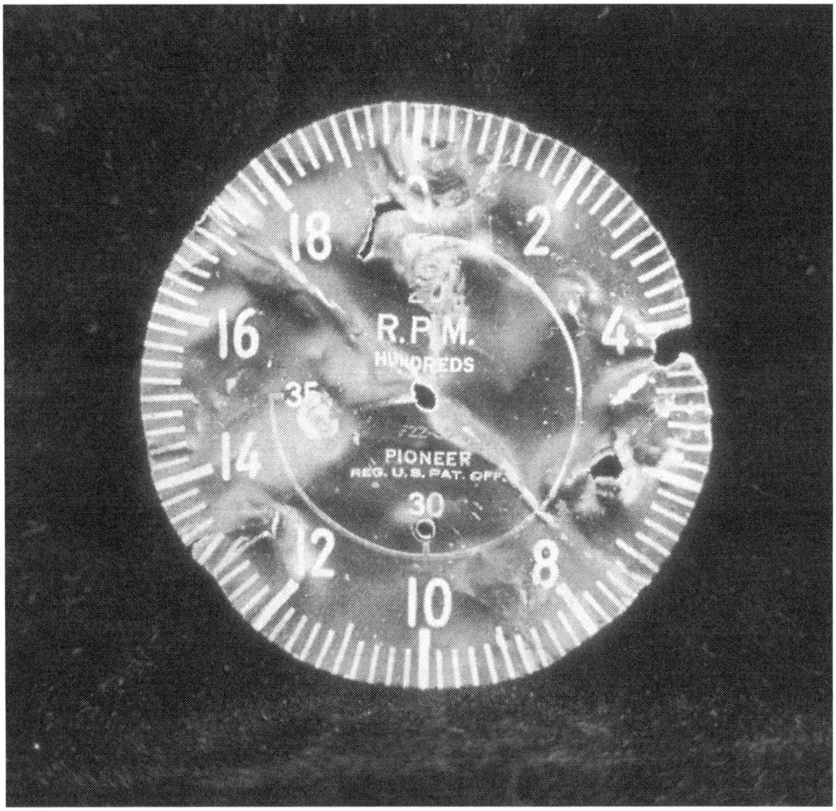

RPM instrument dial from N1946 shows signs of impact damage. (Michael B. McComb)

throughout the western United States. This could have caused confusion in the cockpit as to their location in relation to the mountains. It has been suggested that possibly the crew was adjusting the throttles, in which case the cockpit lights would have been up to make it easier to read the instruments. Some of the pilots who knew Captain Williams had speculated that no sooner had the DC-3 left the ground, that he was back in the cabin visiting with Lombard, leaving an inexperienced co-pilot flying the aircraft. This scenario does not make sense. First, Captain Williams had more then enough time to visit with Lombard between Albuquerque and Las Vegas while it was daylight. Second, as far as the co-pilot being inexperienced, nothing could be farther from the truth. Granted, he did not have the 12,000-plus hours that Captain Williams possessed, but he did have more than 3,000 hours total time; 755 hours had been accumulated during his year and one-half with TWA. He also was rated as a co-pilot on the Boeing 307 Stratoliner, which was a state-of-the-art aircraft in 1942.

The bottom line on this accident is that we never will really know what happened to cause a highly experienced flight crew to fly into a mountain. The official verdict in the CAB report stated: "Upon the basis of the forgoing finding, and of the entire record available at this time, we find that the probable cause of the accident to aircraft NC1946 on

Pilot's wings found at the Lombard crash site were a gold/bronze color showing the air carrier's name on the front and the number "79" on the reverse. (David L. McCurry)

January 16, 1942, was the failure of the captain after departure from Las Vegas to follow the proper course by making use of the navigation facilities available to him."

During the week following the accident, wreckage was examined and the bodies of the passengers and crew were removed. A special effort was made to find several items of jewelry that Carole Lombard had with her. Clark Gable, who had flown up to Las Vegas hours after the accident in a chartered Western DC-3, was particularly interested in recovering two diamond and ruby clips that he had given Lombard for Christmas a few weeks earlier. On January 20, a soldier approached a Gable associate and offered to sell a piece of the jewelry that he had found. This item was confiscated and the incident was reported to the soldier's commanding officer. This was believed to be the only piece of jewelry recovered by the search teams after the accident.

The Crash Site Today

More than half a century has passed since that dark, cold January night claimed those aboard Flight 3. Time has eroded the crash site

Engine and firewall components litter the area more than 65 years after the DC-3 crashed near Las Vegas. (Michael B. McComb)

Large pieces of fuselage skin can still be found at the crash site more than 50 years after the accident.
(Michael B. McComb)

and the memories of those who were involved in the aftermath of the accident. Most of the major figures have been dead for years. Some of the FBI files are sealed to this day, and those that are available have been heavily censored. In researching this accident, extensive use was made of newspaper accounts, government accident reports, and historical records from Clark County, Nevada.

Locating this site was very difficult. In newspaper articles Mt. Potosi goes by several different names including Double-Up Peak, Table Spring Mountain, and Olcott Mountain, to name a few. After viewing old pictures of the site, the location was pinpointed by taking aerial photos of Mt. Potosi and comparing them. No wreckage could be seen from the air.

On October 19, 1992, an expedition was mounted. After a two and one-half hour hike, the lower crest of Mt. Potosi was reached.

From the elevation contour of 7,700 feet, author Michael B. McComb proceeded to hike along the base of the fossil-encrusted cliff that the DC-3 had impacted. The hiking was extremely difficult. There were very few level spots; the ground was crumbly and the incline reached in excess of 50 degrees. Numerous ponderosa pine trees dot the side of the mountain, some reaching upwards of 75 feet. This area of the Mt. Charleston range is considered the most rugged in Nevada, if not the western United States.

After an additional hour of hiking, one could clearly make out the distinctive shape of a Wright Cyclone engine, its cylinders and pistons frozen by the impact. Other bits of airframe could be seen scattered around. In a scrub oak brush lay one of the main gears, its oleo struts still gleaming. Not far away was a prop dome, pointing toward the sky it would never fly in again. Down slope was the flap from the right wing. There were little items too, like a crushed Stanley thermos. Stamped on the base was the company's motto: "It will not break." However in this case, it did. Not far away was a piece of plastic drinking cup with the letters "TWA" on the base.

In early September 1993, another trip was made to the site. The first thing accomplished was to locate the point of impact on the cliff. Next was to determine where the aircraft cabin came to rest and burned. This was accomplished by finding cabin materials, such as silverware, dishes, and personal effects including coins and jewelry.

The tail section with the words "Sky Club" painted on it was no longer there—or was it? While examining some of the wreckage, a piece of airframe about 8-inches by 8-inches was located. The piece had a red stripe with black borders, consistent with the size of the "Sky Club" letters on the tail. The tail section, apparently along with most other larger fragments, had been broken up to avoid being reported as a new crash.

Also among the wreckage a number of shovels and sifting screens were found. These items showed signs of having been there at least a few years, no doubt left at the site by somebody looking for trinkets, or perhaps Carole Lombard's lost jewels. Amid the bits of debris were several Army Air Corps "wings and propeller" collar insignia, an rpm gauge face, and a Sperry Gyro Horizon instrument face.

A few weeks before her fateful departure for Indianapolis, Carole Lombard had finished making a movie with Jack Benny titled *To Be or Not To Be.* When the movie was released in February 1942, the producers edited six words from the original version. Removed from the film was a scene in which Carole Lombard asked Jack Benny, "What could happen on a plane?"

AMERICAN AIRLINES
Air Conditioner
FOR PASSENGER COMFORT
Flagship Skysl
NC
21752
AMERICAN
AIR EXPRESS

Chapter 7

The DC-3 That Crashed and Flew Again

Ed Davies

Having chosen an incident to investigate, the wreckchaser follows the parallel paths of researching the paper trail and pounding the real trail to the scene of the accident. The first steps are determining the exact location of the crash site, obtaining right of entry, and scheduling the often grueling hike in. The reward is experiencing the unbelievable awe of seeing the field of wreckage.

Wearing her original name, Flagship Memphis, *American Airlines DST-217A NC21752, prepares to take on passengers at United Airport, Burbank, California. Note the interesting ground-handling equipment, including a truck to air condition the cabin. (American Airlines via Davies)*

The concurrent detective work needed to re-create the story of the crash may be prolonged, requiring patience and persistence. Using sources outlined in this edition, the wreckchaser can methodically piece together the paper trail and cement it through interviews with the people involved.

Scattered, charred fragments of twisted wreckage are the usual signature of an aircraft disaster. However, once in a while, a sturdy, very lucky aircraft survives complete destruction, is repaired and returns to the airways. The wreckchaser, in this case, may find the aircraft of his story still in operation at a major international airport or a quiet rural airfield.

Costly Boeing 747s have been classic survivors. A Japan Airlines jumbo jet was blown off an icy taxiway at Anchorage in 1975. Eight months and 20,000 new parts later, a Boeing work crew handed it back to the airline. An American Airlines DC-10 suffered a structural failure that caused severe engine and hydraulic damage. The crew eventually got

Flagship San Antonio *on the ground at Saline, December 1944. Work had begun to remove the DST from the corn field for transport to Willow Run. One month later, the DST was back in revenue service. (Davies Collection)*

the crippled aircraft down at Detroit-Metropolitan Airport. There, an American Airlines maintenance crew from Tulsa rebuilt it in place and flew it out to serve for many more years. A DC-8 landed in the water short of San Francisco International Airport's Runway 28 Left. Hauled out of its watery wreck site, it was refurbished and returned to revenue service.

One of the most interesting examples of a survival event involved an American Airlines passenger DC-3. Crippled by a mid-air collision, it crash-landed in a snow-covered cornfield. Leaving no trace for the wreckchaser, it was hauled from the wreck site, repaired, and in less than a month was back in scheduled service.

This particular story began when the author found a single-line entry in the airline's maintenance summary sheet for NC21752. It read: "12-24-44 Saline Mich. Collided with a C.A.A. plane while in flight." Few aircraft have survived a mid-air collision; this one not only did, but is still flying half a century later.

NC21752 was delivered new to American Airlines in August 1939, and was one of the last of 40 "Sleeper Transports" built by the Douglas Aircraft Co. at Santa Monica, California. The second row of tiny rectangular windows that served the upper berths distinguished this type from the regular 21-passenger DC-3. American Airlines used them on their southern transcontinental route, accommodating up to 14 overnight passengers.

The Davis-Douglas Company allocated the Manufacturer's Serial Number (msn) 100 to the Cloudster, the first aircraft they built. The next plane ordered was 101, and until the company was acquired by Boeing in 1997, it continued to assign unique consecutive identification numbers to its commercial aircraft. Though the registration may change many times during the life of the aircraft, the msn remains a constant invaluable identification item when tracing a plane's historic paper trail. DST-217A, NC21752's msn was 2165.

Pearl Harbor dramatically changed the U.S. airline industry, with many civilian planes being pressed into military service. The smaller passenger capacity DSTs were among the first to be released by the airlines. NC21752 had flown 7,956 hours, almost equivalent to non-stop flying day and night for a whole year, when it was purchased by the War Department in March 1942. Painted olive drab, with a "Star in Circle" insignia, it became a U.S. Army Air Corps type C-49E, serial number 42-43620.

Its wartime record, obtained from the U.S. Air Force Historical Research Center at Maxwell Air Force Base (See Appendix VI: *Obtaining U.S. Air Force Aircraft History Cards*), notes that this particular C-49E did not leave the continental United States. Based at Kansas City, Camp Douglas, Sedalia, Cheyenne, and Memphis, it was used for freight, passenger, and medivac assignments.

Setting the Stage for a Mid-Air Collision

In October 1944, American Airlines repurchased NC21752, converting it to a standard 21-passenger DC-3 at its New York base. The distinguishing upper row of windows was plated over, and with 11,822 hours on the clock, it returned to civilian passenger service on November 16, 1944. It was common practice at this time for individual aircraft to be named after cities on the airline's system. NC21752 became *Flagship San Antonio.*

On Christmas Eve 1944, *Flagship San Antonio* was assigned to Flight 21, from New York to Chicago. The airliner departed Detroit City Airport, a scheduled intermediate stop, at 11:28 am Eastern War Time. Piloting the flight was Captain Victor Evans, a nine-year veteran with American Airlines. The final leg of the flight was being flown by the First Officer J.R. Lyons. Stewardess Mary Brauer tended to the 15 passengers, many of them servicemen traveling from New York for Christmas furloughs. The youngest passenger was two-year-old Candace Collet, traveling with her parents to their home in Chicago for the holiday. Other passengers included Elmer Johnson, electrician's mate of Portland, Oregon; Dr. E.G.

Ahrens, Romeo, Michigan; Dr. R.S. Mitchell of Detroit, Michigan; A.S. Tucker, seaman of Milwaukie, Oregon; Ensign R.D. Looney, Oklahoma City, Oklahoma; Lt. R.I. Benson, Glenwood, Minnesota; apprentice seaman P.F. Walker, New Haven, Connecticut; Ensign R.F. Schemanski, Milwaukie, Oregon; Ensign W.W. Korn, Alameda, California; Lt. A.O. D'Armour, Duluth, Minnesota; Ensign J.F. Garcia, Hayward, California; and Mr. G. Kasper, Detroit, Michigan.

The takeoff was routine, weather conditions good, and the aircraft proceeded on a westerly course at the 2,500-foot altitude assigned by the Detroit ATC. Stewardess Brauer served the box lunches to the relaxing passengers.

That same morning at 11:00 am, a two-place Taylorcraft BL-65, fitted with skis and powered by a Lycoming 65 horsepower engine, took off from Ypsilanti Airport, Michigan. Registered NC24403 to Ypsilanti Air Service, it was based at the small airport 35 miles southwest of downtown Detroit. Aboard were Donald J. Gridley, flying instructor and part-time manager for Ypsilanti Air Service, and student pilot Miss Eleanor Cramer. The training was associated with the Civil Air Patrol (CAP). The notation on the American Airlines maintenance summary had wrongly described this as a CAA flight. Cramer already had received five hours of flying instruction, and on this particular day was practicing left and right spins. Parachutes were mandatory for these maneuvers, and Cramer recalled that the chutes would make the small cockpit of the Taylorcraft even more restrictive. The flying lesson proceeded smoothly, and Cramer was flying the aircraft straight and level, about two miles south of Ypsilanti, positioning herself for a return landing.

Both aircraft were at the same altitude, each oblivious of the other's presence, as the faster DC-3 bore down on the small yellow trainer.

Researching the Crash

Perhaps this dramatic moment would be a good time to break, to review how the detailed information was gathered about an incident that took place more than 60 years ago.

Significant clues were the date and location of the incident. The airlines are quite naturally reticent about discussing accidents involving their equipment and thus are not a great source of information. However, knowing the date and location, I sent a letter to the National Transport Safety Board in Washington, D.C. It produced a copy of the Accident Investigation Report. From it, I gleaned many further clues about the people, equipment, and circumstances of the incident. Given the type, registration, and msn, the FAA in Oklahoma City, for a small fee, sent a copy of the microfiche containing the participating aircraft's registration and major maintenance history. Aircraft accidents are a newsworthy event, usually well-documented by the local newspapers. Armed with the accident date, a call to the library in the city nearest the crash scene usually will generate an interested response, with perhaps photocopies from their newspaper microfilm files. In this case, I called the editor of the *Saline Reporter*. He in turn wrote a column on my request for information about the incident that generated several letters from citizens who recalled their participation and memories of that day.

Eventually, the meaningful sources of information began to peter out, and I hadn't found either pilot. It was time for the first barrel of the shotgun research technique. I wrote to Arthur Pearcy, and he included the story as I then knew it in the regular DC-3 column in the popular British aviation magazine *FlyPast*. Within a month, Pearcy sent me a copy of a letter he received from a *FlyPast* subscriber in the United States. It was the Taylorcraft pilot.

Gridley had retired and was living with his wife Lucy in Mackinaw City, Michigan. He still was in touch with his former student pilot, now Mrs. Eleanor Rose, who was living in San Diego, California. I corresponded with both, and they sent me photographs and photocopies of documents relating to the incident.

The shotgun approach proved so successful, I decided to try the other barrel. Co-author Nicholas A. Veronico had just been appointed editor of the first regional edition of *Pacific Flyer*, featuring Northern California and Bay Area aviation news. The story of the mid-air collision ran in the April 1988 issue under the title, "Indestructible DC-3." A Saline, Michigan, reader sent a copy to George Hof, who at that time was Vice President of Flight for American Airlines. He in turn forwarded it to retired American Airlines Captain J.R. Lyons, almost a neighbor of mine, living in nearby Hayward, California. Bull's-eye again.

I became good friends with Dick Lyons and his wife Gloria, and gathered first-hand his recollection of the mid-air incident. He was flying the DC-3 for the Detroit-to-Chicago leg. The pilot-in-command, Captain Vic Evans, had retired from the airlines many years earlier. He had passed away a year or so before I met Captain Lyons.

Diligent research of the paperwork trail was now confirmed by the actual participants in the drama. They, in turn, were discovered by lucky hits from a shotgun approach search for missing information—some of the many ways that the facts of yesterday's drama were slowly pieced together.

Impact! The DST and Taylorcraft Meet

The first officer of the DC-3, leaning forward to tune in the auxiliary receiver for a range position check, saw a flash of yellow to the left and above. A split second later, he felt the impact, but could not recall whether he had intuitively taken any evasive action. The sound and jolt of the impact caused Captain Evans to take over the controls, though it took the combined efforts of both pilots to try to raise the left wing in an attempt to maintain level flight. The first officer used the radio to call the company to inform them of the situation and advise them that they probably would have to make an emergency landing about six minutes west of Romulus Army Air Base. Unable to maintain altitude, Captain Evans turned the aircraft a few degrees to the right for a wheels up, flaps down landing on a snow-covered cornfield on the farm owned by Gilbert Dick. Stewardess Brauer cautioned all passengers to fasten their seat belts tightly and, immediately before the impact, the co-pilot cut all electrical power and pulled the mixture controls to the cut-off position. The crippled airliner plowed through three fences as it careened some 800 feet through the snow before coming to a silent halt.

Meanwhile, aboard the Taylorcraft, Gridley and his young student heard a shattering noise and lost all elevator and rudder control. One of the propellers of the overtaking DC-3 sheared off the right elevator and part of the vertical stabilizer. One of the skis from the Taylorcraft was embedded in the leading edge of the DC-3's left wing. For the first time they saw the airliner about a mile ahead and realized they had been involved in a dreaded mid-air collision. The small plane did not go out of control immediately, but Gridley, who realized that it was only a question of time, began helping Cramer unfasten her seat belt. He quickly coached her on the procedure, telling her to jump, count to 10, then pull the rip-cord of her parachute. She remembers climbing out onto the strut, counting "One, seven, ten," pulling the rip-cord and jumping. With the plane slowly turning north, Gridley jumped at about 1,600 feet. The doomed Taylorcraft plunged vertically to the ground. The tail was found alongside U.S. Highway 112; the remainder was strewn along a field south of the highway.

Tom and Blanche Bennet were startled by the roar of the wounded airliner as it passed low over their house on Willis Road. Donning their winter gear and high boots, Bennett and his father-in-law, Hartley Boutilier, struggled through the snow to where the DC-3 had come to rest. Despite the fact that airport neighborhood disaster drills hadn't been invented yet, the community public safety agencies sprang into action. A Mr. McBride at the Ford Bomber Plant called the Michigan State Police to inform them he had intercepted a radio distress transmission from the airliner. Patrol cars quickly honed in on the crash sites. Francis Lockwood, Saline's funeral director, whose hearse doubled as the local ambulance, raced to the scene.

Cramer floated earthward peacefully. She watched the DST crash land, her instructor's parachute open, and the Taylorcraft plunge into the fields below. Her landing was soft, and as she unbuckled her chute, a group of people came towards her. A young boy, who yelled with surprise, "It's a girl, a sissy," led the crowd. Cramer and Gridley ran towards each

Engine cowls have been removed prior to separating the powerplant and accessory section from the firewall. During the collision, one of the Taylorcraft's skis stuck in the DST's port wing leading edge. (Davies Collection)

other, crying and hugging as they met. They made their way to the home of Edna Murray. From there, they were driven to the State Police Station, where they made their initial statements. Later Cramer went home to a delayed dinner and thankful prayers.

For a moment, silence reigned over the passenger plane as it lurched to a stop. The crew immediately ordered the passengers to evacuate the plane, fearing it might explode. Miraculously, none of the passengers or crew was hurt, nor had there been any panic during the frightening ordeal. Captain Evans led his passengers to the farmhouse, where they made their telephone calls and were supplied with food and coffee by Blanche Bennet and her neighbors. Co-pilot Lyons remained with the silent, wounded plane, guarding the mail and awaiting the authorities. U.S. Army doctors and ambulances arrived from Willow Run and the nearby Romulus Army Air Base, fortunately to find that their services were not required. The mail was off-loaded, and Bennet's nine-year old son Tom hauled it to the house on his sleigh. He carefully watched over it until the postal authorities came to pick it up. They put it on another flight from Willow Run. Tom was rewarded with five dollars for his diligence. A senior inspector from the CAA arrived from Dearborn, and Mr. Tanguay, air safety investigator from the CAB flew in, landing alongside

Douglas Sleeper Transport 217A, msn 2165, at Schellville/Sonoma Valley Airport, California, prior to the major restoration effort. The plane is currently owned by Dr. Lee Schaller, and it wears the paint scheme of Pacific National Airways. Schaller plans to restore this aircraft back to its sleeper transport configuration. (Ed Davies)

the crippled airliner. They began taking statements for their report, which they hoped would identify the cause of the mid-air collision.

Close to 3:00 pm, American Airlines's station manager from Detroit arrived to make arrangements for the stranded passengers. A Ford Motor Company bus took them first to Memorial Hospital in Ypsilanti for physical examinations. All were given a clean bill of health, but in the meantime weather intervened, canceling plans for a back-up plane to Chicago. Perhaps the passengers didn't want to fly again that day anyway. The evening ended with the airline hosting a Christmas Eve party for the crew and passengers at the Book-Cadillac Hotel.

State Police and the Civil Air Patrol maintained a guard over the downed airliner until Christmas Day, when engineers and mechanics from American Airlines arrived to start the recovery process. Engines and outer wing sections were removed. The DC-3 was jacked so the landing gear could be extended. During the evening of December 26 and early morning of the next day, the fuselage was towed to the Willow Run Bomber Plant. Replacement engines and a new left wing were installed, enabling the aircraft to be ferried to the airline's maintenance base in New York. On January 20, 1945, NC21752 was back in scheduled service with American Airlines.

With a mere twelve-thousand flying hours on the airframe and not a scratch on her refurbished fuselage, the rugged DC-3 could look forward to many more years of active flying. American eventually retired her in December 1948, placing the aircraft in storage at Tulsa, Oklahoma, until a buyer could be found. Purchased by Colonial Airlines in February 1949, the veteran DC-3 returned briefly to scheduled airline service before being sold again in August 1950.

Replaced in scheduled airline service by more modern equipment, many DC-3s were converted either for cargo operation or into luxurious corporate aircraft. N21752 was no exception, and in late 1950 it was transformed into corporate configuration by Remmert Werner at Lambert Field, St. Louis. A VIP interior was fitted, and the original Wright Cyclone engines were replaced by the more available Pratt & Whitney Twin Wasp 14-cylinder radials. The new owner was Owens Illinois Glass Co. of Toledo, Ohio.

During the early 1960s, the vintage DST was transformed yet again. Acquiring a high-density 24-seat interior, it became a "Flying Classroom" for Ohio State University at Columbus, Ohio. Re-registered N110SU, the plane was crewed by both faculty and staff pilots, with advanced students serving as co-pilots. Frequent uses included hauling university athletic teams (except the heavy football players) all over the Midwest, flying as an aerial platform for geography and geology studies, and for trips to New York with parties of theater students. Early in 1974, all three of the university's aging fleet of DC-3s were put up for sale.

Nevada Airlines of Las Vegas, operating scheduled passenger services over the Grand Canyon, took ownership in March 1975. Registration was changed once again, to N139D. Pacific National Airways took possession during 1980, but soon afterwards the aircraft was withdrawn from service and stored in Las Vegas. Crocker National Bank offered N139D and her sister ship N74KW for sale, and both were acquired by Dr. Lee Schaller, a San Francisco oral surgeon. Both were flown to Schellville/Sonoma Valley Airport in Northern California. N74KW was refurbished there, sold again, and ferried to new owners in Florida.

For the next 10 years the historic DST, N139D, never flew. It was worked on occasionally, and her colors faded in the hot California sun. It was considered as a possible candidate for flagship of the new C.R. Smith Museum built by American Airlines in Fort Worth, but it was beaten out by a younger ex-American Airlines DC-3. Serious restoration began again in 1994. The work included a rebuilt interior and major work on the engines. As one of the oldest DC-3s in the country, one of the few originally built as a DST, and one of the very few to survive a mid-air collision, it soon may fly again.

History repeated itself on November 27, 1951. An Eastern Airlines DC-3, N25646, msn 2234, flying between Atlanta, Georgia, and St. Petersburg, Florida, was involved in a mid-air collision with an L-4J Piper Cub, again operated by the Civil Air Patrol. The larger aircraft made a normal landing at Taylor Field. The Piper Cub crashed into a heavily wooded area near Ocala, Florida, killing the pilot and only occupant.

Chapter 8

Restricted Medical Certificate Ignored: Robin Airlines C-46

Nicholas A. Veronico

Robin Airlines Flight 416W departed New York on April 17, 1952, at 9:09 pm EST on a cross-country trip to the Los Angeles suburb of Burbank. The plane never made its final destination. Trip 416W ended in the La Puente Hills, near Whittier, California, on April 18, 1952, at 3:34 am PST. The crew of three and 26 passengers perished in the crash.

C-46F N8404C came to grief on the hills of La Puente, east of Los Angeles International Airport, the plane's final destination. The flight's crew of three and 26 passengers perished in the April 18, 1952 crash. (L. Griggers Collection via Macha)

The trip was flown with a war-surplus Curtiss C-46F-1-CU Commando, N8404C, msn 22466. The plane was delivered to the United States Army Air Force on July 23, 1945, as serial number 44-78643. Assigned to Manilla, Philippines, it did not depart the continental U.S. until April 19, 1946. The Commando was posted to Itazuke and Tachikawa, Japan, before its transfer to the Foreign Liquidation Commission on June 17, 1948. The Foreign Liquidation Commission sold the plane to Civil Air Transport, who registered it N8404C in December 1949. The plane was then sold to Air Charters Inc. On March 28, 1952, Robin Airlines leased the plane for a one-year period. Robin Airlines, a non-scheduled carrier, also was doing business under the name North Continent Airlines.

The airplane made one stop at Chicago, Illinois, and then continued on to Kansas City, Missouri, where the plane landed at 4:08 am CST. A new crew boarded to take the flight westward to California. The crew consisted of Captain Lewis R. Powell, reserve Captain John D. Treher, co-pilot Charles K. Waldron, and hostess Dolores A. Bradford. Federal regulations required that a flight of the duration between Kansas City and Burbank required a third relief pilot—thus the inclusion of Captain Treher. He had dead-headed from his home in Chicago to meet the flight at Kansas City.

While preparing to depart Kansas City, the right oil cooler sprang a leak, requiring it to be replaced. This maintenance squawk delayed the flight more than 11 hours. The flight finally left Kansas City at 3:38 pm CST on a VFR flight plan with reserve Captain Treher flying left seat and Waldron sitting in the right seat. Captain Powell sat in the main cabin to relieve Treher on the next leg.

The flight landed at Wichita, Kansas, at 5:00 pm CST, to check the right engine's oil consumption. Thirty-four minutes later the flight departed for the West Coast. Treher was still at the controls when the flight arrived in the vicinity of Tucumcari, New Mexico, where they encountered severe thunderstorms. The plane turned east and flew to Amarillo, Texas, where it landed at 10:14 pm CST to wait out the weather. The plane's tanks were topped with 606 gallons of fuel and 32 quarts of oil.

Captain Treher left the flight and Captain Powell took command, departing at 11:02 pm CST headed for Phoenix, Arizona. The plane landed at Phoenix at 12:30 am PST where three adults and one child deplaned. Flight 416W left Phoenix at 1:43 am on a Defense Visual Flight Rules (DVFR) flight plan. It was instructed to cruise at 8,000 feet

War surplus Curtiss C-46s were plentiful after the war and formed the backbone of numerous non-scheduled carriers' fleets. The aircraft shown is the same type as N8404C. (William T. Larkins)

following Green 5 Airway to Riverside, California, and then direct to the flight's terminus at Burbank.

The morning after the crash: Above, the empennage and one of the R-2800-75 engines and its twisted Hamilton Standard propeller at the point of impact, 980 feet above sea level. (L. Griggers Collection via Macha)

Flight 416W requested the weather at both Los Angeles (Mines Field) and Burbank at 3:13 am PST. The flight was radioed the following information that was current as of 2:28 am: "Burbank closed, visibility one-eighth mile, and Los Angeles measured 700 overcast, visibility two and one-quarter (miles) with haze and smoke, temperature 57 degrees, dew point 54, wind southeast (at) one (mph), altimeter 29.91." The pilots elected to file an IFR flight plan later in their journey. At 3:17 am, Flight 416W reported passing over the Riverside Range Station at 6,000 feet and requested an IFR approach to Los Angeles, giving an estimated time of 3:36 am over Downey, California. Six minutes later, ARTC (Air Route Traffic Control) instructed the flight: "From present position to Downey radio beacon cruise at least 500 on top. Descend VFR and cross Downey and maintain 3,00. Contact Los Angeles Approach Control over La Habra. No delay expected." The pilots acknowledged the clearance and repeated the instructions.

The Final Four Minutes

The log of the Los Angeles Airport Chief Traffic Controller relates the last four minutes of Robin Airlines Flight 416W: "At 3:33 am PST, N8404C called Los Angeles Approach Control on 119.9 mc (very loud

Civil Aeronautics Board Accident Investigation Report 1-0027, released August 21, 1952, determined that the pilot descended too low to clear the terrain en route to Los Angeles International Airport. (Larkins Collection)

SA-259 File No. 1-0027

CIVIL AERONAUTICS BOARD

ACCIDENT INVESTIGATION REPORT

Adopted: August 20, 1952 Released: August 21, 1952

ROBIN AIRLINES, INC., NEAR WHITTIER, CALIFORNIA, APRIL 18, 1952

The Accident

At approximately 0334 PST1/ April 18, 1952, a C-46 aircraft, N 8404C, crashed and burned near Whittier, California, resulting in destruction of the aircraft and death to all persons aboard - 26 passengers and three crew members. The aircraft was operated by Robin Airlines, Inc.,2/ an irregular carrier, under a lease agreement with its recorded owner, Air Charters, Inc., of Carson City, Nevada.

History of the Flight

N 8404C departed New York, New York, at 1809, April 16, as Trip 416W. After making a scheduled stop at Chicago, Illinois, it arrived at Kansas City, Missouri, at 0208, April 17. At this point the flight was taken over by a new crew consisting of Captain Lewis R. Powell, Reserve Captain John D. Treher, Copilot Charles K. Waldron, and Hostess Dolores A. Bradford. The flight time requirements specified by the Civil Air Regulations (Part 42.48) made it necessary to have a three-man flight crew between Kansas City and Burbank because of the expected flight time involved. For this purpose Reserve Captain Treher had deadheaded from Chicago to Kansas City.

Departure from Kansas City was delayed approximately eleven hours when it was found necessary to replace the right engine oil cooler which had developed a leak. The flight departed Kansas City on a VFR (Visual Flight Rules) flight plan at 1338, with Reserve Captain Treher occupying the left pilot seat and Copilot Waldron, the right. Captain Powell occupied a seat in the main cabin.

A precautionary landing was made at Wichita, Kansas, at 1500, to check oil consumption, which was found to be normal, and the flight departed at 1534 on an IFR (Instrument Flight Rules) flight plan, with Captain Treher still flying the aircraft. Upon arriving in the vicinity of Tucumcari, New Mexico, a severe thunderstorm condition was encountered, whereupon the flight turned eastward and landed at Amarillo, Texas, at 1814. Reserve Captain Treher deplaned at this point, and at 2102 the flight again proceeded westward on an IFR flight plan to Phoenix, Arizona, with Captain Powell occupying the left pilot seat and Copilot Waldron still occupying the right.

1/ All times referred to herein are Pacific Standard and based on the 24-hour clock.

and clear) advising he was in the vicinity of La Habra and was having difficulty with his ADF equipment because of static and that he would have to make some other type of approach. The approach controller asked N8404C if he had ILS equipment and whether he believed he could pick up the outer marker satisfactorily. The pilot answered in the affirmative and further said that he could probably find the ILS Glide Path and proceed from there on in. N8404C was then cleared (3:34 am) for a straight-in ILS approach from the Los Angeles Outer Marker and given the current Los Angeles weather and also advised that the Los Angeles Low Frequency Range was inoperative because it had been shut down for maintenance.

"The Los Angeles Approach Controller then immediately began watching for N8404C's appearance within the next few minutes on the Surveillance Radar Scope on the normal setting of 20-mile range as

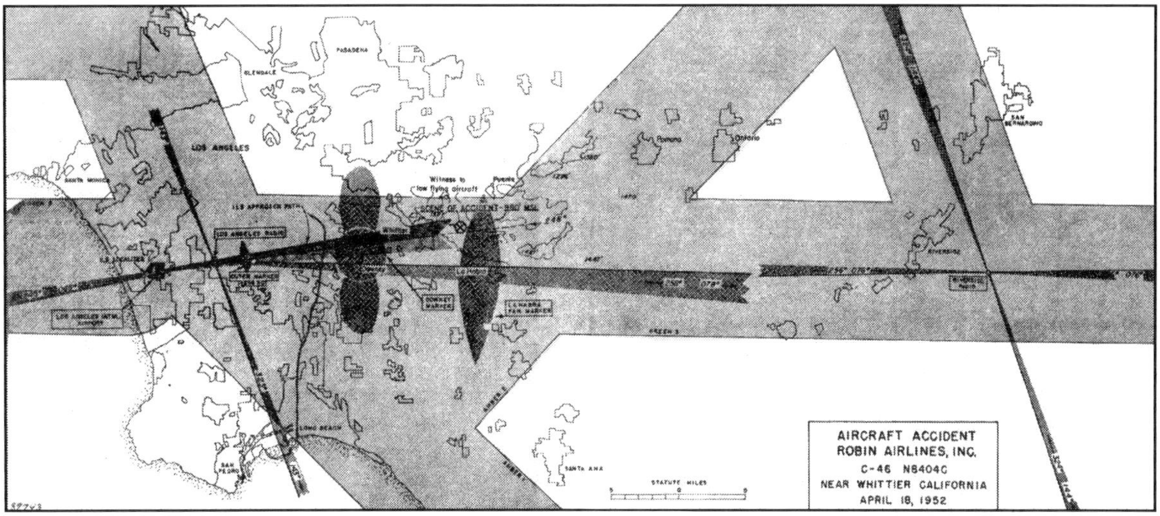

Airway map showing the flight path to Los Angeles International, the La Habra Fan Marker, location of the witnesses, and the crash site. Note that the crash site is just east of the published instrument landing approach path. (Larkins Collection)

the flight continued westbound toward the Los Angeles Outer Marker. When no target appeared on the Surveillance Scope by 3:37 am, several radio calls were directed to N8404C by Los Angeles Approach Control. No response was received."

The Fate of Flight 416W

Hayden Jones, a Puente, California, rancher, found the wreckage in the hills two miles east of Whittier and 22.5 miles east-northeast of Los Angeles Airport. A mass of twisted aluminum that once was Robin Airlines C-46 Flight 416W was scattered on the hillside at an altitude of 980 feet above sea level and headed on a course of 260 degrees magnetic. The wreck site was 2,600 feet north of the ILS approach's centerline, 7.5 miles east of the Downey fan marker.

The landing gear was down, and the flaps were fully retracted at the time of impact. The instrument panel clock was located. Its hour hand was loose on the spindle, the minute hand was stopped at 33 minutes after, and the second hand was frozen at 45 seconds. Examination of the area around the site revealed that the C-46 had struck the top of an adjacent hill, then continued to fly an additional 1,875 feet across a small canyon before impacting on the far side. The plane subsequently burned.

A local couple who lived 2.5 miles northwest of the crash site reported to officials that they had been disturbed from their sleep by a plane flying low overhead. Looking through a window, they saw the navigation lights of an airplane flying to the west. The plane flew out of sight, but not out of hearing range. The couple reported that the plane returned, now flying to the east, then out of hearing range. The Civil Aeronautics Board reported that Robin Airlines Flight 416W was the only airplane in the vicinity of the couple's home in the early morning hours of April 18.

The massive tail of the C-46 remained intact while the fuselage was completely destroyed in the crash and subsequent fire. This wreckage was removed but a number of seat frames and other small pieces from the crash are at the site still. A metal detector is highly recommended to wreckchasers. (L. Griggers Collection via Macha)

Mitigating Factors

The pilot of Flight 416W, Captain Powell, was a very experienced aircraft commander. Powell had accumulated 7,913 hours flight time: 1,500 hours in the Douglas DC-3, 1,900 hours in the Douglas DC-4, and 600 hours in the Curtiss C-46. He held an Air Transport Pilot certificate that originally was issued in December 1945 and was reissued four months before the crash, on December 23, 1951.

Powell had suffered a heart attack on March 30, 1951. He was sent to the hospital by ambulance where he remained until April 13, when he was sent home in an ambulance and confined to bed rest for the next six weeks. He gradually recovered and remained under medical supervision until December 1951. He was last seen by his doctor on April 12, 1952.

During his recovery, Powell saw the physician who usually gave him his CAA medical evaluations, Dr. Francis C. Herzog. During his routine examination on September 1, 1951, Dr. Herzog found no physical irregularities. When asked, Powell responded affirmatively that he had suffered a heart attack during the period since his last flight physical.

Police, firemen, and officials from the medical examiner's office comb through the fuselage for clues to the accident's cause. Note the windscreen panels in the lower left of the photo. (L. Griggers Collection via Macha)

According to federal regulations, Powell was asked to obtain and submit an electrocardiogram and a letter from his doctor for review by the CAA's regional medical officer.

The case was reviewed by the CAA Medical Standards Branch, Washington, D.C., who responded on October 23, 1951: "... Mr. Powell, like others who have coronary artery disease, should not be certified for solo or pilot-in-command flying." Powell was issued a Class One medical certificate that was Restricted for Check Pilot Duties only.

Powell quickly took action in an attempt to convince the medical board that he should be allowed an unrestricted medical certificate. He was unsuccessful, and his restricted for-check-pilot-duties license stood. Powell was examined again by Dr. Herzog on March 14, 1952, to renew his restricted license. Dr. Herzog found no physical irregularities, but because of his heart history, reissued his restricted license.

A CAA aviation safety agent, G.O. Trapp, performed a ramp check on a Robin Airlines flight at Amarillo, Texas, on March 11, 1952. Powell was a crewmember on this flight. Trapp stated in his report that Powell was not carrying the required airman identification card but, in a later statement, said that he did indeed examine Powell's medical certificate and noted no limitations. If the medical certificate was displayed in a wallet, the restrictions could have been folded under and not displayed.

The autopsy that was performed on Powell's body showed that his heart was severely damaged. Apparently it had recently suffered a hemorrhage but the post-mortem examination was unable to conclusively show whether the hemorrhage had occurred prior to the crash. The report stated that this hemorrhage may have "occurred within ... probably a matter of hours, at the outside. It could have been immediately before, or it could have been a matter of several hours before (the crash)."

Photos from the day of the crash should help future wreckchasers locate the crash site. Note the fire truck on the road above and the wreck's proximity to the summit of the hill. (L. Griggers Collection via Macha)

The Official Cause of the Crash

After examining the wreckage and the aircraft's maintenance records, officials determined that there was no evidence of structural or mechanical failure occurring. The resulting fire showed there was fuel aboard. With

this information, the CAB Accident Investigation Report dated August 20, 1952, stated, "... it must be concluded that the cause of the accident was operational rather than mechanical. The board determines that the probable cause of this accident was the action of the pilot in voluntarily descending below the minimum altitude for which he was cleared and attempting an approach at an altitude too low to clear the terrain."

The gruesome task of removing the bodies goes on while investigators examine the wreckage. Note the main landing gear at the bottom of the ravine. (L. Griggers Collection via Macha)

Powell's willful failure to comply with the restrictions placed on his medical certificate caused the deaths of himself, his two crewmates, and 26 passengers.

The Crash Site

The plane went down in the La Puente Hills near Rose Hills Cemetery. The Los Angeles County Sherriff's Office lists the crash site as one-half mile south of the dead end of La Belle Street in the Whittier Hills district. Although the major portions of the aircraft wreckage were removed shortly after the crash, seat frames and other small pieces of this aircraft can still be located. A metal detector is recommended.

VH-BPH
BRITISH COMMONWEALTH PACIFIC AIRLINES

Chapter 9

Resolution: *Aussie Airliner Crash Site Revisited*

Ed Davies, Nicholas A. Veronico

Douglas DC-6 VH-BPH was a sister ship to British Commonwealth Pacific Airlines' VH-BPE Resolution, *which crashed on Kings Mountain on October 29, 1953. (John Wegg Collection)*

Captain Bruce N. Dickson departed Honolulu in command of a British Commonwealth Pacific Airlines DC-6 on October 28, 1953. Known as Flight 304/44, Dickson was bound for San Francisco with eight crewmembers and 11 passengers. Sadly, Dickson, his highly experienced crew, and his passengers became involved in the worst air disaster to occur in San Mateo County.

British Commonwealth Pacific Airlines was founded on June 24,1946, to operate trans-Pacific passenger and mail flights from Australia and New Zealand to the United States and Canada. Share capital to start the airline was raised from the Australian government (50 percent), the New Zealand government (30 percent), and the United Kingdom (20 percent). Commercial service began in September 1946 with a bi-weekly flight from Sydney, Australia, to Vancouver, British Columbia, Canada. Subsequently, Auckland, New Zealand, was added as a departure point, and San Francisco became the U.S. destination. The Sydney/San Francisco flight was known as the "Southern Cross" route.

The first flights were made using Australian National Airways DC-4s under a charter agreement with BCPA. By 1949, BCPA had acquired three DC-4s and was bringing the new pressurized DC-6 on line.

BCPA purchased four new DC-6s. Each of the sleeper-equipped Royal Mail airliners was named after one of the ships (*Resolution, Endeavour, Adventure, Discovery*) commanded by Capt. James Cook (1728–1779) on his voyages of discovery in the Pacific.

Flight 304/44 was being flown by BCPA DC-6 *Resolution*, registered VH-BPE, the jumbo jet of the 1950s. *Resolution* was a Douglas-Long Beach-built DC-6, serial number 43125, completed in 1948. On October 28, 1953, she had 5,904 airframe hours since her last major overhaul. The DC-6 was a large aircraft, measuring 100 feet, 7 inches in length, with a wingspan of 117 feet, 6 inches. This DC-6 was powered by four Pratt & Whitney R-2800-CA15 engines driving Hamilton-Standard propellers.

The flight originated at Sydney, where the following passengers had boarded: Reginald F.K. Eastoe, 50, an engineer from Norfolk, England; William J. Cox, 52, a shopfitter from Neutral Bay, Australia; John W. "Jack" Butterworth, 52, and Cyril G.H. McDonald, 60, engineers from the Victoria State Railway sent to the United States to study U.S. railway technology and to purchase a locomotive; Capt. Paul O. Olsen, 39, a master mariner from Cardiff, Australia, sent to the United States to take command of a new merchant ship; Bernard R. Tischler, 31, a chief passenger clerk from Brighton, Australia; John K. Briscoe, 45, an insurance executive from London, England; William Kapell, 31, a well-respected pianist from New York City returning from a concert tour of Australia; and Janos Feher, 39, a watchmaker and citizen of Hungary, and his seven-year-old son, John, who had been stricken with polio, traveling to New York to see a medical specialist.

Resolution departed from Sydney with stops at Nadi, Fiji Islands, and then on to Canton Island and Honolulu, where a routine crew change took place. Capt. Bruce N. Dickson, 34, assumed command of Flight 304/44. He was a 10,696-hour pilot, with 3,624 hours on instruments and 4,136 hours in type. His crew on October 28, 1953, consisted of First Officer Frank A. Campbell, 28, who held a third-class air transport rating with 3,896 of his 4,782 flying hours in the DC-6. George R. Murtagh, 28, navigator, had 2,482 hours in type, almost all exclusively while flying trans-Pacific flights. Walter B. Knight, 34, purser, had 1,008 hours flying time. Vernon A. Walker, 32, radio Officer, had 5,645 hours, 2,645 of which were in type.

All the crewmembers were Australian, except for Charles N. Cattanach, 31, flight engineer. Cattanach, a Canadian, was one of the first flight engineers hired by BCPA and had 3,118 hours, all in the DC-6.

Rounding out the flight crew were hostesses June F. Elder, 27, and Amy K. Lewis, 32, both unmarried.

Mrs. Jean Chiverton, 65, of Vancouver, B.C., boarded the flight in Honolulu, becoming the eleventh passenger.

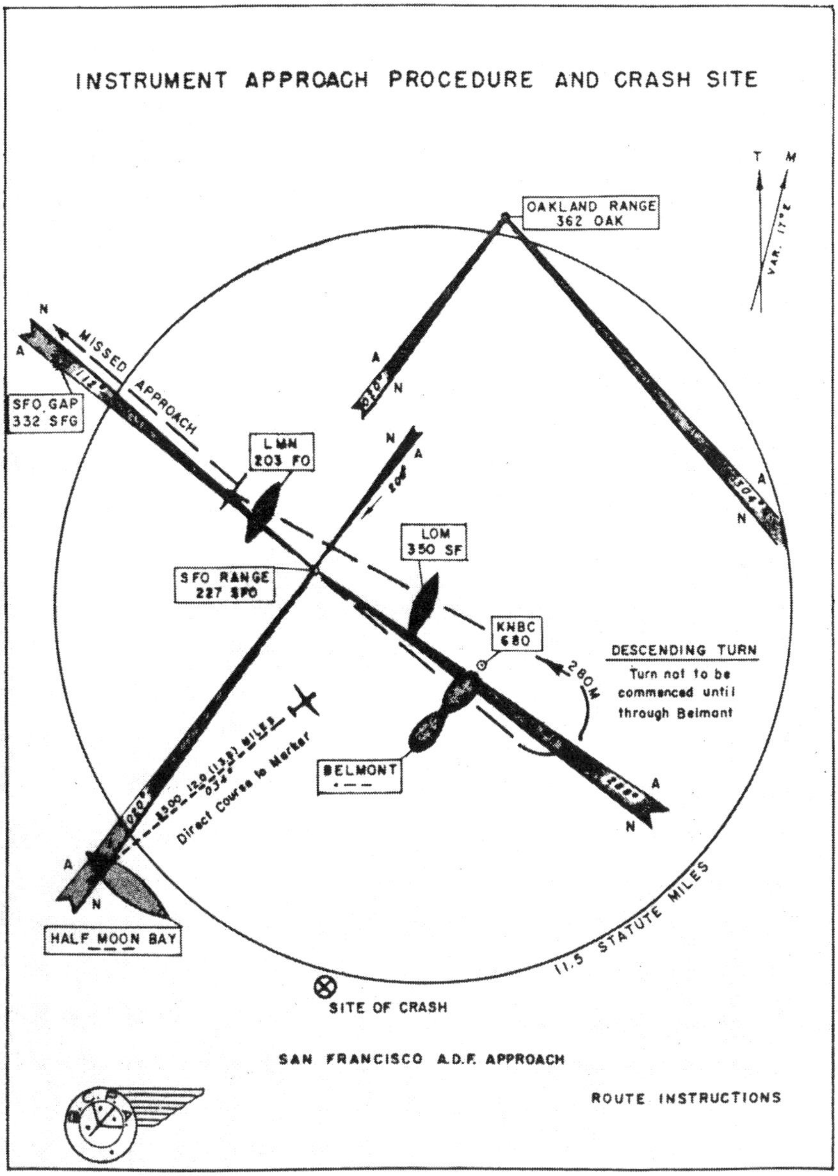

Diagram from the Civil Aeronautics Board showing the crash site of VH-BPE in relation to the approaches to the San Francisco Airport and the Half Moon Bay Fan Marker. (Ed Davies Collection)

The estimated flying time from Honolulu to San Francisco was 9 hours, 25 minutes, with sufficient fuel on board for 12 hours, 53 minutes. The gross takeoff weight was 90,166 pounds, 5,034 pounds below maximum gross takeoff weight.

Flight 304/44 departed Honolulu at 10:59 pm local time on an IFR flight plan to San Francisco. Once airborne, they requested to leave the tower frequency. Three minutes later, Dickson called the tower and said, "We're having a little trouble with one of the props."

Permission was granted for a return to Honolulu, and the IFR clearance was canceled. At 11:05, Dickson reported, "The relay is working okay now; desire to continue flight." The IFR clearance was reinstated, and the flight proceeded towards San Francisco.

The normal radio communications were sent from the plane while en route, and Dickson estimated his arrival at San Francisco to be 8:40 am PST.

At 8:21 am PST, Western Air Defense Force Radar identified VH-BPE. *Resolution* was cleared "to the San Francisco ILS Outer Marker via the Half Moon Bay Fan Maker direct to the San Francisco Outer Marker. Maintain at least 500 feet above all clouds. Contact San Francisco Approach Control after passing Half Moon Bay Fan Marker. Cloud tops reported in the Bay Area: 1,700 feet."

After crossing the coast at the Half Moon Bay Fan Marker, the standard approach directed the aircraft over the San Francisco Airport, followed by a right turn for an approach to Runway 28. Capt. Dickson had flown this route numerous times and was well aware of the procedures.

Eighteen minutes later, *Resolution* advised that they were over Half Moon Bay, 500 on top, and listening on 278 kc. Approach Control responded with the following clearance: "Cleared for an ILS approach to the airport, Runway 28, wind west 15; cross the Outer Marker initially at least 500 on top, report when inbound; ceiling 1,200, visibility nine, altimeter 30.14."

Unique to the microclimates of the San Francisco Peninsula, the coastal range was covered by a tree-clinging fog.

At 8:41 came the last transmission from VH-BPE: "Air Pacific Easy (VH-BPE's radio call sign), Roger, southeast, turning inbound."

A controller quickly added, "Check passing the ILS Outer Marker inbound." *Resolution* was never heard from again, as all subsequent radio calls went unanswered.

Ray Brooks, now living in New Zealand, was the BCPA station manager at San Francisco on October 29, 1953. He had arrived for work at 7:30 am, that day, in plenty of time to meet *Resolution*. Brooks worked closely with United Airlines, which was BCPA's handling agent at San Francisco. At 8:45 am, Brooks was informed that radio contact had been lost with *Resolution*.

Soon after the loss of radio contact, a Coast Guard PB-1 (B-17), piloted by Lt. Cdr. D.M. Reed, was dispatched to search for the wreckage. Reed and his crew spotted the crash site at 10:10 am, 1 hour and 24 minutes after the crash. *Resolution* had crashed on the wooded southwest side of Kings Mountain, west of Redwood City, two miles from the Skeggs Point turnout on Skyline Boulevard.

The first on the scene was Belmont Police Officer James Winters, who discovered a completely demolished aircraft that had caused three forest fires. He noted correctly that none of the 11 passengers or eight crew could have survived.

Officer Winters was followed to the wreck site by the first rescue team led by Deputy Sheriff Joe Kimball, who was accompanied

by *San Mateo Times* reporter Virgil Wilson and photographer Jack Russell. The rescue operation was coordinated by Redwood City Police Chief Stanley Wood.

Paul Jensen, the newly elected coroner, had been in office less than 30 days, and this was to be his first major case. James Alteri was one of the first Red Cross volunteers at the scene.

Upon assessing the situation, bulldozers were called in to cut a road and clear a base of operations for the rescue and recovery operation. Once this base was established, San Mateo County Red Cross volunteer chairman Liz Mack organized canteen operations to feed the firefighters and Red Cross workers.

Mack, now living in San Mateo, said, "We used about 25 to 30 volunteers, nurses aides, a motor service, and a canteen service. We had a phone line set up within hours." She also obtained potable water for the first rescuers from Vic and Alberta Brock, owners of the Kings Mountain Inn, a local restaurant.

As soon as he received confirmation of the crash site, Brooks asked for the United Airlines' crash response team to be sent from Denver.

Award-winning newspaper photographer Reg McGovern rented a plane and flew over the crash site on the afternoon of October 29, 1953. Trees still burn in the heavily forested area on King's Mountain. (Reg McGovern)

This 13-foot section of wing is the largest piece of VH-BPE at the crash site today. The point of impact is directly north on the opposite canyon wall. (Ed Davies)

He then left the airport to set up and coordinate the recovery efforts from Redwood City's National Guard Armory on Valota Road, which was serving as a temporary morgue. Brooks ensured that the mail was recovered, attempted to identify the bodies of the crew, and dealt with the insurance company representative who had come to the site.

The impact and resulting fires rendered most of the bodies unrecognizable. Coroner Jensen called in two physicians, Dr. A.C. Ladd and Dr. Seth Smott, and a dentist, Dr. Donald Allen, to assist in the identification of the bodies. These three men helped form the backbone of San Mateo County's first forensic investigation team.

The Civil Aeronautics Board investigated the crash and found that the aircraft was almost entirely destroyed by impact and the ensuing fire. The left wing first struck a tree at an elevation of 2,020 feet above sea level, severing 13 feet, 4 inches of the wing inboard from the tip. The main wreckage area was located at an elevation of about 1,950 feet.

Examination at this site revealed that the landing gear was down and locked, and the flaps were extended to between 15 and 20 degrees. All propeller blades were found, and from the blade positions, domes and hubs, it was determined that they were set between 29 and 37 degrees at impact. The propeller governors from engines two and three were found, and they indicated settings of about 2,400 rpm.

The CAB report states: "As far as could be determined from an examination of the damaged engines and components, there was no indication that a malfunction or failure had occurred prior to impact."

The probable cause of the accident was given as, "The failure of the crew to follow prescribed procedures for an instrument approach."

After seeing the location of the wreckage in relation to the Half Moon Bay Outer Marker, it is assumed that the aircraft crossed the coast south of the marker and was making a direct approach to Runway 28.

VH-BPE *Resolution* Today

As far as aircraft wrecks go, the final resting place of *Resolution* is accessible, yet strangely removed. The wreck of the *Resolution* is on land belonging to the Midpeninsula Regional Open Space District in the El Corte de Madera Creek Open Space Preserve in the coastal foothills separating the San Francisco Bay from the Pacific Ocean.

Because the area is a park, all artifacts are the property of the Midpeninsula Regional Open Space District. Items recovered and now in the possession of the district include a three-ring notebook, a coroner's glove, suitcase hinges, an aircraft specialty tool, switches, clamps, and cockpit and side window glass. The list is long.

El Corte de Madera Creek Open Space Preserve is open to the public from dawn to dusk. No motor vehicles or pets are allowed. Midpeninsula Regional Open Space District may be contacted at (650) 691-1200 for more information, and downloadable topo maps of the area are available at: www.openspace.org.

There are two ways to get to the wreck site. From Highway 92, drive south on Skyline Boulevard until you come to the Kings Mountain Country Store. Load up on sandwiches, chips and drinks and check out their display of the Kings Mountain area history.

The second route is to drive west on Woodside Road from either Highway 101 or Highway 280 to Skyline Boulevard. Drive the two or three miles north to the parking area at Skeggs Point, walk across the road (to the west), and continue north about 100 yards to the gate at the beginning of the trail to Vista Point. Vista Point is about one-and-a-half miles from Skyline Boulevard, and the trail is marked with signs and mileage estimates. Follow the trail to "Resolution Trail," which passes directly through the crash site and is named in honor of the aircraft. Near the trailhead, a memorial marker has been placed. This was done through the efforts of Christopher O'Donnell, who spent years fighting bureaucracy to get the marker installed in memory of his fellow countrymen and women.

A light-weight, long-sleeved shirt, good shoes, sunglasses or some form of eye protection, and a couple quarts of water are recommended for the hike.

Vista Point is the area cleared by the bulldozers in October 1953 to serve as the base of operations for the recovery effort. When a number of trails were closed by the Open Space District in the 1990s, they opened an equal number of new trails and one was the previously mentioned *Resolution* Trail. Follow the trail to the impact point. Here, a large amount of identifiable debris still exists—a radio rack, an ashtray, you name it. The ground is just littered with airplane parts.

Climbing to the top of the ridge, where the manzanita is very thick, is not recommended, and for those who might think, "there's got to be a road just over the hill," there isn't. There are a number of small pieces of fuselage, and the firewall section of an engine can be seen, but the pain of getting to them is not worth the reward.

The BCPA Fleet
Douglas DC-6

Name/ Registration	Constructor's Number	Delivered To BCPA	Disposition
Resolution VH-BPE	43125	Nov. 26, 1948	Crashed San Mateo, Oct. 29, 1953
Endeavour VH-BPF	43126	Nov. 19, 1948	Crashed Java, Jan. 1, 1971
Adventure VH-BPG	43127	Dec. 17, 1948	To N80MA, Broken up, Chandler, Arizona
Discovery VH-BPH	43128	Sept. 30, 1948	To N90MA, Broken up, Chandler, Arizona. Cockpit reportedly preserved.

BCPA's VH-BPF is seen at Vancouver, British Columbia, Canada in the early 1950s in company with a Trans-Canada DC-3. VH-BPF Endeavour, *flew until it crashed in Java on Jan. 1, 1971. (John Wegg Collection)*

UNITED
United
United

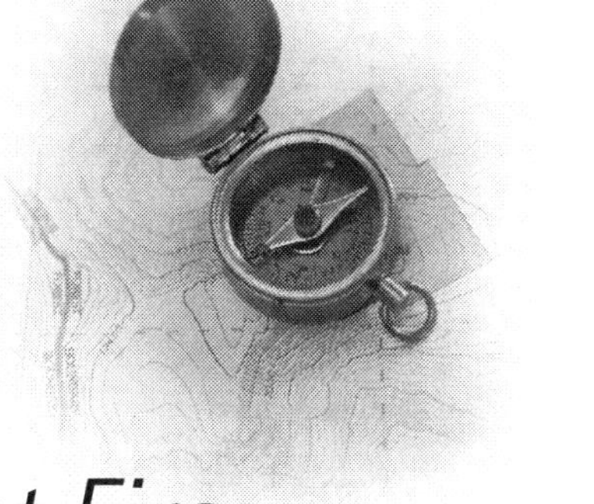

Chapter 10

Fuel Transfer Starts In-Flight Fire: United DC-6 N37503

Michael B. McComb

Since the early days of powered flight, one of the greatest fears for any pilot has been an in-flight fire. Although less likely to happen in modern jet aircraft, the checklist procedure has remained relatively unchanged for more than 75 years. This serious and potentially devastating situation requires one of the quickest and most demanding responsive actions on the flight deck. Modern airline flight simulator sessions provide a number of in-flight fire emergencies such as engine fires, baggage compartment fires, and wheel well fires. Most aircraft fires today can be contained or extinguished by automatic fuel shutoff valves and halon-type fire bottles. These devices can be activated either thermally or manually by the flight crew. However, in the golden age of propliners, fire was fuel-fed. Uncontained and uncontrolled, it could result in an extremely serious life or death situation. Such was the case on October 24, 1947, with United Airlines' Flight 608.

This United DC-6 is similar to the aircraft that crashed at Bryce Canyon. Fuel being transferred from one wing tank to another overflowed into the belly of the aircraft. When the cabin heater was switched on, an explosion and fire began. The pilots bravely attempted to reach the Bryce Canyon Airport, but time ran out for the crew of five and 46 passengers. (UPI/Bettmann)

Shortly after 9:00 am, the crew of Flight 608 arrived via hotel courtesy car at the busy Los Angeles Airport terminal. After checking the en route and forecast weather, Captain E.L. McMillan was busy performing instrument and performance checks while First Officer G.G. Griesbach conducted the walk-around inspection. The aircraft, a Douglas DC-6, was one of United's newest to join the company's

Aerial views of the crash site. The top photo was taken October 25, 1947, one day after the disaster. Highway 12 was then a dirt road. (UPI/Bettmann) Today, bottom photo, it has been paved and runs through the left third of the photo. (Michael B. McComb)

Sister ship to ill-fated N37503, United Airlines DC-6 N5414 is seen on the ramp at Denver's Stapleton Airport. (Robert J. Boser/www.airlinesafety.com/editorials/AboutTheEditor.htm)

mainliner fleet. NC37510 had accumulated only 133 hours operation since its delivery date the previous March. The DC-6 was proudly named *Mainliner Seattle*.

Its four Pratt & Whitney R-2800 engines ensured that it could climb higher and faster than its predecessor, the Douglas DC-4. The manufacturer had also installed the latest, top-of-the-line Sperry autopilot system, and an advanced altitude rate controller for the cabin pressurization system. One major safety improvement was a fire detection and extinguishing system. Considered state-of-the-art for its time, the system could detect a fire in any of the four powerplants as well as both forward and aft cargo and hydraulic accessory compartments, and extinguish the fires with pressurized halon.

Cabin heating systems, on the other hand, remained mostly unchanged since the introduction of the DC-3 in the mid-1930s. The system operated very much like a modern jet engine. Aircraft fuel was fed into a burner can arrangement, while air was ducted via a scoop on the belly of the aircraft. As the cabin temperature dropped, a thermostat closed a switch, igniting the fuel-air mixture in the burner can. The system worked well and is still being used on some light twin-engine aircraft.

Given all the conveniences and technical innovations built into the DC-6, the engineers at Douglas had inadvertently developed and overlooked a sort of Achilles Heel.

Mainliner Seattle to Chicago

Sunlight was beginning to break through the midmorning coastal layer as United began boarding Flight 608. Wearing their blue uniforms, stewardesses Shirley E. Brown, Helen F. Morrisey, and Sabina H. Joswich greeted passengers and directed them to their seats. Up front on the flight deck, McMillan was discussing a change of flight plan with Griesbach. They opted for a cruising altitude of 19,000 feet, which would give the aircraft a little less headwind and reduce the time drain along the usual seven-hour flight to Chicago.

Once all 46 passengers were aboard and their carry-ons placed in the open overhead compartments, Stewardess Brown closed the cabin door of the shiny silver and blue airliner for the last time. After receiving the "cabin secured" signal from the back, McMillan started each of the four gas-guzzling R-2800 engines. Family and friends at the gate watched as each engine roared to life, throwing clouds of oil smoke past the windows and obscuring the smiling faces of friends and loved ones.

Slowly the plane left the gate and taxied to Runway 25L. McMillan read the taxi checklist as Griesbach performed the functions—"hydraulic

The twisted tail section was the largest remaining piece of Mainliner Seattle. *The vertical fin appears to have severe fire damage. (UPI/Bettmann)*

United DC-6 NC37510 Mainliner Seattle *came to rest on the far side of this barbed wire fence, just inside Bryce Canyon National Park. (Michael B. McComb)*

pressure, check ... flaps, set ... fuel ..." Fuel was unbalanced with 2,400 pounds more in the left tank. However, a fuel imbalance was a common inconvenience in the airline industry, and the crew had no reason to suspect a safety concern. McMillan advised his co-pilot they would start a fuel transfer to the right tank upon reaching cruising altitude. Griesbach agreed, and they continued with the checklist.

After taxiing out to the approach end of Runway 25L, and following engine run-up checks, Flight 608 was ready and cleared for takeoff. Griesbach eased the four power levers forward, and the DC-6 began its roll. McMillan called, "Four engines stable ... manifold power set ... 60 knots ... V1 ... V2 ... rotate ... flight in less than 45 seconds." Flight 608 lifted off, leaving behind a cloud of spray from the prior evening's light rain. Upon reaching a positive rate of climb, approximately 1,500 feet per minute, Griesbach called for "gear up" and McMillan complied.

McMillan had given Griesbach his leg to Chicago so Griesbach could add to his hours at the controls of the DC-6. Griesbach, 25, had been hired by United in 1945. He had accumulated more than 3,000 hours flying time, but only 66 hours in the DC-6.

McMillan, 42, had accumulated more than 15,000 hours flying time. He had joined United in 1936, and left during World War II to fly B-17s on bombing missions over Europe. When he returned to United in 1945, he flew DC-3s and DC-4s. Since being on line with the DC-6, he had accumulated 138 hours in the type.

Flight 608 had just passed Fontana, climbing through 10,000 feet, when they made a gradual left turn toward the Daggett navigation station. Below them were the San Bernardino Mountains and to the north, the great expanse of California's Mojave Desert. As the flight progressed in a northeasterly direction, controllers with Los Angeles Center cleared Flight 608 to "climb and maintain 15,000 feet." McMillan acknowledged. The stewardesses had begun making their rounds, serving coffee and preparing lunch.

Passengers were settling down for the trip, some playing cards in the lounge while others, mostly businessmen, were catching up on work. The view outside the window was picture perfect. The scattered cumulus clouds seemed to glide by against the blue sky as the Douglas bore through the sky at more than four miles a minute.

Upon reaching their final cruising altitude of 19,000 feet, McMillan reached over and set cruise power. He began to cross-feed fuel from the left tank to the right tank, speeding up the process by placing the fuel transfer boost pumps on "HI." In this transfer configuration, the process would take less than 40 minutes.

At 11:40 am, Flight 608 reported its position over the gambling mecca of Las Vegas. In the distance on the right, passengers could see the still-forming Lake Mead and the western end of the Grand Canyon. Below lay the Charleston Range, where not more than five years before, actress Carole Lombard had lost her life in a plane crash.

The passengers settled in their seats for lunch and McMillan made an announcement over the public address system that, in a few minutes, they would be passing over the colorful butte and canyons of both Zion and Bryce national parks. For many on board, this was a highlight of the flight, and passengers began loading film into cameras for this and other sights along the way.

McMillan made his position report call with Aeronautical Radio (ARINC), "Salt Lake, United 608, Saint George, estimating Bryce Canyon 1222." It was shortly after this call that McMillan probably noticed that the right fuel tank had not only filled but overfilled. Overfilling was a common occurrence on Douglas aircraft because there were no automatic fuel cross-feed shutoff valves. Though it was something crews always tried to avoid, it would not have bothered either crewmember. Normally, any extra fuel would just drain overboard.

But, unknown to McMillan and Griesbach, the highly volatile fuel was not quite leaving the plane in the 300 mph slipstream. Instead, it was flowing under the belly of the aircraft and directly into the cabin pressurization and heater air scoop at a rate of nearly five gallons per minute. Fuel had entered the compartment, soaking numerous articles of luggage and creating an extremely volatile situation.

Cabin Fire at 19,000 Feet

Meanwhile, oblivious to the situation below, passengers were busy taking pictures of the many brightly hued formations and the tall Ponderosa Pines of the Dixie National Forest. However, some passengers wanted to rest and complained to stewardesses that the cabin was cold. A stewardess told the flight crew, and McMillan made the adjustment on the thermostat. Just then a loud thud was heard and felt.

Many passengers in back thought the jolt was an air pocket. McMillan and Griesbach were puzzled and concerned but also thought it might have been turbulence. They were wrong. When the cabin heater came on, it caused a powerful fuel-air explosion, which completely blew the air scoop from the aircraft and ignited a raging fire underneath.

Soon McMillan and Griesbach were looking at an illuminated aft cargo compartment fire light and hearing the bell. Quickly, McMillan pulled the fire bottle handle, which silenced the bell but did little to put out the fire. At 1228, Griesbach put out a call to Salt Lake ARINC, "United 608, we have a fire in the aft cargo ... unable ... emergency landing Brycc ..." Smoke was beginning to fill the cabin as panic-stricken passengers began to scream. Some passengers in the back of the cabin may have noticed the floor becoming exceedingly warm, while others may have noticed the carpet beginning to smoke as the fire below began to burn through the floor.

McMillan, now at the helm, steeply descended toward the Bryce Canyon Airport, the controls shaking as the fire began to consume the elevators and rudder. As the plane flew over the town of Tropic, Utah, the main cabin door fell from the aircraft, taking with it a burning passenger. Other articles, such as luggage and portions of the aft galley also dropped from the aircraft as it made its fiery attempt to land.

When smoke began to fill the cockpit, McMillan and Griesbach were barely able to breathe and donned oxygen masks as they strained to see the airport. The screams of panic previously heard in the cabin began to subside as each passenger became overcome by fire or smoke.

Nearly six miles from landing, the aircraft was barely controllable, and Griesbach reported, "The tail is going out ... we may get down and we may not."

At 12:26 pm, the last radio transmission was received by Salt Lake controllers. "We may make it ... approaching a strip." However, approximately one and one-half miles southwest of Bryce Canyon Airport, the Douglas' tail section gave way, shearing control cables. Flight 608 pitched into the plateau, sending burning wreckage and bodies flying for more than 1,500 feet.

Although the impact of the explosion could be heard for miles, no one saw the aircraft fall to earth. Charlie Francisco was a boy living on a ranch near the town of Tropic, where he recalls seeing a large plane descending with flames and black smoke coming from it. He also recalls seeing burning fragments falling as it disappeared behind some hills. Then he heard an explosion. His account was like those of many others who witnessed the tragedy. When rescue workers reached the

In his directions to the crash site, author Michael B. McComb states, "Make a left turn on Highway 12, pass the airport turnoff, and continue past the Highway 22 intersection and national park turnoff. In less than one-quarter mile, pull over at a large sign that reads, 'Bryce Canyon National Park.' You are there." (Michael B. McComb)

scene, there was little they could do. What was left of the aircraft was hauled off for scrap.

The Crash Site Today

It was fall when I arrived at Bryce Canyon and began my search for the crash site of Flight 608. Through previous research, I had a general idea of the location, but I did not have aerial photos, which made finding the site more difficult. According to the CAB report, the Douglas DC-6 crashed approximately one and one-half miles southeast of the Bryce Canyon Airport. I concentrated my efforts in this area.

I began a walking ground search. The first few hours were uneventful. However, I eventually crossed Highway 12 (the highway that runs through Tropic), and after climbing over a National Park boundary fence, I soon found myself standing amid the burned aluminum pieces of the once-new propliner. The one thing that surprised me most about the site was the close proximity to a paved road. In fact, after further examination, I found that some pieces of wreckage had actually eroded from the hillside and were lying next to the highway. Unlike many of the other sites I have visited on which engines and large airframe structures remain, the Flight 608 site has none of these large pieces.

Most wreckage at the site measured approximately three- to eight-inches-square, which is not unusual considering the proximity to a paved roadway. The variety of small pieces at the site includes everything from bits of window Plexiglas to fragments of pale blue plastic UAL drinking cups. A closer examination revealed pieces of jewelry, coins, flight instrument parts, and other small remnants from the plane.

Some of the old timers in the area told me how people used to look around the site and find wristwatches and rings. One story I heard occurred sometime between the late 1960s and early 1970s. A road crew was working in an area adjacent to the site across Highway 12 when one worker looked under a ledge and found a very weathered and torn Samsonite suitcase. Upon opening it, they found it contained the personal belongings of one of Flight 608's passengers. After hearing this story, I have no doubt that other items like this continue to lie amid the hills and cliffs of Bryce Canyon today.

However, because the site lies within the northern boundary of the Bryce Canyon National Park, all wreckage is considered federal property and may not be removed. To take anything is a felony. The Park Service does patrol the area, and fines can be very steep.

A visit to the Flight 608 site is a non-strenuous experience, as there are no canyons to crawl down or mountains to climb. From Interstate 15 in Utah, take Highway 20 east to State Route 89, then turn right toward the town of Panguitch and continue south on 89. Make a left turn on Highway 12, pass the airport turnoff, and continue past the Highway 22 intersection and national park turnoff. In less than one-quarter mile, pull over at a large sign that reads, "Bryce Canyon National Park." You are there. (If you continue to drive and start to descend off the plateau, you have gone too far.)

Remember, the crash site is on the south side of the highway (the same side as the park sign). You must climb a four-foot barbed wire fence, but going over it is not illegal if you don't break it. The site lies a short walk further. Once again, don't remove anything you find.

TWA
TRANS
TWA

Chapter 11

Final Destination: Grand Canyon Mid-Air

Donald B. McComb Jr. and Michael B. McComb

The grandfather of all midairs—the collision of Trans World Airlines Lockheed 1049 Super Constellation, N6902C, *Star of the Seine*, and United Airlines DC-7, N6324C, *City of Vancouver*, on June 30, 1956, shocked the world as the worst air disaster in the history of commercial aviation. The public outcry over this accident brought about a complete revamping of the Air Traffic Control (ATC) system, creating new airways and providing radar separation nationwide.

The Constellation involved in the Grand Canyon mid-air, N6902C Star of the Seine, *was similar to the 1049 shown here at San Francisco. (William T. Larkins)*

Early on the morning of June 30, 1956, at Los Angeles International, the passengers preparing to board TWA's Flight 2 and United's Flight 718 were not thinking of radar separation or the ATC system. Undoubtedly, their thoughts concerned the start of vacations, a new job, or the countless other reasons people make cross-country flights. Those passengers that arrived at the airport early might have taken a moment to visit one of the airport concession stands for a pack of gum or a roll of Life Savers, never dreaming that a pack of candy would outlive them by 34 years.

Flight Into Eternity

Just after sunrise, TWA Flight 2, nonstop service for Kansas City, was being readied for departure. The aircraft was a Lockheed Constellation L-1049, N6902C. Delivered new to TWA on May 22, 1952, N6902C

United DC-7 N6324 City of Vancouver, *was similar to the aircraft shown here. At the time of the crash, N6324C had flown 5,115 hours since being delivered new to United. (Michael B. McComb Collection)*

was the second A-model series aircraft delivered to TWA. The plane was named *Star of the Seine* for France's most famous river. After four years, one month, and one week of service, " '02C" had flown 10,519 hours in TWA service. During the night, a line maintenance check had been performed, and the plane had been given a clean bill of health for the cross-country flight.

Several hundred feet away, United Airlines' Flight 718, nonstop service for Chicago, was in the final stages for departure. The aircraft for this flight was a Douglas DC-7, N6324C, which had been delivered new to United on January 10, 1955, and carried the name *City of Vancouver*. In the one year, five months, and twenty days with United, " '24C" had flown 5,115 hours. The day before, N6324C had flown in from Idlewild as Flight 707, arriving at Los Angeles at 3:45 pm The DC-7 also had overnighted for a line maintenance check.

As the final boarding started, both aircraft were in the process of being fueled. The Connie was topped off with 3,300 gallons and the DC-7 with 3,850 gallons of high-octane gasoline. The weather en route was expected to pose no problem. The weather in Los Angeles that morning was typical for late June: coastal clouds and haze that was expected to burn off by mid-morning.

The *Star of the Seine's* doors were closed at 8:50 am. In command of Flight 2 were Captain Jack S. Gandy, Co-pilot James H. Ritner, and Flight Engineer Forrest D. Breyfogle. Captain Gandy had been with the company since 1939, and had a total of 14,922 hours, nearly half piloting Constellations. This trip would be his 178th between Los Angeles and Kansas City. One-by-one the big 2,700-horsepower Wright Cyclone R-3350 engines came to life, blowing clouds of oil smoke across the ramp.

While Flight 2 began its taxi out to Runway 25, United's Flight 718 also had fired up its engines and was making its way to Runway

This 1956 view of the Constellation's tail section shows the rugged, boulder-strewn terrain of the crash site. (Michael B. McComb Collection)

25L. In command of the DC-7 were Captain Robert F. Shirley, Co-pilot Robert W. Harms, and Flight Engineer Gerard Fiore. Though Captain Shirley had fewer hours in DC-7s than Captain Gandy had Connies (1,238 vs. 7,208), he had accumulated 16,492 hours in his 19 years with United and had flown the Los Angeles/Chicago route on a regular basis since October 1, 1955.

Captain Gandy held short at the end of Runway 25 as an American DC-7 touched down. As the American DC-7 cleared the runway,

Captain Gandy received his takeoff clearance. He moved the Connie into position for takeoff. After a short pause, Gandy advanced the throttles. The four Wright R-3350s thundering roar drowned out all other sounds in the immediate area. At 9:01 am, the brakes were released, and the *Star of the Seine* began its final journey. N6902C lifted off easily, roaring over Dockweiller Beach and out over Santa Monica Bay.

The IFR flight plan filed by Captain Gandy called for a cruising altitude of 19,000 feet and a true airspeed of 270 knots. Flight 2 would fly to Kansas City via Green Airway 5, Amber Airway 2, crossing over Daggett direct Trinidad, direct Dodge City, and Victor Airway 10 into Kansas City.

While Flight 2 climbed out over Santa Monica Bay, Captain Shirley guided *City of Vancouver* into position for takeoff. Immediate clearance was given and the DC-7 rumbled off down the runway. At 9:04 am, three minutes after the TWA Connie broke ground, Captain Shirley eased back his control column, and the DC-7 sailed over the low hills that border the western boundary of Los Angeles International Airport.

Flight 718's flight plan would take the DC-7 on a more southerly route than that of Flight 2. Flight 718 was to cruise at 21,000 feet at a true airspeed of 288 knots via Green Airway 5, Palm Springs intersection, direct Painted Desert, direct Durango, direct Pueblo, direct St. Joseph, Victor Airway 116 Joliet, and Victor Airway 84 to Chicago-Midway Airport. However, once United 718 reached the Palm Springs intersection, its route would start to take a more northerly heading. The routes that TWA Flight 2 and United Flight 718 were flying would gradually come together over the Painted Desert. But with the United DC-7 flying 3,000 feet higher than the Connie, this should have posed no problem.

TWA Flight 2 had just reached its cruising altitude of 19,000 feet at 9:20 am near Daggett, California. Captain Gandy, seeing thunderhead

Right forward fuselage section of the Constellation on Temple Butte. (Michael B. McComb Collection)

Fuselage section of the TWA Constellation showing the red cheatline stripes. (Michael B. McComb Collection)

buildups on the far horizon called TWA Flight Operations and requested an altitude change on its IFR clearance from 19,000 feet to 21,000 feet and, if unable, 1,000 on top. The TWA radio operator who received the request called Los Angeles Air Route Traffic Control and at 9:21 am advised, "TWA 2 is coming up on Daggett requesting 21,000 feet." The Los Angeles controller then contacted the Salt Lake ARTC controller and asked, "TWA 2 is requesting two-one-thousand, how does it look? I see he is Daggett direct Trinidad, I see you have United 718 crossing his altitude—in his way at two-one-thousand." Salt Lake replied, "Yes, their courses cross and they are right together."

The Los Angeles controller then called the TWA radio operator and said, "Advisory, TWA 2, unable to approve two-one-thousand." At this time, the radio operator interrupted and said, "Just a minute. I think he wants a thousand on top, yes a thousand on top until he can get it." After determining from the flight, through the TWA radio operator, that he was then 1,000 on top, the Los Angeles controller issued the following amended clearance: "ATC clears TWA 2, maintain at least 1,000 on top. Advise TWA 2 his traffic is United 718, direct Durango, estimating Needles at 9:57 am."

When TWA amended its flight plan from an assigned 19,000 feet to 1,000 feet on top, no information concerning this was given to United 718, nor was it required, even though the flights were in controlled airspace at the time. Neither aircraft was traffic for each other at the time TWA's amended clearance was granted, but in projecting their tracks eastward, both would cross Red Airway 15 with ill-defined horizontal separation.

Aboard both aircraft, people were settling down for the long flight ahead. The stewardesses on United 718 and the "hostesses" (as they were still called by TWA) began serving breakfast to their passengers. A few of

Main impact site of TWA's Star of the Seine. *Note the number of large pieces still at the crash site. (Michael B. McComb Collection)*

the more observant passengers had already spotted the Colorado River up ahead. Beyond lay Arizona and the sweep of the Great Plains.

TWA Flight 2 reported its position to company radio at Las Vegas at 9:59 am. Flight 2 had passed over Lake Mohave at 9:55 am, was 1,000 on top at 21,000 feet, and estimated reaching the Winslow omni station (Painted Desert) at 10:31 am, with Farmington the next reporting position.

At 9:58 am, United 718 made a position report to the CAA communication station at Needles, California. Flight 718 reported that it was over Needles at 9:58 am at 21,000 feet and estimated crossing the Painted Desert at 10:31 am, with Durango next. When the two aircraft crossed the Colorado River, they were about 40 air miles apart. With every mile, the distance between the Connie and DC-7 closed.

As they crossed over the Kaibab Plateau, the two aircraft were less than 10 miles apart. Some of the more keen-eyed passengers on the DC-7 might have seen the white Connie, which would have appeared nearly motionless several miles away. One can also speculate that Flight 2 should have been visible to Captain Shirley from his left seat in the DC-7, but this was in the days before cockpit voice recorders. What was said on the flight decks of both aircraft before the accident will never be known.

The Final Seconds of Flight 2 and Flight 718

Over the Grand Canyon that morning, towering cumulus buildups were forming—in some cases already climbing past 25,000 feet. As the two aircraft approached the eastern section of the canyon, they were probably maneuvering around clouds and, sometimes, punching through them. It is also possible they were banking to give their passengers a better view of the canyon.

What was happening in the last few seconds before impact will never be known. Were they in the clouds, in the clear, giving their passengers a better view of the canyon with a wing dipped, or steering around thunderheads?

What is known is: at 10:31 am at a point just west of the confluence of the Colorado and Little Colorado rivers, the left aileron tip of the United DC-7 struck the leading edge of the center fin of the TWA Constellation. A split second later, the DC-7's lower surface of the left wing outboard of the Number One engine smashed into the upper aft fuselage of the Connie with a shattering impact. This started the breakup of the Connie's fuselage just forward of the pressure dome in the area of the rear galley.

The DC-7 continued to pass laterally over the top of the Connie, the left wing next making contact with the top of the left fin, shearing it off. Before the two aircraft separated—in less than one-half of a second, the propeller on the Number One engine of the DC-7 had inflicted a series of cuts in the aft baggage compartment of the Connie.

Minus its famous triple tail, the Connie pitched into a -8g dive. Passengers without their seatbelts fastened were hurled about the cabin to be pinned to the ceiling. Less than a minute later, the *Star of the Seine* smashed into the jagged rocks of a draw on the northeast slope of Temple Butte.

At impact, the Connie was in a slightly inverted dive going well-over 400 mph. Totally fragmenting on ground contact, what little that was left of the aircraft was destroyed by the intense ground fire. Falling like a giant leaf, the massive triple tail/elevator assembly came to rest about 550 yards northeast of the main impact site. The ground impact knocked off both the left and right outboard fins from the tail assembly.

When the two aircraft separated after the collision, the United DC-7 was missing most of the left wing outboard of the Number One engine. Despite the fact that fuel was pouring from the ruptured wing tanks, there was no in-flight fire. The DC-7 began a turning descent to the left that was a little less rapid but no less fatal than TWA's.

It was at this time that a message was picked up by ARINC in San Francisco and Salt Lake City. The message was not understood when it was received, but by playing it back was interpreted as: "Salt Lake, United 718 ... ah ... we're going in."

Could Captain Shirley have saved the DC-7? If he had cut power on the right wing Number Three and Four engines and increased power on Number Two, would he have been able to maintain some control?

Of those who perished in the mid-air collision, 29 persons from the United aircraft were unidentifiable. They were interred together at the Grand Canyon Cemetery in Grand Canyon National Park. This headstone marks their final resting place. (Michael B. McComb Collection)

Aerial view of the United DC-7 crash site. The arrow indicates point of impact. This site was too remote to travel to in only four days. (Michael B. McComb)

There are a couple of examples of airliners losing most of an outer wing (a TWA 707 and a Pan American 707) and making safe landings. But both were jets and both incidents took place nearly 10 years later.

Some passengers on the left side of the DC-7, who just happened to be looking out the window, must certainly have had a "front row" seat to observe the collision as it occurred. Others seated on the left side, hearing the shouts and cries of fellow passengers were greeted with the sight of the twisted and stilled Number One propeller and fuel streaming from the torn wing. The rapidly increasing turning descent was an advance notice that the end was near.

As the DC-7 screamed downward, the aircraft shed bits and pieces of the elevators and rudder. As its speed approached Mach 1, the control surfaces encountered compressibility—where the airflow became greater than the control surfaces could act against. Captain Shirley had only one hope left. The faster the aircraft flew, the greater the lift generated, which could in theory pull up the nose of the aircraft into a climb that would slow the aircraft enough to break the sonic airflow grip on the control surfaces—provided there was enough airspace for this to occur.

Out the cockpit windows of the DC-7, Captain Shirley and First Officer Harms faced the imposing buttes and chasms of the Grand Canyon with plateaus nearly a mile above sea level. The collision occurring at 21,000 feet gave the DC-7 a little more than three miles of altitude to work with, and it looked like they might just make it. The rate of descent was slowing; the nose was starting to come up ever so slightly. For the crew of the DC-7, there was hope that they might just pull it off, just get the ship into a positive rate of climb to bleed off the excess airspeed. If they could get the plane under control, they could either head for an airport or make an emergency landing in the Painted Desert just beyond the Grand Canyon.

Another couple of thousand feet of altitude might have made the difference. But fate was not kind to United DC-7, N6324C, that day. Through the front cockpit windows, the crew watched with horror as the jagged sheer cliffs of a butte filled the windows. About a half second before impact, the DC-7 lost its left elevator due to the aerodynamic overload. With the nose down about 20 degrees and the left wing in a 10-degree bank, the DC-7 slammed into Chuar Butte just 10 feet below the top of the 4,050-foot ridge.

Most of the wreckage fell onto the ledges and into the 500-foot deep chimneys below the crash site. Some of the wreckage, such as the vertical fin, landing gear, and major parts of engines and propellers, came to rest on the south slope below the vertical butte face. Other major components, such as the horizontal stabilizers, elevator, and one engine, cleared the summit and came to rest on the northeast slope of the butte. Like the Connie, the ground fire was intense at the impact site, however, a great deal of the DC-7 wreckage fell away unburned.

Later that afternoon, one of the tour operators flying out of Grand Canyon Airport spotted smoke drifting up from the eastern part of the canyon. Having heard earlier in the day that two airliners were missing in the area, he decided to investigate. In a few minutes, he was flying over the two burned out crash sites. Confirmation came moments later when he spotted the Connie's tail section nearby.

The next day, rescue personnel from the Arizona National Guard made hazardous landings with helicopters at both crash sites. It was quickly determined that there was no hope for any of the passengers or crew from either aircraft. Rescue crews from the National Guard, U.S. Park Service, and a Swiss mountain climbing team were brought in to remove bodies and essential wreckage.

Based on the examination of the Connie's tail section, recovered sections of the Connie's fuselage and baggage door, and recovered sections from the DC-7's outer left wing (some of which was recovered at the TWA site), it did not take the investigators from the Civil Aeronautics Board long to figure out that a collision had occurred. This investigation, in fact, led to the creation of the Federal Aviation Administration (FAA).

In the official report released by the CAB on April 17, 1957, the probable cause of the collision was as follows: "The board determines that the probable cause of the midair collision was that the pilots did not see each other in time to avoid the collision. It is not possible to determine why the pilots did not see each other, but the evidence suggests that it resulted from any one or a combination of the following factors: Intervening clouds reducing time for visual separation, visual limitations due to cockpit visibility, preoccupation with normal cockpit duties, preoccupation with matters unrelated to cockpit duties, such as attempting to provide the passengers with a more scenic view of the Grand Canyon area, physiological limits to human vision reducing the time opportunity to see and avoid the other aircraft, or insufficiency of en route air traffic advisory information due to inadequacy of facilities and lack of personnel in air traffic control."

R-3350 engine cylinder at the Constellation site. (Michael B. McComb)

The Crash Site Today

Over the years, the canyon has gradually reclaimed the crash sites. Rain and snow have washed and worn the fire-blackened rocks to the point where you really have to know where to look in order to spot the sites. With the exception of most human remains and pieces of debris essential to the investigation, everything else was left where it had fallen. Since then, people on rafting trips down the Colorado have had the crash sites pointed out by their guides, and occasionally, sunlight reflects off pieces of the DC-7 high on the ledges of Chuar Butte.

In an effort to discourage souvenir hunters and to generally remove what some would call an eyesore, in 1976 and again in 1980, the Park Service contracted with the Arizona Air National Guard to remove most of the large items of wreckage. Large military helicopters were utilized in the removal process. Gone were the Connie's tail section and detached fins, landing gear, and large sections of the fuselage. The Connie's engines were blown up and most of the pieces removed. From the DC-7 site, only the large pieces that were projected down onto the lower ledges and slopes were removed in these operations. For the most part, more than 40 percent of the L-1049 remains on site, with more than 85 percent of the DC-7 still on Chuar Butte.

To a marine archaeologist, there are shipwrecks ... and there are *shipwrecks*, like the *Titanic* or the *Atocha*. This accident is the aviation archaeologist's version of the *Titanic*. It is a very well-preserved site, and considering that aviation itself is less than a century old, it is a very old site. It has one other thing in common with the *Titanic* ... it is very difficult to reach. Without a Jet Ranger III, reaching the sites meant hiking a roundtrip distance of just over 45 very hard miles, plus crossing rivers, and running rapids.

Author Donald B. McComb was unable to hike to the crash site due to an injury suffered in a motorcycle accident. His involvement was in the planning, research, and documentation of all data and photographs obtained. Michael B. McComb was uniquely qualified to conduct this expedition. He holds an Air Transport Pilot (ATP) certificate and, at the time, was a senior pilot for Air Grand Canyon. He flew daily over Temple and Chuar buttes. In addition, he is a trained archaeologist, having done work with the Bureau of Land Management on many important Indian archaeological sites. Donald B. McComb picks up the story:

Decaying TWA flight schedule recovered from the purse found at the Connie crash site. (Michael B. McComb)

While Mike and I had discussed going to the Connie and DC-7 crash sites for years, it was not until Mike started flying for Air Grand Canyon that planning for the trip started in earnest. As he put it, "Every day I flew what we called our Grand Tour. I could look down and see the reflections off the wreckage strewn across the slopes of Temple Butte and high on the cliffs of Chuar Butte. None of my passengers ever asked about the reflections on the rocks below. Of course, this is one bit of Grand Canyon history that I never mentioned unless asked."

Our initial plans called for a four-day trip, which included one day to reach the confluence of the Colorado and Little Colorado rivers. The second day would be spent crossing the river and setting up a camp near Chuar Butte. Since it was not expected to take very long to reach Chuar Butte, Mike planned to spend a good portion of the second afternoon examining the United site. The plan for day three was to get up at daybreak and spend about six hours photographing and documenting finds. Camp would be broken around noon, and a short rafting trip down river would be made to a point near Temple Butte. Camp would be set up at once, and an examination would be made of the TWA site, photographing whatever wreckage was visible.

To enter the canyon in the first place, we had to obtain a backcountry permit, which works just like a flight plan and specifies a certain time period. In order to be out of the canyon by late afternoon on the fourth day, as required by the permit, Mike would have to make an early morning departure. This was vital, because permit holders who are not out of the canyon by the time specified are looked for and better have a good reason for being late.

This was a compressed schedule to be sure, but four days was all we had to work with at the time. Also, our main intention was to make this first trip an "inspection" tour to see if the sites were worthy of a longer expedition in the future. However, as we had discovered while investigating the Air West DC-9 crash site in the mountains above Los Angeles (see Chapter 18: *Air West Mid-Air with F-4 Phantom*), trying to determine the difficulty in reaching a crash site and actually doing it are two different things. Our well-organized four-day plan was doomed from the beginning.

Heading to the Crash Site

Before dawn on October 26, 1990, Mike parked at Lippan Point near the head of the Tanner Trail, equipped with more than 60 pounds of gear in a backpack—cameras, food for a week, inflatable raft, emergency survival gear including aerial flares, and just about everything you would rather have and not need, than need and not have. The first leg of the trek was a 12-mile hike to the end of Tanner Trail at the Colorado River.

The first few miles went fairly smoothly, then the trail disappeared, becoming just a little less rocky than the rest of the terrain. The expected six-hour hike to the river took the whole day, and Camp One had to be set up next to the river at the end of Tanner Trail. The next morning, now several hours behind schedule, Mike set off down the Beamer Trail. He was climbing away from the river on a trail in no better condition than the Tanner Trail. About halfway along the Beamer Trail, Mike found the first evidence of the midair collision.

"The Beamer Trail portion of the trip, 12 miles in length, was much worse than I thought it would be," Mike said. "Even though I had topped off all my water bottles at the river, my water supply was going down much faster than expected. About halfway along the trail, I saw something reflecting sunlight some 50 feet

Michael B. McComb near the Constellation crash site with his one-man raft used to travel the Colorado River. (Michael B. McComb)

McComb holds a piece of the aircraft's skin at the Constellation crash site. (Michael B. McComb)

off to the left. On closer inspection, I discovered what must have been part of the cabin interior trim from the fuselage of the Connie. This find consisted of a small piece of weathered plywood with an aluminum strip screwed along one edge. It measured about four feet long. This wreckage is consistent with some of the lighter debris that spilled out of the L-1049 after the collision. The sighting of this simple piece helped give me the added energy to continue on."

When Mike reached the end of the Beamer Trail, he had nearly exhausted his water supply and his daylight. He inflated his raft to cross the Little Colorado River, refilling the water bottles midstream, and setting up camp on the other side. At dawn the next morning, he crossed the Colorado River itself. The raft was beached for a few minutes while photos were shot of Chuar Butte. Because the window on the time he had available in the canyon was closing, Mike decided to bypass the planned inspection of the United site. However, an examination of the cliff face of Chuar Butte through binoculars revealed several large pieces of DC-7 wreckage high on the ledges. On one of the pieces the distinctive white and blue United paint scheme was still visible. Regretfully, the United site would have to wait.

Mike reboarded the raft for the short one-and-a-half mile trip down river, beaching on the shore near Temple Butte. This point was about 500 yards downhill from the Connie crash site. After the raft was unloaded, Mike nearly had a major disaster, courtesy of mother nature. "As I turned away from the now-empty raft, a gust of wind came up. I turned back to the raft just in time to see it 20 feet in the air and nearly 15 feet out over the water. It had just touched down when I was halfway out to it. The water was freezing cold, but that raft was the only way out of the canyon. It was well anchored before I left it again."

A purse found at crash site held a TWA flight schedule, a roll of Life Savers, and coins. (Michael B. McComb)

Once camp was set up, Mike started for the impact site. There was no trail, only a very hard climb up a rugged slope. Just before reaching the main impact site itself, there is a narrow little canyon. It was here that first signs of the crash site were spotted. Pieces of what could have been parts of the wings or fuselage littered the ground.

"I promptly dubbed the narrow canyon 'Connie Canyon,'" Mike said. "When I reached the end of Connie Canyon, the main impact site spread out before me. Matching the terrain to several photographs that were taken at the site in 1956, it was easy to see that the Connie had hit at the top of a small hill, spraying wreckage downhill towards the small canyon I had just come through."

For a couple of hundred feet in every direction, the ground was littered with pieces. Most were unidentifiable, but some were very easy to identify—crushed flight instruments, a massive cylinder from one of the R-3350 engines, bent and twisted silverware with the TWA logo still visible, an exhaust stack from one of the engines. Coins littered the site, none with a date later than 1956. A purse was visible sticking out of a pile of dirt and aircraft pieces.

The purse was carefully extracted and opened. Inside were the remains of a badly decayed TWA flight schedule, a roll of Life Savers, a book of three-cent stamps, a pencil, lipstick, Max Factor makeup, $1.05 in change, and a Gulf Oil Company credit card. The name on the credit card matched a name on the passenger list. Because this accident occurred in a National Park, nothing could be removed without a collection permit. Due to the various delays in getting to the TWA site, Mike only had about three hours on site. But it was enough time to decide that the TWA site—and the much harder to reach United site—were of prime interest for aviation archaeologists.

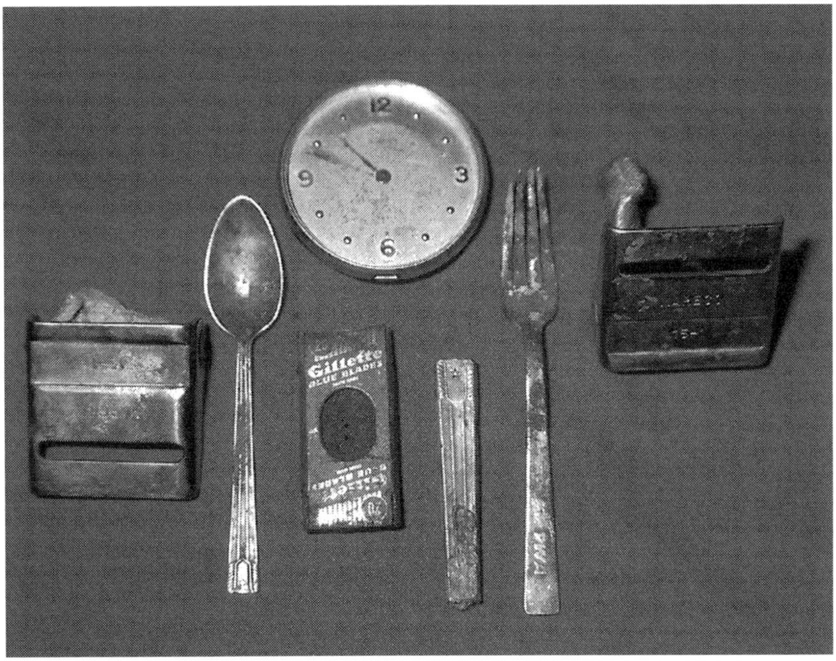

Articles found at the crash site include silverware, razor blades, seat belt buckles, and a travel clock.
(Harvey Gardner Collection)

The next morning, after a rafting trip further down the river and through a couple of small rapids that nearly swamped the raft, Mike crossed to the other side of the river to pick up the Beamer Trail for the long hike home. To sum up the whole experience, Mike said, "Throughout that long hike home, I made plans about what to do and what not to do on the next expedition into the canyon. But even more than that, my thoughts turned to the stark desolation and stillness of the crash site at Temple Butte. I think I now know how Ballard felt when he first looked down on the deck of the *Titanic.*"

United
United
Mainliner

Chapter 12

Cross Country to Disaster: United Flight 615

Nicholas A. Veronico

United Airlines Flight 615, a Douglas DC-6B, N37550, left Boston, Massachusetts, at 5:32 pm EST on August 23, 1951, en route to San Francisco. Three stops were made as the plane traveled westward; first at Hartford, Connecticut, next at Cleveland, Ohio, and finally at 9:59 pm CST, at Chicago, Illinois. During the layover at Chicago, Flight 615 changed crews.

This United DC-6B is identical to the plane that crashed in the hills behind Union City, California, on the morning of August 24, 1951. (William T. Larkins)

When the flight departed Chicago at 10:59 pm CST, Captain Marion W. Hedden, 42, was at the controls. His first officer was George A. Jewett, 35, assisted by Flight Engineer Marion A. Durante, 36, and Assistant Chief Flight Engineer Arthur W. Kessler, 43. Seeing to the passenger's needs were stewardesses Marilynn Murphy, 24, and La Verne Sholes, 22.

Captain Hedden began his career with United Airlines on November 1, 1939, and held an Airline Transport rating. He had accumulated 12,032 flight hours, including 417 in the DC-6 and 14 in the new DC-6B. He was granted a DC-6 rating on January 15, 1951, and qualified on the DC-6B on April 26, 1951. The airplane Hedden was flying on the night of August 23/24, was delivered new to United Airlines on April 14, 1951. It had accumulated 361 hours total time without any engine changes or major mechanical problems.

An interesting aerial view of the crash site with the aircraft's flight path was created by newspaper graphic artists with the arrow ending by pointing into Dry Creek Gulch. Vehicles are parked on the saddle area, which is east of Tolman Peak. In the area near the large column of white smoke, center, a number of large pieces of wreckage were found 44 years after the crash. (San Francisco Chronicle)

Upon takeoff from Chicago, Flight 615 carried 44 passengers, including two infants, and six crewmembers. The flight to California was filed as an instrument flight plan from Chicago to Oakland and then under visual flight rules across the bay to San Francisco. The flight plan's assigned altitude for the route was 18,000 feet, passing Denver, Colorado, and Milford, Utah, before heading direct to Oakland. The flight from Oakland to San Francisco was to be accomplished at an altitude ranging from 300 to 500 feet.

The cross-country flight was uneventful. All radio transmissions were routine and at 3:54 am PST, Flight 615 was cleared to the Newark (California) fan marker with instructions to maintain 6,000 feet and to contact Oakland Approach Control over the 1,009-foot high Altamont Pass, which separates the San Francisco Bay Area from California's fertile San Joaquin Valley. Although some 40 miles from the San Francisco Bay, the Altamont Pass area and its low-lying Livermore Valley are less than 15 miles from the Sacramento River Delta. During the summer months this area is often blanketed by a marine layer with ground-hugging fog. When flying over the Altamont Pass, United Flight 615 would have been in clear air with a thick undercast a couple of thousand feet below.

The flight reported over Stockton, California, at 4:11 am, at an altitude of 9,500 feet and descending. United 615 was radioed the Oakland altimeter setting of 29.88 inches, which was acknowledged. Five minutes later, the flight reported passing the Altamont Intersection, and then contacted Oakland Approach Control for the first time. Approach Control cleared Flight 615 to the Oakland radio range station with instructions to remain no less than 500 feet above the cloud tops. United 615 then requested direct clearance to Newark with a straight-in range approach. The DC-6B reported that it was approaching the Hayward compass locator (between Altamont and Newark), and requested a

straight-in Instrument Landing System (ILS) approach to Oakland. Flight 615 was instructed to stand-by for clearance until another aircraft in the area cleared. Captain Hedden then requested Oakland Approach Control to cancel his ILS approach request.

Oakland Approach Control's last instructions to the flight came at 4:25 am The plane was cleared to fly from Newark on a straight-in approach on the southeast course of the Oakland radio range beacon. No further transmissions were received.

Crash investigators and firemen examine the remains of United's DC-6B on the saddle area behind Tolman Peak. The brush line in the lower right corner leads down into Dry Gulch Canyon. This area was pasture land and all debris on the grassy area havs been removed. (San Francisco Chronicle)

14.8 Miles Short of Oakland

The *San Francisco Chronicle's* banner headline on the morning of August 25, 1951, read: "Air Crash Kills 50: Big Liner Rams East Bay Hill." United Flight 615 crashed 14.8 miles short of Oakland Airport in the hills behind Union City, California, at an altitude of 983 feet above sea level. The plane was on a course of 296 degrees, flying straight, and descending at the time of impact. A descent was confirmed by the fact that the hill it passed over prior to the crash was taller than the hill of impact. The DC-6B impacted, then cartwheeled over the peak and scattered itself across a small saddle and then into the canyon beyond. The wreckage field was 900 feet wide and 1,640 feet long. The fuel tanks exploded upon impact, causing a small grass fire.

The CAB report stated, "the main landing gear was extended at the time [of impact], and reasonable proof exists that the nose wheel was retracted, or nearly retracted. The main landing gear on this model extends before the nose gear and retracts after it. Wing flaps were between

Civil Aeronautics Board report on the crash of United Airlines' Flight 615 from Boston to San Francisco. (William T. Larkins Collection)

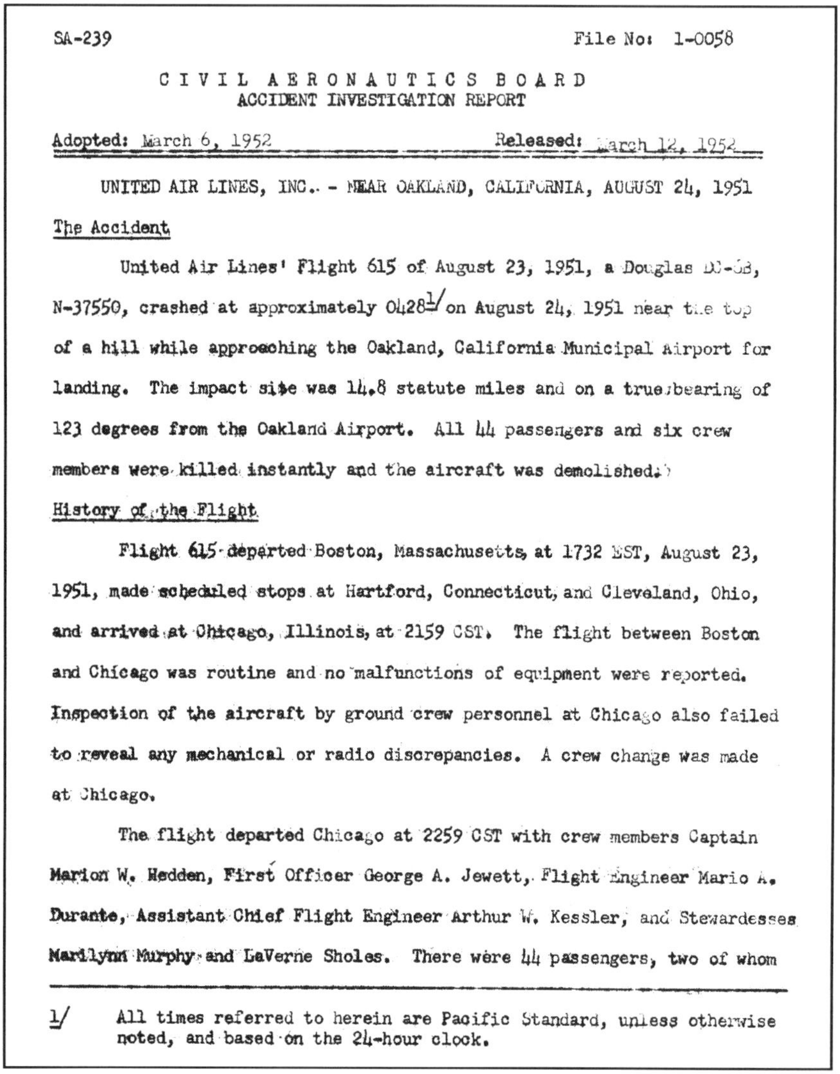

SA-239 File No: 1-0058

CIVIL AERONAUTICS BOARD
ACCIDENT INVESTIGATION REPORT

Adopted: March 6, 1952 Released: March 12, 1952

UNITED AIR LINES, INC. - NEAR OAKLAND, CALIFORNIA, AUGUST 24, 1951

The Accident

United Air Lines' Flight 615 of August 23, 1951, a Douglas DC-6B, N-37550, crashed at approximately 0428[1] on August 24, 1951 near the top of a hill while approaching the Oakland, California Municipal Airport for landing. The impact site was 14.8 statute miles and on a true bearing of 123 degrees from the Oakland Airport. All 44 passengers and six crew members were killed instantly and the aircraft was demolished.

History of the Flight

Flight 615 departed Boston, Massachusetts, at 1732 EST, August 23, 1951, made scheduled stops at Hartford, Connecticut, and Cleveland, Ohio, and arrived at Chicago, Illinois, at 2159 CST. The flight between Boston and Chicago was routine and no malfunctions of equipment were reported. Inspection of the aircraft by ground crew personnel at Chicago also failed to reveal any mechanical or radio discrepancies. A crew change was made at Chicago.

The flight departed Chicago at 2259 CST with crew members Captain Marion W. Hedden, First Officer George A. Jewett, Flight Engineer Mario A. Durante, Assistant Chief Flight Engineer Arthur W. Kessler, and Stewardesses Marilynn Murphy and LaVerne Sholes. There were 44 passengers, two of whom

1/ All times referred to herein are Pacific Standard, unless otherwise noted, and based on the 24-hour clock.

the fully retracted and 30 degrees extended position. All four engines were producing substantial power at the time of impact. Examination of propeller blade cuts in the earth and blade index settings showed that the blades were in the forward thrust range. Evidence indicated that the ground speed upon impact was between 225 and 240 miles per hour."

Weather conditions at the time of the crash were low broken stratus clouds with ceilings between 1,000 and 1,500 feet. Visibility below the clouds was better than six miles. Winds were reported below 10 knots and icing was not a factor as the freezing level was reported to be at 13,000 feet. The crew should have been able to see lights through the undercast from the towns of Niles, Centerville/Fremont, and Newark. The CAB went on to report, "the crash occurred during morning twilight and some light was also available from the moon. As Flight 615 broke out under the stratus at about 1,500 feet, downward visibility was possible,

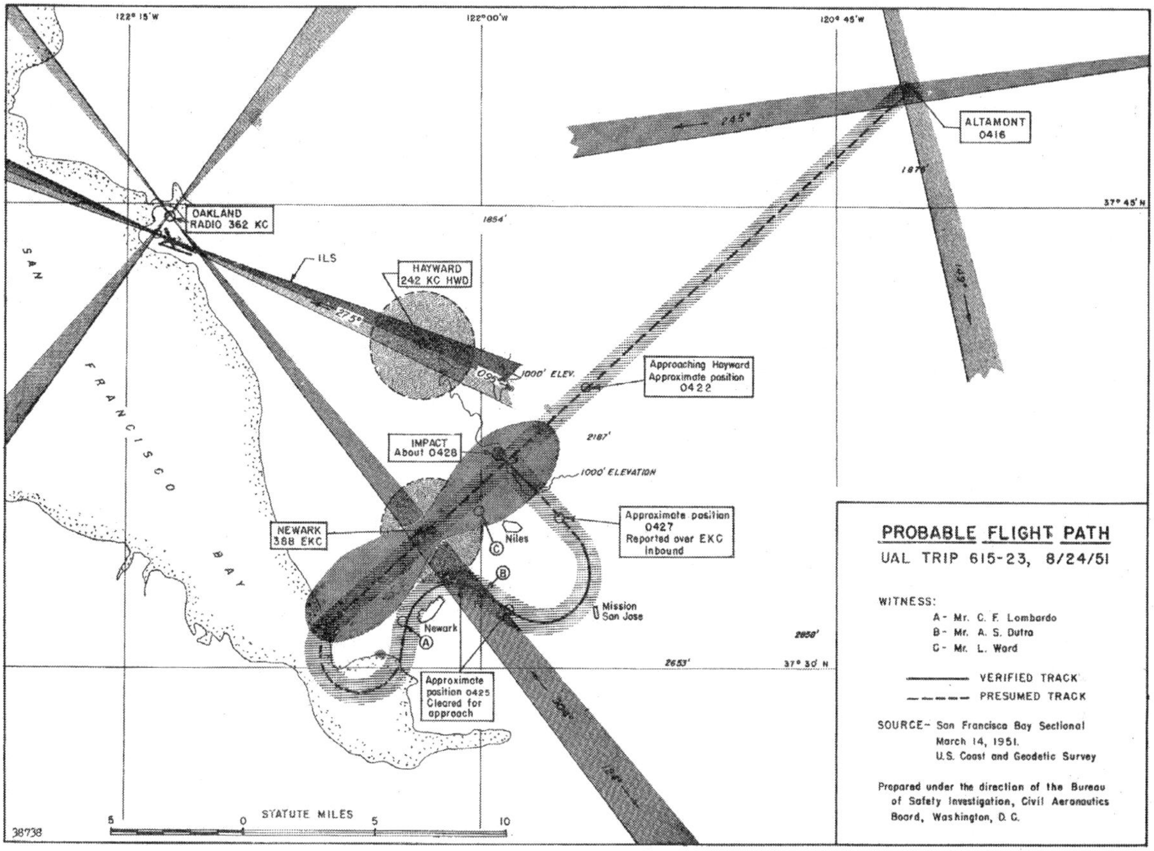

Probable Flight Path map from Civil Aeronautics Board Accident Investigation Report SA-239, released March 12, 1952. Flight 615 approached from the east over the Altamont Pass en route to the Newark fan marker during the early morning hours of August 24, 1951. After being cleared for an approach to Oakland, the plane struck coastal foothills east of Union City at 4:28 am. (William T. Larkins Collection)

but ground objects and contours were probably difficult to recognize and identify. For this reason, it is believed that weather conditions were closer to Instrument Flight Rules (IFR) than VFR at the time of the accident.

"Three witnesses saw the flight in the vicinity of Newark. They stated that it was flying in and out of low clouds and noted nothing abnormal except that it was low. The impact site was shrouded in wisps of fog."

The Crash Site Today

Flight 615 crashed in the rising foothills on the eastern side of the San Francisco Bay near the borders of Hayward and Union City, California. The crash site is 14.8 miles from Oakland Airport on a true bearing of 123 degrees. The DC-6's final resting place is at the top of Dry Gulch Canyon on the eastern side of Tolman Peak.

In August 1951, the area was pasture land and the geographic features had not yet been named. The crash site is only 1.5 miles from Mission Boulevard, as the crow flies, at the southeastern end of Dry Creek Pioneer Regional Park. Dry Creek Pioneer and its adjoining Garin Regional Park are part of the extensive and well-managed East Bay Regional Park system. This system has preserved large amounts of open space and ridge tops in the East Bay hills.

The difficulty of getting to this wreck is about a three on a ten-point scale. Depending on how adventurous you are once at the wreck site, going home can be a one (all downhill), or a seven if you decide to explore the wreckage that landed on the canyon sides of Dry Gulch.

Before making the journey, be sure to study the topo map for this crash site well in advance. Remember to carry the map. Two U.S. Geologic Survey 7.5 Minute Quadrangle maps will be required (See Appendix VII, *Obtaining USGS Topo Maps*). First obtain the Newark, California, quad for the walk into the wreck site. The crash site is located on the Niles, California, 7.5 Minute Quad in the upper left-hand corner at Tolman Peak.

Also highly recommended is a copy of the Garin & Dry Creek Pioneer Regional Parks guide map available from the East Bay Regional Park District. These maps can be found in a stand at the park's entrance gate, but do not count on it. Obtain one prior to your trek at: www.ebparks.org/parks/garin or call (510) 582-2206 to order one by phone.

Getting to the Site

Driving to the starting point of this wreckchase is relatively simple. From San Jose, travel north on Highway 880, or from San Francisco/Oakland drive south on 880 to the Whipple Avenue offramp. Proceed

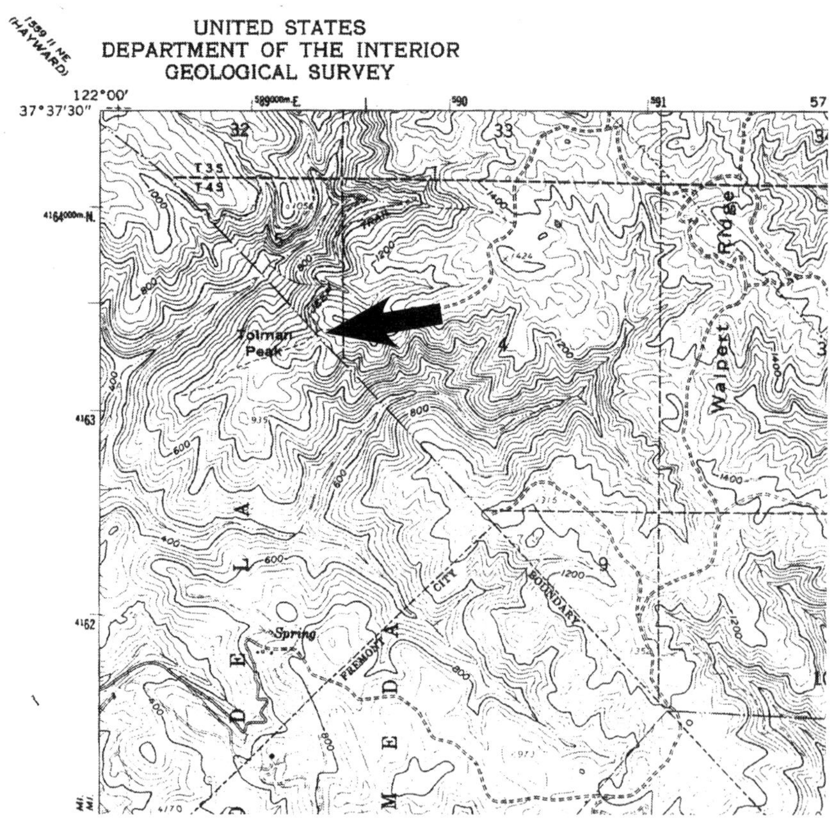

Prominently displayed in the upper left-hand corner of the Niles, California, 7.5 Minute Quad is Tolman Peak. United DC-6B N37550 came to rest east of the peak on a saddle (see arrow). This is a relatively easy site to reach on groomed East Bay Regional Park trails. (USGS)

The crash site today: "A" shows the Tolman Peak Trail and the location of the Tolman Peak marker. "B" indicates the point where emergency vehicles parked during the rescue and post-crash investigation (shown in photos on pages 162 and 163). "C" is the area where the majority of the wreckage impacted after striking the hill from where this photo was taken, and "D" is positioned just south of the Oakland Airport, the flight's intended destination. (Nicholas A. Veronico)

east toward the hills until coming to Mission Boulevard. Turn left (north) and continue about one-half of a mile to Tamarack Drive. Turn right and follow the street to the end where you will come to the Dry Creek Pioneer Regional Park gate. Find a place to park on the street as there is no parking lot at this gate.

Even though this crash site is "near civilization," proper precautions must be taken and common sense heeded. First, never hike alone. Wear long pants, a hat, and carry a long-sleeved shirt to avoid poison oak—there's lots of it! Carry enough water for the hike. Double what you consider to be an adequate amount of water. Bring a camera and, if you own or can rent one, a metal detector—for this expedition it is highly recommended.

From the Tamarack Drive gate take the High Ridge Loop Trail for about half a mile. Then continue toward the right onto the Tolman Peak Trail. This will take you to Tolman Peak. It is a five-mile walk, relatively easy as hikes go. The trails are wide and well-marked.

Once at the summit of Tolman Peak, continue to the saddle just behind it. The trail makes a 90-degree turn to the right at the saddle, leaving you facing a flat area with the brush-filled canyon to the left and small peaks to the right.

The DC-6 impacted the peaks to the right and continued over to crash on the saddle in front of you. A number of large engine and firewall parts continued on into the canyon and are still there today.

Arriving at the saddle, my hiking companions and I agreed, "This is the place." Unable to locate any witnesses from the crash, we used aerial photos obtained from the *San Francisco Chronicle* to determine our position.

Splitting our hiking party into three groups, Ed Davies gave the saddle a "once over" for any items visible through the tall grass—a long shot, as the property had been grazing land before becoming a park. The surface debris had been cleaned out years before, but it was worth a look. Ken Miller and Bob Swanson headed to the end of the saddle and proceeded to look down into Dry Gulch Canyon. Ian Abbott and this

Bob Swanson found this engine mount on the far side of Dry Gulch, about 50 feet up from the bottom. (Ian Abbott)

Author Veronico, left, and Ken Miller inspect a number of firewall forward parts and an engine magneto. These parts were located on the far side of Dry Gulch Canyon. (Ian Abbott)

author took the near and middle of the saddle and began to comb the brush on the rim of the canyon. Abbott was the first to locate debris, a small stringer with rivets on it, which confirmed the site.

Miller and Swanson came across a rattlesnake and an old encampment of some kind, probably supplies left by the rescuers during the crash clean-up. The rattler was guarding a number of discarded cans, bottles, and ceramic dishes. While avoiding the snake, Miller noticed a shiny piece of metal on the far side of the canyon. Through binoculars the item looked round and spoked, like a wheel. The group put off the decision to investigate the "wheel" until it was time to depart the crash site. It would be a long slide down the near side and a real adventure to try and locate the wheel from the canyon bottom.

A seat pan was found at the eastern end of the saddle area. Numerous large pieces can be found after a dedicated search. (Jim Rowan)

After searching the canyon side of the saddle, numerous small pieces of wreckage were found including an instrument case, stringers, and small sections of engine cylinders.

Once the decision to head back was made, our group headed, or more accurately, slid down the hill into Dry Gulch Canyon. More parts were found including an oil tank and assorted rubber seals, a watchband, and a Zippo lighter with one of the passenger's initials engraved on it. At the canyon bottom, we split into two groups in an attempt to find the wheel. It was located without too much effort, but turned out to be a magneto. Other firewall forward parts including an engine mount and cowl flaps were found there.

Following the contour of the canyon's bottom, the group was able to exit directly onto the Tolman Peak trail. This shaved about 30 minutes off the hike out.

Postscript

The August 28, 1951, issue of the *Oakland Tribune* reported, "... Fifty persons might be alive today if radar surveillance equipment had been functioning in the Oakland Municipal Airport control tower ..." Installation of the equipment had been delayed by the Korean War as well as production setbacks. Radar would have instantly told controllers that the DC-6 was off course during its descent, and this information could have been relayed to the crew.

EASTERN AIRWAYS INC
EASTERN AIRWAYS INC

Chapter 13

Training Flight Mid-Air: Cal Eastern and Overseas National

Nicholas A. Veronico

The early 1950s were heady days in commercial aviation. Thousands of experienced pilots were home from World War II seeking employment. The Korean conflict was on and hundreds of non-scheduled carriers flew cargo and passengers to feed the war effort. Two such carriers were California Eastern Airways and Overseas National Airways (ONA). Both airlines were incorporated in Delaware-Cal Eastern in 1946 and Overseas National in 1950. Each maintained a base at Oakland Municipal Airport, California. Cal Eastern's primary business was flying passengers and freight on "mid-Pac" routes as part of the Pacific Airlift for the Military Air Transport Service (MATS). Overseas National also flew government contracts.

N79993 Fern M., *sister ship to ill-fated Overseas National DC-4 (C-54D-10-DC) N79992 (msn 10832)* June S., *in front of California Eastern Airway's facility at Oakland Municipal Airport. (William T. Larkins)*

On the morning of November 17, 1951, each carrier sent a DC-4 aloft to give pilots their six-month instrument competency checks. Before lunch one aircraft would be destroyed and the second flyable, but heavily damaged. Three highly experienced Overseas National captains would lose their lives.

The Aircraft, Carriers, and Their Crews

Ill-fated Overseas National DC-4 (C-54D-10-DC) N79992 (msn 10832) was delivered as serial number 42-72727 to the U.S. Army

A Douglas DC-4 in an early California Eastern Airways color scheme. Captain Ralph A. Shope was able to maintain control of his aircraft and land it successfully at San Francisco. (William T. Larkins)

Air Force (AAF) on July 16, 1945. The plane was leased to ONA and registered in 1947. In September 1947, the aircraft's owners, the AAF, became the U.S. Air Force. In 1949, Transocean Air Lines subcontracted to operate Overseas National's aircraft. This agreement was short-lived and the company was again flying its own equipment by April 1950. The plane had flown 5,257 hours since its last major overhaul. Although leased to ONA at the time of the crash, it was still owned by the Air Force. ONA's fleet name for N79992 was *June S.*

Crew for this flight included Captain Marion Harvey Click, 31, ONA's assistant chief pilot. Click was trained by the Army Air Force during World War II and went on to fly with a couple of carriers before joining the company on June 16, 1950. He had accumulated 7,871 hours, 5,028 in type. Captain Warren Cecil Gessner, 27, was trained by the U.S. Navy and flew with Alaska Airlines, Near East Transport, and Westair Transport prior to hiring on with ONA. His flying time was 3,590 hours, just over 1,900 in DC-4s. The third member of the crew was Captain Hammond Garrard, 32. His employment with the carrier was somewhat turbulent. He was hired on July 6, 1950, promoted to captain on July 17, 1950, but was then furloughed until November 15, 1950. Like Gessner, he earned his wings of gold with the Navy, then flew for Capital Airlines, and Cal Eastern. Also very experienced, he had amassed 5,879 hours, 3,100 in type, yet only 330 while flying on instruments. Click would serve as examiner while Garrard and Gessner performed their instrument proficiency checks.

Cal Eastern's DC-4 (C-54B-1-DC) N4002B (msn 10474), was delivered to the Army Air Force as serial number 42-72369 on December 12, 1944. Just over one year later, on December 20, 1945, Douglas repurchased the aircraft and converted it to civilian DC-4 standards, assigning the plane conversion Number 15. It returned to the

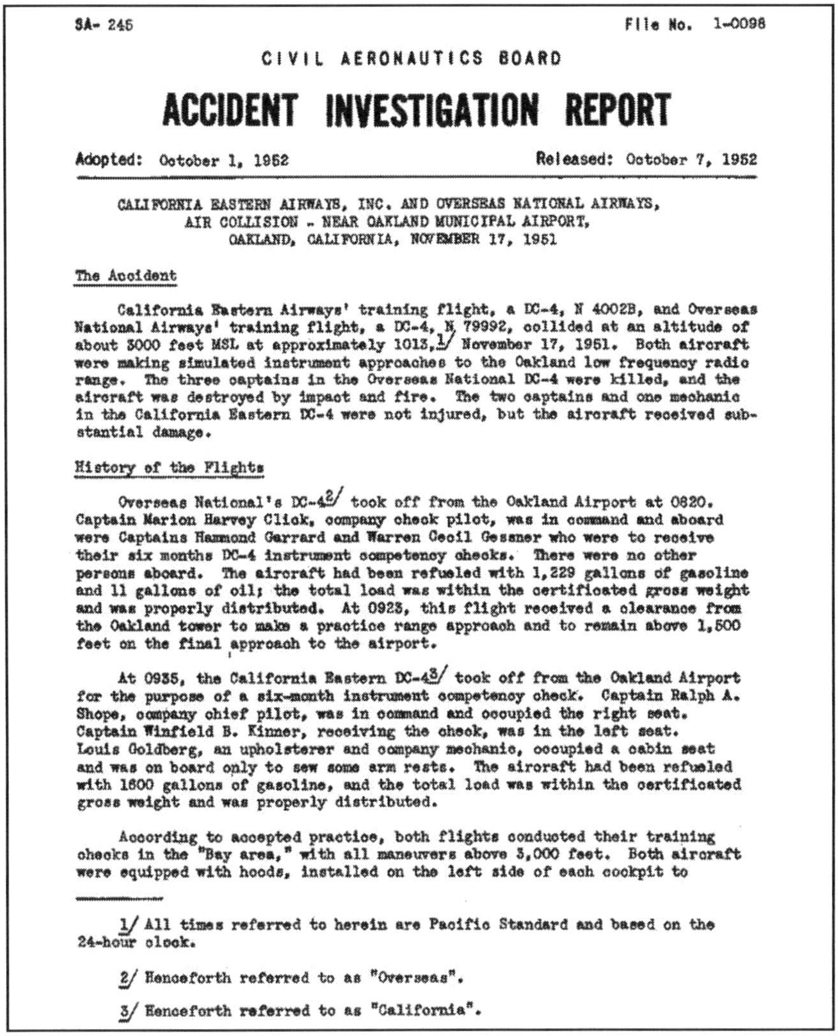

SA- 245 File No. 1-0098

CIVIL AERONAUTICS BOARD

ACCIDENT INVESTIGATION REPORT

Adopted: October 1, 1952 Released: October 7, 1952

CALIFORNIA EASTERN AIRWAYS, INC. AND OVERSEAS NATIONAL AIRWAYS,
AIR COLLISION - NEAR OAKLAND MUNICIPAL AIRPORT,
OAKLAND, CALIFORNIA, NOVEMBER 17, 1951

The Accident

California Eastern Airways' training flight, a DC-4, N 4002B, and Overseas National Airways' training flight, a DC-4, N 79992, collided at an altitude of about 3000 feet MSL at approximately 1013,1/ November 17, 1951. Both aircraft were making simulated instrument approaches to the Oakland low frequency radio range. The three captains in the Overseas National DC-4 were killed, and the aircraft was destroyed by impact and fire. The two captains and one mechanic in the California Eastern DC-4 were not injured, but the aircraft received substantial damage.

History of the Flights

Overseas National's DC-42/ took off from the Oakland Airport at 0820. Captain Marion Harvey Click, company check pilot, was in command and aboard were Captains Hammond Garrard and Warren Cecil Gessner who were to receive their six months DC-4 instrument competency checks. There were no other persons aboard. The aircraft had been refueled with 1,229 gallons of gasoline and 11 gallons of oil; the total load was within the certificated gross weight and was properly distributed. At 0923, this flight received a clearance from the Oakland tower to make a practice range approach and to remain above 1,500 feet on the final approach to the airport.

At 0935, the California Eastern DC-43/ took off from the Oakland Airport for the purpose of a six-month instrument competency check. Captain Ralph A. Shope, company chief pilot, was in command and occupied the right seat. Captain Winfield B. Kinner, receiving the check, was in the left seat. Louis Goldberg, an upholsterer and company mechanic, occupied a cabin seat and was on board only to sew some arm rests. The aircraft had been refueled with 1600 gallons of gasoline, and the total load was within the certificated gross weight and was properly distributed.

According to accepted practice, both flights conducted their training checks in the "Bay area," with all maneuvers above 3,000 feet. Both aircraft were equipped with hoods, installed on the left side of each cockpit to

1/ All times referred to herein are Pacific Standard and based on the 24-hour clock.

2/ Henceforth referred to as "Overseas".

3/ Henceforth referred to as "California".

The CAB report detailing the mid-air collision and its aftermath was released nearly one year later on October 7, 1952. (William T. Larkins Collection)

skies for Western Air Lines on August 8, 1946, as N88701, then was acquired by United Airlines and christened *Mainliner Hoover Dam* one year later. Cal Eastern acquired the aircraft in 1950. Then title passed to TACA Airlines, Cal Eastern leasing the plane back on April 5, 1951. On the day of the mid-air collision, N4002B had flown 16,435 hours total, 6,484 hours since its last major overhaul.

Captain Ralph A. Shope, 40, Cal Eastern's chief pilot, began his flying career in 1934. He was an Army flying instructor, flew for TACA, and TWA-ATC (Air Transport Command) during World War II. Of his total 11,225 hours flight time, 4,733 were in type with 1,009 on instruments. On November 17, 1951, he was flying as check pilot for Captain Winfield B. Kinner, 40, who began his flight training in 1928 and also was an instructor for Army cadets during the war. He later flew for ATC before joining a number of non-scheduled carriers. Kinner had accumulated 5,000 hours, 3,500 in type and 350 on instruments.

This is how the crash site looked once the smoke had cleared. The tail (1), fuselage (2), wing and nose section (3) fell separately near Doolittle Drive. A car driven by Robert Leibel (4) struck the aircraft. Two other cars swerved into the parking lot at right as the wreckage fell toward them. Norman Barnes' car (5) was scorched, but he and his son escaped injury. (photo at right by Bob Hofford, top photo by San Francisco Chronicle)

After the fire was put out, the fuselage and wing sections were pushed off of Doolittle Drive and into a parking lot near the water's edge. The tail section can be seen in the background sitting right side up. (Bob Hofford)

While the two pilots performed their flying and checkride duties, Louis Goldberg, a Cal Eastern mechanic and upholsterer, flew in the cabin repairing the seats.

November 17, 1951, a Beautiful Day

Being a Saturday, commercial traffic was light at Oakland. The weather was pleasant with thin broken clouds at 25,000 feet, visibility of seven miles, and a light breeze blowing from the south. ONA's N79992 took off at 8:20 am More than an hour later, at 9:35, Cal Eastern's N4002B also departed from Oakland Municipal. Once at altitude, the pilot's side windows were covered with a "hood" to simulate Instrument Meteorological Conditions (IMC). The check pilot observed from the right seat and the third captain on board N79992 acted as observer.

Both aircraft were flying at 3,000 feet, approaching the Oakland low-frequency radio range station at 10:13 am—Overseas' N79992 on a magnetic heading of 124 degrees; Cal Eastern's N4002B's heading was 75 degrees. Observers on the ground saw both aircraft flying toward each other and converging without taking evasive action. ONA was slightly above Cal Eastern's flight path whose vertical stabilizer struck

A police officer examines the clipped tail of Cal Eastern's DC-4 at San Francisco Airport. (San Francisco Chronicle)

just forward of N79992's horizontal stabilizer. As the tail sliced through ONAs' fuselage, the control cables were severed followed by separation of the entire empennage. N79992 nosed-over and dove out of control toward the ground, impacting in the middle of Doolittle Drive, a road that runs parallel to the Oakland Airport and onto the island of Alameda. The tail section floated down aimlessly and landed in the marshland next to the road, 100 yards north of the impact area.

Traffic was light on Doolittle Drive, but the wreckage dropped in front of Robert Leibel, 20, and his car struck the debris. He was severely burned. In another car, Norman Barnes and his son were able to stop short of hitting the crashed plane and escaped injury. The paint on their auto was scorched. Frank Ormerod, his wife, and daughter were also able to stop their car, which was showered by debris.

Bob Way, an employee at the Oakland Naval Medical Supply Center, was driving 10 members of the Junior Air Force section of Oakland's Junior Hi-Y, who were riding in the back of his pickup truck. Young Don Gaskin Jr. was quoted in the November 18, 1951, *San Francisco Chronicle*,

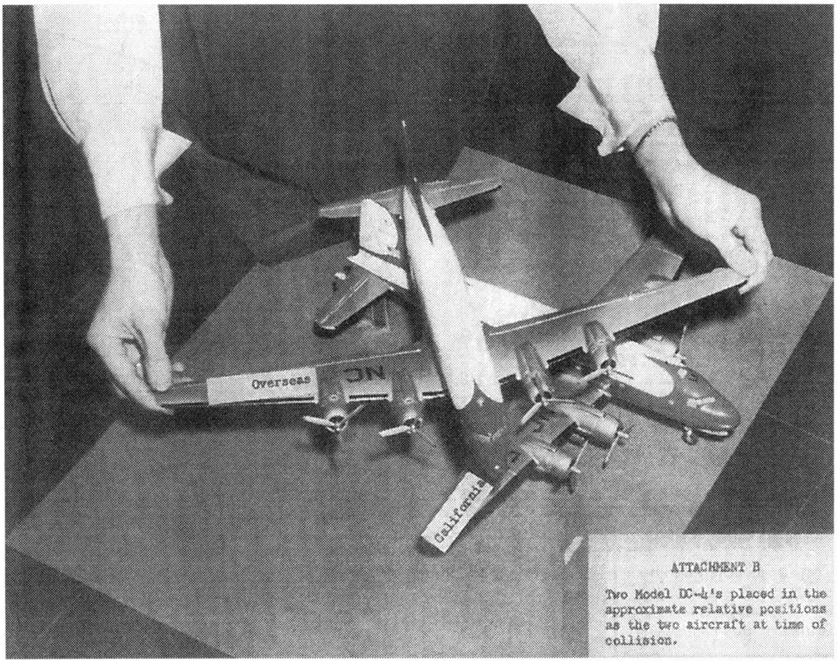

This Civil Aeronautics Board photo shows the relative proximity of the two aircraft at the time of impact. (CAB)

"First a small piece of the tail fell off, then the whole tail broke, but the heavy plane beat it to the ground, catching fire on the way down.

"When it hit, fire and smoke went up like an atomic bomb. Then red hot metal shot all around us like bullets. When it hit, I screamed and dropped down in the truck, but it didn't save me. A piece of the plane tore off one fender of the truck. Then a streak of flame shot out at us and burned the paint off the back of the truck. That was the one that burned me and the other boys." All occupants of the pick-up were treated for burns and shock.

On board the Cal Eastern DC-4, Captain Shope immediately took the controls after the collision. The impact had spun the plane from a northerly heading to the south and tore off the tail (rudder and vertical stabilizer) 20 inches above the center rudder hinge. Shope was able to maintain control of the aircraft above 160 knots and requested permission to land on Oakland's Runway 9R with crash trucks standing by. Because all available airport emergency equipment was then en route to the Overseas National crash, Shope was diverted to San Francisco. Although he landed "hot," at 140 knots, the crew and aircraft survived to fly again.

The Aftermath

The wreckage of Overseas National's N79992 burned for hours and even threatened a gasoline pipeline supplying the Naval Reserve Air Base on the field. Once the fire was out, the twisted mass of metal was pushed off the road into a parking lot. Examination of the ONA tail revealed a 20-foot piece of antenna wire and paint marks from Cal Eastern's DC-4.

Two other pieces of Cal Eastern's tail were found in the vicinity of the crash site.

Both aircraft were operating with pilots "under the hood" simulating instrument flying conditions. Fabric covered the left windscreen and side windows, thus requiring the pilot to fly completely blind. This also limited the check pilot's view out the left side of the cabin. Under existing aviation regulations, neither flight was required to be in contact with the field's tower while approaching the Oakland radio range station. Overseas National's company rules stated that its check pilots should look for traffic out the astrodome while making turns, but allows them to be in the cockpit while flying straight and level. Even if the third captain had been in the astrodome, it is unlikely that he would have seen the Cal Eastern DC-4 approaching from below and to the rear. After the accident, Cal Eastern immediately changed its company policy to include a third crewmember to serve as safety observer on instrument check flights.

The CAB filed a report of violations against the captains of each aircraft, faulting them for failing to see the other aircraft, and Shope was reprimanded for not having a third pilot on the flight deck watching for traffic. As any pilot will tell you, it all boils down to, "See and Be Seen."

Coincidentally, three additional Overseas National captains were scheduled to be on board for flight checks but failed to arrive on time and the flight left without them. How lucky can you get?

The crash site today: Doolittle Drive facing northwest. N79993 came to rest approximately where the white arrow points. (Nicholas A. Veronico)

N4002B's Subsequent Career and the Crash Site

N4002B was repaired and subsequently sold to TACA, registered YS-04C. During the opening days of 1952, RANSA acquired and re-registered it TI-1046C. On April 4, 1952, Transocean Airlines bought the plane and its new registration became N4664S. Nine years later, in October 1963, Lineas Aereas Paraguayas obtained title to the DC-4 and re-registered it ZP-CAR. One year later, its registration changed once again, this time sold to Paranese, a Brazilian company. Reports state that it was stored at Sao-Paulo and eventually broken up by 1980.

Thousands of cars pass directly over N79992's crash site each day. Probably less than 1 in 100,000 know that an aviation accident occurred at that location, or that three men lost their lives there. Little has changed. The road is still in the same place and the site where the tail section landed is still a marsh. The parking lot next to where N79992 came to rest is now gone. This entire waterfront area has been redeveloped into a park complete with boat launch ramp. A soil berm has been erected between the water and the road, but one can still locate the crash site through pictures. The road has been paved over numerous times, but that will never hide the scars where a DC-4 and its crew came to rest in the winter of 1951.

AVE.
UNITED
STOP
U.S. MAIL

Chapter 14

Collision Course: New York Mid-Air

Donald B. McComb Jr.

On June 30, 1956, a mid-air collision occurred over the Grand Canyon, in Arizona, involving a United Airlines Douglas DC-7 and a Trans World Airlines Lockheed 1049 Constellation. Because of this accident, many improvements to the air traffic control system were implemented. While these changes were sweeping, they were not a panacea.

Nearly four and one-half years later, a midair collision occurred over New York City. As with the 1956 accident, the airlines involved were United and TWA, and in the case of TWA, the same aircraft type was involved. The combined death toll between the two aircraft came to 128 passengers and crew, which, believe it or not, was the same total for the 1956 accident. The New York accident also took the lives of six persons on the ground.

United Airlines DC-8-11 N8013U, *Mainliner Will Rogers*, departed Los Angeles International Airport (LAX) on December 16, 1960, at 12:20 am, designated as Flight 856, en route to New York's Idlewild Airport (IDL). Flight 856, truly a "red-eye," thundered out over Santa Monica Bay into the darkness and turned east heading for Chicago O'Hare (ORD), its only stop-over. N8013U, msn 45290, had been delivered new to United on December 22, 1959, and just a few days short of its first year in service, had accumulated 2,429 hours of flight time.

A stop sign on the corner of 7th Avenue and Sterling Place is dwarfed by the tail section of United Airlines' DC-8-11 N8013U, Mainliner Will Rogers. *The plane crashed into a residential section of Brooklyn following a mid-air collision with Trans World Airlines' Super Constellation* Star of Sicily. *(UPI/Bettmann)*

The crash site at the intersection of 7th Avenue and Sterling Place bears no scars of the aviation tragedy that touched this peaceful corner of Brooklyn more than 40 years ago. (Bill Hough)

The cockpit crew of Flight 856 was headed by Captain Robert Sawyer, assisted by First Officer Robert Fiebing, and Second Officer Richard E. Pruitt. Captain Sawyer was 46 years old and was employed by United Airlines on January 2, 1941. Type-rated on the Boeing 247, Douglas DC-3, DC-4, DC-6, DC-7, and DC-8, Sawyer had logged a total of 19,100 hours. He passed his DC-8 flight check on June 6, 1960, and had accumulated 344 hours in the type as of December 16, 1960.

First Officer Fiebing was 40 years old and was employed by United Airlines on May 1, 1951. He was rated in the DC-3, DC-4, DC-6, DC-7, and DC-8 aircraft and had accumulated 8,400 hours, of which 416 were in DC-8s. Second Officer Pruitt was 30 years old and joined United Airlines on September 15, 1955. He held both an Airline Transport Certificate and a Flight Engineer Certificate for Douglas' DC-6, DC-7, and DC-8. He had a total flight time of 8,500 hours, of which 379 hours were as flight engineer on DC-8 aircraft. If the crew's flight time in DC-8 aircraft seemed low, keep in mind that the DC-8 had only entered service in May 1959. Even the highest-time DC-8 pilots in 1960 would have had no more then 1,000 hours by December 1960.

Flight 856 climbed rapidly to 33,000 feet (FL330) en route to Chicago. The plane arrived at 5:56 am CST after an uneventful flight. Following a two-hour stopover in Chicago, the same flight crew reboarded the aircraft. The flight attendants who had staffed the cabin from LAX were replaced by a fresh crew for the final leg of the trip into Idlewild.

TWA was a very progressive airline, as shown in this June 1954 advertisement. The company built customer loyalty around the comfort offered by the Lockheed Constellation and also marketed itself directly to women. Star of Sicily *was delivered to the carrier two years before this ad appeared. (Veronico Collection)*

Fuel, food, and liquor were loaded, and N8013U departed from Chicago at 8:11 am CST. Flight time to New York was estimated to be one hour and 29 minutes. The assigned cruising altitude of 27,000 feet (FL270) was reached at 9:36 am. On board the DC-8, making his first flight in a jet, was Stephen Baltz, age 11. Baltz had been seen off at Chicago by his father and was to be met at Idlewild by his mother and sister.

At 9:00 am EST, 11 minutes before the United DC-8 left the ground at Chicago, a Trans World Airlines Lockheed 1049 Super Constellation, N6907C *Star of Sicily*, departed Port Columbus Airport, Columbus, Ohio, as Flight 266, for a one hour and 32 minute flight to New York's La Guardia Airport. N6907C, msn 4021, delivered new to

TWA's Star of Sicily *N6907C, a Lockheed 1049 Super Constellation, was delivered to the airline on August 11, 1952. The Connie is shown here at an unidentified location midway through her career. (Donald B. McComb Jr. Collection)*

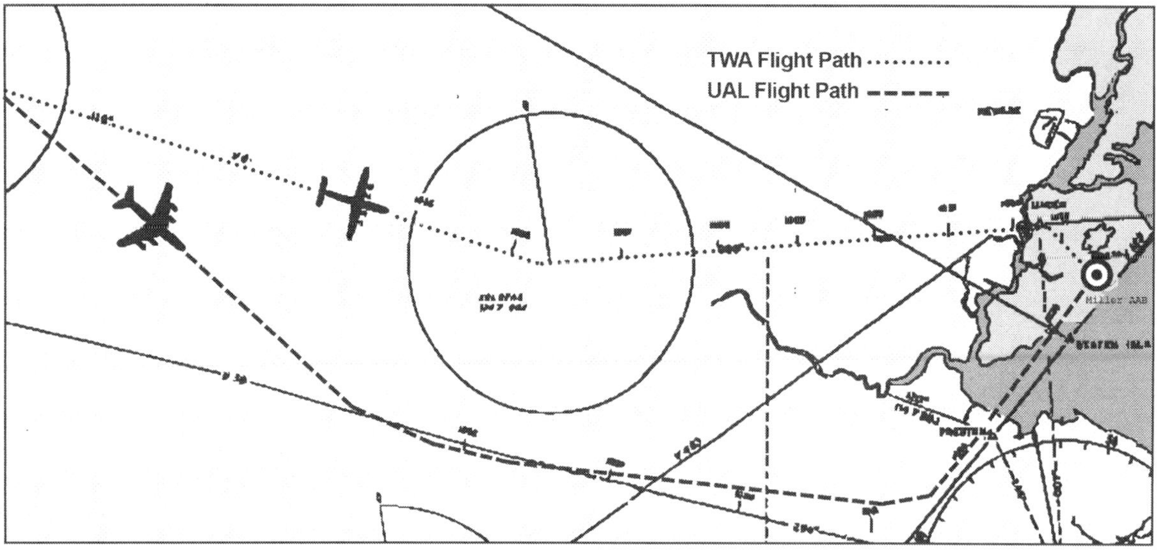

The Civil Aeronautics Board (CAB) issued this map showing the flight paths of the two airliners and the crash site on Staten Island. (CAB)

Trans World Airlines on August 11, 1952, had been in service for eight years, four months. N6907C had flown 21,555 hours.

In command of Flight 266 was Captain David A. Wollam, assisted by First Officer Dean T. Bowen and Second Officer LeRoy L. Rosenthal. Wollam was 39 years old, had joined Trans World Airlines on May 23, 1945, and was rated in the DC-3, Martin 202/404, and the Lockheed Constellation. He had a total flight time of 14,583 hours, of which 267 were in the Constellation.

First Officer Bowen, 32, was employed by Trans World Airlines on July 13, 1953. He was rated in the 202/404 and the Constellation, and had a total of 6,411 hours, of which 268 were in the Connie. Flight Engineer Rosenthal was 30 years old and had been hired by TWA recently, on January 3, 1956. He held a current airframe and powerplant certificate

Accident investigators gather the wreckage of Star of Sicily *that crashed near Miller Field, Staten Island, New York. A horizontal stabilizer is on truck bed in foreground. Note the rudder collapsed over on its side. (UPI/Bettman)*

Firemen stand amid the wreckage of TWA Flight 266, Star of Sicily. *The Constellation broke into three pieces and came to rest in a Staten Island neighborhood. (UPI/Bettmann)*

and a flight engineer certificate. Rosenthal qualified as a flight engineer with TWA on May 9, 1956, and had a total of 3,561 hours, of which 204 were in Constellation aircraft.

After an uneventful flight, United 826 contacted New York Air Route Control Center at 10:12 am. The center answered, "United 826, New York Center, Roger. Have your progress, radar service not available. Descend to and maintain flight level 250 (25,000 feet)." Captain Sawyer reported leaving 27,000 feet at 10:14 am One minute later, New York Center advised: "United 826 clearance limit is Preston intersection via Jet 60 Victor to Allentown, direct to Robbinsville, via Victor 123. Maintain flight level 250." United 826 acknowledged this message.

At 10:21 am United 826 contacted ARINC operator of United Airlines' company communications system, and advised them that the "number two navigation receiver accessory unit is inoperative." This message was acknowledged by ARINC and reported to United Airlines. As soon as Captain Sawyer finished with this message, New York Center issued further clearance to descend to 13,000 feet. United 826 replied, "We'd rather hold upstairs." At 10:22 am, New York Center called Flight 826, "United 826 New York Center, radar contact." United 826 replied, "Roger, we're cleared to 13,000 to maintain 25,000 until we had conversation with you. If we're going to have a delay, we would rather hold upstairs than down. We're going to need three-quarters of a mile visibility; do you have the weather handy?" The center replied, "No, but I'll get it. There have been no delays until now."

At 10:23 am, Captain Sawyer reported over Allentown, Pennsylvania, at Flight Level 250. New York Center acknowledged, and at 10:24 am, advised that the Idlewild (now Kennedy International) weather was "... 1,500 feet overcast, one-half mile, light rain, fog, altimeter 29.65." Shortly thereafter Captain Sawyer advised, "We're starting down."

In the rear of the DC-8's cabin, passengers noticed that the aircraft had started its descent and were busy turning in cups and other service items in preparation for landing. In the rear of the cabin Stephen Baltz watched as the cloud deck loomed closer and closer, finally engulfing the big jet in a sea of white.

Minutes earlier, at 10:19 am, the TWA Constellation reported to New York Center that it was "passing Allentown at 11,000 feet." Starting at 10:05 am, when the flight had been cruising at 19,000 feet, Captain Wollam had been descending in stages. New York Center advised that radar contact had been established, cleared the flight to Linden (New Jersey) Intersection, and requested the pilot to stand by for descent. At 10:21 am, New York Center further cleared TWA 266 to descend to and maintain 10,000 feet, then to 9,000 feet and to report leaving 10,000. TWA 266 acknowledged Center's call. At 10:27 am, TWA 266 advised that it was past the Solberg (New Jersey) VOR. The center acknowledged and advised that radar service was terminated, and to contact La Guardia Approach. The crew acknowledged by repeating the frequency. At 10:29 am Approach Control cleared the flight to descend to 6,000 feet. One minute later the controller advised TWA 266 to maintain its present heading for a radar vector to the final approach course. At 10:30:49, Flight 266 was advised to reduce to approach speed. Less than two minutes later, the controller advised TWA 266 to turn right to a heading of 130 degrees. The crew acknowledged the transmission by repeating the heading. La Guardia Approach then cleared the flight to descend to 5,000 feet.

As the DC-8 flew through the heavy overcast, Air Route Traffic Control Center (ARTCC) amended the ATC clearance as follows, "826 cleared to proceed on to Victor 30 until intercepting Victor 123 and that way to Preston. It'll be a little bit quicker." This new routing shortened the distance to the Preston intersection by 11 miles. Because of this amended clearance, two things happened: Captain Sawyer had refused clearance to a lower altitude when it was first offered, so he now had to quickly lose a lot of altitude in a high-speed descent. Furthermore, because one of the two VOR receivers on the DC-8 was inoperative, the crew had to use the serviceable one to get a crossbearing with the VORs at Colt's Neck,

The DC-8's number four engine ingested a passenger from the Constellation during the collision. The engine broke away and fell into this playground of the General Berry houses in Dongan Hills, Staten Island. Patrolman William P. Pierce examines the twisted JT3C. (UPI/Bettmann)

and Solberg, New Jersey, which would identify the Preston intersection. Because of the high-speed descent and the limited time available, this would be very difficult to accomplish.

United 826 called Idlewild Approach Control at 10:33:28: "United 826 approaching Preston at 5,000 feet." This was the last communication from the flight. Flying at nearly 400 miles per hour, the DC-8 shot through the Preston intersection like a car running a red light. At 10:33:32, at an altitude of 5,200 feet over Staten Island, the DC-8's outer right wing and number four turbojet engine slammed into the cabin of the Constellation just aft of the right wing. Ripped from its mounts by the tremendous impact, the 6,000 pound Pratt and Whitney JT3C turbojet hurtled through the cabin of the Constellation, sucking a passenger into the turbine blades before flying out the other side of the fuselage. The DC-8 continued toward the triple tails of the Constellation, clipping off the right fin before the two aircraft separated. TWA 266 broke up at once. The fuselage tore into three pieces as the aircraft fell, the right wing separating from the center section of the fuselage just before impact with the ground.

The number four-engine from the DC-8 arced into a one-mile free fall, digging a crater in a schoolyard. Witnesses on the ground dove for cover as fragments from the two aircraft hurtled earthward.

Though the end came quickly for those on TWA 266, the next few minutes held great terror for those aboard United 826. Missing most of the right outer wing and the number four engine, the big DC-8 was on fire and descending toward heavily populated Brooklyn, New York. At the intersection of Brooklyn's 7th Avenue and Sterling Place, it was a typical Friday morning. Because of the cold and the snow, few cars were on the streets and even fewer people. Suddenly the peace and quiet of the morning was shattered.

The DC-8 screamed in low over the Park Slope section of Brooklyn, missing a school by a few hundred feet. Just before ground impact, the left wing clipped the roof of a building at 126 Sterling Place. Less than a second later the DC-8 slammed into the ground at the intersection of 7th Avenue and Sterling Place. The ground impact snapped off the tail section of the aircraft, which came to rest in the middle of the street.

The fuselage, with the cockpit and the majority of the right wing still attached, smashed into the Pillar of Fire Church. An intense ground fire consumed most of the wreckage and the church. Six bystanders on the ground were killed, including one of the church's caretakers who died as the building collapsed around him.

As rescue personnel and local residents converged on the area, movement was seen under the tail section of the DC-8. Incredibly, 11-year-old Stephen Baltz, who had been seated in the rear of the aircraft, survived. As the doctors fought to save his life, he told them that before the crash, "New York looked like a picture out of a fairy book. It was a beautiful sight." Unfortunately, his injuries were too severe, and he died 26 hours after the accident.

This accident, the first in which a U.S.-built passenger jet was lost carrying passengers, shook the nation. As a result of the crash, a further overhaul of the air traffic control system was enacted. The most important development was the implementation of a "positive control" system. Under this new system, aircraft flying above 24,000 feet would be under radar control that would extend down to 8,000 feet on high-density airways. In addition, a speed limit of 250 knots below 10,000 feet was implemented. Another change was the requirement that all aircraft weighing over 12,500 pounds must carry two pieces of electronic hardware—a transponder and Distance Measuring Equipment (DME). The transponder identifies the aircraft on controller's radar, while DME provides the flight crew with the exact distance to various navigational aids.

Just as the 1956 accident started the overhaul of the ATC system by controlling high-altitude air traffic, the DC-8/Constellation crash fine-tuned the system to protect aircraft in crowded skies.

Chapter 15

Christmas Eve Disaster: Flying Tigers Connie Flight 282

Nicholas A. Veronico and Ed Davies

Rain, low clouds, fog, and mist covered the San Francisco Bay Area in the late evening and early morning hours of December 23-24, 1964. The day would dawn as Christmas Eve, but for three families this day would become a sad anniversary. The official weather called for scattered clouds at 700 feet under an 1,800-foot overcast ceiling. Visibility was six miles in light rain.

Flying Tiger Line Lockheed 1049H Constellation, similar to the aircraft shown in flight, crashed into Sweeny's Ridge shortly after takeoff from San Francisco on Christmas Eve, 1964. (Lockheed)

Flying Tiger Line Flight 282 was scheduled to depart December 23, at 9:00 pm, on a domestic cargo trip from San Francisco to New York (JFK). The trip would be flown with Lockheed 1049H, N6915C, msn 4812. The scheduled departure time came and went as the company did not have a flight engineer available. A request was made to the Los Angeles, California, station and Flight Engineer Paul M. Entz, age 37, deadheaded on the next flight into San Francisco, arriving at 11:15 pm He was an experienced crewmember having 4,113 hours of flight time, nearly 93 percent in the 1049H. Entz, having given up Christmas with his family, joined Captain Jabez A. Richard, 49, and Co-pilot Daniel W. Hennessy, 33, in preparing for the flight. Richard joined Flying Tigers on December 4, 1950, and had accumulated 14,911 hours, of which 3,942 were in Lockheed's Super Constellation. Hennessy went to work for the carrier on April 24, 1955, and had accumulated 3,636 hours with 1,277

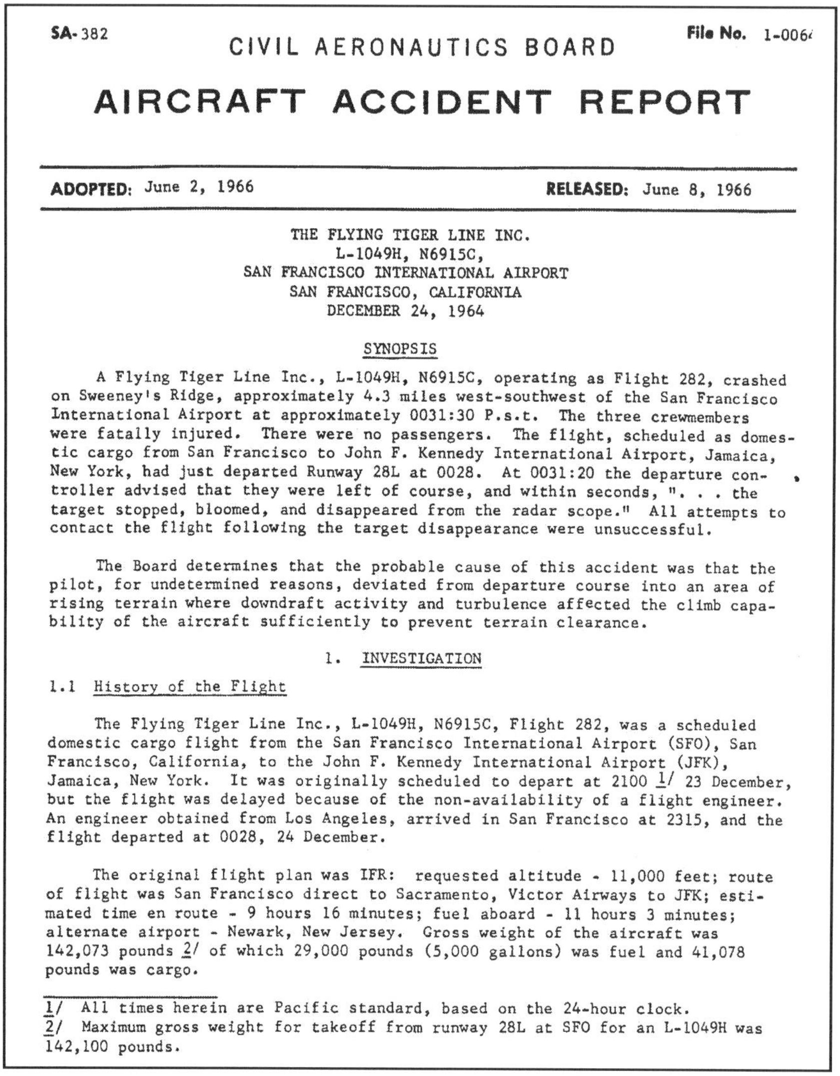
SA-382 **CIVIL AERONAUTICS BOARD** File No. 1-006

AIRCRAFT ACCIDENT REPORT

ADOPTED: June 2, 1966 **RELEASED:** June 8, 1966

THE FLYING TIGER LINE INC.
L-1049H, N6915C,
SAN FRANCISCO INTERNATIONAL AIRPORT
SAN FRANCISCO, CALIFORNIA
DECEMBER 24, 1964

SYNOPSIS

A Flying Tiger Line Inc., L-1049H, N6915C, operating as Flight 282, crashed on Sweeney's Ridge, approximately 4.3 miles west-southwest of the San Francisco International Airport at approximately 0031:30 P.s.t. The three crewmembers were fatally injured. There were no passengers. The flight, scheduled as domestic cargo from San Francisco to John F. Kennedy International Airport, Jamaica, New York, had just departed Runway 28L at 0028. At 0031:20 the departure controller advised that they were left of course, and within seconds, ". . . the target stopped, bloomed, and disappeared from the radar scope." All attempts to contact the flight following the target disappearance were unsuccessful.

The Board determines that the probable cause of this accident was that the pilot, for undetermined reasons, deviated from departure course into an area of rising terrain where downdraft activity and turbulence affected the climb capability of the aircraft sufficiently to prevent terrain clearance.

1. INVESTIGATION

1.1 History of the Flight

The Flying Tiger Line Inc., L-1049H, N6915C, Flight 282, was a scheduled domestic cargo flight from the San Francisco International Airport (SFO), San Francisco, California, to the John F. Kennedy International Airport (JFK), Jamaica, New York. It was originally scheduled to depart at 2100 1/ 23 December, but the flight was delayed because of the non-availability of a flight engineer. An engineer obtained from Los Angeles, arrived in San Francisco at 2315, and the flight departed at 0028, 24 December.

The original flight plan was IFR: requested altitude - 11,000 feet; route of flight was San Francisco direct to Sacramento, Victor Airways to JFK; estimated time en route - 9 hours 16 minutes; fuel aboard - 11 hours 3 minutes; alternate airport - Newark, New Jersey. Gross weight of the aircraft was 142,073 pounds 2/ of which 29,000 pounds (5,000 gallons) was fuel and 41,078 pounds was cargo.

1/ All times herein are Pacific standard, based on the 24-hour clock.
2/ Maximum gross weight for takeoff from runway 28L at SFO for an L-1049H was 142,100 pounds.

Front page of the report detailing the crash of 1049H N6915C. (CAB)

in type. He was a Korean War veteran and his wife Lorie was a former Flying Tiger stewardess.

The crew had filed an Instrument Flight Rules (IFR) flight plan from San Francisco to Sacramento, then to JFK following Victor Airways, all at 11,000 feet. Flight time was expected to be 9 hours, 16 minutes, but the plane carried enough fuel (5,000 gallons or 29,000 pounds) for 11 hours, 3 minutes aloft. The flight's alternate landing field was Newark, New Jersey. Cargo for the flight weighed 41,078 pounds—bringing the total weight to 142,073 pounds—only 27 less than its maximum allowable gross takeoff weight.

San Francisco Ground Control granted N6915C permission to taxi toward Runway 28L at 12:13 am. Winds were reported as 15 knots with gusts to 23 from 210 degrees, creating a strong crosswind on takeoff. The Clearance Delivery Controller granted the flight its IFR flight plan

The Connie door rests on Sweeney's Ridge. The door and other large pieces can still be found in the thick underbrush. (Ian E. Abbott)

indicating that the departure would be along the 287-degree radial also known as the "Golden Gate One" departure. From Runway 28, the Golden Gate One departure takes an airplane through a "gap" between the San Bruno Mountains on the bay side of the peninsula and the coastal foothills to the west. Flight 282, callsign "Tiger Niner Fifiteen," read back the clearance including the climb-out on the 287-degree radial, at 12:21 am.

Tiger Niner Fifteen advised the tower that they were ready for takeoff 6 minutes and 45 seconds later. At 12:28, Flight 282 reported to the tower that they were "rolling." The tower controller noted that the aircraft passed in front of the tower and became airborne at 12:30 am.

Witnesses on the ground later said that Tiger Niner Fifteen veered to the right and then made a steeper turn to the left before leveling its wings and continuing to climb. They said the plane entered the clouds wings level. These turns were probably course corrections to return to the correct heading after encountering strong crosswinds.

The tower controller instructed the flight to contact Departure Control at 12:30:22 am. Thirty seconds later, Flight 282 made contact and said, "Departure, Tiger Nine One Five, you got us—ah, over?" Departure Control acknowledged the transmission five one-hundredths of a second later and advised the flight to report its progress to 11,000 feet in 1,000-foot increments. The crew responded at 12:31:05, "Roger, how do you have us tracking toward the, ah, gap?" The controller switched radar modes, from 30- to 10-mile scan setting, and asked the crew to report its altitude. They replied, "Nine Hundred" at 12:30:16. Departure Control quickly responded by saying, "... you're left of course of the San Francisco two-eight-seven (radial)."

Flight 282 did not respond, nor did it answer any subsequent calls. The Departure Controller said, "... within seconds after the second

Another view of the Connie door showing the outer fuselage skin and locking handle. (Ian E. Abbott)

transmission, the target stopped, bloomed, and disappeared from the radar scope."

The flight lasted a mere 3 minutes and 30 seconds; it was estimated that the plane crashed at 12:31:30 am, December 24, 1964. The Constellation had indeed veered left of its intended course and struck Sweeney's Ridge approximately 4.3 miles from the San Francisco International Airport bearing 257 degrees (roughly 2.5 miles left of its intended course). The left wing struck the east side of Sweeney's Ridge at 840 feet above sea level, cartwheeling the fuselage into the hill at 860 feet, narrowly missing a U.S. Coast Guard radio station. The plane exploded and momentum carried parts up and over the 925-foot summit. The CAB report stated that all four engines were producing power and that none of the control surfaces had separated in flight. Both the ADF and VOR receivers were set correctly.

The Constellation was carrying 41,000 pounds of "general merchandise" and electronics equipment plus 136 pounds of Christmas mail. It was reported that hundreds of "brightly colored women's scarves were found scattered about the area."

Authors Veronico, left, and Davies display a number of artifacts found at the Connie crash site. Veronico holds the fuel tank cap and the blade antenna can be seen leaning against the door. (Ian E. Abbott)

This gear section was found partially buried on the hillside. Rumors persist that one of the Connie's engines remains on the far side of Sweeney's Ridge. (Ian E. Abbott)

Determining the Cause

Local Sheriff Earl B. Whitmore was quoted in December 24, 1964's *San Mateo Times*, "Had it been 20 feet higher, it might have cleared the ridge." A little bit of an exaggeration but, as always, had it been 100 feet higher it would indeed have cleared the ridge.

A number of factors contributed to this crash. First, the heavily loaded Constellation faced winds and crosswinds from 30 to 35 knots with gusts to 45 knots. As the plane few closer to Sweeney's Ridge, it would encounter turbulence and possibly severe downdrafts.

Second, false VOR indications may have been presented to the crew by a faulty radio transfer switch assembly (or more precisely, the deviation indicator transfer switch) that displays readings from co-pilot's VOR onto the pilot's. The CAB flew a similar "ghost ship" over the crash route in an effort to determine a possible cause, but it was a report from another Flying Tiger Connie that experienced a VOR deviation that led investigators to look at the crash as a possible contributing factor.

In addition, the co-pilot's request for tracking information may have been an indication of a navigational aid problem or failure. In an effort to ensure this type of accident did not happen again, Flying Tiger Line inspected all radio transfer switch assemblies in its Connie fleet. Three aircraft were found to have faulty switches. Subsequently, the FAA issued an Airworthiness Directive (AD) requiring that each switch be pulled and inspected before it had accumulated 300 hours in service.

Third, the aircraft executed a 55-degree left turn after takeoff. This will never be explained—considering the departure Tiger Niner Fifteen was approved for calls for a slight veering to the right. The CAB report stated, "Since no reason is apparent why the left turn would not have been displayed on the instrument panel, the Board concludes that the crew apparently failed to refer to the total instrument portrayal in the cockpit."

The probable cause for the crash was cited as, "... the pilot, for undetermined reasons, deviated from departure course into an area of rising terrain where downdraft activity and turbulence affected the climb capability of the aircraft sufficiently to prevent terrain clearance."

The Crash Site Today

Sweeny's Ridge is sometimes known as the "Plymouth Rock of the West Coast." From here, explorers of the Spanish Portola expedition had their first views of San Francisco Bay in November 1769. At the time of the crash, the area was a U.S. Coast Guard reserve, off limits to the public. When the Coast Guard decommissioned the site it was dedicated as a part of the Golden Gate National Recreation Area on May 8, 1984. This location offers tremendous unobstructed views of both the ocean and San Francisco Bay, and is home to mule deer, coyotes, bobcats, and mountain lions.

Problems quickly arose when attempting to locate this crash site. The official coordinates were off—way off. The CAB's position put the wreck across the valley, or gap, below 600 feet in elevation and the plane could not have crashed there. A study of aerial photographs was made available by Tom Northop and Pacific Aerial Surveys of Oakland, California. Northrop was able to locate aerial photos taken two years after the crash that still showed the burned foliage around the wreck site. This started the expedition off in the right direction.

After viewing the photos, we decided to put the "TOPO!" CD-ROM of USGS maps to the test. The product billed itself as "The Ulitmate Tool for Planning Outdoor Activities Around the Bay Area." After reading the manual and quickly installing the software, the crash coordinates from the CAB report were entered. Using the software, coupled with the aerial photographs, we were able to plot the crash site and determine the correct topo, San Francisco South 7.5 Minute Quadrangle Map. Viewing the topo on the screen, the Coast Guard reservation and its buildings were clearly marked. The map was printed and the group headed for the site.

We proceeded to Skyline Junior College, parked in the southernmost parking lot near the trailhead and the school's maintenance yard. Although Sweeney's Ridge is not marked on the topo, it is part of the Golden Gate National Recreation Area and is listed in its publications.

This section, possibly from the flaps or wing area, is nearly three feet long. It was found 100 yards from the top of the hill. (Ian E. Abbott)

The group started up the well-marked and maintained trail. At the top of the trail, approximately one-half mile, the trail forks. Heading to the right to the top of Sweeney's Ridge, we walked another one-tenth of a mile before turning off the trail to the east. From this point, the San Francisco Jail could be seen below the hillside. All of the Coast Guard buildings were torn down in the 1950s.

The first pieces of wreckage were found 50 yards down the face in an area of thick ground cover. Be aware that parts of the old Coast Guard reservation and radio station have been mixed in with the Connie's remains. This material is primarily electrical components, street lights, and wood. Many people have ventured into this area not knowing its significance. Dozens of beer cans and bottles litter the area.

Once clear of the recent debris, a number of large pieces can be quickly located. One or two flaps, a door complete with latch, handle, and locking-mechanism, and the radio blade antenna were found. A portable am/fm radio that was brutally twisted bore the scars of the crash, including a small pebble imbedded in its face. One of the wing fuel cell caps, still wearing a top coat of red paint, turned up. Dozens of pieces with Lockheed part numbers were found, making the wreck even more interesting. Portions of Flight 282's cargo still can be found with a little digging. Blue beads from the costume jewelry plus gloves and scarves still wrapped in plastic—some with melted or scorched packaging—were found in large numbers.

Flying Tiger N6915C is one of the most accessible crash sites anywhere, with a walking trail less than 25 yards from the point of impact. Its proximity to the coast, coupled with the site's thick vegetation, calls for layers of long-sleeve shirts and good eye protection. No poison oak was noticed during our visit, but at other times of the year it can be extremely thick. Sweeney's Ridge is a popular hiking area, yet hundreds of pieces still littered the site more than 50 years later.

This wreck was also the acid test of "TOPO!" software (www.topo.com). Did it work? Outstanding is the answer. After returning to the office, the precise location was entered into the database and the correct coordinates were provided: latitude: 37°37'28" by longitude 122°27'45".

G-APFE
B O A C

Chapter 16

Severe Turbulence Ends BOAC Flight 911 Over Mt. Fuji

Donald B. McComb

In the early afternoon of March 5, 1966, a BOAC (British Overseas Airways Corporation) Boeing 707-436 G-APFE sat patiently on the ramp at Tokyo International Airport awaiting service. On March 4, the 707 had flown from San Francisco to Honolulu and was scheduled to arrive in Tokyo late in the afternoon, where it would overnight. However, because of bad weather in Tokyo, the flight diverted to Itazuke, arriving at 6:00 pm, local time. The flight, now at the midpoint of a round-the-world service that had originated in London, would continue on to Tokyo in the morning. Flight 911 was scheduled to arrive in Hong Kong that afternoon.

British Overseas Airways Corporation (BOAC) publicity shot of Boeing 707-436 G-APFE (msn 17706). This aircraft crashed March 5, 1966, on the slopes of Japan's Mt. Fuji. The crew of 11 plus 113 passengers perished in the disaster. (BOAC)

Seventy-five American tourists who would board the flight in Tokyo were on the trip of a lifetime. They were dealers and executives of Thermo King, based in Minneapolis, Minnesota, and were finishing a 14-day, all-expenses-paid trip that had been their reward for a sales campaign.

That night a Canadian Pacific DC-8-43 (CF-CPK) undershot the approach into Tokyo International Airport. CF-CPK's initial touchdown was 2,800 feet short of the runway threshold. It then hit a seawall, coming to rest near the end of the runway. The DC-8 exploded, killing 64 of the 72 on board.

Upon learning of the crash, there certainly was some apprehension among the passengers as they packed for the flight to Hong Kong, the last city on the tour.

Flight 911 took off from Itazuke at 11:25 am, local time, arriving at Tokyo's Haneda airport at 12:43 pm. While the 707 was being serviced with fuel, food, and liquor, Captain Bernard Dobson and First Officer Malony received a weather briefing for the Tokyo-to-Hong Kong segment of the of the flight that was due to depart at 1:45 pm. The weather briefing consisted, in part, of the following: "A depression intensified during the night and moved rapidly northeast across Japan. High pressure is developing over the Asian continent in conjunction with a low-pressure area over the sea to the east of Japan. This is causing a steep pressure gradient from west to east over Japan at low levels." According to the observations taken at the Fuji-san weather station at the summit of Mt. Fuji, the wind was 60 to 70 knots out of the northwest and the temperature was 18 degrees Fahrenheit.

While the flight's crew of 11 and 113 passengers made their way out to the 707, someone paused for a moment to capture the scene with a camera. Taken from the observation deck, the photo shows G-APFE, its company colors of blue, white, and gold resplendent in the afternoon sunshine. Surrounded by a sea of baggage carts, catering trucks, and power carts, it looked well-cared for. The scene must have inspired confidence in even the most nervous passenger. The 707 was one of the finest airliners around and BOAC was one of the safest airlines in the world.

With passengers and crew on board, G-APFE began communications with air traffic control at 1:42 pm. First, permission was requested to start engines. Then the crew asked for clearance to amend the planned departure route asking instead for permission to climb initially in Visual Meteorological Conditions (VMC), undoubtedly to give the passengers a view of Mt. Fuji. This was approved and Flight 911 started its taxi to Runway 33L.

Flight 911 received takeoff clearance at 1:58 pm. Captain Dobson advanced the throttles and four Rolls Royce Conway 508s rapidly increased power output to 17,500 pounds of thrust each. G-APFE accelerated down the runway, lifting off and climbing out over Tokyo Bay. After making a wide right turn, Flight 911 flew south towards Yokohama and made a gradual turn southwest on a course that would take the 707 near Mt. Fuji. Approaching 17,000 feet, most of the passengers probably were starting to relax. Soon the drink cart would make its rounds through the cabin. One passenger seated on the right side of the aircraft over the wing took out his 8mm movie camera and started filming the breathtaking view outside. Investigators who later recovered this camera found footage of Tokyo airport, the Tanzawa Mountains, Lake Yamanaka, and after skipping two frames, something that looked like passenger seats and carpet.

Mt. Fuji from the starboard side of a Boeing 707 similar to BOAC's G-APFE that crashed on March 5, 1966. Struck by a meteorological phenomenon known as a "mountain wave," this mass of air hit the 707 broadside with the force of 7.5Gs. (Donald B. McComb Jr. Collection)

When the 707 flew near the top of Mt. Fuji, it encountered a condition known as a "mountain wave." This phenomenon forms behind a mountain and flows at high speed down the leeward side. Often these invisible waves are noticeable by the presence of a type of altocumulus cloud known as a "lenticular cloud." Easy to spot, they are shaped like a giant lens with smooth edges. Today, however, no such clouds were present. This flow of air "broadsided" the 707 with a "wall of air" moving nearly 100 mph, from right to left across the path of the 707. Striking broadside, the aircraft was subjected to a 7.5G shock, which snapped the vertical stabilizer off at its mounts—mounts that had been tested to take a 100,000-pound side load. The tail fin then fell, destroying the left horizontal stabilizer. The aircraft immediately pitched up and rapidly decelerated from 350 knots to less then 100 knots. It was at this point that the passenger filming lost control of the movie camera. Those standing or walking in the aisle were thrown into the cabin walls.

As G-APFE pitched up, all four engine pylons failed at the wing-to-pylon attach points. Simultaneously, the right wing failed outboard of the number-four engine and the rear fuselage failed at the aft main door. What was left of the 707 entered a flat spin falling nearly straight down, spilling fuel from fractured wing tanks. At around 6,000 feet, the fuselage

Blanket-covered bodies of crash victims lie on the ground at Gotemba, Japan, on March 5, 1966, after being recovered by police and troops from Japan's Self-Defense Forces. This was Japan's second major airline disaster in two days, following the crash of a Canadian Pacific DC-8-43 CF-CPK. (UPI/Bettmann)

forward of the wings, weakened by spin forces, broke away from the falling hulk. As this section failed, the center fuel tank fractured, flooding the forward baggage compartments and the electronics bays below the flight deck. This section went into a free fall and was destroyed and consumed by fire upon impact. Falling more slowly, the center section impacted in a forest at the base of Mt. Fuji. While this section did not burn, those alive after the in-flight breakup were killed by the ground impact.

Originally, investigators were puzzled by the fact that a modern jetliner had literally fallen apart on a clear day. Their attention quickly turned to the weather as a possible cause as mountain wave conditions were perfect that day. In addition, metallurgical tests showed fatigue cracks in the right attachment mount of the vertical stabilizer, though it could not be determined that these cracks had led to the structural failure. The best clue of all was the recovery of the 8mm movie camera from the wreckage. Tests were performed on the camera to determine what amount of force would cause the camera to skip two frames and be pulled from the hands of the photographer. It was determined that a force of 7.5Gs would cause the camera to skip two frames.

From an investigator's standpoint, there was not much to work with. The aircraft was not equipped with a cockpit voice recorder and the flight data recorder, primitive by today's standards but state-of-the-art in 1966, was mounted in the aircraft's nose below the cockpit floor. It was completely destroyed by the post-crash fire that also consumed the aircraft's instrumentation. In addition, a U.S. Navy Skyhawk, which overflew the site of the accident shortly after it occurred, encountered turbulence so severe that the aircraft was grounded for inspection after landing. The official report as issued by the Japanese government listed the possible cause of the accident as follows: "The probable cause of the accident is that the aircraft suddenly encountered abnormally severe turbulence over Gotemba City, which imposed a gust load considerably in excess of the design limit."

In terms of wreckchasing, getting to this accident site should be simple. Do your homework thoroughly. Then hop a flight to Tokyo, rent a car, and drive to Gotemba City. There, in the shadow of Mt. Fuji, ask the locals about the air disaster that happened in 1966. This part might take some time, language problems and all, but once you get proper directions you should be able to pinpoint the site. Is there anything left on the site? Most certainly you should be able to find something, even if it's only a small piece of metal with a couple of rivets. Experience shows that rarely is an accident site totally cleaned up. Recently, I received a phone call from a gentleman who informed me that while stationed in Japan back in 1969-'70, as a crewman on helicopters, he had over-flown the crash site several times. Cruising over the eastern slopes of Mt. Fuji, he spotted large pieces of the 707. Its blue-and-white paint was still visible.

PAN AM
N708PA
PAN AMERICAN

Chapter 17

Lightning Strike Ignites Explosion, Downing Pan Am Flight 214

Donald B. McComb Jr.

Sunday morning, December 8, 1963, dawned no different then any other at Philadelphia International Airport. Among the many airliners being made ready for flight was Pan American Boeing 707-121 N709PA (msn 17588), *Clipper Tradewind*. It would operate Flight 213, service to San Juan, Puerto Rico, with an en route stop at Baltimore. After spending a couple of hours on the ground at San Juan, the 707 would return as Flight 214, stopping once again in Baltimore before arriving back at Philadelphia at 8:30 pm local time. Truly an historic aircraft, N709PA was the third-production 707, and on August 15, 1958, it became the first jetliner delivered to a U.S. air carrier. On December 8, after five years and four months in service, N709PA had flown 14,602 hours.

Boeing 707-121 N709PA (msn 17588) was lost on December 8, 1963, over Elkton, Maryland, when a lightning strike ignited fuel fumes in the left wing. (Donald B. McComb Jr. Collection)

Only one incident had marred an otherwise trouble-free flying career. During a training flight on February 25, 1959, while flying near its minimum controllable airspeed at 8,000 feet over France, N709PA was allowed to stall. During the recovery, one of the engines and most of the pylon separated from the aircraft, landing in a farmer's field. The plane continued on to Heathrow, where it was inspected and repaired.

That December morning, Flight 213 departed Philadelphia prior to 10:00 am local time. In command was Captain George F. Knuth, 45 years old, a veteran Pan American pilot with 17,049 hours, 2,890 of which were in the 707. In the right seat was First Officer John R. Dale, employed since 1955, who had 13,963 hours, of which 2,681 were in type. Second Officer Paul L. Orringer was the navigator, but also was rated as a pilot on the 707. He had logged 10,008 hours, of which 2,808 were in 707s. John R. Kantlehner served as flight engineer. He had flown 6,066 hours, of which 76 were in the 707. The flight to San Juan was without incident and arrived shortly after 2:00 pm local time.

While on the ground, the captain was briefed on the weather along his intended route back to Philadelphia. The crew was provided with a flight folder containing the required weather documents. As the crew was being briefed, N709PA was being prepared for the return flight. Flight 213 landed with 25,500 pounds of Jet-A fuel remaining aboard and took on an additional 52,500 pounds of Jet-B fuel. The difference between the two fuels is that Jet-A is standard aviation kerosene, not much different then what is used in kerosene heaters, and Jet-B is a wide-cut gasoline-type fuel with a very low flash point and a maximum vapor pressure of three-pounds per square inch. When the fueling was completed, the wing tanks of the 707 contained between 64 and 69 percent Jet-B fuel, while the center tank, which on the 707 holds 7,306 gallons of fuel, was 100 percent Jet-B.

At 4:10 pm local time, the 707 departed San Juan as Flight 214. The flight north was uneventful, the 707 skirting the eastern coast of the United States with the late-afternoon sunshine turning to twilight. At 7:35 pm, *Clipper Tradewind* touched down at Baltimore's Friendship International Airport. Seventy-one passengers deplaned and none were boarded for the short flight to Philadelphia.

At 8:25 pm, N709PA thundered off into the night for the short 20-minute flight to Philadelphia. As the aircraft climbed out, Baltimore Departure Control provided radar vectors to the Victor 44 airway where control of the flight was passed to New Castle Approach Control. Communication was established and the 707 was cleared to descend to 5,000 feet, then to the New Castle VOR. Captain Knuth reported over the VOR at 8:42 pm and was transferred to Philadelphia Approach Control that advised, "Philadelphia weather now 700 scattered, measured 800 broken, 1,000 overcast, six miles visibility with rain showers. Altimeter 29.45. The surface wind is 280 degrees at 20 knots, with gusts to 30 knots. I've got five aircraft holding until the extreme winds have passed ... Do you wish to be cleared for an approach, or would you like to hold until the squall line ... passes Philadelphia?"

The crew advised approach control that they would hold. Flight 214 was instructed to hold west of the New Castle VOR on the 270-degree radial and was given an expected clearance time of 9:10 pm. The crew requested and received permission to use two-minute legs in the holding

pattern. Flight 214 advised that that they were ready to start the approach at 8:50 pm. Approach control instructed them to continue holding and they would be cleared as soon as possible. Flight 214 acknowledged with, "Roger, no hurry, just wanted to let you know that ... we'll accept a clearance."

The cockpit crew of National Airlines Flight 16, a Douglas DC-8-51 N875C (msn 45635), witnessed the death plunge of Pan Am Flight 214 on the night of December 8, 1963. (ATP/Airliners America)

For the next eight minutes, Flight 214 flew through the rainy night in a holding pattern near the small community of Elkton, Maryland. Also in the holding pattern, but 1,000 feet higher, was National Airlines Flight 16, operated by N875C, a Douglas DC-8-51.

At 8:58 pm, the following transmission was heard on Philadelphia Approach Control frequency. "MAYDAY, MAYDAY, MAYDAY, Clipper 214 out of control ... here we go." Overhead, the first officer of National 16 watched in horror as the Boeing 707 spun out of control. "Clipper 214 is going down in flames," he radioed tersely.

One thousand feet below, a lightning bolt had struck the left wing of the 707, resulting in an explosion that caused the wing to fail between the Number One and Two engines. Flight 214 began spinning earthward trailing a streamer of fire. At nearly 500 mph, it fell into a cornfield near Red Hill, two and one-half miles northeast of Elkton. The main wreckage missed a farmhouse by 100 feet. While the majority of the wreckage was located at the main impact point, parts were strewn as far away as three and one-half miles.

At first, crash investigators were hard pressed to believe that lightning indeed had caused the demise of Flight 214. Only once before in the history of commercial aviation was it proven that lightning had caused an accident. This was the loss of a TWA 1649 Constellation near Milan, Italy, in 1959.

After an extensive investigation it was determined that two factors, the fuel type and lack of static wicks, were instrumental in the cause of this accident. It was determined that the outer left wing tank was empty. The lack of static wicks allowed the static charge on the aircraft to build up as the aircraft flew in and out of the clouds. Recovered wreckage showed a lightning strike on the left wing tip and on the tip of the high-frequency antenna probe located at the top of the 707's vertical stabilizer. Whether it was the lightning strike itself that caused the explosion, or the static build-up, will never be known for sure. However, gasoline vapors in the left surge tank did ignite, causing a greater explosion in the left outer wing tank. At the time of the accident, N709PA was one of ninety-seven 707s flying that had not had the static wicks installed. The end result was that the use of gasoline type turbine fuels became almost obsolete in commercial aviation, and static wicks became standard equipment on every airliner in service.

Notes for Wreckchasers

In December 1990, I attempted to locate this accident site. This was a spur of the moment trip. At the time I was visiting a friend in Glen Burnie, Maryland, and was armed only with photocopies of the accident report. My goal was to take a look at the town itself and ask around to see if someone could point me in the right direction. Elkton is located about an hour north of Baltimore near the Delaware border.

Once in Elkton, I stopped at a small store. The clerk remembered the accident and gave general directions that took me three miles east of town. (Note, if you cross into Delaware you've gone too far!) I located a cornfield next to a farmhouse that matched the general description of the crash site. This location also matched the store clerk's description. Unfortunately, it was getting dark and there was no time to pursue things further. Satisfied that I had at least found the general area of the accident, if not the actual site, I prepared to return to Baltimore. As a general observation, everything in Elkton looks like it has not changed in 40 years. In all likelihood, the impact site still is a cornfield so there is some potential for wreckchasing. Since this area is predominantly farmland, written permission to enter fields should be obtained and carried when searching for this site.

Pan Am 707 Fleet Losses

Pan American World Airways was the first U.S. airline to introduce jet aircraft service on Oct. 26, 1958. The carrier eventually operated 149 Boeing 707 type aircraft, placing an order for twenty 707-121s on Oct. 13, 1955. The 707-121 could seat 165 passengers in an all-economy class configuration.

The airline later acquired 707-321 aircraft, fitted with more powerful engines and capable of a greater range. When flown on Pan Am's "Clipper Cargo" service, the -321 could carry 38 tons of cargo. Nine Boeing 720s—a shorter fuselage 707—were also acquired. The last of the 707s were retired on Jan. 26, 1981, with a number of them sold to provide parts for the U.S. Air Force for its KC-135 tanker upgrade program. In all, 12 of the type were lost in Pan Am service. The details of these aircraft follow.

Dec. 8, 1963
Boeing 707-121 N709PA (msn 17588); *Clipper Tradewind*
Elkton, Maryland
Route: Washington, D.C. to Philadelphia
Fatalities: 81
Probable Cause: Lightning caused vapors in the fuel tanks to ignite

Sept. 17, 1965
Boeing 707-121B N708PA (msn 17586); *Clipper Constitution*
Montserrat, British West Indies
Route: Montserrat to Antigua
Fatalities: 30
Probable Cause: Controlled flight into terrain; aircraft struck a mountain at 2,760 feet.

Dec. 12, 1968
Boeing 707-321C N794PA (msn 19696); *Clipper Malay*
Into the sea on approach to Caracas, Venezula
Route: New York (JFK International) to Caracas, Venezuela
Fatalities: 51
Probable cause: Controlled flight into terrain; aircraft descended into the sea 12 miles short of the airport.

Dec. 26, 1968
Boeing 707-321C N799PA (msn 18824); *Clipper Racer*
Anchorage, Alaska
Route: Anchorage, Alaska to Tokyo, Japan
Fatalities: 3
Probable cause: Aircraft took off with flaps retracted.

June 12, 1968
Boeing 707-321C N798PA (msn 18790); *Clipper Caribbean*
Calcutta, India
Route: Bangkok, Thailand to Calcutta, India
Fatalities: 6
Probable cause: Controlled flight into terrain; altimeter set incorrectly. In bad weather, aircraft descended too low, clipped a tree, and crashed 3,500 feet short of the runway.

Dec. 1, 1969
Boeing 707-321B N892PA (msn 20029); *Clipper Star King*
Sydney, Australia
Route: Sydney, Australia to Honolulu, Hawaii
Fatalities: none (125 passengers and 11 crew on board)
Probable cause: Birds ingested in number two engine, take off rejected, aircraft over-ran runway. Aircraft a total loss.

July 25, 1971
Boeing 707-321C N461PA (msn 19371); *Clipper Rising Sun*
Guam
Route: San Francisco, California, via Honolulu, Guam, and Manila, to Saigon
Fatalities: 4
Probable cause: Controlled flight into terrain; aircraft descended into Mount Kamunay, Guam, striking the earth at 2,525 feet above sea level.

July 22, 1973
Boeing 707-321B N417PA (msn 18959); *Clipper Winged Racer*
Papeete, French Polynesia
Route: Auckland, New Zealand to Los Angeles, California, via Papeete, French Polynesia, Honolulu, Hawaii, and San Francisco, California.
Fatalities: 78
Probable cause: Unknown. Aircraft departed Papeete and began a left turn at 300 feet. Bank angle became too great and the aircraft fell into the ocean.

Nov. 3, 1973
Boeing 707-321C N458PA (msn 19368); *Clipper Titian*
Boston, Massachusetts
Route: New York (JFK International) to Glasgow/Prestwick, Scotland
Fatalities: 3
Probable cause: Smoke in the cockpit.

Dec. 17, 1973
Boeing 707-321A N407PA (msn 18838); *Clipper Celestial*
Rome, Italy
Route: Rome, Italy to Beirut, Lebanon
Fatalities: 30
Probable cause: Hijackers killed one crew and 29 passengers, and destroyed the aircraft using grenades.

Jan. 30, 1974
Boeing 707-321B N454PA (msn 19376); *Clipper Radiant*
On approach to Pago Pago, American Samoa
Route: Auckland, New Zealand to Los Angeles, California, via Pago Pago, and Honolulu, Hawaii
Fatalities: 97
Probable cause: Controlled flight into terrain; aircraft crashed short of the runway on approach

April 22, 1974
Boeing 707-321B N446PA (msn 19268); *Clipper Climax*
Denpasar, Indonesia
Route: Hong Kong to Denpasar, Indonesia
Fatalities: 107
Probable cause: Controlled flight into terrain on approach.

AIR WEST
AIR WEST

Chapter 18

Air West Mid-Air with F-4 Phantom

Nicholas A. Veronico and Donald B. McComb Jr.

Among the many airliners preparing to depart at Los Angeles International Airport (LAX) in the late afternoon of June 6, 1971, was Air West Flight 706. It was Air West's daily service from Los Angeles to Seattle with stops at Salt Lake City, Utah; Boise and Lewiston, Idaho; and Pasco and Yakima, Washington.

Equipment for Flight 706 was N9345, a DC-9-31 (msn 47441). Delivered new to Air West on June 4, 1969, the 503rd DC-9 off the line at Long Beach, it had flown 5,542 hours with Air West.

In command were Captain Theodore Nicolay and First Officer Price Bruner. Between them, the Seattle-based flight crew had nearly 30,000 hours of flying experience. At 6:02 pm local time, N9345 departed LAX with 44 passengers and a crew of five. Taking off to the west into the setting sun, the DC-9 headed out over Santa Monica Bay for approximately five miles before making a right turn to heading 040 degrees. This course took the DC-9 over Santa Monica, Beverly Hills, and just to the north of Dodger Stadium, before heading out over the rugged San Gabriel Mountains.

While the DC-9 was climbing out from LAX, a Marine Corps McDonnell Douglas F-4B Phantom II (Bureau Number 151458) was passing over Palmdale, California, en route to Marine Corps Air Station

Air West DC-9-31 N9345 (msn 47441) taxies out for takeoff at Los Angeles International Airport (LAX) during its brief career. The plane was delivered new to Air West on June 4, 1969, and collided with a Marine Corps F-4B Phantom II on June 6, 1971. Forty-four passengers and five crew on board the DC-9, as well as the pilot of the F-4, perished in the accident. Only the Phantom's rear-seat Radar Intercept Officer survived. (ATP/Airliners America)

El Toro, east of Orange County Airport. First Lt. James R. "Rick" Phillips was the pilot in command and First Lt. Christopher E. Schiess, in the rear seat, was RIO (Radar Intercept Officer). "At the time, Rick was 28 years old. He had previously been enlisted and then went back through OCS (Officer's Candidate School). Rick got a commission and went through flight training," Schiess said. "We were flying by ourselves that day because the other plane had been down for maintenance troubles. They went back down (to MCAS El Toro) the day before." The F-4B was returning to El Toro, its home base, after an overnight cross-country flight to McChord Air Force Base, Washington.

On the way back to El Toro, the Phantom made a stop for fuel at Mountain Home Air Force Base, Idaho. While the aircraft was on the ground, the crew had the radio inspected because it had failed during the landing approach. Maintenance personnel at Mountain Home replaced a fuse in the radio. However, they could not fix a small oxygen leak that they discovered. In addition, the transponder was inoperative. The Phantom's crew decided to file a VFR (Visual Flight Rules) flight plan to Naval Auxiliary Air Station (NAAS) Fallon, Nevada, to see if repairs could be made on the oxygen system. During the flight to Fallon, the oxygen leak increased. Ground personnel at NAAS Fallon were unable to make repairs. Phillips phoned his duty officer at El Toro for instructions and was advised to proceed home at low altitude.

After refueling, the crew filed a VFR flight plan to El Toro. Takeoff was delayed from Fallon because El Toro was holding an airshow, so 151458 did not depart until 5:16 pm. The Phantom's route was to fly direct to Fresno, then follow Airway J-65 to Bakersfield, next to J-5

The F-4B Phantom II that collided with Air West N9345 was similar to the Air Force examples shown here patrolling the Air Defense Identification Zone off the California coast. (Nicholas A. Veronico)

taking the jet fighter to Los Angeles, then transitioning Los Angeles's airspace direct to El Toro.

Once airborne, 151458 climbed to 15,500 feet to clear the eastern Sierra Mountains. On the western side of the range, 151458 descended to 5,500 feet and followed J-65 to Bakersfield. At this point the Phantom's crew elected to deviate from the flight plan. "We had filed to go a route that would have taken us right over Los Angeles," Schiess said. "And then we were talking back and forth and thought, 'Oh, geez, it's so crowded. Why don't we cut west of Los Angeles.' That's what took us to the east about 30 to 40 miles. (Looking back today,) it would have been a lot safer if we had flown right over the top of Los Angeles at 15,000 feet instead of being out where we were that put us in line with a SID (Standard Instrument Departure)." They flew east of the planned course over Palmdale. Because of decreasing visibility at the lower altitudes and the fact that the San Gabriel Mountains were looming ahead, 151458 climbed once again to 15,500 feet. This was accomplished using maximum engine power without afterburner and took less than two minutes. Shortly after leveling off, and with the Distance Measuring Equipment (DME) indicating 50 miles to El Toro, Phillips executed a 360-degree aileron roll. This maneuver could be considered a questionable thing to do approaching the crowded skies of Southern California, and much was made of it in the press, although it had little, if any bearing on the event that was to follow.

While the Phantom was executing its climb to 15,150 feet, Air West Flight 706 was sprinting upwards at nearly 1,500 feet per minute en route to the Daggett VOR, its first checkpoint.

Close-up of the F-4B's left wing with the main gear still retracted. The tip was torn away when the two aircraft collided. (Christopher E. Schiess)

Both aircraft were closing very quickly. At one minute to impact, the two were nearly 10 miles apart. Thirty seconds to impact, 5.3 miles apart. If visible to each other, they would have appeared nearly stationary. In fact, the two aircraft were closing the distance at better then 1,050 feet per second, the speed of a .22-caliber bullet. Fifteen seconds before impact they were 2.6 miles apart. The smoky trail of the F-4B might have been visible at this point. Ten seconds prior, 1.8 miles apart, and five seconds before, less then one mile to impact.

Lt. Schiess Describes the Next Fateful Seconds

"It had probably been just a matter of minutes, like one to three, that we had been at that altitude (15,500 feet). We had been doing a low-level flight, 500 to 1,000 feet AGL (Above Ground Level), and then we just popped up. We probably went from 4,000 to 15,000 feet in a minute or two to get up top before we started our descent into El Toro. We got to the very top, did an aileron roll, and then that's when I got on the radar (and started) ground mapping," Schiess said.

In mapping mode, the RIO's head is down in the cockpit looking at the screen—only seeing what the radar is focused on. Schiess said, "You see the scope and the image of the ground and where it rises, depending on where you have the antenna pointed. This was equipment that was 40 years old at the time, and it did not provide high-definition or high-resolution images like they have today. That antenna had a three-degree

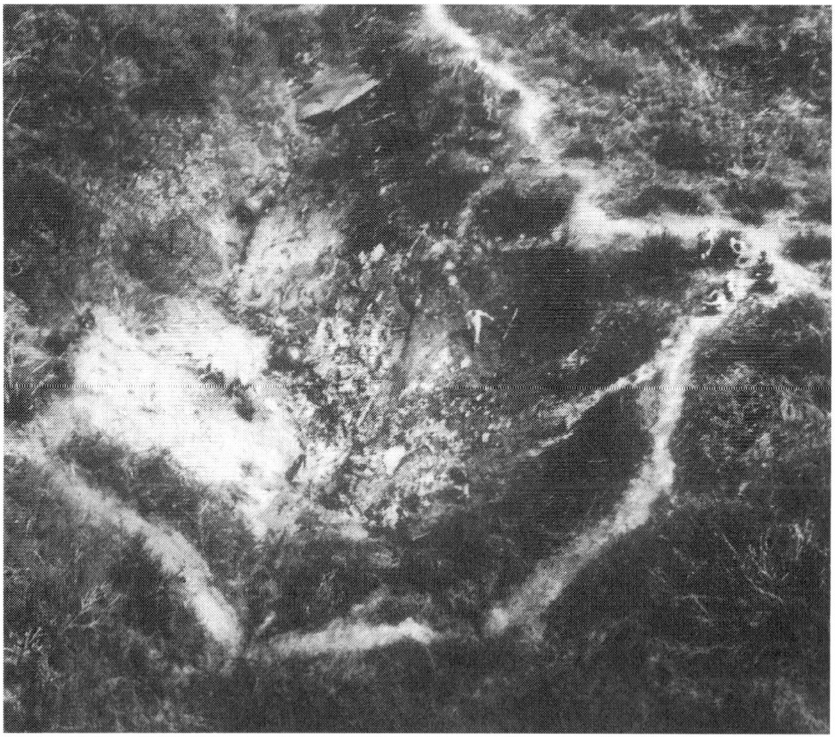

Investigators pore over the F-4B crash site. One engine and a wing panel are visible in the upper center. (NTSB)

National Transportation Safety Board photo of the DC-9 impact point. Note the investigators on the 60-degree slopes of the canyon. The tail section is at the bottom of the gulley on its left side. (NTSB)

beam. At a couple miles, if you are at 15,000 feet, that might paint something up to 18,000 and down to 12,000 feet. You had to put the antenna where you want to see.

"I had my head down in the cockpit for 45 seconds to a minute, as if you were reading something, and looked up to give my eyes a rest. I just happened to look up—I saw [the DC-9] and yelled instantly. I think the pilot probably saw it at the same time because his reaction was too quick for it to be a response to my yell. I shouted, 'Watch it Rick!' and he max'd left aileron deflection—slammed it against the left hand stop. We rolled extremely hard and nose low a little bit. I was watching and, for a millisecond, I did not know if we had missed or not.

"Then we hit. The back part of our airplane collided with the underneath of the DC-9 and it severed our jet in half.

"The NTSB report says that we were in a 28-degree roll when we hit, and I think that report is wrong. I know I lost sight of the airplane, and I know I could not have possibly lost sight of them if we were only at 28 degrees of roll. We had to be over 90. It is sort of amazing to me that science comes out wrong on that because they do have a lot of accuracy (in the report). But I would go to my grave saying they missed that one because I vividly remember losing sight of the airplane and wondering for a millisecond what was going to happen.

"There was absolutely no doubt there was a collision. Our airplane started tumbling, almost somersaulting. I said to myself, 'This airplane

Shortly after the crash, an attempt was made to remove the wreckage. A helicopter reportedly picked up the tail section and began to fly it out to be scrapped. The tail section, loaded in a sling, began to lift and the helicopter crew was forced to drop it about one-half mile from its original resting point. (Michael B. McComb)

Ground view of the DC-9 vertical and horizontal tail some distance away from the main impact point. (Michael B. McComb)

isn't going to fly!' Because I was getting bounced around a lot—my head was slamming against the canopy, I saw not only my warning lights (I had eight to twelve), I saw a bunch of warning lights in the front. I thought to myself, 'Oh my God, Rick's already out.' That's when I pulled my ejection ring.

"Our airplane was going down in a fireball. I think your instinct is to just get out before weighing the consequences of what had just occurred. Your instinct is to get out of the airplane that you know is on fire and is destroyed.

"I reasoned incorrectly with respect to the fact that Rick would be out because the sequence is the back canopy goes, then the back seat goes, then the front canopy goes, then the front seat. The only way he would have been out was if my seat had malfunctioned. The best knowledge is that Rick did not try to get out before I got out. The reason he did not get out is one of three possibilities: he didn't try to get out and rode it in; he was knocked unconscious by the collision—but that's very unlikely in my opinion although I never attempted to talk to him after the collision because things happened so quickly; and the third, and most likely reason in my opinion, is that his seat malfunctioned. When my canopy went off, it caused a pressure differential and he was stuck in the aircraft. After that accident they put charges on the canopies so that, if in fact that was the case, it would not happen again.

"The seats had a barometer that was set to separate it from the pilot at a certain altitude. It should deploy at about 15,000 feet. I remember hearing the canopy blow off, going up and getting caught in the wind stream. I tucked my arms in as hard as I could so they would not get blown off, and then I opened my eyes, looked down, and saw the ground. I had enough time to realize that I still had my seat with me. It had not separated automatically and I got to thinking, 'Ok, I'd better try to do this manually.' At that time it separated automatically.

"I'm coming down in my chute and I've got airplane parts all around me—part of the vertical stabilator fell—I don't know how close, but it wasn't very far from me. Then I looked down in time to see our airplane that was totally on fire. The first thing I started looking for was another chute. Then I watched our airplane until it hit the ground. At that point I started looking for the DC-9. I saw it and I watched it for 10- or 20-seconds. It looked like a leaf falling from a tree, just oscillating about 20 degrees on the vertical yaw axis. Nose level, going left and right, all the way down at a 60- to 70-percent rate of descent. Everything looked fine but it did not have any power. Everything I could see from looking above it was totally intact."

Having had most, if not all of its control cables and electrical systems from the cockpit to the rest of the aircraft severed, the DC-9 was doomed. Flight 706 entered a flat spin and impacted into the bottom of a

An engine cowl from the Air West DC-9 rests in the thick undergrowth. (Michael B. McComb)

One of the DC-9's main landing gear appears in a brush clearing near the point of impact. (Michael B. McComb)

steep canyon leading off of Mt. Bliss, about three-quarters of a mile from where the F-4B crashed. There were no survivors on the DC-9.

"I landed three or four miles from the DC-9 and one or two from our airplane," Schiess said. "I tried to have some control over my descent because I was coming down right on top of these huge powerlines. I thought, 'What an irony. I survived this collision and now I'm going to get fried by these powerlines.' I started yanking on the chute cords trying to change my angle of descent. It seemed to have no effect, but then I drifted off of them a little bit. I landed 50, maybe 75 yards below this Forest Service road. I just sat there and contemplated what had happened for a while and then a truck came by and picked me up."

The NTSB's Findings

The NTSB lists the probable cause of this accident as the failure of both crews to see and avoid each other, but recognizes that they only had marginal capability to detect, assess, and avoid the collision. Other factors include a very high closure rate, the combination of IFR and VFR traffic in an area where the limitation of the ATC system precludes effective separation of such traffic, and the failure of the crew of 151458 to request radar advisory service, particularly considering the fact that they had an inoperable transponder. If 151458 had requested the radar advisory there is a very good chance that the accident never would have occurred.

Schiess debates those points and said, "There was nothing wrong with the airplane that had any impact whatsoever with respect to the

N9345's tail section at rest on the slopes of Mt. Bliss in this photo taken from a Cessna 172 in December 1987. (Michael B. McComb)

accident. That was overplayed by the news media. The transponder was not working, but I don't think it would have mattered. I don't believe they had altitude on transponders back then, so that would be total conjecture. To conjecture [sic] that the transponder could have prevented the collision means that somebody on the ground would have noticed the signal and then alerted the other aircraft to our presence. Maybe it would have happened and maybe it wouldn't. It would have been extremely lucky for me to have picked up that airplane on radar because at the time of the accident I was trying to do some ground mapping with it. So I did not have the antenna aimed at where that aircraft was coming from. That probably had nothing to do with it. The oxygen system squawks were not a factor because the cabin was pressurized."

Follow-up and the Crash Site Today

Schiess stayed with the same squadron and continued his training until "combat qualified." This takes about a year while completing a syllabus in the aircraft type assigned. "I was about halfway through the syllabus when the accident occurred," Schiess said. "Six months later when I became combat qualified, I went to a group billet. At that time, one-third to one-half of the crews were getting orders to go overseas for eventual duty in Vietnam. Six months earlier everybody got orders to go to Vietnam. Six months later, nobody did. Because there was all this litigation due to the crash, I was held back. A few months later it did not make any difference because nobody was going over there. It was all winding down."

After leaving the Marine Corps, Schiess went onto a successful career in the pharmaceutical industry. He now is married with three children.

Michael B. McComb located the wreckage of Air West Flight 706 in fall 1987 while scouting the area in a Cessna 150. He captured the tail section's coordinates in his Loran at 34 11'30" north 117 56'10" west.

McComb said, "The aerial search lasted a mere 45 minutes. However, I had invested many hours of research in the area's libraries reading through newspaper microfilm.

"I obtained a USGS Azusa topographic map and then went to work. I located Mt. Bliss, a prominent geographic feature mentioned in the newspapers and official reports. Once the approximate location and elevation was determined, I set out from the Upland/Cable Airport. Flying northwesterly toward the heart of the rugged San Gabriel Mountains, I began to see the silhouette of Mt. Bliss through the late-afternoon smog.

"At first I made a series of orbits around the mountain, making sure I kept a safe distance between myself and the terrain. During several turns around the mountain, I failed to see any metal fragments on the brush- and tree-covered slopes. The sun was beginning to set and I decided to return to the airport, 15 miles away. It was shortly after I made the turn that I looked down one more time and saw the unmistakable view of a DC-9 tail section sitting upright among the tall trees.

"I quickly logged the location and began a descent toward the find. Because of the terrain, I had to plan every turn I made within the narrow canyons. The tail section was within a ravine on the eastern face of Mt. Bliss facing Fish Canyon. I made several passes taking pictures and searching for additional wreckage. During these observations and later examining the photographs, I noticed that the Air West livery has been erased by the elements."

Mt. Bliss is 3,720 feet tall and the tail section rests between 2,600 and 2,800 feet. Shortly after the accident, an attempt to remove the tail section was made. Using a helicopter, the tail was being flown out from the crash site when it gained lift and was dropped before the helicopter became unstable and crashed. Thus, there are now three sites to investigate—the impact points of the F-4B, the DC-9, and the tail section. Schiess describes the F-4B's crash site, "I saw the pictures of my aircraft and there wasn't anything very big left. Of course, half of it was gone before it hit the ground."

This is rough country, but most wreckchasers will find the trip worthwhile.

Chapter 19

The Search for Pearl Harbor Veterans in Hawaiian Waters

Nicholas A. Veronico

During World War II a number of aircraft crashed on the Hawaiian Islands and in the waters around them. In an effort approved by the U.S. Park Service, in conjunction with the USS *Arizona* Memorial, the University of Hawaii, the Oregon Air Museum, and benefactor Erickson Air Crane from Central Point, Oregon., a massive aircraft location project was begun.

A two-month search of the waters off Oahu led the Erickson search team to the wrecks of two Mitsubishi A6M Zero fighters, one Kate torpedo bomber, a Corsair, an SBD Dauntless, a B-24 Liberator, and a pair of F6F Hellcats, plus a number of other rare aircraft.

Several World War II aircraft wrecks were also located on land, including an F6F, an F4U Corsair, and a P-47 Thunderbolt. A Republic P-47 and a Douglas B-18 Bolo, both originally discovered in the late 1970s, were also resurveyed for possible recovery.

Recovery efforts for the three veterans of the Japanese attack on Pearl Harbor began in August 1992. The Kate, which rests in 110 feet of water with its torpedo still attached, and the two Zeros, each in just over 100 feet of water, are slated to be recovered, pending final arrangements, and displayed at the USS *Arizona* Memorial. National Park Service divers

An overview of the sunken Corsair shows the fuselage, engine and propeller, and right wing. (Erickson Air Crane)

also may survey one of the Japanese Zero fighters and possibly recover an outer wing panel.

The University of Hawaii leased one of its two deep-submersibles, the Pisces V, to Erickson to aid the search team's recovery efforts. The three-man mini-sub is operated by the university's Hawaiian Undersea Research Lab. The Pisces V is towed to the dive area on a catamaran barge, which lowers itself under the surface to allow the mini-sub to float free.

During a recovery operation, divers attach air bags and harnesses to an aircraft, which then float it up to a depth of about 10 feet. Once the aircraft is stabilized just under the surface, the submersible catamaran barge is lowered beneath the aircraft. Then the platform ascends to the surface, where it is either towed to shore with the aircraft secured to the barge, or lifted from the barge by helicopter and flown to a nearby pier.

The Pisces V is also planned to be used in the recovery of a Douglas SBD Dauntless dive bomber, which lies in 680 feet of water off the Oahu coast.

A B-24 Liberator was located in the Maui Channel, resting on its belly in 180 feet of water. All four engines are still attached, and although the fuselage is complete, the forward area took a tremendous beating during the aircraft's successful ditching. The tail turret is covered in black coral, and its guns point upwards toward the surface.

The Corsair found at the bottom of Maunalua Bay may have come from one of the many aircraft carriers that have operated in Hawaiian waters, like the USS Intrepid, *shown here during World War II. (U.S. Navy)*

Cockpit section of an F4U Corsair in 110 feet of water. (Erickson Air Crane)

A Corsair was found intact in Maunalua Bay, covered with marine growth at a depth of 105 feet. The tail wheel and hook are down, and the canopy is open, as if the pilot ran out of gas or could not extend his main landing gear and elected to ditch the Navy fighter. This aircraft will not be recovered, as it provides a source of income for local dive shops and freelance dive guides who take scuba enthusiasts to the fighter wreck.

Aside from the three aircraft planned for display at the USS *Arizona* Memorial, discussions are underway to display several of the other recovered aircraft permanently at other locations in the Hawaiian Islands.

U.S. NAVY

Chapter 20

U.S. Navy Examines Historic Airship Wreck

Nicholas A. Veronico

The USS Macon weathervanes from the mooring mast at Moffett Field. The airship was powered by eight Maybach engines contained within the airship. The engines drove transmissions and shafts to turn the propellers and rotate them relative to the direction of flight. (U.S. Navy)

The U.S. Navy located and photographed the wreckage of the airship USS *Macon* and two of her F9C-2 Sparrowhawk fighters in 1,500 feet of water north of Point Sur, California, on June 24, 1990, and again on September 18-22, 2006. For its initial investigation of the *Macon*, the Navy was aided by historical information and ocean current calculations provided by the Naval Postgraduate School and the Monterey Bay Aquarium Research Institute (MBARI).

Searchers used the world's deepest-diving manned submersible, the *Seacliff* (DSV-4), in their efforts. The *Seacliff* is a 32-foot-long, titanium-hulled, three-man vehicle capable of depths up to 20,000 feet. For the 2006 expedition, MBARI employed a Remotely Operated Vehicle (ROV) called *Tiburon*, to make a photographic mosaic of the wreck site.

The *Macon* was returning from maneuvers with the Pacific Fleet on February 12, 1935, when she encountered a squall. The turbulence broke the airship's vertical fin, tearing the spine of the airship and deflating the craft's helium cells, which caused the airship to lose control. It eventually crashed into the sea southeast of Monterey near Point Sur. Only two of the crewmen aboard the *Macon* at the time of the crash were killed. The crash of the *Macon* ended the "Zeppelin era" for the United States and its military forces, and was the last rigid airship in the Navy's inventory.

The USS *Macon*, Navy designation ZRS-5, was commissioned on June 23, 1933. She was powered by eight 560-horsepower Maybach engines with a maximum speed of 84 mph and a range of 9,200 miles at a cruising speed of 60 mph. The *Macon* carried a crew of up to 91, and was 785 feet long, 132.9 feet in diameter, and held 6.5 million cubic feet of helium.

The *Macon* was the sister ship to the USS *Akron*, ZRS-4, which was lost during night exercises in the Atlantic on April 3/4, 1933. Both airships were designed as flying aircraft carriers to scout ahead of the fleet and were equipped with four F9C-2 Sparrowhawk biplane fighters for defense.

The Sparrowhawks were lowered into the air by a trapeze and then launched for scouting missions or defense of the mother ship. When a mission was completed, the Sparrowhawks would return to the airship and, by means of a large hook mounted to the upper wing, were recovered by flying the hook onto the trapeze. Once tethered to the airship, the aircraft were hoisted into the 70-by-58-foot hangar deck.

Seen from inside Hangar One, Macon *rides the south mooring mast. Expeditions to the* Macon *by the Monterey Bay Research Institute (MBARI) in 1990 and 2006 examined the dirigible's wreckage and the condition of its Sparrowhawk fighters. (U.S. Navy)*

A trio of Sparrowhawks passes over Moffett Field's massive Hangar One, built in 1932 to house the USS Macon. *(U.S. Navy)*

Since the airship's crash into the cold Pacific Ocean, there have been a number of unsuccessful attempts to search for the wreckage. Then MBARI talked to a fisherman, Dave Canepa, who had netted a "piece of aircraft wreckage" during the 1970s. Canepa gave the location where he had found the piece of metal to MBARI, which in turn contacted the Naval Postgraduate School. Using this information as a starting point, the *Seacliff* was able to locate, photograph, and recover small pieces of the airship's framework for study during the first expedition to the site.

The *Seacliff* and her mothership, the M/V *Laney Chouest*, went to Monterey to survey the underwater damage and to relocate submerged oceanographic instruments that were moved during the October 17, 1989, Loma Prieta earthquake. According to the Naval Postgraduate School, some of the instruments that were anchored in the undersea Monterey Canyon moved more than 600 feet.

The F9C-2 Sparrowhawk fighters carried aboard the *Macon* are very significant, as only one example is known to survive—a composite

One of the Macon's *four Sparrowhawk fighters is perched on the "trapeze" that raised and lowered the fighters from the hangar deck. Note the shadow of the* Macon *above the aircraft's left wing. (U.S. Navy)*

aircraft currently on display at the National Air and Space Museum's Hazy Center in Virginia.

After the Navy's success in recovering the Grumman F3F-2 off the coast of San Diego (see Chapter 21, *Rare Grumman Fighter Recovered from the Pacific)*, enthusiasts had hoped that the Navy would attempt to raise at least one of the *Macon's* Sparrowhawks, but this does not look likely to occur as the wreck site was added to the National Register of Historic Places on January 29, 2010.

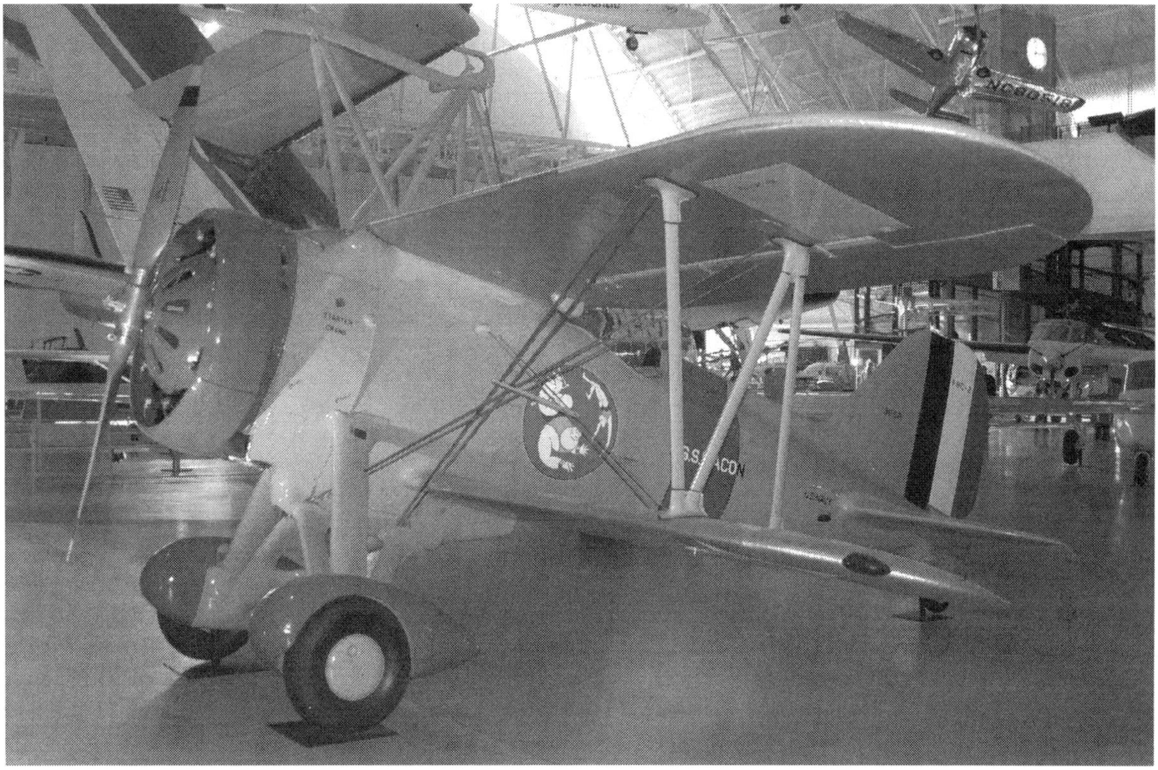

The sole remaining Curtiss F9C-2 Sparrowhawk fitted with trapeze gear resides at the National Air and Space Museum's Steven F. Udvar-Hazy Center in Chantilly, Virginia.
(Nicholas A. Veronico)

F3F-2
0972
2-MF-3
U.S. MARINES

Chapter 21

Rare Grumman Fighter Recovered from the Pacific

Thomas Wm. McGarry

On Tuesday, August 29, 1940, a young U.S. Marine Corps pilot attached to VMF-2 ran short of fuel just 200 yards from the deck of the USS *Saratoga* (CV-3) and ditched his Grumman F3F-2 biplane, serial number 0976, into the waters of the Pacific Ocean.

This Grumman F3F-2, serial number 0972, was photographed at Oakland, California, in April 1938. She served in the same squadron as the F3F-2 that was recovered off the coast of Del Mar, California, in April 1990. (William T. Larkins)

During the first week of April 1990, that same aircraft was raised from the ocean off Del Mar, California, with the pilot watching. Recovery of this aircraft was the first step in a restoration process, with a goal to place the rare, original biplane fighter on static display at the National Museum of Naval Aviation in Pensacola, Florida.

The aircraft was discovered on a routine training exercise and was recovered in conjunction with a salvage effort to retrieve a UH-1N helicopter, which ditched in October 1989.

The Marine Corps Grumman F3F-2 was one of only 82 built (including the first "X" model) and first flew in March 1935 as the improved version of the F2F, having a more powerful 750-horsepower Wright Cyclone engine. Although the F3F-2 served only in small numbers, it saw prewar duty in Marine Corps units on both coasts and at various Naval air stations.

The Marine Corps received most of the 81 production aircraft, though the Navy did equip VF-6 with the F3F-2. Most of the F3F-2s

Fifty years after ditching in the Pacific Ocean, F3F-2, serial number 0976, rests on her landing gear at NAS North Island, San Diego. The Grumman biplane was transferred to the San Diego Aerospace Museum for restoration by its volunteer staff. (U.S. Navy)

were withdrawn from front-line service in May 1941, and were replaced by the Grumman F4F Wildcat. There was, however, at least one F3F-2 in Hawaii on December 7, 1941, but its fate is unknown.

The discovery and recovery of the F3F-2 has left some aviation historians, "very excited," according to retired U.S. Marine Corps Maj. John Elliot, former head of the Aviation Branch, Naval Historical Center at the Washington Navy Yard. When originally discovered, the aircraft was viewed through a remote underwater television camera at a depth of more than 2,000 feet. The aircraft was remarkably well preserved, with the original paint and markings clearly visible.

At that time, the aircraft was almost completely intact. However, between the time it was discovered and recovered, some significant damage occurred, probably due to the aircraft's being caught and dragged by a fishing net. In the process, the plane's right wings, the canopy, and the tail were either torn off or damaged.

Robert Rasmussen, director of the Naval Aviation Museum, said, "It was very, extremely disappointing to have it on the bottom for 49 years in absolutely perfect condition and then come back to find that it's been torn apart by a fishing net."

The aircraft originally was delivered to the Marine Corps on December 21, 1937, at the Marine Corps Air Station Quantico, Virginia, and spent its entire service life on duty with the Marine Corps. The aircraft was so well-preserved that the yellow stripe on the fuselage, indicating the sixth section's leader, was still bright, as were the squadron markings, 2-MF-16, and the national and Marine Corps insignia.

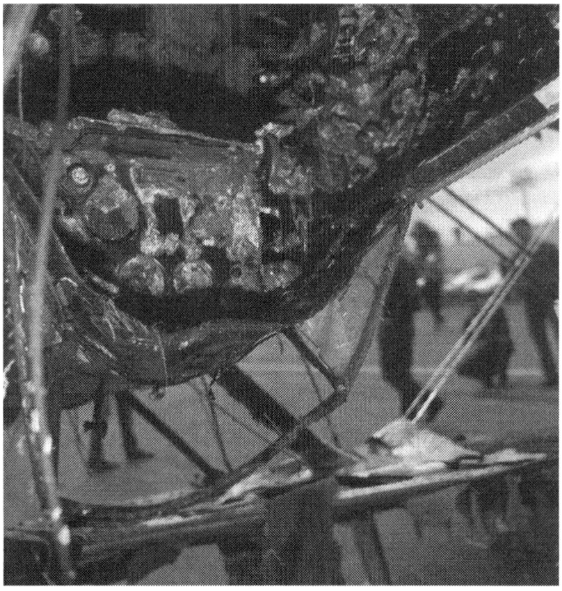

As the F3F was lowered to the dock to be righted so it could sit on its landing gear, Navy personnel reached into the cockpit and removed the pencil used by the aircraft's pilot, then First Lt. Robert E. Galer. Compare the cockpit photo to the shot of the aircraft's restored instrument panel. (U.S. Navy and Nicholas A. Veronico)

When 1st Lt. Robert E. Galer, then 27, experienced fuel problems and was forced to ditch, the aircraft had flown some 836.2 hours. Galer was on hand for the recovery and received a pencil that was found in the cockpit.

The former pilot was quoted as saying of the accident: "I just wanted to get down, then worry about being sorry. I was on the downwind leg when I switched on the reserve tank, and the engine just quit. There is not much you can do at 1,000 feet but go down.

"There were destroyers following the aircraft carrier on plane guard duty, and the landing speed was only 60 mph. The aircraft landed, nosed over, and then settled back. It floated for a while, and I got picked up."

Galer recovered from the mishap and went on to receive the Medal of Honor for his destruction of 11.5 Japanese aircraft while flying a Grumman F4F Wildcat over Guadalcanal in October 1942. He ended the war with 13.5 enemy aircraft to his credit. He later flew jet fighters during the Korean War and retired from the U.S. Marine Corps in 1957 as a brigadier general and director of the Navy's guided missile program. Galer passed away on June 27, 2005.

The stubby little Grumman was one of the Navy's last biplane fighters. Streamlined with an enclosed cockpit and retractable landing gear, the F3F-2 epitomized both the peak of biplane design and the twilight of the biplane era. The F3F-2 was proudly displayed by the Navy at the 1938 Cleveland Air Races.

F3F-2 Buno. 0976 is now on display at the National Museum of Naval Aviation in Pensacola, Florida, where the aircraft sits in a place of honor in the museum's South Wing. (Nicholas A. Veronico)

After recovery, the biplane was restored by volunteers at the San Diego Aerospace Museum. The Navy retrieved the aircraft in 1995 for permanent display in Pensacola.

The only other aircraft of this type is a Grumman G.22 Gulfhawk II, which spent its life with Gulf Oil as an aerobatics aircraft. The G.22 Gulfhawk II is a hybrid aircraft with the fuselage of an F3F-2, the wings of an F3F-1, and a 1,000-horsepower Wright R-1820 engine. The plane is now on display at the National Air and Space Museum, Washington, D.C.

Details of MBARI's expeditions to the Macon, specifically the 2006 trip, can be seen on the Internet at: www.mbari.org/expeditions/Macon/index.htm.

TF
F-708

Chapter 22

TF-51H Returns from Arizona Hillside

Robert A. Kropp

Lt. Robert G. Westlund had no way of knowing that he was making his final flight as he warmed up the Merlin engine in his TF-51H Mustang, serial number 44-64697, on a cold morning in December 1951.

Lt. Robert G. Westlund in the cockpit of a TF-51H, the same model Mustang in which he perished on an Arizona hillside. (Robert A. Kropp Collection)

Westlund took off on a cross-country navigation flight from Fresno, California, to his duty station, the 3625th Air Force Central Training Squadron at Tyndall Air Force Base, Florida. Several hours into his flight, military officials in Arizona picked up a final radio transmission from him. He reported an oxygen system failure at high altitude and requested clearance for an emergency landing at Davis-Monthan Air Force Base in Tucson.

A rancher told military authorities he heard a shriek and then an explosion that sounded like a bomb when the airplane impacted with the earth. Several weeks later, the pilot of a small plane reported sighting the wreckage of the fighter deep in a canyon on a remote mountainside in southern Arizona.

Air Force officials sent an accident investigation team into the area, recovered the remains of the pilot, and photographed the wreckage. Within a month, the incident was entered into the military files and written off as an unfortunate and one of many all-too-frequent mishaps.

Lt. Robert G. Westlund.

Arizona resident Richard Johnson, a budding aviation enthusiast and military historian, was intrigued by the story of this missing Mustang, and he was determined to find the airplane. In June 1991, Johnson not only located the rare Mustang, but spent several days with a group of men removing the warbird from its remote crash site.

Johnson said he made the recovery with the hope that the vintage fighter would return to the air again one day. "Whether it can be restored or used as a parts source for another P-51H restoration project, the end result justifies this endeavor. Mustangs were meant to fly, and I think Lt. Westlund would have wanted it this way," he said.

The deceased pilot's family members agreed and traveled to Scottsdale, Arizona, from California to view the remains of Lt. Westlund's Mustang. "It was a very moving experience," Johnson said. "I had been in contact with Lt. Westlund's family about six months prior to the discovery of the airplane. I had spoken with them to tell them about my intention of placing a memorial plaque in a town not far from the crash site in the mountains, and they were pleased that I cared about something that had happened such a long time ago.

"They were kind enough to send me copies of the military accident report and the pieces of this puzzle started to come together. I searched for the Mustang on several occasions before I actually found it, and after coming upon something like this that was the scene of a tragedy 40 years ago, I had my reservations about trying to remove the airplane. I came to the conclusion that a person can still show reverence to the misfortune of others and help preserve a little piece of aviation heritage at the same time."

The P-51 Mustang, developed during World War II for its role as bomber escort, is perhaps the best-known fighter plane of the war. The first Mustangs arrived in England in December 1943, and after a series of production line refinements, the fighters were instrumental in reversing the Luftwaffe's air superiority in the skies over Europe.

Both the Army Air Forces and the Royal Air Force used the Mustang in a variety of combat roles. The early variants were powered by 12-cylinder, inline Allison engines and the later models by the Rolls-

North American TF-51H Mustangs line up on the ramp at Tyndall Air Force Base, Florida. Lt. Westlund's AAF SN44-64697 is the first from left.
(Robert A. Kropp Collection)

Royce-pattern Packard-Merlin. The final production P-51, designated as an "H" model, was the Cadillac of Mustangs. A refinement of the P-51D, the "H" was a completely new and different airplane, and only the engine spacers of the earlier variant were interchangeable.

A sleek and fast-flying gun platform, the "H" model was longer, lighter, and took command of the sky with a 1,490-horsepower V-1650-9 Packard-Merlin, with water injection and improved cooling for extended operation at war emergency power settings. Developed late in the war, 555 "H" model Mustangs were built and delivered to the Army Air Forces by November 1945. North American Aviation had a standing contract for an additional 1,445 "H" model Mustangs, but the agreement was canceled in September 1945 with the surrender of Japan.

The Mustang saw combat again in the Korean War, but while the earlier models were pressed into service under a fighter-bomber role, the "H" models remained stateside and were used as trainers. The Air Force redesignated the P-51 (the "P" for "Pursuit") as F-51 (the "F for "Fighter").

The "H" model's light weight was seen as a drawback in a ground attack role, and the Mustang continued in service with Air National Guard units before being phased out completely in 1957. Lt. Westlund's Mustang was listed on the government rosters as a "TF-51," the "T" prefix indicating the airplane was a training ship and was not armed.

During the mid-to-late 1950s, most of the "H" model Mustangs succumbed to the scrapper's torch. Of the 555 "H" models built, only six are known to remain, and only two of that half-dozen are in flyable condition.

Johnson at first searched on foot for the Mustang, which was located on federal land. "I had a friend call me and tell me that he had found the wreck," Johnson said. "He had gone into the area and had found some small pieces of metal, but nothing like what I saw in the fuzzy pictures in the military accident report. It just didn't jive."

An R22 Robinson helicopter was chartered for the reconnaissance mission, and after four hours over the crash site on a warm June morning, the Mustang was spotted. "It was really like looking for a needle in a haystack," Johnson said.

The wreckage of 44-64697 yielded two rebuildable wings, the tail section, and numerous cockpit and fuselage parts. The Mustang will undergo extensive restoration in Texas. (Robert A. Kropp Collection)

“There’s an awful lot of mountain, scrub oak and chaparral bushes out there that can hide an airplane. You can literally be within several feet of something and not see it. When I saw a little tiny piece of aluminum wing root glinting in the sun, I knew we had found what we were looking for.”

The accident report indicated the Mustang had broken apart in a supersonic dive, a fact confirmed by Johnson and his two partners, Neil Jones, chief helicopter pilot for Arizona Wing and Rotor, and Scott Urschel of Urschel Manufacturing Inc. The Mustang’s wings were hidden in underbrush several miles apart from one another, and the rest of the wreckage was scattered over several miles.

The trio then chartered a trip to the wreckage and spent two days photographing and cataloging their find. Although the Mustang had suffered extensive damage in the crash, some items were found in relatively good condition.

“I had never been to an airplane wreck that hadn’t been picked through by souvenir hunters before,” Johnson said. “We found everything just as the military had left it; the throttle was cracked wide open, the radios were still tuned to their final frequencies, and the Merlin crankcase contained gummy oil. The armor windscreen was up against a bush, and the pilot’s seat armor was resting against a rock. Access panels could still be opened with a Dzus tool.”

The feeling of elation in finding this undisturbed wreckage was sobered by the discovery of Lt. Westlund’s parachute harness and the remains of his parachute. “It put things into perspective pretty darn quick.”

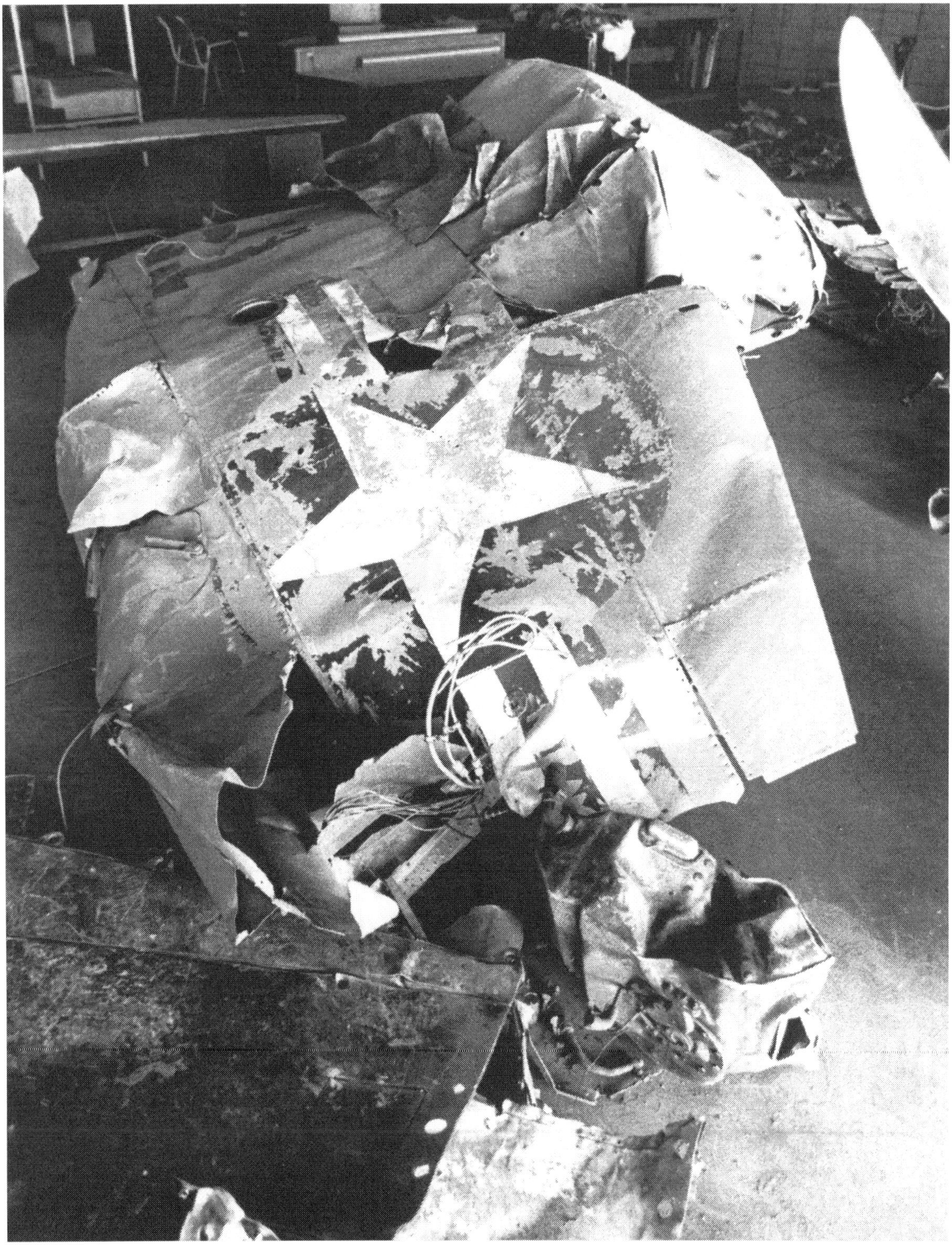

The Mustang was transported to a covered hangar in Scottsdale, Arizona, where Johnson and his partners examined and inventoried their find. Original ammunition boxes were still in place and undamaged, although the original armament group of .50-caliber Browning machine guns had been removed before the final flight. (Robert A. Kropp Collection)

Aviation historian Richard Johnson stands near the vertical stabilizer of the TF-51H Mustang he helped to recover. Despite almost 40 years of exposure under the Arizona sun, unit markings are still discernable. (Robert A. Kropp Collection)

Johnson and his two partners decided the Mustang was worth saving and then went through a six-week process to obtain the airplane legally. "It was a real paper chase," Johnson said. "Because the airplane was located on wilderness land, I first approached the United States Forest Service to gauge their feelings on a cleanup of this site. Surprisingly enough, they were most agreeable, but only if I was able to get a release from the government for what they called 'government property on government land.'"

Forest Service officials knew about the wreck—it was one of several airplanes that dotted the mountaintops in the area—and were more than amenable to the cleanup. Many years ago, it was standard procedure for rangers or Forest Service employees to remove, dismantle, destroy or mark airplane wreckage that would otherwise tempt curious hikers into dangerous areas or fool pilots into thinking the area was the site of a recent aviation incident.

The "H" model Mustang escaped scrapping and destruction because of its remoteness, but either the military or the Forest Service had marked the fuselage and wings with a thick, latex-type paint to indicate the aircraft was listed on crash rosters in case it was spotted from the air.

The Legal Office of the U.S. Air Force eventually released the airplane to the trio, but only after the crash paperwork was pulled out of the archives and reviewed—even though it had been forgotten for almost 40 years. Johnson said the request was examined by historians at Wright-Patterson Air Force Base, who decided to release the rare Mustang because of "its extensive damage and the cost and effort that would be involved in the recovery."

Neil Jones, in a Bell JetRanger, lowers a wing of the recovered TF-51H Mustang. (Robert A. Kropp Collection)

Wing gun ammunition boxes look as good as the day Lt. Westlund took off from Fresno, California. (Robert A. Kropp Collection)

"There were times when I thought we were going to be denied, and then everything started happening at once," Johnson said. "Within a couple of days, we had lined everything up, and we were hoping the weather was going to hold so we could operate the helicopter. It was touch and go. We were fighting temperatures in the high 90s in the mountains—not very conducive to operating helicopters."

A team of eight men worked several days at the crash site, all while being observed by the Forest Service to make sure the sanctity of the wilderness area was not disturbed. Johnson said 20 loads of parts were removed from the mountainside by a Bell JetRanger helicopter.

"We used nets and nylon cargo slings and everything we had at our disposal to remove the wreckage," he said. "We used gloves to clean up small parts from rocks and trees, and the only thing we left behind was the Merlin. It is heavily damaged, but it's worth saving, and we hope to get it out [later], even if we have to disassemble it into components."

The wreckage was flown from the mountainside into a nearby valley, where it was loaded onto trucks and transported into a covered hangar in Scottsdale. The tension of removing some of the more unwieldy parts from the mountainside was broken when a family of chipmunks (flying squirrels?) evacuated a wing in droves as the JetRanger pulled it airborne.

A post-recovery inspection uncovered perfect ammunition boxes in the gun bays, although all weapons had been removed during the training airplane's service days and the gun ports were faired over with stainless steel. Hydraulic lines were found to contain fluid, and radio sets still had tuners and crystals intact.

The landing gear, which was still tucked up in one of the wings, could be fully extended; wiring in electrical junction boxes still smelled of

Wing section and propeller after recovery. (Robert A. Kropp Collection)

fungicide preservative; and data plaques, painted stenciling, and pencil-marked inspection notes were still legible in the crumpled fuselage. When a fuel cap was removed in a wing section, the intact rubber fuel cell still emitted a faint scent of aromatic fuel vapors.

Lt. Westlund's family members were presented with a North American Aviation-marked rudder pedal and some cockpit items when they visited the airplane. Ironically, the family had talked about the possibility of visiting Arizona to conduct their own search for the wreckage of the Mustang to put a chapter in their family history to rest.

"We'll all never know just what happened during those last few moments as the Mustang fell to earth," Johnson said. "The accident report indicated Lt. Westlund tried to bail out of the stricken airplane, but got tangled up in the wreckage. His family told me that the plane allegedly had been back at the field twice before his fateful trip for repairs to the oxygen system.

"It was really a strange twist of fate. Lt. Westlund was a World War II combat pilot. His family showed me gun camera footage taken in some of his P-38 missions in Europe. The man survived some brutal aerial combat over Axis skies, and then he died in a freak mishap after stopping over in California to visit his sick grandmother and attempting to make an everyday cross-country navigation run.

"The accident report indicates he suffered oxygen deprivation and blacked out in flight. He came to with the airplane in a dive he couldn't bring under control, so he tried to get out of the airplane, and the Mustang just broke up around him. We'll never know just what happened up there, and perhaps it's better that way."

Although the trio had discussed keeping the Mustang for restoration, the rarity of the airplane and the great expenses borne in recovering the wreckage prompted them to sell it to a Southwest-based Mustang restorer. The rare Mustang was crated and shipped to Texas where the new owner, who has asked to remain anonymous, plans to rebuild and mate the wings and tail section to a P-51H fuselage currently under restoration.

The fuselage of the wrecked fighter will yield many valuable parts to the restoration, and the composite aircraft will reportedly be registered with the Federal Aviation Administration using the serial number of Lt. Westlund's former mount. The owner believes the P-51H Mustang eventually will return to the skies.

Arizona's rugged Galiuro Mountains also have claimed a BT-13 trainer, a Boeing B-50, and a B-24 Liberator over the years.

17246

Chapter 23

Bell P-39 Airacobra Recovered from Canadian Lake

Nicholas A. Veronico

During World War II, the United States lend-leased the Russians 4,924 Bell P-39 Airacobras. The 25th Ferrying Squadron, 7th Ferrying Group of the Air Transport Command (ATC), was responsible for delivering lend-lease aircraft to Nome, Alaska, where the Russian pilots would then fly them to the battlefields in Europe.

This Factory-fresh Bell P-39 Airacobra is ready to go to war. An Airacobra similar to this aircraft was recovered from a lake in Canada for restoration. (Warren M, Bodie Collection via A. Kevin Grantham)

However, 178 of the P-39s that left the factory to serve with the Soviet air force did not reach Alaska. These lost aircraft are a wreckchaser's dream come true—somewhere between Buffalo, New York, and Nome, Alaska, lie the remains of these fighters.

Two Russia-bound Airacobras took off from Fort Nelson, British Columbia, Canada, on the morning of December 6, 1943. Second Lt. Hal Coons and his wingman, Second Lt. Delos R. Carpenter, were airborne at 11:05 am MWT. Their first stop was Whitehorse, Yukon Territory, Canada, with a final destination of Ladd Field in Nome.

For this flight, Lt. Carpenter was flying P-39Q-15, serial number 44-2485. He had logged 475 hours flight time while in the Army Air Forces, 40 of those hours in the P-39.

Once airborne, both planes climbed through the "high overcast" and headed toward Fort Nelson on course. One hour later, Lt. Coons decided to let down through a hole in the overcast. As the aircraft descended, they became separated.

After making a number of 360-degree turns in an attempt to locate Coons, Lt. Carpenter, who was now low on fuel, decided to belly land on a frozen lake. He jettisoned his drop tanks and landed the aircraft with only minor damage to the propeller, but the right wing had buckled. The aircraft broke through the ice but remained afloat.

Lt. Carpenter removed his survival gear, which consisted of a shovel, an axe, rope, and smoke flares, and then headed to the shore, where he managed to build a fire. At approximately 8:30 pm, he made contact with Lake Army Airways.

The following day at about 3:00 pm, Lt. Carpenter was rescued by a "ski plane." The Army Air Forces reported that the ice was so thin and the lake so short, fuel had to be drained from the ski plane to get him out.

Lt. Coons had decided to set down because he had suffered a compass failure. Unable to locate Lt. Carpenter, he had followed a valley until he flew out from under the clouds, where he recognized his position as south of Fort Laird. Coons returned safely to his point of origin, Fort Nelson, to attempt the flight to Whitehorse another day.

Former U.S. Navy SEAL divers George Carter, left, and Wayne Lloyd, near the Airacobra's tail section after recovery. Carter and Lloyd unbolted the tail section under water to lighten the load when the helicopter lifted the wings and center section out of the water. (Gary Larkins)

Lifting the fuselage, center section, and wings back into the air after more than 47 years. (Gary Larkins)

Forty-seven years later, warbird restorer Gary Larkins of Auburn, California, set out in search of Lt. Carpenter's P-39. Larkins began by looking for the aircraft at the coordinates listed on the Air Force crash report. At the time of the crash, this area was "uncharted."

The Air Force listed the crash location as 120 miles due north of the Smith River, so Larkins' first two trips were spent searching all the lakes north of the reported crash site. Although these first two trips were unsuccessful, he secured the necessary permits from the Canadian Ministry of Transport—for the P-39Q-15 and two other P-39s—in anticipation of a successful recovery of this aircraft.

On Larkins's third trip he located 44-2485 in Carpenter Lake, 240 miles from Watson Lake, Yukon Territory, Canada. The aircraft was recovered on July 19 and 20, 1990, at the tail end of a 10-day trip into the Canadian wilderness.

Upon arriving at this particular lake, Larkins and his crew immediately knew that they had found the crash site. The area was littered with 55-gallon drums, the remnants of tents, wood stoves stenciled with U.S. Army Corps of Engineers, and a medical kit.

George Carter and Wayne Lloyd, both former U.S. Navy SEALs, worked with Larkins on the recovery effort. They are also the same divers

Bell P-39Q Airacobra, serial number 44-2485, on a trailer at Watson Lake. The helicopter flight from the crash site to Watson Lake took more than nine hours and covered 240 miles in the air. (Gary Larkins)

who had dived through two inches of ice to locate a PBM Mariner in Chesapeake Bay, only to find out that the aircraft was not worth recovering.

Larkins, Carter, and Lloyd arrived at the lake in a de Havilland Beaver fitted with floats. Aside from the regular camping gear, they took a rowboat, six dive tanks, a pair of lift bags, tools and a sonar scanner. Because of space limitations, they could not get an outboard engine on board the Beaver, but a set of oars fit nicely.

Their first two days at the site were spent rowing the scanner the length of the lake. Once contact was made with the aircraft, they began diving on the Airacobra. They placed a buoy on the fuselage and then began to search for other parts underwater.

The nose of the aircraft was at a depth of 60 feet, and the tail was at 30 feet. While the aircraft was underwater, the divers removed the empennage. Carter and Lloyd had to work fast as they only had six air tanks, two of which were expended in the removal and recovery of the tail.

Larkins raised the tail to the surface with a rope and then towed it to shore, stroke-by-stroke, with the rowboat. On shore, the horizontal was removed and readied for transport.

Next they raised the airframe with lift bags. Again using only the rowboat, Larkins towed it into shallow water where they rigged it with a harness so that the helicopter could pick it up. Once rigged, the air was let out of the bags, setting the P-39 back on the lake bottom.

After finding the P-39, Larkins radioed for the helicopter. It took three days for the Bell 205 to reach the wreck site at the right time of day. Once over the lake, a diver in the water coordinated with the helicopter pilot to pick up the P-39. It took an hour to get the hook to the diver and onto the airplane.

After this hour of maneuvering, fuel for the helicopter was getting critical. Once the hook was secured to the P-39, the fuselage and wings were lifted onto shore. While buckets full of mud were removed and the harness was double checked, the helicopter pilot took a well-deserved rest.

When the Army Air Forces salvaged the aircraft, they had removed the engine, cockpit instrumentation, and the landing gear, flying those items out to Fort Nelson. In the process of salvaging the P-39, the Army Air Forces had removed numerous pieces, setting them on the ice near the airplane.

When spring came, the ice thawed, and all the parts left behind sank straight down to a depth of 60 feet. Divers Carter and Lloyd recovered a number of inspection panels and the cowling, located the bent prop, and brought a number of other small parts to the surface.

Netting was rigged over the fuselage and wings to foil the lift, and a drag chute was deployed for directional stability during the airlift to Watson Lake. Once the P-39 was ready to be transported, the Beaver was dispatched to drop fuel at two locations while en route to pick up the divers, their gear, and the P-39's empennage.

Transporting the P-39 over the 240 miles to Watson Lake took 9.5 hours. The Bell 205 was only able to make 60 knots and, at times, had to clear mountain ridges as high as 14,000 feet.

Once at Watson Lake, the wing was demated from the fuselage, and all the aircraft components were packed into shipping containers. P-39Q 44-2485 is in excellent shape. Both the Bell data plate and the Russian export data plate are still in the aircraft. The Russian red star is still visible on the empennage and the wings.

An Allison engine has already been acquired, and Larkins plans to recover two more P-39s to provide enough parts for a flyable restoration. Currently 44-2485 is located at the Tillamook Air Museum in Tillamook, Oregon. It can be viewed on the web at: www.tillamookair.com.

The X-31 Enhanced Fighter Maneuverability program was run out of Edwards Air Force Base, California, during the early 1990s. The Defense Advanced Research Projects Agency, NASA, the U.S. Air Force, U.S. Navy, the German Federal Ministry of Defense, Rockwell International's North American Aircraft Division, and Deutsche Aerospace collaborated to build this high-maneuverability fighter test bed. The aircraft flew at 70 degrees angle of attack for the first time on Sept. 18, 1992. Nearly three years later, on Jan. 19, 1995, pilot Karl-Heinz Lang was forced to abandon the aircraft after it became uncontrollable approximately 1.5 miles north of Edwards AFB, California. The wreckage was recovered for the accident investigation. (top: NASA, bottom: NASA/Tony Landis)

Part III:

Wreckchasing Resources

On Aug. 18, 1943, two P-38 Lightnings collided in the skies above San Diego, California. Both Lightnings were from the 329th Fighter Squadron, 330th Fighter Group, based at NAS San Diego. P-38H-5-LO 42-66814, piloted by Keith Mahon, fell into a home in the Linda Vista area of San Diego. Mahon was killed along with three children in the home. The second aircraft, P-38H-5-LO 42-66806, was piloted by William P. Jones. He bailed out of the stricken fighter, and it crashed into a nearby canyon. (Veronico collection)

Appendix I

Military Aircraft Wrecks by State

This listing of known aircraft wrecks was taken from the Civil Air Patrol's list of aircraft wreckage, as well as from the Department of the Air Force, Headquarters Western Aerospace Rescue and Recovery Center's Aircraft Wreckage Locator for California. Most smaller civilian aircraft types, e.g., Cessnas, Pipers, etc., have been removed from the list. This is a partial listing and is in no way complete. It is a common practice to delete aircraft from the crash locator lists as they become overgrown and unrecognizable. Note that these coordinates are intended as a starting point for research and in no way are they exact, nor is there a guarantee that any wreckage can be found at these sites.

Aircraft Type	Date	Latitude	Longitude	Remarks
Alabama				
T-34A	01/09/84	3118N	08647W	Wreck probably removed
Navy TH-57	10/27/82	3148N	08638W	2 miles south of Greenville
USAF T-37B	06/26/72	3214N	08655W	Details unknown
Arizona				
F-4	06/24/70	3131N	10940W	Bu. 637609, unmarked
AD-7	——	3139N	11025W	Scattered, unmarked
T-33A-1-LO	06/26/69	3145N	11018W	USAF 52-9496, silver
F4U/FG-1	——	3157N	10917W	7,000 ft. level, N.Y. Reserve markings
B-24	——	3210N	11053W	Fuselage at 6,000 ft. level
F-4	——	3210N	11316W	Details unknown
B-29/B-50	——	3217N	11146W	Scattered, unmarked
F-86D	——	3227N	11040W	7,000 ft. level of Mt. Lemon
B-50	——	3228N	11016W	USAF 46-04, scattered, unmarked
TF-104G-LO	10/29/69	3228N	11238W	USAF 63-8466, silver, scattered
F-14	02/28/83	3229N	11357W	Wreckage probably removed
P-51D-10-NA	——	3233N	11017W	USAF 44-14697, Bassett Peak
F-104	05/28/66	3234N	11243W	Silver
F4U	01/24/66	3236N	11225W	Marked
F-8C	04/07/65	3240N	11406W	Unknown
F-100C-25-NA	04/24/64	3243N	11251W	USAF 54-2067, burned
F-4C	05/06/65	3243N	10851W	Details unknown
DC-3	——	3244N	11003W	N127G, silver with red trim
BT-13	——	3246N	11027W	Oak Grove Canyon, Air Force markings
Interstate	03/16/65	3248N	11208W	N37292
BT-13	——	3250N	11051W	Unmarked pieces, Putnam Wash
FM-2	——	3250N	10938W	Bu. 55096, Safford
F-86	——	3257N	11043W	Wreckage marked
F-86	——	3302N	11432W	Scattered, unmarked
T-37	02/27/70	3305N	11111W	Silver, marked with yellow

Aircraft Type	Date	Latitude	Longitude	Remarks
P-51	——	3306N	11259W	Scattered, unmarked, Citrus Valley
AT-6D-NT	——	3311N	11211W	Burned parts visible
P-51	——	3311N	11230W	In small gully
T-33	——	3317N	11057W	AF098 marked
F-80	——	3319N	11139W	Details unknown
F-86F-30-NA	——	3320N	11012W	USAF 52-5100, silver
F4U	——	3320N	11111W	Broken up, marked
F4U	——	3320N	11218W	N9409, marked
F-104	04/17/65	3320N	11218W	Details unknown
AT-6	——	3321N	11110W	Burned, marked
B-24	——	3324N	11432W	Burned, unmarked, Mule Wash
F4U	——	3330N	11116W	Broken up, scattered, Weavers Needle
F-100D-25-NA	02/26/64	3334N	11245W	USAF 55-3605, scattered
TBM-3E	——	3336N	11106W	N8037E, wreck probably removed
AT-6	——	3338N	11137W	Adams Mesa
B-18	02/17/70	3340N	10955W	N230C, Bonito Prairie, white
T-33	——	3342N	10945W	Air National Guard, unmarked
F-80	——	3343N	11310W	USAF 669, scattered
P-51	01/01/52	3345N	11340W	Tail intact
C-47	——	3349N	11101W	Tail visible, scattered
P-80C-5-LO	——	3351N	11229W	USAF 47-547, scattered, unmarked
B-17	——	3354N	10929W	Scattered
C-45	——	3355N	10934W	Silver with Air Force star
AT-6	——	3355N	11213W	413283, unmarked
BT-13	——	3402N	11127W	Tail intact
F8F	——	3404N	11152W	N5151, top of peak, burned
BT-13	——	3405N	11127W	White/red, scattered
B-25	——	3405N	11214W	Unmarked
F-100	——	3406N	11315W	Scattered
BT-13	——	3407N	11125W	Unmarked
AT-6	——	3412N	11222W	Details unknown
F-84	——	3413N	11222W	Details unknown
T-33	12/08/76	3414N	11126W	N29147, unmarked
F-104	03/03/66	3415N	11252W	Silver
F-84	——	3415N	11357W	N69911, scattered
P-51 Mustang	——	3420N	11100W	N4893, unmarked
T-33	——	3420N	11133W	Marked yellow
Timm	——	3425N	11235W	NC6298, unmarked
F-100	04/16/66	3426N	11127W	Scattered
F-100	04/10/70	3427N	11122W	Camouflaged markings, burned
AT-6	——	3430N	11155W	Marked
B-25	——	3430N	11244W	In draw near top of mountain
F-84F	——	3431N	11220W	Unmarked
T-33	——	3432N	11154W	Details unknown
F8F	——	3432N	11246W	Scattered, exploded on impact
B-25	02/04/77	3433N	11412W	Scattered, Crossman Peak
F-8	08/02/69	3446N	11209W	Green
UC-78	——	3456N	11307W	Southeast slope of Mt. Hope

Aircraft Type	Date	Latitude	Longitude	Remarks
P-51	——	3500N	11124W	Ashurst Lake area
BT-13	——	3520N	11208W	NC6737, unmarked
T-33A-5-LO	06/24/70	3540N	11225W	USAF 57-0766, silver
T-33 or F-89	——	3540N	11353W	Marked
P-38	——	3550N	11150W	NX5101, unmarked
AT-6	——	3551N	11229W	Partially covered
P-47	——	3552N	11223W	NC9475, scattered
F4U Corsair	08/18/83	3509N	11212W	Wreck probably removed
California				
P-51	——	3152N	11451W	Details unknown
FJ-4	08/24/61	3233N	11642W	Bu. 139290, burned, unmarked
C-46	——	3235N	11649W	Details unknown
FJ-4	03/27/61	3236N	11651W	V-39291, at 2,500 ft. level
SNB	——	3236N	11614W-1/2N	NC68228, marked
F9F-2	——	3238N	11650W	Bu. 125142, NAS San Diego on tail
F4U	——	3240N	11700W	Bu. reported as 81140
F6F-3	11/30/43	3240N	11641W-1/2N	Bu. 66141
B-52	——	3247N	11515W	Marked
PBY	——	3248N	11614W	Details unknown
DC-3	——	3248N	11624W	Unmarked
F4U-1D	——	3251N	11612W	Bu. 57325
A4D	01/09/61	3254N	11543W	Unmarked
P-39	——	3254N	11627W	USAAF 42-6695
F4U	——	3255N	11504W	Marked
F4F	——	3259N	11550W	Marked
P-51	——	3310N	11438W	Unmarked, listed as AF2120
F8U	06/31/63	3302N	11553W	Bu. 146977, marked
UC-78	——	3302N	11707W	NC44000, marked
F8U-1	02/17/60	3304N	11504W	Bulldozed over
L-19	10/20/63	3305N	11634W	USAF 40088
F8D	——	3310N	11720W	Details unknown
SNJ	——	3325N	11615W	Details unknown
F8U-2NE	09/03/64	3322N	11531W	Bu. 150881, scattered, unmarked
F8U	03/27/63	3322N	11648W	Scattered
AD	——	3322N	11731W	Marked
FG-1	——	3329N	11542W	Marked
F8U-1	08/03/60	3330N	11633W	Bu. 145504
FJ-3	——	3331N	11517W	Listed as NGG5814
F-80A-1-LO	——	3332N	11620W	USAAF 44-85208
TBF	1950	3332N	11747W	Underwater, not visible
T-33	09/18/64	3332N	11729W	USAF 52-9670
F8U	09/20/61	3333N	11626W	Burned, unmarked
AD-5	1960	3334N	11619W	Marked
SBD	——	3334N	11732W	Marked
F8U-1	11/15/62	3335N	11618W	Bu. 143728, marked yellow
B-24	——	3339N	11449W	Details unknown
AD	——	3340N	11745W-1/2W	USMC, unmarked

Aircraft Type	Date	Latitude	Longitude	Remarks
AD	——	3341N	11646W	Details unknown
PT-26	——	3342N	11637W	NC60506, unmarked
C-45	1948	3342N	11733W	Marked, yellow X
UH-1	04/13/67	3342N	11732W	USMC markings
BT-13	——	3344N	11635W	Details unknown
P2V	05/29/63	3344N	11734W	Scattered
BT-13	——	3346N	11637W	Details unknown
F9F	——	3346N	11726W	Details unknown
F9F	——	3346N	11740W	Details unknown
F3F	——	3347N	11743W	Bu. 5843, marked
P-38	——	3348N	11726W	Marked
C-47	12/14/61	3348N	11737W	Burned
PT-19	——	3349N	11658W	N48588, unmarked
F-86	——	3355N	11611W-1/2W	Details unknown
F-89	——	3358N	11743W	Unmarked
P-51	——	3400N	12000W	Listed as AF4542
AT-6	——	3401N	11545W	Details unknown
F9F	06/23/61	3402N	11601W	Listed as Bu. 147380
PT-19	——	3402N	11648W	NC56575
BT-15	——	3403N	11556W	USAAF 42-1833, marked
B-25	01/26/55	3404N	11648W	USAF 44-86805, marked
C-47	12/01/52	3406N	11649W	USAF 45-1124, marked
PT-17	——	3408N	11646W	Details unknown
BT-13	——	3408N	11711W	NC69500, marked
A-26	——	3410N	11735W	N717L, unmarked
BT-13	——	3410N	11717W-1/2N	Details unknown
B-26	——	3411N	11815W-1/2N	Details unknown
SNJ-5	1944	3412N	11652W-1/2N	Marked yellow
F-100C-25-NA	09/21/56	3412N	11711W	USAF 54-2027
F-100	05/27/64	3412N	11722W	Scattered, unmarked
C-47	——	3412N	11732W	Marked
SNJ	——	3412N	11759W	Marked
C-45	——	3412N	11816W-1/2W	Details unknown
P-38L-VN	——	3413N	11819W	USAAF 44-24918, marked
AT-6	——	3413N	11807W-1/2N	Marked
BT-13	——	3414N	11647W	Marked
A-26	——	3414N	11733W	Listed as 5488, marked
BT-13	——	3415N	11815W	Details unknown
B-24	——	3416N	11722W	Details unknown
P-51	——	3416N	11722W	Details unknown
F6F	——	3416N	11736W	Details unknown
UC-78	1952	3416N	11808W-1/2W	Unmarked, scattered
F-89	01/31/57	3416N	11822W	Scattered
C-45	1945	3417N	11725W	Details unknown
T-33	02/10/59	3417N	11740W	USAF 56-3683, scattered
F9F-5	02/02/57	3417N	11742W	Bu. 125559
F6F (2)	——	3417N	11739W	Marked
C-46	——	3418N	11739W	Reported as 15190, unmarked

Aircraft Type	Date	Latitude	Longitude	Remarks
B-24	——	3419N	11809W	Reported as 42-90434, marked
H-19	1954	3422N	11744W	Marked
C-47	09/21/61	3420N	11836W	N16002, marked
F-86	10/24/56	3421N	11722W	Details unknown
P-80A-1-LO	——	3421N	11729W	Reported as 51371
AT-6	05/14/60	3421N	11825W	N2801G, unmarked
F-84F	02/27/57	3422N	11428W	Reported as AF065, bailout
B-57E-MA	05/03/63	3422N	11924W	USAF 55-4296, scattered
T-34	12/31/64	3423N	11755W	N5506V, yellow with black trim
B-25	——	3423N	11814W	Scattered, silver
C-46A-10-CU	——	3423N	11752W	USAF 41-12363, marked
SBD	——	3424N	11822W	Marked
T-33	——	3425N	11910W	Details unknown
AT-6	——	3427N	11859W	Details unknown
F-86 (2)	09/04/56	3428N	11803W	61338 and ANG 48313, unmarked
P-51	——	3430N	11900W	Details unknown
C-47	——	3432N	11841W	Details unknown
H-34	07/08/64	3432N	11859-1/2W	Bu. 145714, red & black #5 on side
BT-13	——	3432N	11859W	Burned, unmarked
DC-3	——	3432N	12001W	NC63107, marked
Curtiss Jenny	——	3432N	12001W-1/2N	Details unknown
B-24	——	3434N	11943W	Scattered, unmarked
B-26 (2)	——	3434N	11735W-1/2N	AF677 & AF174, unmarked
F4F	——	3434N	12013W	Details unknown
Howard DGA	——	3435N	11905W	NC69965, marked
BT-13	1957	3435N	11905W	N63118
A-1	08/19/65	3436N	11621W	Reported as 35331, white
P-38	08/04/65	3437N	12012W	Burned
P-51	——	3438N	11719W-1/2W	AF978, may have been removed
Stinson	——	3440N	11923W	Unmarked, in river
DC-3	——	3441N	11858W	NC18645, unmarked
P-38	05/28/56	3442N	12009W	N504MH, removal attempted
A-4C	08/18/66	3443N	11617W	Details unknown
F4F	10/31/59	3443N	11907W	Reported as aircraft #259
T-33	12/23/65	3446N	11523W	USAF 53-5956, marked
AD-5	08/25/61	3448N	11755W	Reported as aircraft #33876
F-4	07/10/67	3449N	11722W-1/2W	65-0675, silver, burned, marked
C-47	——	3449N	11911W	Aircraft #KC345
Howard	11/18/61	3451N	11501W	N1441
P-51	——	3451N	11535W	N7369B, unmarked
F-4D-28-MC	05/18/67	3453N	11558W	USAF 65-0668, silver, burned
HH-43B	12/07/62	3455N	11830W	USAF 60-286, slated to be removed
F6F (2)	——	3455N	11900W	Mid-air collision
T-33	——	3455N	11916W	Navy, wing only, unmarked
AT-6	——	3455N	11956W	Unmarked
C-47	——	3456N	11532W	Reported as 112363, marked
B-26	01/31/56	3456N	11556W	Tail only, thought to be an A-26
UC-78	——	3456N	11837W	Reported as 298831

Aircraft Type	Date	Latitude	Longitude	Remarks
AT-10	——	3457N	11835W	Reported as 23512, unmarked
AT-6	——	3458N	12013W	Details unknown
BT-13	——	3502N	11831W	USAAF 41-1500, marked
BT-13	——	3502N	11833W	Reported as 63334
F4U	——	3502N	11850W	Reported as 1542
A-20	——	3502N	11829W-1/2N	Reported as USAAF 41-1564
P-51	04/04/51	3504N	11718W	Possibly removed
XB-70/F-104	06/08/66	3505N	11703W	Silver
F-10	02/11/64	3506N	11640W	Scattered
F4U	——	3512N	11823W-1/2N	Marked
T-34	11/18/60	3513N	12006W	N5507V, marked
F-104C	04/12/63	3515N	11610W	56-896, details unknown
C-45	12/16/61	3517N	11635W	N16020, burned
Aeronca	——	3520N	12038W	NC31994, unmarked
Howard	——	3522N	11825W	N67764, unmarked
UC-78	——	3522N	12037W-1/2W	UC69080, unmarked
HRS-2 (S-55)	——	3535N	11529W	Marked
P-38L-1-LO	——	3531N	11612W	USAAF 44-24790
PT-19	——	3528N	12059W	NC48885, marked
Single-Engine Fighter		3528N	11700W	3500 ft. level, silver wing, orange wingtip
Stinson	10/12/47	3533N	11531W	NC591000, unmarked
AT-6	10/26/45	3538N	11535W	AF2913, unmarked
KC-135	07/08/64	3537N	11647W-1/2N	Widely scattered, burned, visible
F-105	07/08/64	3541N	11644W	Partially removed
F-100	——	3542N	11657W	Marked yellow
PQ-14	——	3543N	11646W	USAAF 43-4439, unmarked
JRB-4 (C-45F)	02/03/49	3543N	11759W	Bu. 90550, unmarked
F-4C	02/20/67	3547N	11556W	Reported as 65-0656, marked
B-25	1944	3547N	11838W	USAAF 41-30140, marked
AD-5Q	04/11/61	3550N	12110W	#134988, burned
Stearman	08/02/57	3557N	12112W	NC5722B, unmarked
F-104	——	3557N	11831W	Scattered, turbine visible
AD-4	12/17/61	3606N	11641W	Reported as 42203
FG-1	06/13/47	3603N	11636W	Marked yellow
WACO	1947	3606N	11807W	NC17745, marked
Stinson	05/14/53	3607N	12100N	N9890, marked
UC-78	1946	3611N	11822W	NC1342, marked
PT-17	06/06/46	3612N	11820W	NC6454, marked
BT-13	1951	3613N	11806W	Wreckage is orange
F-100	08/18/58	3615N	11645W	Scattered
F-100	10/22/56	3618N	11643W	AF654, details unknown
A-4	10/15/65	3622N	11850W	White, aircraft #504
B-17	1942	3622N	12045W	Unmarked
F6F-5	1945	3623N	11813W	Bu. 71033
SA-16	——	3625N	11719W	Details unknown
A-20	——	3626N	12154W	Marked
C-45	04/08/64	3629N	11814W	Marked, 7 SW of Mt. Whitney
C-46	01/13/59	3634N	11843W	N1240N, marked

Aircraft Type	Date	Latitude	Longitude	Remarks
R4D (C-47)	02/02/45	3635N	11820W	Navy 39584, marked
SNJ	08/23/52	3642N	11821W	Navy 0994, marked
P-40C	10/24/41	3642N	11831W	USAAF 39-287, details unknown
U-3B	06/18/66	3643N	11823W	Blue/white, AF06081, visible
H-19	06/26/66	3644N	11821W	Bu. 130222, blue, submerged in lake
P-38	1942	3644N	12108W	Marked
B-24	10/20/44	3645N	11751W	Reported as 42-41444, marked
SA-16A	05/25/53	3654N	11829W	AF7173, marked
B-52B-BO	09/17/56	3655N	12000W	USAF 53-0393
F2H-3	08/02/56	3656N	11822W	Unmarked
F-86	11/23/54	3704N	12051W	Reported as 3766, unmarked
B-18	1940	3705N	11825W	"Army" on wing
TV-2	10/07/56	3706N	12151W	Reported as 8060
F9F-8	——	3707N	12138W	Bu. 146374
F3H-2	09/20/60	3708N	12012W	Bu. 143442, marked
F3H	10/07/61	3708N	12212W	Navy 3766, marked
C-47	——	3712N	12130W	White, marked
TV-2	04/14/55	3712N	12205W	Bu. 138055, marked
P-51	——	3714N	11851W	Details unknown
A3D	10/26/62	3714N	12055W	Possibly removed
F2H-4	02/22/59	3717N	12207W	Reported as 127614
A-4	07/08/65	3722N	12121W-1/2N	Navy NF461
F8J (2)	03/24/59	3727N	12134W	Bu. 144448 & 144451, wing section visible
PT-19	——	3729N	12141W	USAAF 41-25537, marked
PT-19	09/25/60	3730N	12220W	NC69086
T-33	01/11/65	3734N	12157W	Reported as 41506, scattered
F4H-2B	10/29/56	3734N	12144W	N125651, unmarked
A-4E	02/20/64	3736N	11852W	Bu. 150077
R5D	02/17/56	3737N	12156W	Bu. 39116
BT-13	08/08/48	3738N	12158W	NC57365, marked
T-28	02/17/55	3743N	12159W	Bu. 17602
A-4D	02/20/64	3744N	11904W	Navy 504, scattered
F-101	01/10/64	3747N	12205W	Reported as USAF 15438, burned
FJ-3	10/26/56	3751N	12212W	Bu. 135978
C-47	03/16/45	3751N	11912W	USAAF 43-3067, 9,000 ft. level, marked
UC-78	06/04/47	3745N	12038W	NC5458, marked
F9F-6	10/30/56	3755N	12210W	Reported as 12758
TV-2	06/29/56	3801N	12128W	Navy 750, unmarked
P-61	08/28/44	3804N	11926W	Known dynamited by USAAF late 1940s
C-45	——	3804N	12238W	Details unknown
P-39 or P-63	——	3804N	12255W	Details unknown
A-4	07/10/66	3807N	11935W	Navy 2789, scattered
H-34	03/23/65	3821N	11939W	Reported as 48935, intact
T-28	07/02/65	3823N	11204W-1/2W	N8321H
F4U	01/29/52	3825N	11933W	Bu. 82067, marked
F2H	08/25/55	3831N	12236W	Bu. 123344, unmarked
B-24D-20-CO	1942	3835N	12310W	USAAF 41-24262, unmarked
T-33A	02/19/56	3839N	12237W	USAF 51-9307, unmarked

Aircraft Type	Date	Latitude	Longitude	Remarks
Fighters (2)	08/26/54	3839N	12239W-1/2N	AF5254 & 5264, marked
T-33	04/12/61	3842N	12132W	Details unknown, burned
S-2	01/16/66	3855N	12014W	Bu. 136542, gray, scattered
Fighter	02/13/58	3855N	12332W	Bu. 135048, marked
Constellation	03/09/64	3900N	11953W	N86504, Paradise Airlines
C-46	Apr 1944	3901N	12056W	Marked
P-39	03/21/43	3901N	12222W	USAAF 42-9120, scattered
BT-13	10/25/50	3904N	12049W	N56639, marked
AT-11	12/17/49	3912N	12052W	AF9564, unmarked
BT-13	03/07/47	3913N	12033W	NC58661, marked
BT-13	01/13/47	3915N	12116W	NC62742, marked
Stinson	05/30/47	3916N	12101W	NC97999, marked
T-33	11/13/55	3925N	12020W	Reported as 4339, unmarked
T-33	02/27/57	3925N	12043W	Reported as 51-4495, unmarked
BT-13	12/03/45	3927N	12242W	Reported as AF9669, marked
TBM-3U	Aug 1960	3928N	12016W	NC109Z, probably removed
Navy Jet	——	3939N	12116W	Scattered, unmarked
BT-13	——	3939N	12251W	Scattered, burned
B-17F	05/30/43	3955N	12306W	42-5318, Leech Lake Mountain
B-29	1944	3957N	12144W	May be B-29A-50-BN, USAAF 44-61843
A-4C	08/19/66	4004N	12404W	Details unknown
L-20	01/12/59	4032N	12047W	Reported as 43-2086, marked
BT-13	11/13/47	4039N	12112W	NC58778, marked
B-26	1944	4059N	12250W	Details unknown, marked
B-26	——	4101N	12253W	Reported as 42-87186
BT-13	12/16/49	4107N	12126W	NC56865, marked
T-34	02/27/60	4107N	12144W	N6186C, unmarked
F6F	11/14/45	4110N	12230W	Covered, unmarked
TBM	06/06/47	4121N	12300W	Unmarked
F-101B-70-MC	05/09/62	4147N	12143W	USAF 57-0271
Colorado				
B-24	——	3715N	10510W	Marked, visible
T-29	02/25/62	3725N	10803W	91931
BT-13	——	3727N	10513W	Scattered
L-1049	12/15/65	3734N	10530W	N6914C, scattered, burned
L-5	01/15/44	3751N	10500W	AF8693
A-4C	09/14/69	3755N	10723W	Gray with black tail
AT-6	03/25/67	3830N	10603W	N6973C
C-47B-1-DK	09/24/56	3831N	10618W	43-48416
T-33A-5-LO	09/12/74	3840N	10539W	58-0528, silver, burned
L-19E-CE	08/16/51	3840N	10503W	56-2669
U8F	09/14/70	3843N	10505W	A23859, olive drab
B-25	04/29/58	3845N	10503W	29785
B-58	04/22/58	3849N	10503W	AF8102
C-47	10/14/47	3851N	10504W	AF3503, marked
B-17	——	3858N	10509W	Marked
C-49	12/01/45	3858N	10503W	Burned

Aircraft Type	Date	Latitude	Longitude	Remarks
C-46	12/07/63	4002N	10538W	N609Z, silver and blue
DC-3	01/21/48	4003N	10538W	N206, silver
F-100	01/30/67	4025N	10553W	USAF 54-2015
Unknown	——	4025N	10544W	Radial engine, stabilizer visible
Unknown	——	4025N	10555W	Military, human remains recovered
B-17	——	4029N	10526W	Marked
B-17	06/14/47	4031N	10538W	AF0891, marked
B-24	09/18/45	4035N	10707W	AF8549
C-46	11/16/63	4037N	10529W	N130N
A-7 Corsair II	12/10/81	4039N	10357W	Wreckage probably removed
DC-6	06/30/51	4045N	10544W	Silver
T-34 Mentor	08/01/62	4047N	10705W	N0828
Connecticut				
Cessna 150	——	4132N	07327W	Details unknown
Cessna 182	01/03/86	4140N	07235W	N3349R, white/gold, probably removed
Delaware				
A-7B Corsair	01/15/83	3341N	07856W	In water
A-7B Corsair	01/15/83	3341N	07856W	Wreck probably removed
Florida				
F-4	07/11/83	2439N	08023W	Crashed in water
Navy Corsairs	01/01/54	2527N	08051W	Details unknown
DC-3	——	2625N	08037W	Marked
DC-3	03/20/77	2634N	08111W	N101MX, white
F-4	09/07/71	2641N	08055W	Details unknown
DC-3	——	2658N	08034W	Silver wing and tail
DC-3	——	2705N	08135W	White
F-4	06/28/73	2735N	08117W	Camouflage
F-100C-20-NA	04/22/68	2738N	08109W	USAF 54-1914
T-33	——	2803N	08057W	Details unknown
Unknown	12/08/81	2804N	08006W	Crashed in water
A-5	10/04/69	2853N	08048W	Details unknown
F4U Corsair	——	2902N	08116W	Unmarked
F-101	12/14/71	2938N	08518W	Details unknown
T-33	——	3004N	08535W	Details unknown
F-101B-115-MC	12/04/75	3019N	08522W	USAF 59-0406, tail intact
T-33	12/22/82	3021N	08526W	Markings: 28N Tyndall AFB
T-28	03/11/68	3040N	08656W	Marked as 2W216
A-6 Intruder	02/12/82	3047N	08226W	USMC, Okefenokee Swamp
Georgia				
T-33	——	3135N	08337W	AF1964
P-40	——	3137N	08110W	Given as 0244
F-4	04/30/41	3426N	08442W	Probably removed
F-101	——	3438N	08433W	Details unknown
UH-1B	03/22/76	3447N	08405W	USAF 63-8762, green

Aircraft Type	Date	Latitude	Longitude	Remarks
Idaho				
RF-4C-26-MC	10/04/69	4223N	11603W	USAF 65-0889
C-140	11/26/53	4231N	11205W	C76661
AT-6	12/01/63	4313N	11528W	Visible, Bennett Mountain
T-33A-1-LO	09/06/62	4317N	11432W	USAF 51-17419, scattered
BT-13	02/31/46	4324N	11553W	C325
P-38	03/11/45	4325N	11535W	Unmarked
L-19	12/13/55	4336N	11526W	Intact, unmarked, Trinity Mountain
B-47	01/01/62	4413N	11605W	Burned
C-43	04/05/43	4430N	11510W	Cape Horn Lakes area, unmarked
C-47	01/01/58	4445N	11648W	USFS, aluminum, Advent Gulch area
C-45	07/09/65	4450N	11450W	Scattered
B-24	01/27/43	4509N	11550W	Loon Lake area, visible, unmarked
Taylorcraft	10/12/45	4511N	11451W	Visible, unmarked
L-5	06/28/63	4521N	11529W	58-995, yellow and blue
TBM	——	4537N	11353W	Marked
B-17	11/01/62	4702N	11640W	Details unknown
B-24	06/16/41	4737N	11700W	"4443," Rockford Bay area
BT-13	04/29/47	4741N	11629W	C56962
Iowa				
B-23	02/15/67	4212N	09045W	N2318Q, white with blue trim
Louisiana				
BT-13	——	3003N	08945W	Aircraft on its back
H-34	——	3005N	09027W	N46755
Maine				
F-101	11/14/67	4458N	07006W	Details unknown
TBM Avenger	05/18/72	4656N	06939W	Details unknown
Montana				
TBM	08/27/64	4537N	11353W	Unmarked
T-33	05/05/65	4701N	11101W	Tail number "079"
F-101	05/19/66	4802N	11149W	Silver
Nebraska				
A-26	09/18/65	4153N	10333W	Executive conversion
New Mexico				
B-25	——	3211N	10458W	Not visible from air
AT-11	——	3212N	10633W	Details unknown
B-25	——	3217N	10633W	Details unknown
Unknown	——	3225N	10558W	Military, silver
BT-13	——	3231N	10628W	Details unknown
C-140	——	3246N	10544W	On bombing range
T-34	08/04/81	3301N	10745W	Forest Service aircraft
T-33	05/26/81	3320N	10503W	USAF, 25 miles west of Roswell
OV-10	08/06/81	3328N	10708W	At the end of Elephant Butte
T-33	07/28/67	3336N	10412W	USAF, silver
F-4C-26-MC	12/06/69	3357N	10527W	USAF 64-0969, camouflage

Aircraft Type	Date	Latitude	Longitude	Remarks
B-17	——	3406N	10710W	Details unknown
A-70	——	3423N	10349W	Details unknown
T-37A-CE	02/23/69	3440N	10625W	USAF 57-2301, silver and black
AT-11	——	3446N	10626W	Details unknown
Unknown	——	3909N	10624W	N8414E, Navy
AT-6	——	3515N	10553W	Details unknown
C-47	——	3515N	10611W	Details unknown
B-24	——	3624N	10503W	Details unknown
Navy PBM	01/01/64	3629N	10528W	Marked yellow
C-47	——	3647N	10527W	Marked
B-17	——	3647N	10531W	Details unknown
B-24	——	3653N	10521W	Visible from air near peak
B-17	——	3655N	10830W	Details unknown
North Carolina				
F-11	05/20/69	3502N	07715W	Bu. 138639
T-34	11/19/73	3530N	07737W	Details unknown
F8F	01/01/64	3608N	07726W	USMC
Oklahoma				
F-105	09/13/80	3419N	09535W	Details unknown
Oregon				
A-6	09/20/73	4306N	12026W	Navy 28314, silver and white
A-6	05/31/73	4318N	12242W	Navy 52907, gray
F-101	04/06/65	4324N	12055W	Details unknown
DC-9	10/02/66	4515N	12158W	N9101, marked
Culver	12/08/68	4547N	12257W	NC4461
Pennsylvania				
T-34	10/23/82	4007N	07916W	Navy
Texas				
T-38	04/06/83	2951N	10041W	USAF 1591
S-2	05/23/65	3014N	10108W	V33111, gray
T-38A-50-NO	05/26/65	3027N	10129W	63-8244, scattered
B-24	——	3131N	10534W	Scattered
B-29	——	3146N	10446W	Scattered on west slope
Lockheed 12	——	3150N	10630W	Scattered
TV-2 (T-33)	——	3157N	10427W	Aircraft in gully
P-51	10/15/75	3159N	10053W	N651D
T-33	——	3234N	09725W	Details unknown
T-37	12/17/69	3256N	10112W	USAF 58-1913
F-100	02/09/69	3418N	10100W	Red, white, blue
Utah				
UC-78	——	3731N	11358W	Details unknown
T-33	——	3820N	10939W	Details unknown
T-28	07/02/65	3823N	11204W	Reported intact
F-4E-51-MC	12/03/77	3947N	11403W	USAF 72-0134

Aircraft Type	Date	Latitude	Longitude	Remarks
F-111	03/01/69	3955N	11245W	Details unknown
V-1 Rocket	——	4026N	11333W	Intact, unmarked
Mace Missile	——	4033N	11335W	Scattered
V-1 Rocket	——	4034N	11353W	Intact unmarked
T-34	11/22/65	4039N	11044W	N6826E, silver
Virginia				
A-6 Intruder	06/27/83	3636N	07725W	Wreck probably removed
FB-111	——	3656N	08153W	Wreck marked with white/yellow
S-2	02/12/69	3700N	08010W	Details unknown
T-28B	05/01/64	3756N	07854W	USMC Bu. 137731

Appendix II

Propliner Crashes

This list is intended as a starting point for research purposes only. It does not list every aircraft of a particular type that has crashed. The authors/publishers make no guarantees that wreckage still exists at these sites. Wreckchasers are cautioned to do their research and be prepared before setting out on an adventure.

Type	MSN	Reg.	Date	Airline	Nearest Major City
Airspeed Ambassador 2					
AS.57	5211	G-AMAD	07/03/68	BKS Air Transport	London-Heathrow, England
AS.57	5217	G-ALZU	02/06/58	British European Airways	Munich, West Germany
ATL.98 Carvair					
ATL.98	3/18339	G-ARSF	12/28/62	Channel Air Bridge	Rotterdam, The Netherlands
ATL.98	6/7480	CF-EPU	09/28/68	Eastern Provincial Airways	Twin Falls, Labrador
ATL.98	16/10485	HI-168	06/23/69	Dominicana	Miami, Florida
Avro Tudor					
688 Tudor I	1235	G-AGSU	08/23/47	Ministry of Supply & Aircraft Production	Woodford, Manchester
688 Tudor I	1253	G-AGRE	01/17/49	British South American Airways	into sea en route Bermuda to Jamaica
688 Tudor I	1255	G-AGRG	01/27/59	Air Charter	Brindisi, Italy
688 Tudor I	1256	G-AGRH	04/23/59	Air Charter	Mount Suphan, Turkey
688 Tudor I	1349	G-AHNP	01/30/48	British South American Airways	into Atlantic Azores to Bermuda
689 Tudor 2	1417	G-AkBY	03/12/50	Airflight Ltd.	Llandow, South Wales, England
Avro York					
C.1	1210	G-AGJD	02/01/49	BOAC	Castel Benito, Libya
C.1	MW136	CF-HMW	09/26/56	Maritime CentralnAirways	Chimo, Quebec, Canada
C.1	MW147	CF-HMZ	04/11/55	Associated Airways	Yellowknife, NWT, Canada
C.1	MW193	G-ANSY	02/25/56	Scottish Aviation	Luqa, Malta
C.1	MW231	EP-ADA	09/15/55	Persian Air Services	Basra, Iraq
C.1	MW248	———	07/04/48	Royal Air Force	mid-air with SAS DC-6 SE-BDA Middlessex, England
C.1	MW294	CF-HIQ	01/08/57	TransAir	Rankin Inlet, Hudson Bay, Canada
C.1	MW295	EP-ADE	07/15/59	Persian Air Services	Kuwait City, Kuwait
C.1	MW308	G-AMUL	04/30/56	Scottish Airlines	Stansted, Essex, England
C.1	MW321	G-AMUN	12/23/57	Scottish Airlines	Stansted, Essex, England
C.1	MW327	G-ANRC	09/22/54	Scottish Aviation	Stansted, Essex, England
C.1	MW332	G-AMUM	04/13/54	Scottish Aviation	Luqa, Malta
C.1	1218	OD-ACZ	03/15/63	Middle East Airlines	Karai, Iran
C.1	1219	G-AGNR	07/16/47	BOAC	AZ-Zubair, Basra, Iraq
C.1	1222	OD-ACO	05/24/61	Trans Mediterranean Airways	AZaiba, Muscat
C.1	1226	G-AGNY	06/26/54	Skyways Ltd.	Kyritz, Germany
C.1	1227	ZS-BRB	08/24/52	BOAC	Gatow, West Berlin
I	1300	G-AHEW	09/07/46	British South American Airways	Bathhurst, The Gambia
I	1301	G-AHEX	01/05/49	British South American Airways	Natal, Brazil
I	1303	G-AHEZ	04/13/47	British South American Airways	Dakar, Senegal
I	1304	G-AHFA	02/02/53	Lancashire Aircraft Corp.	into sea between Newfoundland to Jamaica
I	1307	OD-ADB	09/29/58	Middle East Airlines	into sea between Beirut to Rome
I	1311	OD-ADA	09/11/62	Middle East Airlines	Azaiba, Saudi Arabia
I	1316	G-AFHI	03/15/49	Skyways Ltd.	Gatow, West Berlin

Type	MSN	Reg.	Date	Airline	Nearest major city
I	1354	G-AMGL	03/11/52	Air Charter Ltd.	Hamburg, West Germany
I	1365	LV-XIG	12/23/46	Flota Aerea Mercante Argentina	Rio de Janeiro, Brazil
I	1366	LV-XIH	07/25/47	Flota Aerea MercanteArgentina	Buenos Aires, Argentina
C.1	PC4494	G-ALBX	06/19/49	Skyways Ltd.	Nuestadt, Germany
Boeing 377 Stratocruiser					
377-10-26	15932	N1032V	03/26/55	Pan Am	into sea off Seattle, Washington
377-10-26	15933	N1033V	04/10/59	Pan Am	Juneau, Alaska
377-10-26	15939	N1039V	04/29/52	Pan Am	Carolina, Brazil
377-10-28	15943	G-ALSA	12/25/54	BOAC	Prestwick, Scotland
377-10-30	15954	N74608	04/02/56	Northwest	into sea off Seattle, Washington
377-10-29	15959	N90943	10/16/56	Pan Am	into sea between Honolulu and San Francisco
377-10-29	15960	N90944	11/09/57	Pan Am	into sea between Honolulu and San Francisco
377-10-34	15970	N31230	09/12/51	United Airlines	Redwood City, California
Bristol 170 Freighter					
MK.IIB	12731	F-BHVB	11/04/58	Cle Air Transport	Le Touquet, France
Mk.IIA	12734	G-AHJB	07/04/46	Bristol Aeroplane Co.	into sea near Aracaju, Brazil
Mk.II	12738	F-BENF	07/28/50	Cle Air Transport	Tanezrouft, Tunbukta
Mk.II	12739	HC-SBU	08/06/49	Shell Co. of Ecuador	East Cordilleras, Ecuador
Mk.IIA	12742	G-AHJJ	03/21/50	Bristol Aeroplane Co.	Cowbridge, Glamorgan, Wales
Mk.21	12756	G-AICM	01/19/53	Silver City Airways	Templehof, West Berlin
Mk.21	12757	EC-ADI	05/09/57	Aviacion y Comercio	Barajas, Madrid, Spain
Mk.21E	12762	G-AICS	02/27/58	Manx Airlines	Horwich, Lancashire, England
Mk.21	12766	G-AIFF	00/00/49	Bristol Aeroplane Co.	into English Channel
Mk.21E	12772	HZ-AAC	10/08/57	Saudi Arabian Airlines	Taraif, Saudi Arabia
Mk.21	12779	VR-NAD	02/05/55	West African Airways Corp.	Calobar, Nigeria
Mk.21	12782	F-BECR	03/10/50	Ste Indochinoise de Transportes Aeriens	Siagon, South Vietnam
Mk.I	12788	F-BCJN	10/16/47	Societe Aerienne du Littoral	into sea Cartagena, Spain
Mk.XI	12792	SE-BNG	11/18/47	Trafik Turist Transportflyg	Revello, Italy
Mk.21	12797	EC-AEG	12/04/53	Aviacion y Comercio	Guaderrama Mtns. Spain
Mk.IIA	12802	F-BCJA	01/25/48	Ste IndoChinoise de Transports Aeriens	into sea en route Cyprus to Baghdad
Mk.21E	12807	VH-SJQ	05/10/75	Jetair Australia Party Ltd.	into Bass Strait, Victoria, Australia
Mk.21E	12809	F-VNAI	08/16/54	Air Vietnam	Pakse, Laos
Mk.21E	12812	F-BENG	04/11/48	Cie Air Transport, Los Barrios	Algecivon, Spain
Mk31	12828	ZK-AYH	11/21/57	Straits Air Freight Express	Christchurch, New Zealand
Mk.31	13073	G-AMWA	09/24/63	Bristish United Air Ferries	Guernsey, Channel Islands
Mk.31E	13076	EI-APM	06/12/67		Dublin, Eire
Mk.32	13078	CF-QWJ	03/00/77	Lambair Ltd.	Rankin Inlet, Canada
Mk.31M	13134	C-CYQY	06/21/88	Trans Provincial Airlines	Bronson Creek, B.C., Canada
MK.32	13260	G-ANWL	11/01/61	Silver City Airways	Les Prevosts, St Savior, Guernsey, Channel Islands
Britten-Norman Trislander					
BN-2A Mk.III-2	1051	XA-JPE	05/05/89	Aerocozumel	Chichen Itza, Yucatan, Mexico
Canadair Argonaut					
DC-4M1	103	CF-TEL	08/12/48	Trans Canada Airlines	Sydney, Nova Scotia, Canada
DC-4M2	128	CF-TFD	12/09/56	Trans Canada Airlines	Mount Siesse, BC, Canada
DC-4M2	137	I-ACOA	10/11/66	Hank Wharton	Garoua, North Cameroons
C-4-1	147	YV-C-LBV	07/06/62	Linea Expressa Bolivar	into sea off Caracas, Venezuela
C-4-1	148	CF-CPR	02/09/50	Canadian Pacific Air Lines	Tokyo, Japan
C-4-1	150	CF-TFW	04/08/54	Trans Canada Air Lines	mid-air with RCAF Harvard, Moose Jaw, Saskatchewan, Canada
C-4	151	G-ALHE	06/24/56	BOAC	Kano, Nigeria
C-4	153	G-ALHG	06/04/67	British Midland Airways	Stockport, Manchester
C-4	158	G-ALHL	09/21/53	BOAC	Idris, Tripoli, Libya
C-4	161	VP-KNY	04/11/62	East African Airways	Nairobi, Kenya

Type	MSN	Reg.	Date	Airline	Nearest major city
Convair 240					
240-1	3	N55VM	10/20/77	L&J Co.	Gillsburg, Mississippi
240-0	6	PP-CEV	01/15/65	Cruzeiro do Sul	Jabaguara, Brazil
240-1	22	N8405H	02/13/58	Western Air Lines	Garnet, California
240-0	25	PP-CEZ	05/09/52	Cruziero do Sul	Vitoria, Espirito Santo, Brazil
240-1	27	JA5088	05/29/65	Japan Domestic Airlines	Obihiro, Japan
240-1	37	N8407H	02/26/54	Western Air Lines	Wright, Wyoming
240-8	38	N7177B	09/04/78	Mission Air Lift	Clewiston, Florida
240-2	39	PP-VCK	09/22/58	Varig	Brasilia, Brazil
240-0	40	N94221	08/04/55	American Airlines	Fort Leonard Wood, Missouri
240-2	49	N90662	09/02/51	Pan Am	Kingston, Jamaica
240-7	52	AP-AEH	05/15/58	Pakistan Int'l Airlines	New Delhi, India
240-0	53	JA5098	02/27/64	Fuji Airlines	Oita, Japan
240-0	54	N94229	01/22/52	American Airlines	Elizabeth, New Jersey
240-2	55	JY-ACB	01/22/59	Air Jordan	Dabouk, Jordan
240-2	59	N90664	02/27/51	Mid-Continent Airlines	Tulsa, Oklahoma
240-4	61	HB-IRW	06/19/54	Swissair	into sea off Folkstone, England
240-0	66	N94234	03/20/55	American Airlines	Springfield, Missouri
240-2	71	XC-DOK	01/25/70	Carrier unknown	Poza Rica, Mexico
240-6	72	ZP-CDP	05/26/67	Lineas Aereas Paraguayas	Buenos Aires, Argentina
240-6	77	LV-ADQ	10/16/54	Aerolineas Argentinas	Capila del Senor, Argentina
240-4	78	D-BELU	07/31/60	Deutsche Flugdienst	Rimini, Italy
240-7	82	AP-AEG	03/14/53	Orient Airways	Kalahasahar, India
240-0	88	N94244	01/20/54	American Airlines	Buffalo, New York
240-2	90	N90670	08/15/58	Northeast Airlines	Nantucket, Massachusetts
240-2	103	PP-VCQ	12/22/62	Varig	Brasilia, Brazil
240-0	115	N300GR	05/24/80	Charles Clay	Spruce Creek, Florida
240-0	116	N94255	09/16/53	American Airlines	Albany, New York
240-0	117	N94256	02/19/61	Lyndon B Johnson	Johnson City, Texas
240-4	125	PH-TEI	05/25/53	KLM Royal Dutch Airlines	Amsterdam, The Netherlands
240-12	128	OO-AWO	12/19/53	Sabena	Zurich, Switzerland
240-0	139	N94266	06/22/49	American Airlines	Memphis, Tennessee
240-0	141	N777DC	04/01/78	Thrifty Threads	Ungula, Columbia
240-0	150	N94273	03/25/59	American Airlines	Chicago, Illinois
240-12	154	OO-AWQ	10/14/53	Sabena	Frankfurt, Germany
240-12	155	SP-LPB	04/11/58	LOT-Polish Airlinesn	Warsaw, Poland
240-12	157	N270L	01/17/70	Aspen Airways	Aspen, Colorado
240-13	158	N91238	01/14/52	Northeast Airlines	Flushing Bay, New York
240-13	161	N91241	08/11/49	Northeast Airlines	Portland, Maine
240-23	172	PK-GCB	02/27/62	Garuda Indonesian Airways	Palembang, Indonesia
240-23	175	PK-GCE	08/17/62	Garuda Indonesian Airways	Ambon, Indonesia
T-29B/VT-29B	261	XA-JOU	03/15/84	Aero Cozumel	Cancun, Mexico
T-29B/VT-29B	322	N155PA	06/19/85	Combs Airways	Trenton, Canada
Convair 340/440					
340-35	44	N90853	03/16/54	Continental Air Lines	Midland, Texas
340-32 (440)	45	N3414	11/29/66	Allegheny Airlines	Harrisburg, Pennsylvania
340-31	59	N73130	12/21/62	Frontier Airlines	Grand Island, Nebraska
340-32	71	N3422	07/17/55	Braniff Airways	Chicago, Illinois
340-38 (440)	95	N4809C	07/14/78	Charlie Inc.	South Caicos
340-41 (440)	112	YU-ADL	02/04/61	Jugoslovenski Aerotransport	Titograd, Yugoslavia
340-47 (440)	125	N8415H	07/23/65	Allegheny Airlines	Montoursville, Pennsylvania
340-38 (440)	138	N4819C	03/13/74	Sierra Pacific Airlines	White Mountain, Bishop, California
340-48 (440)	143	TG-ACA	04/27/77	Aviateca	Guatemala City, Guatemala
340-38	152	N4820C	03/20/68	Delta Air Lines	Evansville, Indiana
340-59	159	PP-CDW	05/03/63	Cruzeiro do sul	Sao Paulo, Brazil
340-58	162	YU-ADA	12/22/56	Jugoslovenski Aerotransport	Grub, Germany
340-68B	174	HZ-AAT	02/04/72	Saudi Atabian Airlines	Sanaa, Yemen
340-58	178	YU-ADC	10/10/55	Jugoslovenski Aerotransport	Vienna, Austria
340-62	191	PP-YRB	06/24/60	Real SA	Guanabara Bay, Rio De Janeiro, Brazil
340-62 (440)	195	SE-CCK	11/20/64	Linjeflyg	Angelholm, Sweden
340-68 (440)	210	N477KW	08/25/82	National Flight Services	Wolf Creek Pass, Colorado
340-68/C-131D	219	HZ-AAZ	07/08/68	Saudi Arabian Airlines	Dhahran, Saudi Arabia
440-35	319	CP-1489	04/20/85	Carga Aereo Transporta da Santa Rosa	

Type	MSN	Reg.	Date	Airline	Nearest major city
					Beni, Bolivia
440-75	325	N21DR	01/17/82	Island Airlines Hawaii	Pearl Harbor Channel, Oahu
440-11	327	XA-KEH	05/21/81	Aero Leon SA	Oaxaca, Mexico
440-11	335	HB-IMD	07/17/56	Swissair	Shannon, Eire
C-131E	342	N121CA	06/03/81	Command Aviation	Dillingham, Alaska
440-11	355	HB-IMF	02/10/67	Swissair	Regensberg, Switzerland
440-38	378	N102US	00/00/80	Farm-Kem	Colombia
440-62	388	EC-ATH	03/31/65	Iberia	into sea off Tangier, Morocco
440-75	395	SE-BSU	11/01/69	Linjeflyg	Arlanda-Stockholm, Sweden
440-11	414	CP-1358	01/11/80	Carga Aero Transportadora	Camiare, Beni, Bolivia
440-86	415	CP-1078	03/26/76	San Francisco Servicio Aereos	into Pacific, near Chile
440-86	416	N9302	05/12/78	Argosy Air Lines	Skippingport, Pennsylvania
440-86	425	CP-924	09/06/78	North East Bolivian Airways	El Desengano, Yacuma, Bolivia
440-62	443	EC-ATB	11/12/62	Iberia	Carmona, Seville, Spain
440-88	448	N985	11/30/76	OMCO Petroleum Co.	Cairo, Egypt
440-62	456	PP-AQE	09/18/57	REAL SA	Montevideo, Uruguay
440-0	464	D-ACAT	01/28/66	Lufthansa	Bremen, Germany
440-59	493	PP-CEP	06/16/58	Cruziero do Sul	Curitaba, Parana, Brazil
de Havilland DH-114 Heron					
1B	14001	G-APJS	02/19/58	Gulf Aviation	Mount Saraceno, Italy
1B	14004	PP-SLG	03/27/53	Transportes Aereos Salvador	Itapebi, Bahia, Brazil
2 (2D)	14007	G-AMTS	07/10/61	Metropolitan Air Movements	Biggin Hill, Kent, England
1B	14009	HR-SAN	05/26/70	Aeroservice S de RL	Tegucigalpa, Toncontin
1B	14010	F-BGOI	04/18/55	Union Aeromaritime de Transport	Kupe Mountain
1B	14017	G-AMYU	08/15/58	Jersey Airlines	Guernsey, Channel Islands
1B	14026	JA6159	08/17/63	Fuji Airlines	Mount Hachijo, Fuji, Japan
1B	14028	JA6158	02/23/62	Toa Airways	Mount Ohira, Hofu-shi, Yamaguchi, Japan
1B	14033	VQ-FAL	12/11/65	Fiji Airways	Tavenni
1B	14034	TN-ABA	07/11/69	Cogair	Rudddervoorde, Belgium
1B	14040	F-OCED	01/27/68	Air Comores	Moroni, Comores
2B	14052	VP-BAO	08/23/59	LIAT	St Kitts
2B	14056	DQ-FEF	12/27/86	Sunflower Airlines	Nadi, Fiji
2	14067	VH-CLS	10/23/75	Connair	Cairns, Australia
2B	14085	N554PR	06/24/72	Prinair	Mercedita Airport
1B	14099	G-AOFY	09/28/57	British European Airways	Port Ellen, Isle of Islay
2D	14109	N19D	03/29/72	Air Pacific	location unknown
2	14111	N998SA	12/18/78	Fisher Bros Aviation	Cleveland, Ohio
2D	14113	EC-ANJ	04/14/58	Aviaco	Barcelona, Spain
2D	14117	EC-ANZ	11/15/57	Aviaco	Palma deMajorca, Spain
2D	14125	N563PR	03/05/69	Prinair	San Juan, Puerto Rico
2D	14127	LN-NPH	08/04/68	Norflyselskap	Bodo, Norway
2D	14132	CR-TAI	01/26/60	Transportes Aereos de Timor	into sea off Timor
Douglas DC-4					
C-54-DO	3060	NC88839	04/18/57	Capital Airlines	Pittsburgh, Pennsylvania
C-54A-DO	3065	7T-VAU	04/11/67	Air Algerie	Tamanrassett, Algeria
C-54A-DO	3076	N79998	08/15/49	Transocean Air Lines	into sea off Lunga Point, Ireland
C-54A-DO	3079	F-BDRI	07/18/51	Transports Aeriens Intercontinentaux	Tananarive, Madagascar
C-54A-DO	3084	F-BELB	12/08/50	Transports Aeriens Intercontinentaux	Bangui, Central Africa
C-54A-DO	3094	VT-DIA	09/08/58	Indian Airlines	Madras, India
C-54A-DO	3098	XW-TDE	02/11/72	Royal Air Lao	between Saigon and Vientiane, Laos
C-54A-DO	3099	OO-SBL	04/22/60	Sobelair	Bunia, Belgian Congo
C-54A-DO	3106	PI-C100	01/11/47	Far Eastern Air Transport	Lasaq
C-54-DO	3112	N88842	06/13/47	Pennsylvania Central Airlines	Lookout Rock, West Virginia
C-4-DO	3114	41-32939	01/15/43	Trans Continental & Western	Paramaribo, Surinam
C-54-DO	3123	N88852	11/17/55	R.R. Kerkorian	Seattle, Washington
C-54A-1-DO	7445	LV-ABI	09/27/49	Flota Aerea Mercante Argentina	Castilla, Argentina
C-54A-1-DO	7449	N68736	05/13/57	U.S. Overseas Airlines	Narssarssuaq, Greenland
C-54A-1-DO	7459	D-ALAF	11/03/57	Karl Herfurtner	Dusseldorf, Germany
C-54A-1-DO	7462	OB-R247	12/30/76	Faucett	Andes Mountains, Peru

Type	MSN	Reg.	Date	Airline	Nearest major city
C-54A-1-DO	7464	G-AJPL	02/04/49	Skyways Ltd.	Castel Benito, Lybia
C-54A-5-DO	7467	PP-AXS	11/04/57	REAL,	into sea off Praia de Balaia, Brazil
C-54A-5-DO	7468	LV-ABQ	06/17/53	Aerolineas Argentinas	Cordova, Argentina
C-54A-5-DO	7473	TJ-ABC	06/13/61	Air Cameroon,	Douala, Cameroon
C-54A-5-DO	7479	LV-AFG	01/13/48	Flota Aerea Mercante Argentina	Ponta Galeria, Italy
C-54A-1-DC	10270	N05425	06/23/50	Northwest Airlines	Benton Harbor, Lake Michigan
C-54A-1-DC	10274	CP-717	05/29/64	Transportes Aereos	Benianos, Trinidad, Bolivia
C-54A-1-DC	10277	OB-PAZ-228	10/02/55	Faucett	Pico Oiriruma-Vinac, Peru
C-54A-1-DC	10279	G-APYK	06/03/67	Air Ferry	Mount Canigou, France
C-54A-5-DC	10280	HK-172	01/15/76	Taxi Aereo	Bogota, Columbia
C-54A-5-DC	10284	OB-R-148	12/08/67	Faucett	Carpich Huanuco Mountain, Peru
R5D-1	10290	F-BFGR	02/07/53	Compagnie Autrex-Lopez-Loreta-Lebreton	Eysines, France
R5D-1	10294	CP-747	05/29/64	Transportes Aereos Benianos	location unknown
C-54A010-DC	10310	VR-HEU	07/23/54	Cathay Pacific	into sea off Hainan Island, China
C-54A-10-DC	10315	N4726V	03/28/64	Facilities Management Corp.	into sea between San Francisco and Hawaii
C-54A-10-DC	10317	N88920	10/26/47	Pan Am	Annette Island, Alaska
R5D-1	10319	CU-T-397	12/06/52	Cubana	Bermuda
R5D-1	10320	N48762	10/28/60	Northwest Airlines	Missoula, Montana
R5D-1	10327	CF-CPC	07/21/51	Canadian Pacific Air Lines	en route Sitka-Yakutat, Canada
C-54A-10-DC	10328	LV-JPG	02/19/71	Aero Palas	Cervo Huaycas, Peru
C-54A-10-DC	10331	N30061	11/14/61	Zantop	Cincinnati Airport, Kentucky
C-54A-10-DC	10339	N90439	02/05/50	El Al	Lydda, Israel
R5D-1	10341	F-BFCQ	04/04/54	Compagnie Autrex-Lopez-Loreta-Lebreton	Gian Lan, Vietnam
R5D-1	10342	N91068	09/12/46	Pennsylvania Central Air Lines	Washington, D.C.
C-54A-15-DC	10346	F-BFCP	05/28/69	Air France	Paris, France
C-54A-15-DC	10347	N5519V	03/22/61	Seven Seas Air Lines	Nagpur, India
C-54A-15-DC	10356	N3821	03/09/69	Continental Air Transport	into Atlantic
C-54A-15-DC	10359	G-ASOG	01/21/67	Air Ferry	Frankfurt, West Germany
C-54A-15-DC	10360	CF-ILI	11/04/59	Wheeler Airlines	St. Cleophas, Quebec, Canada
C-54A-15-DC	10376	VT-DIC	05/07/62	Indian Airlines	Haveri, India
C-54A-15-DC	10384	EP-ADK	08/04/61	Iran Air	location unknown
C-54A-15-DC	10387	HP-382	07/10/63	Aerovias Panama Airways	into sea off South Caicos Island
C-54A-15-DC	10388	N30065	05/29/46	United Air Lines	Chicago, Illinois
C-54A-15-DC	10391	F-BELO	11/28/49	Air France	St Just Chalignin, France
C-54A-15-DC	10403	HK-1309	06/30/75	Taxi Aereo El Canado	Saravena Arauca, Columbia
C-54A-15-DC	10406	N88785	10/27/48	Northwest Airlines	Edmonton, Alberta, Canada
C-54A-15-DC	10410	N90433	09/24/55	Flying Tigers	into sea off Honolulu, Hawaii
C-54A-15-DC	10418	HK-135	06/23/59	Avianca	Cerro Baco Mountain, Peru
C-54A-15-DC	10424	OD-AEB	12/12/63	Trans Mediterranean Airways	Koh Mountains, Kabul, Afghanistan
R5D-2	10431	N98AS	03/28/81	Caribbean Air Cargo	into sea off St. Croix, Virgin Islands
C-54B-1-DC	10439	C-114	02/15/47	Avianca	Sabana Mountains, Columbia
C-54B-1-DC	10441	9Q-CAM	11/26/77	African Lux	Tete Province, Mozambique
C-54B-1-DC	10445	N90427	09/28/68	Pan African Airlines	Port Harcourt, Nigeria
C-54B-1-DC	10450	N30050	12/24/46	United Air Lines	Los Angeles, California
C-54B-1-DC	10452	9Q-CBG	08/23/88	Kinair Cargo	River Zaire, Zaire
C-54B-1-DC	10469	HK-130	01/28/62	Avianca	Cucuta, Columbia
C-54B-1-DC	10471	N30051	10/08/46	United Air Lines	Cheyenne, Wyoming
C-54B-1-DC	10486	N63396	09/24/59	Reeve Aleutian Airways	Adak, Alaska
C-54B-1-DC	10493	XA-FOW	06/25/46	Mexicana	Mexico City, Mexico
C-54B-1-DC	10498	F-BFVO	11/06/52	Union Aeromaritime de Transport	Lake Chad, Chad
C-54B-1-DC	10503	N88899	04/11/52	Pan Am	into sea off San Juan, Puerto Rico
C-54B-1-DC	10504	N88900	09/12/59	Pan Am	Tegucigalpa, Honduras
C-54B-1-DC	10506	PP-BTQ	04/04/64	Paraense	Belem, Brazil
C-54B-1-DC	10507	HK-728	07/24/74	Aeronorte Columbia	Bogota, Columbia
C-54B-1-DC	10510	CP-609	02/05/60	Lloyd Aero Boliviano	Laguna de Juana-Costa, Bolivia
C-54B-1-DC	10512	4X-ADN	11/24/51	El Al	Zurich, Switzerland
C-54B-1-DC	10513	N9982H	05/24/69	Pan African Airlines	Port Harcourt, Nigeria
C-54B-1-DC	10518	CF-EDN	11/13/50	Curtiss Reid Flying Svce.	Grenoble, France
C-54B-1-DC	10530	D-ABEB	06/17/61	Cont. Deutsche Luftreederei	Kano, Nigeria
C-54B-1-DC	10544	PP-LEQ	08/12/58	Loide Aereo Naciona	Belem, Brazil
R5D-3	10559	CP-1206	03/24/84	Frigorifico Reyes	Rurrenabaque, Bolivia

Type	MSN	Reg.	Date	Airline	Nearest major city
R5D-3	10563	N8060C	11/19/79	Tiburon Aircraft Inc.	McCormick, South Carolina
R5D-3Z	10576	CP-1404	06/08/83	Frigorifico Reyes	Trinidad, Bolivia
C-54D-1-DC	10588	XV-NUH	09/24/72	Air Vietnam	Ben Cat, South Vietnam
C-54D-1-DC	10591	OB-R-776	01/14/70	Faucett	Mount Pumacona, Lima, Peru
C-54D-10-DC	10761	CP-1352	01/12/79	Trak Airways	San Borja, Bolivia
C-54D-10-DC	10832	N79992	11/17/51	Overseas Nat'l Airways	mid-air with DC-4 N4002B
C-54D-10-DC	10853	FAC-1106	12/18/79	Satena	Cerro Toledo Mountain, Columbia
C-54B-1-DO	18325	HK-730	01/15/66	Avianca	into sea off Cartagena, Columbia
C-54B-5-DO	18330	N95412	06/01/47	Northwest Airlines	Chicago, Illinois
C-54B-5-DO	18336	PP-LEM	02/01/58	Loide Aereo Nacional	Rio de Janeiro, Brazil
C-54B-5-DO	18348	N8342C	12/21/48	Civil Air Transport	Basalt Island, Hong Kong
C-54B-10-DO	18350	N86574	01/07/53	Flying Tigers	Issaquah, Washington
R5D-2	18365	N88727	11/01/49	Eastern Air Lines	mid-air with P-38 NX26927, Wash., D.C.
C-54B-10-DO	18367	YA-BAG	11/21/59	Ariana Afghan Airlines	Beirut, Lebanon
C-54B-15-DO	18374	CF-MCF	08/11/57	Maritime Central Airways	Issoudun, Quebec
C-54B-15-DO	18379	N384	03/10/64	Slick Airways	Boston, Massachusetts
R5D-2	18380	N88814	05/30/47	Eastern Air Lines	Havre de Grace, Maryland
C-54B-15-DO	18384	OO-DEP	11/29/64	Belgian Int'l Air Svcs	Leopoldville, Belgian Congo
C-54B-15-DO	18386	N44567	02/06/47	Aerovias Cuba Int'l	Pedro Bernados, Spain
C-54B-15-DO	18389	N30062	10/06/55	United Air Lines	Laramie, Wyoming
C-54B-15-DO	18390	N37478	03/10/48	Delta Air Lines	Chicago, Illinois
R5D-2	18396	N88729	10/11/46	Eastern Air Lines	Alexandra, Virginia
C-54B-15-DO	18397	N88939	01/00/85	BIF Air Inc	South Caicos, Caicos Islands
C-54D-15-DC	22174	XV-NUI	03/19/73	Air Vietnam	Ban e Thout, South Vietnam
C-54B-20-DO	27229	N88911	09/20/47	Pan Am	New York, New York
C-54B-20-DO	27239	N90449	03/02/57	Alaska Airlines	Blyn, Washington
C-54B-20-DO	27240	TF-RVC	09/14/50	Loftleidir	Catna Jokull Glacier, Iceland
C-54B-20-DO	27242	A2-ZER	03/04/74	Wenela	Francistown, Botswana
C-54E-5-DO	27279	N45342	01/19/52	Northwest Airlines	Sandspit, British Columbia, Canada
C-54E-5-DO	27290	N90904	10/03/46	American Overseas Airlines	Stephenville, Newfoundland
R5D-4R	27368	N96361	12/23/86	Central Air Service	Arlington, Washington
C-54E-15-DO	27374	F-RAFA	01/21/82	Aeronavale	Noumea, Tahiti
C-54D-10-DO	36061	N3373F	07/14/81	Aero Union	Kenai, Alaska
C-54G-10-DO	36072	N300JT	06/29/83	Pacific Air Express	Kahului, Hawaii
C-54D-10-DO	36076	N88942	03/20/53	Transocean Air Lines	Alvarado, California
DC-4-1009	42910	VH-ANA	06/26/50	Australian National Airways	York, Western Australia
DC-4-1009	42912	F-BBDB	01/22/50	Air France	Paris, France
DC-4-1009	42918	OD-AEC	07/09/62	Trans Mediterranean Airways	Brindisi, Italy
DC-4-1009	42930	SE-BBG	10/20/47	AB Aerotransport	Athens, Greece
DC-4-1009	42932	OO-CBE	05/13/46	Sabena	Magazini, Congo
DC-4-1009	42935	F-BBDC	04/10/48	Air France	Kano, Nigeria
DC-4-1009	42937	F-BBDE	06/12/50	Air France	Bahrain, Saudi Arabia
DC-4-1009	42950	VH-AND	10/16/52	Australian National Airlines	Sydney, Australia
DC-4-1009	42982	JA6011	09/30/57	Japan Air Lines	Itami, Osaka, Japan
DC-4-1009	42986	OO-CBG	09/18/46	Sabena	Gander, Newfoundland
DC-4-1009	42989	F-BBDL	07/12/48	Air France	Paris, France
DC-4-1009	42990	F-BBDM	05/14/60	Air France	Bahrain, Saudi Arabia
DC-4-1009	42991	SR-MAD	07/19/67	Air Madagascar	Tanararive, Madagascar
DC-4-1009	42992	F-BBDO	02/03/51	Air France	Mount Cameroun, Nigeria
DC-4-1009	43065	VH-TAA	05/24/61	Trans Australia Airlines	Buiwer Island, Brisbane, Australia
DC-4-1009	43072	HB-ILA	05/15/60	Ballair AG	Jebbel Marra, Sudan
DC-4-1009	43073	HB-ILE	12/13/50	Swissair	Sydney, Nova Scotia
DC-4-1009	43095	9Q-CBH	04/07/74	Air Zaire	Gemena, Zaire
DC-4-1009	43097	YK-AAR	09/01/60	Syrian Airways	Kinshasa, Congo
DC-4-1009	43098	HB-ILO	12/14/51	Swissair	Schiphol, Amsterdam
Douglas DC-6					
XC-112A	35325	N901MA	02/08/76	Mercer Airlines	Van Nuys, California
DC-6	42871	N37506	06/17/48	United Air Lines	Mount Carmel, Pennsylvania
DC-6	42875	N37510	10/24/47	United Airlines	Bryce Canyon, Utah
DC-6A	42901	N90806	07/12/53	Transocean Air Lines	Wake Island
DC-6	42902	PI-C294	01/14/54	Philippine Air Lines	Rome, Italy
DC-6	43001	N37512	04/04/55	United Air Lines	Ronkonkoma, New York
DC-6	43031	LV-ADS	09/07/60	Aerolineas Argentinas	Salto, Uruguay

Type	MSN	Reg.	Date	Airline	Nearest major city
DC-6	43034	LV-ADV	06/10/58	Aerolineas Argentineas	Rio de Janeiro, Brazil
DC-6	43043	CP-926	06/17/71	Savco	Arica, Chile
DC-6	43055	N90891	02/11/52	National Airlines	Newark, New Jersey
DC-6	43057	N90893	02/14/53	National Airlines	Mobile, Alabama
DC-6	43059	XA-LAU	01/30/67	Mexicana	Merida, Mexico
DC-6	43112	PT-TKW	05/01/48	KLM-Royal Dutch Airlines	Amsterdam, The Netherands
DC-6	43114	PT-TPJ	03/22/52		Frankfurt, Germany
DC-6	43119	SE-BDA	07/04/48	Scandinavian Airlines	mid-air with Avro York MW248, Northwood, Middlesex, England
DC-6	43125	VH-BPE	10/29/53	BCPA	Woodside, California
DC-6	43126	XW-PEH	02/01/72	Penas	Tegal, Java
DC-6	43133	XA-NAH	06/29/67	Saesa	Mazatlan, Mexico
DC-6	43136	LV-ADW	07/19/61	Aerolineas Argentinas	Azul, Argentina
DC-6	43144	N37543	06/30/51	United Air Lines	Fort Collins, Colorado
DC-6	43212	XA-JOS	09/01/51	Mexicana	Mexico City, Mexico
DC-6	43215	I-LUCK	12/23/51	Linee Aeree Italiane	Milan, Italy
DC-6B	43260	N37550	08/24/51	United Air Lines	DeCoto (Union City), California
DC-6B	43270	HI-146	10/19/71	LADECO	Mendoza, Argentina
DC-6B	43273	CP-698	09/26/69	Lloyd Aereo Boliviano	La Paz, Bolivia
DC-6B	43519	HK-1359	02/04/76	LAC Columbia	Santa Maria, Columbia
DC-6B	43520	N77DG	02/17/75	Pacific Alaska Airlines	Fairbanks, Alaska
DC-6B	43526	HP-539	04/10/72	Inair Panama	Manaus, Brazil
DC-6B	43531	TG-ADA	06/08/78	Aviateca	Guatemala City, Guatemala
DC-6B	43538	N37559	11/01/55	United Air Lines	Longmount, Colorado
DC-6B	43556	PH-DFO	08/23/54	KLM-Royal Dutch Airlines	into North Sea off The Netherlands
DC-6B	43559	SE-BDY	09/18/61	United Nations	Ndola, Zambia
C-118A	43565	HK-1705	04/29/78	LAC Columbia	Bogota, Columbia
R6D-1	43685	131582	02/25/60	U.S. Navy	mid-air with DC-3 PP-AXD, Rio de Janeiro
C-118A	43717	C-GBYA	06/26/89	Conifair Aviation	location unknown
DC-6B	43742	N8225H	01/06/60	National Airlines	Wilmington, North Carolina
DC-6B	43823	N91303	04/20/53	Western Air Lines	Oakland, California
DC-6B	43829	OO-ABG	02/18/66	Belgian Int'l Air Services	Milan, Italy
DC-6B	43834	F-ABAE	04/22/85	Securite Civile	Perpignan, France
DC-6B	43835	F-BGOD	02/20/56	Transports Aeriens Intercontintaux	Cairo, Egypt
DC-6B	43843	CF-CUP	08/29/56	Canadian Pacific Airlines	Cold Bay Alaska
DC-6B	43844	CF-CUQ	07/08/65	Canadian Pacific Airlines	Dog Creek, British Columbia
DC-6B	44057	N371	12/02/89	Gomes & Warra Aircraft Corp.	Bahamas
DC-6B	44058	N90773	09/10/61	President Airlines	Shannon, Eire
DC-6A	44069	TF-OAE	05/06/74	Fragtflug,	Nuremberg, Germany
DC-6B	44113	N6113C	11/16/70	Transportes Aereos Latin America	Antigua
DC-6B	44168	HK-1706	02/19/82	LAC Columbia	Cerro del Tablazo, Subachoque, Columbia
DC-6B	44418	I-LINE	12/18/54	Linee Aeree Italiane	Idlewild, New York
DC-6A	44421	N844TA	11/28/80	Miami Air Lease	Bimini Island, Bahamas
DC-6B	44425	N9018N	09/15/80	JMG Inc.	into sea off Haiti
DC-6B	44426	N5026K	06/22/59	Pan Am	Shannon, Ireland
C-118A	44615	N33VX	07/21/88	TACA Int'l Airlines	Golden Meadows, Louisiana
C-118A	44630	N3493F	05/05/78	Surinam Airways	Paramaribo, Surinam
C-118A	44657	N43865	07/20/79	Kimex Inc.	Kingston, Jamaica
C-118A	44659	N96040	12/08/76	Aerovias Las Minas	down between Bogota and Trinidad
C-118A	44660	N2878F	07/06/85	Northern Pacific Transport	Egelik, Alaska
C-118A	44670	HK-1702	02/10/91	Air Colombia	Bogota, Colombia
DC-6A	44678	N34954	02/01/57	Northeast Airlines	La Guardia, New York
DC-6B	44687	HK-1707X	12/08/78	LAC Colombia	Sierra Cucuy, Colombia
DC-6B	44698	CF-PWA	08/02/74	Conair Aviation	Kamloops, British Columbia, Canada
DC-6A	44914	N90779	09/18/60	World Airways	Agana, Guam
DC-6B	45064	N614SE	10/26/73	Span East Airlines	Biscayne Bay, Miami, Florida
DC-6B	45075	I-LEAD	11/24/56	Linee Aeree Italiane	Paris, France
DC-6B	45108	TR-LXN	02/26/79	Air Gabon	Monda, Gabon
DC-6B	45200	N575	08/28/58	Northwest Orient	Minneapolis-St. Paul, Minnesota
DC-6A	45243	N6118C	07/21/61	Slick Airways	Shemya, Alaska
DC-6B	45323	YS-35C	05/02/76	TACA Int'l Airways	Altaverapaz, Guatemala
DC-6B	45324	YN-BFO	12/21/87	Aeronica	Costa Rica
DC-6B	45327	N122A	08/27/78	New World Air Charter	Seeb, Oman

Type	MSN	Reg.	Date	Airline	Nearest major city
DC-6A	45369	N6541C	04/23/65	Aaxico Airlines	Mount Rainer, Washington
DC-6A	45475	N640NA	01/31/67	Saturn Airways	San Antonio, Texas
DC-6A	45476	HR-TNO	01/27/73	TAN Airlines	Tegucigalpa, Honduras
DC-6B	45479	F-BIAO	05/03/63	Air Afrique	Buca, Cameroon
DC-6A	45480	N6579C	05/10/65	Aaxico Airlines	Whiteman AFB, Missouri
DC-6A	45504	OD-AEL	03/10/66	Trans Mediterranean Airways	Athens, Greece
DC-6B	45513	CC-CCG	02/06/65	LAN Chile	Oziebrada Lo Valdes, Chile
DC-6A/C	45532	HB-IBT	05/07/69	Int'l Red Cross	Uli, Biafra
DC-6B	45537	YS-05C	06/29/88	Aerolineas El Salvador	Comalapa, El Salvador
DC-6B	45540	SX-DAE	12/08/69	Olympic Airways	Athens, Greece
Douglas DC-7					
DC-7	44275	N68N	04/00/64	Federal Aviation Admin.	Deer Valley, Arizona
DC-7	44287	N4SW	09/05/79	Butler Aircraft Co.	Klamath Falls, Oregon
DC-7	44288	N6324C	06/30/56	United Airlines	mid-air with Lockheed 1049 N6902C, Grand Canyon, Arizona
DC-7C	44872	PP-PDO	11/01/61	Panair do Brasil	Recife, Brazil
DC-7C	44876	N244B	09/05/78	Advance Aviation	Farmerville, Louisiana
DC-7C	44876	N73675	00/00/77	Consolidated Air	South Carolina
DC-7C	45071	N5903	10/09/86	T&G Aviation	Dakar, Senegal
DC-7C	45072	N5904	03/25/58	Braniff	Miami, Florida
DC-7B	45084	N815D	11/30/62	Eastern Air Lines	New York, New York
DC-7B	45085	N816D	11/28/80	Central Air Services	Pecos, Texas
DC-7C	45090	N7466	09/27/68	Universal Airlines	Cherry Point, North Carolina
DC-7C	45128	N2282	09/12/66	Airlift Int'l	Tachikawa AFB, Japan
DC-7	45142	N6328C	04/21/58	United Airlines	mid-air with F-100F s/n 56-2755, Arden, Nevada
DC-7C	45157	OO-SFA	05/18/58	Sabena	Casablanca, Morocco
DC-7C	45160	G-ARUD	03/04/62	Caledonian Airways	Douala, Cameroon
DC-7B	45192	N8210H	01/31/57	Douglas Aircraft Co.	mid-air with F-89 s/n 52-1870, Sunland, California
DC-7C	45204	N285	10/22/62	Northwest Orient Airlines	Borka Island, Alaska
DC-7C	45209	N290	06/03/63	Northwest Orient Airlines	Annette Islands, Alaska
DC-7C	45214	N8219H	00/00/80	Aero Services	Colombia
DC-7C	45229	N357AL	06/24/79	Go Transportation	Barstow, California
DC-7C	45231	I-DUVO	02/26/60	Alitalia	Shannon, Eire
DC-7B	45355	N4891C	11/15/59	Delta Air Lines	New Orleans, Louisiana
DC-7	45359	N6314J	09/11/77	Safe Air Cargo	Yakutat, Alaska
DC-7C	45366	F-BIAP	09/24/59	Transports Aeriens Intercont.	Bordeau, France
DC-7B	45452	N846D	03/10/58	Douglas Aircraft Co.	unknown
DC-7B	45455	N849D	02/08/65	Eastern Airlines	Jones Beach, New York
DC-7C	45462	N292	07/14/60	Northwest Orient Airlines	Luzon, Philippines
DC-7C	45466	N296	06/21/73	Transair	Miami, Florida
DC-7C	45467	TZ-ARC	10/04/76	Emirates Air Transport	Nairobi, Kenya
Handley Page Hermes					
Hermes I	HP.68/1	G-AGSS	12/03/45	Handley Page Ltd.	Radlett, Herts, England
Hermes IV	HP.81/7	G-ALDF	08/25/52	Airwork Ltd.	Trapani, Sicily
Hermes IV	HP.81/15	G-ALDN	05/26/52	BOAC	Atar, Libya
Hermes IV	HP.81/22	G-ALDV	04/01/58	Skyways Ltd.	Bishops Stortford, Herts, England
Lockheed 049 Constellation					
049	1968	4X-AKC	07/27/55	El Al	Petrich, Bulgarian/Greek border
C-69/049	1976	N2737A	11/08/61	Imperial Airlines	Richmond, Virginia
C-69/049	1978	N2735A	05/12/59	Capital Airlines	Charleston, West Virginia
049	2025	N86504	03/01/64	Paradise Airlines	Lake Tahoe, California
049	2026	N86505	12/28/46	Transcontinental & Western Air	Shannon, Eire
049	2028	N86507	11/18/47	Transcontinental & Western Air	Newcastle, Delaware
049	2029	N86508	05/11/47	Transcontinental & Western Air	Cape May, New Jersey
049	2032	PP-PDJ	06/12/55	Panair do Brasil	Asuncion, Paraguay
049	2034	N86510	03/29/46	Transcontinental & Western Air	Washington, D.C.
049	2035	N86511	10/01/61	Trans World Airways	Chicago-Midway Airport, Illinois
049	2037	PP-PDG	05/29/72	Amazonense Imortacao e Exportacao Ltd.	Cruziero do Sul Acre, Brazil

Type	MSN	Reg.	Date	Airline	Nearest major city
049	2039	N86512	10/12/46	Transcontinental & Western Air	Newcastle, Delaware
049	2040	N86513	07/11/46	Transcontinental & Western Air	Reading, Pennsylvania
049	2046	N88846	06/22/51	Pan Am	Monrovia, Liberia
049	2047	PP-PDE	12/14/62	Panair do Brasil	Parana de Eva, Manaus, Brazil
049	2058	N88858	04/15/48	Pan Am	Shannon, Ireland
049	2062	PP-PCG	07/28/50	Panair do Brasil	Porto Alegre, Brazil
049	2066	PP-PDA	06/17/53	Panair do Brasil	Sao Paulo, Brazil
049	2083	PH-TEN	10/20/48	KLM-Royal Dutch Airlines	Prestwick, Scotland
Lockheed 649/749 Constellation					
749	2506	VT-CQP	11/03/50	Air India	Mont Blanc, Swiss/French border
649	2521	OB-R-771	04/27/66	Lansa	Tomas, Peru
749A	2527	F-BAZX	12/24/58	Air France	Vienna, Austria
649/749A	2533	N112A	12/21/55	Eastern Airlines	Jacksonville, Florida
749	2541	PH-TER	06/23/49	KLM-Royal Dutch Airlines	Bari, Italy
749	2545	F-BAZM	01/11/63	Air France	Perpignan, France
749	2546	F-BAZN	10/28/49	Air France	St. Miguel Island, Azores
749A	2554	EI-ADA	03/13/54	BOAC	Kallang Airport, Singapore
749A	2555	N1554V	06/14/60	Pacific Northern Airlines	Mount Gilbert, Alaska
749	2558	PH-TDF	07/12/49	KLM-Royal Dutch Airline	Bombay, India
749	2560	YV-C-AMA	11/27/56	Linea Aeropostal Venezolana	Caracas, Venezuela
749	2607	HI-328	10/26/81	Aerolineas Argo	St. Thomas, Virgin Islands
749	2608	ET-T-35	07/10/57	Ethiopian Airlines	Khartoum, Sudan
749A	2611	N116	04/26/62	Federal Aviation Admin.	Canton Island
749A	2615	HH-ABA	11/11/61	Air Haiti Int'l	San Juan, Puerto Rico
749A	2616	N119A	10/19/53	Eastern Airlines	New York, New York
749A	2617	N120A	08/04/69	Trans Southern Corp.	Sao Paulo, Brazil
749A	2628	F-BAZS	08/03/53	Air France	Castellorizo, Turkey
749A	2636	N6004C	08/31/50	Trans World Airlines	Wadi Natrum, Egypt
649A	2662	5N-85H	11/28/69	Air Interamerica	Algeria
749A	2664	HK-163	08/09/54	Avianca	Terceira Island, Azores
749A	2665	XA-MEV	06/02/58	Aeronaves de Mexico	Guadalajara, Mexico
749A	2666	VT-DEP	04/11/55	Air India	Great Natuna Islands, Sarawak, South China Sea
749A	2674	F-BAZZ	09/01/53	Air France	Mont Cemet, French Alps
Lockheed 1049 Super Constellation					
1049	4015	N6901C	03/06/66	Lineas Aereas Patagonicas Argentinas	Callao, Peru
1049	4016	N6902C	06/30/56	Trans World Airlines	mid-air with DC-7 N6324C
1049	4021	N6907C	12/16/60	Trans World Airlines	mid-air with DC-8 N8013U
1049D	4165	N6503C	11/10/58	Seaboard & Western Airlines	New York, New York
C-121C	4192	HI-515CT	04/05/90	Aerolineas Mundo	Puerto Rico
1049C	4504	PH-LKT	07/15/57	KLM-Royal Dutch Airlines	Biak, New Guinea
1049C	4509	PH-LKY	09/05/54	KLM-Royal Dutch Airline	Shannon, Eire
1049E	4512	F-BGNC	08/09/69	Catair	Douala, Cameroon
1049C	4526	N6218C	12/04/65	Eastern Airlines	mid-air with Boeing 707 N748TW, North Salem, New York
1049G	4541	N189S	05/28/63	Standard Airways	Manhattan, Kansas
1049G	4550	EC-AIN	05/05/65	Iberia	Tenerife, Canary Islands
1049G	4552	EC-AIP	03/06/61	Iberia	Sao Paulo, Brazil
1049E	4556	HK-177	01/21/60	Avianca	Montego Bay, Jamaica
1049E	4561	YV-C-AMS	06/20/56	Linea Aeropostal Venezolana	New York, New York
1049E	4564	CF-TGG	12/17/54	Trans Canada Airlines	Toronto, Canada
1049G	4575	YV-C-ANC	10/14/58	Linea Aeropostal Venezolana	Maracaibo, Venezuela
1049G	4602	D-ALAK	01/11/59	Lufthansa	Rio de Janerio, Brazil
1049G	4606	VH-EAC	08/24/60	Qantas	Plaisance Airport, Mauritius
1049G	4610	PP-VDA	08/16/57	Varig	Cabarete, Dominican Republic
1049G	4622	F-BHBC	08/29/60	Air France	Dakar, Senegal
1049H	4636	N174W	05/05/70	North Slope Supply Co.	Barrow, Alaska
1049G	4645	5T-TAC	01/00/68	Biafran Government	Port Harcourt, Biafra
1049G	4652	N7125C	11/08/60	Iberia	Barcelona, Spain
1049G	4667	VT-DIN	07/19/59	Air India	Bombay, India
1049G	4670	F-BHMK	12/06/57	Air France	Paris, France

Type	MSN	Reg.	Date	Airline	Nearest major city
1049G	4673	N8021	06/07/70	Aviaco	La Rioja, Argentina
1049H	4674	N173W	06/09/73	Aircraft Specialties Co.	Montreal, Canada
1049G	4678	HP-467	03/30/68	RAPSA	Panama City, Panama
1049H	4810	N6913C	12/14/62	Flying Tiger Line	Burbank, California
1049H	4811	N6914C	12/15/65	Flying Tiger Line	Alamosa, New Mexico
1049H	4812	N6915C	12/24/64	Flying Tiger Line	San Francisco, California
1049H	4815	N6917C	12/16/73	Andes	Miami, Florida
1049H	4817	N6921C	03/15/62	Flying Tiger Line	Guam
1049H	4822	N6920C	09/09/58	Flying Tiger Line	Mount Oyama, Japan
1049H	4824	N102R	11/23/59	Trans World Airlines	Chicago-Midway, Illinois
1049H	4827	N6923C	09/23/62	Flying Tiger Line	near Shannon, Eire
1049H	4828	CF-NAJ	08/03/69	Canairelief Air Ltd.	Uli Airstrip, Biafra
1049H	4834	N564E	10/20/71	Balair Inc.	near Great Inagua, Bahamas
1049H	4838	N566E	09/24/73	The Holy Nation of Islam,	Gary, Indiana
1049H	4840	N45516	05/11/75	Aircraft Specialties	Mesa, Arizona
1049H	4841	PH-LKM	08/14/58	KLM-Royal Dutch Airlines	near Shannon, Eire
1049H	4849	N6936C	06/22/67	Airlift Int'l	mid-air with RF-4C, Saigon, Vietnam
1049H	4850	N74CA	06/22/80	Air Traders Int'l	Columbus, Ohio
1049H	4851	N9740Z	02/03/63	Slick Airways	San Francisco, California
Lockheed 1649 Starliner					
1649A	1002	N7301C	12/18/66	Aerocondor Colombia	Bogota, Columbia
1649A	1008	LV-GLI	09/03/64	Federal Aviation Admin.	Deer Valley, Arizona
1649A	1015	N7313C	06/26/59	Trans World Airlines	Milan, Italy
1549A	1027	F-BHBM	05/10/61	Air France	Edjele, Libya
Martin 202, 404					
202	9134	N93050	03/07/50	Northwest Orient Airlines	Minneapolis-St. Paul, Minnesota
202	9144	N93054	01/16/51	Northwest Orient Airlines	Reardon, Washington
202	9158	N93037	10/13/50	Northwest Orient Airlines	Almelund, Minnesota
202	9159	N174A	12/01/51	Allegheny Airlines	Williamsport, Pennsylvania
202	9160	N93039	11/05/51	Transocean Airlines	Tucumcari, New Mexico
202	9161	N93040	11/07/50	Northwest Orient Airlines	Butte, Montana
202	9164	N94043	04/09/52	Transocean Airlines	O'Shuma Island, Japan
202	9165	N93044	08/29/48	Northwest Orient Airlines	Winona, Minnesota
202A	14081	N93211	01/12/55	Trans World Airlines	mid-air with DC-3 N999B, Covington, Kentucky
404	14101	N40401	08/22/62	Piedmont Airlines	Wilmington, North Carolina
404	14103	N40403	04/01/56	Trans World Airlines	Pittsburgh, Pennsylvania
404	14114	CP-1440	12/12/79	Camba Ltd.	Apolo, Bolivia
404	14116	N40412	05/30/70	Le High Acres Dev. Co.	Atlanta, Georgia
404	14120	N40416	02/19/55	Trans World Airlines	Albuquerque, New Mexico
404	14122	N445A	02/17/56	Eastern Airlines	Ownesboro, Kentucky
404	14140	N449A	07/02/63	Mohawk Airlines	Rochester, New York
404	14151	N464M	10/02/70	Golden Eagle Aviation	Silver Plume, Colorado
404	14170	N40406	11/20/66	Piedmont Airlines	New Bern, North Carolina
404	14173	N40438	11/16/79	Nevada Airlines	Grand Canyon, Arizona
404	14228	N40443	06/27/86	Frontier Airways	Buffalo, New York
404	14290	N13415	11/10/78	J. Whaley	Punta Fija, Venezuela
SAAB Scandia					
90A-2	90.103	PP-SQE	12/30/58	VASP	Santos Dumont, Brazil
90A-1	90.106	PP-SQV	09/23/59	VASP	Sao Paulo, Brazil
90A-1	90.107	PP-SRA	11/26/62	VASP	mid-air with Cessna 310, Paraibuna, Brazil
Scottish Aviation Twin Pioneer					
1	503	G-AOEO	12/07/57	Scottish Aviation	Tripoli, Libya
1	509	JZ-PPX	08/30/57	Nederlands Nieuw Guinea	Japen Island, New Guinea
1	511	PK-GTB	09/20/63	Garuda Indonesian Airlines	location unknown
1	517	VR-OAE	09/16/63	Borneo Airways	Siba, Sarawak
1	519	9M-ANC	05/17/67	Malaysian Airways	Limbang, Malaysia
1	523	5N-ABQ	04/04/67	Bristow Helicopters	Ughelli, Nigeria
1	526	5N-ABQ	01/16/63	Bristow Helicopters	Chepbeica, Morocco

Type	MSN	Reg.	Date	Airline	Nearest major city
Vickers Viking					
621/1A	127	G-AIJE	09/02/58	Independant Air Travel	London-Heathrow, England
614/1	142	G-AHPI	02/17/52	Hunting Air Travel	Monte la Cinta, Sicily
610/1B	148	G-AHPK	01/06/48	British European Airways	Finebush Lane, Ruislip, England
610/3B	152	G-AHPM	08/09/61	Cunard Eagle Airways	Holthei, Norway
610/1B	155	G-APHN	10/31/50	British European Airways	London-Heathrow, England
616/1B	159	VP-YEX	03/17/55	Central African Airways	Belvedere, Salisbury, England
628/1B	196	SU-AGN	03/07/58	Misrair	Port Said, Egypt
628/1B	197	OD-DLI	12/29/47	DDL	Copenhagen, Denmark
628/1B	199	OD-DLU	02/08/49	DDL	Landskrona, Denmark
632/1B	205	VT-CLY	02/06/48	Air India	Bombay, India
634/1B	210	SU-AFM	08/24/60	Don Everall Aviation	Heraklion, Crete
634/1B	213	SU-AFK	12/15/53	Misrair	Cairo, Egypt
610/1B	216	F-BJER	09/11/63	Airnautic	Pyrenees, France
610/1B	229	C-AIVP	04/05/48	British European Airways	mid-air with Yak, Berlin, Germany
644/1B	231	YI-ABQ	10/10/55	Iraqi Airways	Baghdad, Iraq
610/1B	241	G-AJBO	05/01/57	Eagle Aviation Ltd.	Blackbushe, Hampshire, England
610/1B	248	F-BFDN	09/05/59	Airnautic	Traliceto, Southern Corsica
610/1B	262	G-AJDL	01/05/53	British European Airways	Nutts Corner, Belfast, Northern Ireland

The tail section of Air West DC-9-31, msn 47441, is still fitted with the lifting straps used by a helicopter in the attempt to remove this piece of wreckage. This jetliner collided with an F-4 Phantom II in mid-air over the San Gabriel Mountains in Southern California. For more information, please see Chapter 18. (J. Douglas Scroggins III)

Appendix III

Jet And Turbo-Prop Crashes

This list is intended as a starting point for research purposes only. It does not list every aircraft of a particular type that has crashed. The authors/publishers make no guarantees that wreckage still exists at these sites. Wreckchasers are cautioned to do their research and be prepared before setting out on an adventure.

Type	MSN	Reg.	Date	Airline	Nearest Major City
Hawker Siddeley HS 748					
HS 748	1536	G-ARMV	07/11/65	Skyways Coach Air	Lympne, Kent, UK
HS 748	1539	LV-HGW	02/04/70	Aerolineas Argentinas	Corrientes, Argentian
HS 748	1540	LV-HHB	04/15/76	Aerolineas Argentinas	Neuquen, Argentina
HS 748	1546	LV-HHH	01/20/71	Aerolineas Atgentinas	Sarmiento, Argentina
HS 748	1560	G-ASPL	06/26/81	Dan-Air	Nailstone, England
HS 748	1568	HS-THB	04/27/80	Thai Airways	Bangkok, Thailand
HS 748	1580	YC-C-AMY	08/20/68	Linea Aeropostal Venezolana	Maturin, Venezuela
HS 748	1582	C-GDOV	01/12/89	Bradley Air Services	Dayton, Ohio
HS 748	1586	RP-C1029	05/10/75	Philippine Airlines	Manila, Philippines
HS 748	1590	RP-C1028	02/03/75	Philippine Airlines	Manila, Philippines
HS 748	1598	XA-SEV	01/06/72	SAESA	Chetumal, Mexico
HS 748	1617	C-GQTH	11/10/93	Northland Air Manitoba	Sandy Lake, Ontario, Canada
HS 748	1618	C-GQSV	12/03/88	Air Creebec	Waskaganish, Canada
HS 748	1620	PK-IHE	01/09/93	Bouraq Indonesia Airlines	Surabaya-Juanda, Indonesia
HS 748	1625	PP-VDN	06/17/75	VARIG	Pedro Afonso, Gioias, Brazil
HS 748	1632	PP-VDU	02/09/72	VARIG	Porto Alegre, Brazil
HS 748	1633	PK-IHK	02/09/77	Bouraq Indonesia Airlines	Ujung Pandang, Indonesia
HS 748	1635	C-GEPH	XX/29/81	Eastern Provincial Airways	Sydney, Nova Scotia
HS 748	1637	RP-C1015	06/26/87	Philippine Airlines	Crashed Mt. Pugo, Baguio, Philippines
HS 748	1643	RP-C1022	04/21/70	Philippine Airlines	Manila, Philippines
HS 748	1673	XA-SAB	07/27/73	SAESA	Acapulco, Mexico
HS 748	1683	HC-AUE	01/20/76	TAME Ecuador	Andes Mts. near Guayaquil, Ecuador
HS 748	1704	FAC-1103	01/09/74	SATENA	Florencia, Columbia
HS 748	1705	FAC-1104	08/07/83	SATENA	Pasto, Columbia
HS 748	1789	C-GFFA	09/15/88	Bradley Air Services	Ottawa, Canada
BAe Jetstream 31					
Jetstream 31	623	N823JS	02/09/88	Jetstream Int'l Airways	Springfield, Ohio
Jetstream 31	683	N165PC	03/12/92	CCAir	Knoxville, Tennessee
Jetstream 31	706	N334PX	12/01/93	Express Airlines	Hibbing, Minnesota
Jetstream 31	742	N331CY	05/26/87	Air New Orleans	New Orleans, Louisiana
Jetstream 31	776	N410UE	12/26/89	North Pacific Airlines	Pasco, Washington
Jetstream 31	787	N131CA	04/20/93	Westair Commuter Airlines	Merced, California
Bristol Britannia 102					
102	12903	G-ANBB	09/01/66	Britannia Airways	Ljublijana Airport, Yugoslavia
253 C Mk1	13448	G-BRAC	02/16/80	Red Coat Air Cargo	Boston, Massachusetts
Canadair CL-44-6/CC-106					
	1	HK-1972	02/22/75	Aerocondor Columbia	Alto de Toledo, Columbia
CL-44-6/CC-106	12	OB-R1104	08/27/76	Aeronaves del Peru	Lima, Peru

Type	MSN	Reg.	Date	Airline	Notes
CL-44D4-2	22	N453T	03/21/66	Flying Tiger Lines	Norfolk, Virginia
CASA 235					
CASA 235-10	14	PK-MNN	10/18/92	Merpati Nusantara Airlines	Mt. Papandayan, Western Java
Convair 580					
Convair 580	23	N73130	03/05/67		Marseille, Ohio
Convair 580	56	LN-PAA	09/08/89		Hirtshals, Denmark
Convair 580	83	N90858	06/29/72	North Central Airlines	mid-air with Air Wisconsin DHC-6 N4043B
Convair 580	98	N25278	09/19/91	Canair Cargo	Burlington, Vermont
Convair 580	157	YV-84C	05/28/85	AVENSA	Cabimas, Venezuela
Convair 580	180	ZK-FTB	07/31/89	Fieldair	Auckland, New Zealand
Convair 580	380	N4825C	07/24/78	North Central Airlines	Kalamazoo, Michigan
Convair 580	384	N5832	06/07/71		New Haven, Connecticut
Convair 580	386	N5825	01/06/69	Allegheny Airlines	Bradford, Pennsylvania
Convair 580	410	N5802		Allegheny Airlines	Bradford, Pennsylvania
Convair 580	452	N67701	12/12/63	Union Oil Co. of California	Midland, Texas
Convair 640					
Convair 640	9	N862FW	02/09/92		Cape Skirrinng, Senegal
DHC-6 Twin Otter					
DHC-6-100	5	N7705	05/25/73	Air Central	Savoy, Illinois
DHC-6-100	6	VH-TGR	04/28/70	Trans Australia Airlines	Kainatu, New Guinea
DHC-6-100	13	N4043B	06/29/72	Air Wisconsin	mid-air with North Central Convair 580 N90858, Neenah, Wisconsin
DHC-6-100	18	XA-BOP	09/09/78	Lineas Aereas del Centro	Mexico City, Mexico
DHC-6-100	19	C-FAJB	12/16/72	Airwest Airlines	Vancouver Island, British Columbia
DHC-6-100	30	I-CLAI	03/11/67	Aeralpi	Mt. Visentin, Borga Prigola, Italy
DHC-6-100	31	D-IDHC	05/27/67	General Air	Heligoland, Germany
DHC-6-100	34	C-FAUS	11/11/84	Labrador Airways	Mealy Mtns., Goose Bay, Newfoundland
DHC-6-100	38	N2711H	09/09/69	Interior Airways	Sagwan, Alaska
DHC-6-100	39	BR-GCP		Guyana Airways	Georgetown, Guyana
DHC-6-100	56	67-056	07/11/72	Royal Norwegian Air Force	Harstad, Norway
DHC-6-100	58	CF-WGF-X	06/13/87	Athabaska Airways	Maudsley Lake, Canada
DHC-6-100	63	67-063	10/29/90	Royal Norwegian Air Force	Honningsvaag, Norway
DHC-6-100	67	CF-AWF	09/22/76		Mosher Creek, Bella Coola, British Columbia
DHC-6-100	68	N202RH	06/17/88	Samoa Aviation	Tau Manua, American Samoa
DHC-6-100	70	PK-NUC	02/28/73	Merpati Nusantara Airlines	Nabire, Indonesia
DHC-6-100	76	PK-MAM	05/25/87	Missionary Aviation Fellowship	Ilaga, Indonesia
DHC-6-100	83	N6383	01/09/75	Golden West Airlines	mid-air Whittier, Calif., Cessna 120 N11421
DHC-6-100	84	P2-RDE	02/28/78	Talair	Garaina, Papua New Guinea
DHC-6-100	85	ST-ADB	03/18/75	Sudan Airways	Khartoum, Sudan
DHC-6-100	95	CF-QBT	03/06/93	Kenn Borek Air	Baffin Island, NWT, Canada
DHC-6-100	100	C-GPBO	12/01/77	Airwest Airlines	Satuma Island, British Columbia
DHC-6-100	102	9N-RF9	02/27/70	Nepalese Royal Flight	Jomson, Nepal
DHC-6-100 (-300)	105	N127PM	02/21/82	Pilgrim Airlines	Providence, Rhode Island
DHC-6-200	122	C-FWAF	09/30/79	West Coast Air Services	Porpoise Bay, British Columbia
DHC-6-200	125	N4048B	10/13/78	Artic Guide	Barrow, Alaska
DHC-6-200	131	N187SA	04/18/90	Aeroplerlas	Contadora, Panama
DHC-6200	141	N141VP	04/22/92	Perris Valley Aviation Services	Perris, California
DHC-6-200	142	CF-MHU	09/30/75	Northern Thunderbird Air	Klua Tan Tan, British Columbia
DHC-6-200	159	N996SA	01/19/88	Mountain Air Cargo	Charlotte, North Carolina
DHC-6-200	166	OH-KOA	02/05/73	Kar-Air Finland	Pudasjarui, Finland
DHC-6-200	175	N558MA	07/15/60	New York Airways	New York, New York
DHC-6-200	183	N103AQ	05/16/82	Kodiak Aviation	Hooper Bay, Alaska
DHC-6-200	192	N3257	10/11/85	Mountain Air Cargo	Homer City, Pennsylvania
DHC-6-200	195	N7267	07/20/88	Fairways Corp.	Dulles, Washington, D.C.
DHC-6-200	196	N563MA	09/06/77	Alaska Aeronautical Industries	Mt. Iliamna, Alaska
DHC-6-200	203	N958SM	11/09/70	Mississippi Valley Airlines	La Crosse, Wisconsin
DHC-6-200	213	C-FGIK	12/17/83	Inuvik Coastal Airways	Paulatuk, NWT, Canada
DHC-6-200	215	C-FAIV	09/03/78	Stanley Park	Vancouver, British Columbia
DHC-6-200	227	VH-PAQ	02/13/79	Pan-Air	Yarra Creek, King Island, Tasmania
DHC-6-200	230	T-87	08/07/77	Lineas Aereas del Estado	Bariloche, Comodoro Rivdavia, Argentina

Type	MSN	Reg.	Date	Airline	Nearest major city
DHC-6-300	236	N76214	07/13/78	Coastair	Gander, Newfoundland
DHC-6-300	246	CF-QDG	08/23/78	Bradley Air Services	Frobisher Bay, Canada
DHC-6-300	248	N76GC	06/18/86	Grand Canyon Airlines	near Grand Canyon Airport, Arizona
DHC-6-300	251	N389EX	04/28/74	Air America	Laos
DHC-6-300	252	HK-1710W	12/19/79	Am Son Drilling Co.	Bogota, Columbia
DHC-6-300	256	H4-SIB	09/27/91	Solomon Islands Airlines	Honiara, Solomon Islands
DHC-6-300	258	F-OGFE	12/21/72		Crashed off St. Martin
DHC-6-300	262	N101AC	12/12/76	Atlantic City Airlines	Wildwood, New Jersey
DHC-6-300	278	CF-ABW	12/21/77	Kenn Borek Air	Namisivik, NWT, Canada
DHC-6-300	294	N8061V	12/03/79	Evergreen Helicopters	Nome, Alaska
DHC-6-300	302	9N-ABB	07/05/92	Royal Nepal Airlines	Jumia, Nepal
DHC-6-300	326	N5662	07/25/72	Air America	Laos
DHC-6-300	333	VP-FAP	01/24/77	British Antartic Survey	Antartica
DHC-6-300	341	8Q-GIA	02/07/87	Inter Atoll Air	Maldives Islands
DHC-6-300	345	PK-NUE	09/15/89	Merpati Nusantara Airlines	Manokwasi-Benuti, Indonesia
DHC-6-300	346	PK-NUG	08/12/85	Merpati Nusantara Airlines	Mulia, Iran Jaya, Indonesia
DHC-6-300	349	C-FWAB	06/06/90	Ptarmigan Airways	Thistle Lake NWT, Canada
DHC-6-300	354	C-FCSV		Canadian Dept. Trans	Galt, Ontario, Canada
DHC-6-300	361	N361V	02/15/83	Sierra Pacific Airlines	Sun Valley, Idaho
DHC-6-300	363	CP-1018	05/19/87	YPF Bolivianos	El Trompillo, Santa Cruz, Bolivia
DHC-6-300	366	P2-RDW	07/21/89	Air Guadeloupe	Porega, Papua New Guinea
DHC-6-300	370	9N-ABG	10/15/73	Royal Nepal Airlines	location unknown
DHC-6-300	376	9N-ABH	12/22/84	Royal Nepal Airlines	Bhojpur, Nepal
DHC-6-300	387	N25RM	12/04/78	Rocky Mountain Airways	Steamboat Springs, Colorado
DHC-6-300	391	PK-NUL	06/17/93	Merpati Nusantara Airlines	Nibire, Irian Jaya, indonesia
DHC-6-300	392	9N-ABI	05/03/86	Royal Nepal Airlines	Sanphe Bagar, Nepal
DHC-6-300	393	6V-ADE	12/10/93	Air Senegal	mid-air with YS-11, Dakar, Senegal
DHC-6-300	394	TZ-ACH	06/21/83	Air Mali	Bamako, Mali
DHC-6-300	395	YA-GAZ	03/10/83	Bakhtar Afgan Airlines	Shashgow Ghazni, Afghanistan
DHC-6-300	400	N707PV	10/28/89	Aloha Island Air	Molokai, Hawaii
DHC-6-300	401	N540N	03/12/85	Seair Alaska Airlines	Barter Island, Alaska
DHC-6-300	408	LN-BNM	10/27/93	Wideroes Flyveselskap	Namsos, Norway
DHC-6-300	416	TJ-CBC	10/31/81	Cameroon Airlines	Bafoussam, Cameroon
DHC-6-300	417	C-GKBM	07/14/88	Kenn Borek Air	John Day, Oregon
DHC-6-300	419	HK-2920	10/11/87	Aerojecutivos Columbia	El Poleo, Columbia
DHC-6-300	428	C-GDHA	05/03/76	deHavilland Canada	Monze, Zambia
DHC-6-300	431	N23BC	11/05/79	South Pacific Island Airways	Tau Island, American Samoa
DHC-6-300	439	N75GC	09/27/89	Grand Canyon Airlines	Grand Canyon, Arizona
DHC-6-300	452	TN-ACX	03/12/92	Lina Congo	Estouali, Congo
DHC-6-300	457	HC-BAX	05/22/81	TAME Ecuador	Zumba, Ecuador
DHC-6-300	459	PK-NUY	12/30/87	Merpati Nusantara Airlines	Samarinda-Berau, Indonesia
DHC-6-300	463	C-GNTB	01/14/77	Northern Thunderbird Air	Terrace, British Columbia
DHC-6-300	465	N982FL	01/18/78	Frontier Airlines	Pueblo Memorial Airport, Colorado
DHC-6-300	469	F-OGHD	11/18/78	Air Guadeloupe	Marie Galante Island, Guadeloupe
DHC-6-300	473	PK-NUT	09/16/93	Merpati Nusantara Airlines	location unknown
DHC-6-300	474	PK-NUW	05/23/87	Merpati Nusantara Airlines	Ruteng, Flores Island, Indonesia
DHC-6-300	486	PK-NUP	03/29/77	Merpati Nusantara Airlines	Bainaha Valley, Sulawesi, Indonesia
DHC-6-300	488	PK-NUQ	04/03/90	Merpati Nusantara Airlines	Lebuhanraio, Indonesia
DHC-6-300	497	HK-1910	01/23/85	Aces Columbia	Quibdo-Medelin, Columbia
DHC-6-300	501	XY-AEB	08/12/82	Burma Airways	Mindat, Burma
DHC-6-300	512	XY-AEE	10/08/83	Burma Airways	Lonkin Airfield, Burma
DHC-6-300	526	YV-30C	04/17/78	Linea Aeropostal Venezolana	Vrima, Venezuela
DHC-6-300	536	LN-BNS	04/12/90	Wideroes Flyveselskap	into sea, Vaeroey, Loften Islands
DHC-6-300	540	XY-AEH	09/08/77	Burma Airways Corp.	Monghsa-Keng Tung, Burma
DHC-6-300	541	XY-AEI	08/26/78	Burma Airways Corp.	Papun, South Burma
DHC-6-300	568	LN-BNK	03/11/82	Wideroes Flyveselskap	North Cape, Norway
DHC-6-300	581	5H-MRD	12/20/84	Air Tanzania	Dares Salaam, Tanzania
DHC-6-300	606	HK-2889X	07/04/91	Helicol Columbia	El Yopal, Casnare, Columbia
DHC-6-300	609	HK-2216	12/18/81	Aces Columbia	Sanantero, Columbia
DHC-6-300	622	7P-LAA	07/13/84	Lesotho Airways	Mokhotiong, Lesotho
DHC-6-300	630	C-GTJA	11/01/79	Austin Airways	Big Trout Lake, Ontario, Canada
DHC-6-300	632	C-GTLA	11/23/83	Austin House	Lansdowne House, Thunder Bay, Canada
DHC-6-300	670	5A-DDD	11/30/88	Aero Club Libya	Hamada Oilfield, Libya
DHC-6-300	676	HK-2486	06/11/89	Aerotaca	Caribabre, Columbia

Type	MSN	Reg.	Date	Airline	Nearest major city
DHC-6-300	699	ET-AIL	08/07/89	RRC Air Service	Fugnido, Ethiopia
DHC-6-300	713	HK-2536	11/29/82	Aces Columbia	Cerro Pan de Azucar, Columbia
DHC-6-300	737	TY-BBL	02/24/83	Air Benin	Koko, near Beteron, Benin
DHC-6-300	771	HK-2759	06/06/93	Aces Columbia	El Yopal, Columbia
DHC-6-300	780	HK-2761	04/27/86	Aces Columbia	Saravena, Columbia
DHC-6-300	785	V2-LCT	08/03/86	LIAT	St. Vincent-Amos Vale
DHC-6-300	819	ET-AIQ	06/22/86	Ethiopian Airlines	Dembidollo, Ethiopia
DeHavilland DHC-7					
DHC-7 102	028	LN-WFN	05/06/88	Wideroes Flyveselskap	Broennoysund, Norway
DeHavilland DHC-8					
DHC-8-102	061	N819PH	04/16/88	Horizon Airlines	Seattle-Tacoma, Washington
DHC-8-311	210	D-BEAT	01/06/93	Contactair Flugdienst	Paris, France
Dornier 228					
228-100	4358	D-IFNS	03/26/82	Dornier	Igenhausen, Augsburg, Germany
228-201	8052/0052	VT-EJF	09/24/89	Vuyadoot	Lake Indopur, Pune, India
228-201	8110/0110	B-12238	02/28/93	Formosa Airlines	into sea off Green Island, Taiwan
228-201	8151/0151	B-12298	06/14/93	Formosa Airlines	into sea off Green Island, Taiwan
228-212	8196/0196	F-OHAB	04/19/91	Air Tahiti	into sea off Nuku Hive Island
Embraer Emb.110 Banderiante					
110C	110004	PT-TBA	10/28/76	Nordeste Linhas Aereas	Petrolia-Pemanbuco, Brazil
110C	110005	PT-TBB	02/03/92	Nordeste Linhas Aereas	Caetite, Bahia, Brazil
110C	110010	PP-SBB	02/08/79	TAM Linhas Aerea Regional	Bauru, Adudos, Brazil
110C	110011	PT-TBD	01/22/76	Transbrazil	Chapeco, Santa Catarina, Brazil
110C	110013	PP-SBC	06/28/84	TAM Linhas Aerea Regional	Sao Pedro d'Aldeia, Brazil
110C	110021	PP-SBE	02/27/75	VASP	Sao Paulo, Brazil
110C	110037	PP-SBJ	03/23/93	TAM Linhas Aerea Regional	Tangara de Serra, Cuiba, Brazil
110P	110063	PT-GJN	06/23/85	TABA	Cuiaba, Brazil
110EJ	110088	PT-GJZ	08/14/84	VOTEC	mid-air with PT-GKL (msn 110107) near Imperatriz, Maranhao State, Brazil
110C	110090	PT-GKA	10/09/85	Nordeste Linhas Aereas	Vitoria, Brazil
110P	110092	PT-GKC	05/22/82	Rio Sul del	Florianopolis, Brazil
110P	110107	PT-GKL	08/14/84	VOTEC	mid-air with PT-GJZ
110P	110130	PT-GKT	01/31/78	Rio Sul del	Eirunepe, Brazil
110P1	110206	HK-2651	09/02/81	El Venado	Paipa, Columbia
110P1	110226	PT-GMS	11/14/88	Wasa Wings	Ilmajoki, Finland
110P1	110275	N731A	10/08/91	BAC Charter	Narssarssuaq, Greenland
110P1	110294	G-HGGS	11/19/84	Euroair Transport	Inverness, Scotland
110P1	110302	HK-2593	08/04/85	Aires Columbia	Mocoa, Columbia
110P1	110314	PT-SCU	11/11/91	Uniao Taxi Aereo	Recife, Brazil
110P1	110330	N95PB	05/06/89	Southern Express	Mt. Pleasant, Tennessee
110P1	110341	HK-2638	01/23/85	Aires Columbia	Buga, Columbia
110P1	110365	N96PB	12/06/84	Provincetown-Boston Airline	Jacksonville, Florida
110P1	110366	HK-2743	--/--/85	Tavina	location unknown, Columbia
110P1	110368	PT-FAW	09/20/90	Sudene	Fera de Noronha, Brazil
110P1	110370	N1356P	03/13/86	Simmons Airlines	near Alpena-Phelps Collins Airport, Mississippi
110P1	110389	N65DA	05/24/88	Atlantic Southeast Airlines	Lawton, Kansas
110P1	110391	G-ZAPE	01/13/93	Titan Airways	Sellafield, Cumbria, England
110P1	110402	ZS-LGP	03/01/88	Bopair	Johannesburg, South Africa
Embraer Emb.120 Brasilia					
120RT	120019	N219AS	09/19/86	Atlantic Southeast Airlines	San Jose dos Campos, Brazil, on delivery
flight 120RT	120033	F-GEGH	12/21/87	Air Littoral	Bordeaux, France
120RT	120077	N33701	9/11/90	Continental Express	Eagle Pass, Texas
120RT	120218	N270AS	04/05/91	Atlantic Southeast Airlines	Brunswick, Georgia
Fairchild/Swearingen Merlin/Metro					
SA226AT	AT-005	N960M	04/14/75		Southern Pines, North Carolina
SA226AT	AT-008	N577KA	05/07/86	Career Aviation Academy	Billings, Montana
SA226TC	TC-228	N650S	06/12/80	Air Wisconsin	Valley, Nebraska

Type	MSN	Reg.	Date	Airline	Nearest major city
SA226TC	TC-231	N200KC	08/17/93	Aviation Services	Hartford, Connecticut
SA226TC	TC-240	N63Z	01/30/84	Britt Airways	Terre Haute, Indiana
SA226TC	TC-275	VH-SWO	05/13/80	Skywest Airlines	Esperence, Western Australia
SA226TC	TC-327	N163SW	01/15/87	Skywest Airlines	mid-air with Mooney M.20C N6485U, Salt Lake City, Utah
SA226TC	TC-334E	F-GCPG	11/18/88	Air Littoral	Lepaud-Montlucon, France
SA227AC	AC-449	N30093	12/07/82	Pioneer Airlines	Pueblo, Colorado
SA227AC	AC-457	N68TC	01/19/88	Trans-Colorado Airlines	Durango, Colorado
SA227AC	AC-481	C-GSLB	09/26/89	Skylink Airlines	Terrance, Canada
SA227AC	AC-500	D-IABB	02/08/88	Numberger Flugdienst	Dusseldorf, Germany
SA227AC	AC-545	N342AE	08/25/92	Lone Star Airlines	Hot Springs, Arkansas
SA227AC	AC-622	N622AV	02/19/88	AVAir	Raleigh-Durham, North Carolina
SA227AC	AC-653	N2689E	09/29/87	Horizon Airlines	Twin Falls, Idaho
SA227AC	AC-683	N683AV	02/01/91	Skywest Airlines	Ground collision with USAir Boeing 737-3B7, msn 23310, N388US, at LAX
SA227AC	AC-716	N2721M	01/15/90	Skywest Airlines	Elko, Nevada
Fairchild F-27					
F-27A	1	HC-ADV	11/07/60	AREA Ecuador	Quito, Ecuador
F-27	6	N2703	01/17/63	West Coast Airlines	Great Salt Lake, Salt Lake City, Utah
F-27	19	PI-C871	03/08/68	Air Manilla Int'l	into sea off Ibajay Village, Manilla-Cebu
F-27B	21	N4904	08/30/75	Wein Air Alaska	Gambell Airport, St. Lawrence Island
F-27A	29	N745L	11/15/64	Bonanza Air Lines	Las Vegas, Nevada
F-27	32	N2707	08/24/63	West Coast Airlines	Calgary, Canada
F-27A	36	N2770R	05/07/64	Pacific Air Lines	San Ramon, California, crew shot in flight
F-27	47	CF-QBL	03/29/79	Quebecair	Quebec City, Canada
F-27B	49	N4905	12/02/68	Wein Consolidated Airlines	Spotsy Lake, Alaska
F-27A	63	CC-CJE	12/09/82	Aeronor Chile	La Serena, Chile
F-27J	113	CF-GND	06/12/68	Great Northern Airways	Resolute Bay, Canada
F-27J	118	CP-1117	06/02/80	Lloyd Aereo Boliviano	Tapecua Hills, Yacuiba, Bolivia
F-27F	123	N27W	05/04/68	Eastex Inc	Rancho-Paisano Airport, Bruni, Texas
F-27F	125	CF-PAP	02/08/69	Stanair Ltd.	Mikaa Lake, Canada
F-27J	127	CP-862	03/16/84	Lloyd Aereo Boliviano	El Pilon Hill, San Borja, Bolivia
Fairchild FH-227					
FH-227C	517	N380NE	10/25/68	Northeast Airlines	Moose Mountain, Lebanon Airport, N.H.
FH-227B	522	PT-LCS	01/25/93	TABA	Oeiras-Pa, Belem, Brazil
FH-227B	531	N7811M	11/19/69	Mohawk Airlines	Mount Pilot, Glenn Falls, New York
FH-227B	532	F-GGDM	04/10/89	Uni-Air	Valence, France
FH-227B	536	PT-LBV	06/12/82	TABA	Tabatinga, Brazil
FH-227B	541	N7818M	03/03/72	Mohawk Airlines	Albany, New York
FH-227B	546	F-GCPS	03/04/88	Transport AerienTransregional	Fontainebleau, France
FH-227B	556	PP-BUF	03/14/70	Paraense Transportes Aereos	Baja de Guajara Bay, Belem, Brazil
FH-227B	557	N712U	08/10/68	Piedmont Ailines	Charleston, West Virginia
FH-227B	570	PT-ICA	06/06/90	TABA	Altamira, Brazil
Fokker F.27					
F.27-100	10108	N148PM	01/13/84	Pilgrim Airlines	New York, New York
F.27-100	10112	VH-TFB	06/10/60	Trans Australia Airlines	Mackay, Queensland, Australia
F.27-100	10118	YN-BZF	04/20/85	Aeronica	Kulsuk, Greenland
F.27-100	10119	J5-GBB	08/15/91	TAGB Air Bissau	Dori, Burkina Faso, Africa
F.27-100	10123	TC-TEZ	02/17/70	Turk Hava Yollari	Samsun, Turkey
F.27-100	10141	HB-AAI	09/13/64	Balair AG	Malaga, Spain
F.27-100	10142	PK-KFR	11/04/76	Bali Int'l Air	Sjamsuddin Noor, Banjar-Masin, Indonesia
F.27-100	10147	PI-C501	02/28/67	Philippine Airlines	Mactan Cebu, Philippines
F.27-200	10163	AP-ALM	08/06/70	Pakistan Int'l Airlines	Islamabad, Pakistan
F.27-100	10173	VT-DMC	10/19/88	Indian Airlines	Gauhatu, India
F.27-100	10174	VT-DMD	07/24/76	Indian Airlines	Bhubaneshwar, India
F.27-100	10175	VT-DME	08/12/72	Indian Airlines	Maqsoodpur, Delhi-Palam, India
F.27-200	10180	VH-FNH	03/17/65	Ansett ANA	Launceston, Australia
F.27-100	10182	TC-TAY	09/23/61	Turk Hava Yollari	Ankara, Turkey
F.27-200	10188	AP-ALX	12/12/71	Pakistan Int'l Airlines	Karachi-Zahedan, Pakistan
F.27-100	10191	PI-C503	10/12/62	Philippine Airlines	Paranaquerizal, Manilla, Philippines
F.27-200	10193	ST-AAR	07/02/85	Sudan Airways	location unknown

Type	MSN	Reg.	Date	Airline	Nearest major city
F.27-200	10194	ST-AAS	10/05/82	Sudan Airways	Merowe, Sudan
F.27-200	10205	CR-AIB	03/27/70	Mozambique Airlines	Gago Coutinho, Lourenco Marques, Mozambique
F.27-200	10206	PT-LCG	02/12/90	Brazil Central	Bauru, Brazil
F.27-200	10207	PH-FDW	08/25/89	Pakistan Int'l Airlines	Gilgit-Islamabad, Pakistan
F.27-200	10235	XY-ADK	03/25/78	Burma Airways	Rangoon, Burma
F.27-200	10250	AP-ATO	12/15/78	Pakistan Int'l Airlines	Karachi, Pakistan
F.27-200	10251	I-ATIP	04/16/72	Aero Trasporti Italiani	Ardinello di Amasend, Grasinone, Italy
F.27-200	10271	PH-SAB	02/02/66	Indian Airlines	Srinagar-Juma, India
F.27-400M	10273	ST-ADX	05/10/72	Sudan Airways	El Obeid, Sudan
F.27-200	10279	AP-ATT	10/08/65	Pakistan Int'l Airways	Naran, Kaghan Valley, Pakistan
F.27-400M	10282	ST-ADW	06/06/77	Sudan Airways	Fasher, Sudan
F.27-100	10285	PI-C527	07/06/67	Philippine Airlines	Bacolod, Negros Island, Philippines
F.27-400	10306	PK-PFB	04/27/67	Fokker	Malaybalay, Philippines
F.27-200	10308	S2-ABG	11/18/79	Bangladesh Biman	Savar Bazar, Dacca, Bangladesh
F.27-200	10309	VT-DVG	06/07/70	Indian Airlines	Agartala, India
F.27-100	10311	PI-C532	05/09/70	Philippines Airlines	Iligan Airport, Philippines
F.27-400	10313	XY-ADO	08/19/80	Burma Airways	Moulmein, Burma
F.27-600	10314	AP-AUS	12/08/72	Pakistan Int'l Airlines	Rawalpindi, Pakistan
F.27-600	10325	XY-AEK	02/03/89	Burma Airways	Rangoon, Burma
F.27-200	10330	AP-AUV	12/30/70	Pakistan Int'l Airlines	Shemshemagar, Pakistan
F.27-600	10335	AP-AUX	10/23/86	Pakistan Int'l Airlines	Peshawar, Pakistan
F.27-400	10336	VT-DWT	08/29/70	Indian Airlines	Kumbhirgram, Silchar, India
F.27-300	10356	TF-FIL	09/26/70	Icelandair	Myggenaes, Faroe Islands
F.27-200	10357	XY-ADP	06/21/87	Burma Airways	Hopong, Burma
F.27-600	10395	9Q-CLO	03/03/76	Air Zaire	locations unknown
F.27-600	10399	PK-MFD	05/09/91	Merpati Nusantara Airlines	Manado, Sulawezi, Indonesia
F.27-600	10402	9Q-CLP	02/08/80	Air Zaire	Kinshasa-Ndjili, Zaire
F.27-400M	10404	TC-72	03/16/75	Lineas Aereas del Estado	San Carlos de Bariloche, Argentina
F.27-600	10406	9Q-CLR	01/06/76	Air Zaire	Kisangani, Zaire
F.27-600	10410	PK-JFF	06/05/91	Sempati Air Transport	Gresik, Indonesia
F.27-400M	10411	TC-75	06/10/70	Lineas Aereas del Estado	Lima, Peru
F.27-400M	10416	TC-77	12/02/69	Lineas Aereas del Estado	Marambia, Antarctica
F.27-600	10422	PK-GFJ	09/07/74	Garuda Indonesia Airways	Tanjung Karang, Indonesia
F.27-500	10426	OY-APB	12/27/69	Maersk Air	Ronne, Denmark
F.27-500	10428	HL5212	01/23/71	Korean Air	Kansong, Korea
F.27-200	10439	CR-LLD	05/21/72	DTA Angola Airlines	Lobito, Angola
F.27-600	10443	OY-APE	05/26/88	Starair	Hannover, Germany
F.27-600	10452	XY-ADQ	06/16/88	Burma Airways	Putao, Burma
F.27-600	10453	S2-ABJ	08/05/84	Bangladesh Biman	Dhaka Airport, Bangladesh
F.27-500	10456	ZK-NFC	02/17/79	Air New Zealand	Auckland, New Zealand
F.27-600	10462	PK-GFP	09/26/72	Garuda Indonesian Airways	Jakarta, Indonesia
F.27-500	10463	9V-BCU	11/23/71	Malaysai-Singapore Airlines	Kota Kinabalu, Sabah
F.27-500	10473	C-GSFS	09/04/89	Securite Civile	La Grande Combe, Arles, France
F.27-600	10501	XY-ADS	10/12/85	Burma Airways	Putao, Burma
F.27-600RF	10557	6O-SAY	07/20/81	Somali Airlines	Balad, Sommali
F.27-600RF	10559	6O-SAZ	08/02/77	Somali Airlines	Borama, Somali
F.27-600	10562	D-AELB	02/24/90	FTG Air Service Flugcharter	Bergisch Gladbach, Germany
F.27-500	10570	F-BYAH	01/27/79	Air Rouergue	Rodez Airfield, France
F.27-600	10572	XY-ADY	10/03/78	Burma Airways	Mandalay, Burma
F.27-600	10573	TU-TIF	07/25/86	Air Ivoire	Tabou, Ivory Coast
F.27-600	10588	5A-DDV	06/06/89	Libyan Arab Airlines	Zella, Libya
F.27-400M	10649	9Q-CBH	12/13/92	Scibe Airlift Zaire	Goma, Zaire
Government Aircraft Factories Nomad					
22	4	ZK-NOM	10/25/93	Hibiscus Air Service	Franz Joseph Glacier, New Zealand
22B	14	9M-ATZ	06/06/76	Sabah Air	Kota Kinabafu, Sabah
22B	28	PK-MAJ	07/23/79	Missionary Aviation Fellowship	West Irian, Indonesia
22B	39	P2-DNL	12/23/79	Douglas Airways	Menari, Papua Nugini
24A	44	N8071L	06/12/91	Tri Air	ditched off Great Inagua
24A	89	N418NE	05/04/90	Tar Heel Aviation	Wilmington, North Carolina
Grumman G-159 Gulfstream I					
Gulfstream I	24	HK-3315	02/05/90	Helicol Columbia	Mt. El Saludo, Ibague, Columbia

Type	MSN	Reg.	Date	Airline	Nearest major city
Gulfstream I	59	HK-3316	05/02/90	Helicol Columbia	Los Garcones, Monteria, Columbia
Handley Page HPR.7 Herald					
HPR.7-100	150	HK-718	02/11/73	La Urraca	Villavicencio, Columbia
HPR.7-101	152	HK-721	05/07/72	La Urraca	Valledupar, Columbia
HPR.7-201	157	B-2009	02/24/69	Far Eastern Air Transport	Kaohsiung, Taiwan
HPR.7-211	160	CF-NAF	03/17/65	Eastern Provincial Airways	Musquodoboit, Nova Scotia
HPR.7-203	168	I-TIVE	Apr 1971	Itavia	Rome, Italy
HPR.7-207	170	JY-ACQ	04/10/65	Alia Royal Jordanian Airlines	Damascus, Syria
HPR.7-401	178	HK-2701X	09/16/91	LACOL Columbia	Barranquilla, Columbia
HPR.7-401	180	HK-2702X	11/05/89	Aerosucre Columbia	Bogota,Columbia
HPR.7-214	190	PP-SDJ	11/03/67	SADIA	Marumbi Peak, Brazil
Handley Page HP.137 Jetstream					
Mk.1	205	D-INAH	03/06/70	Bavaria Fluggesellschaft	Samedan, Switzerland
Mk.1	238	N11360	04/17/81	Air US	mid-air Cessna 206G N4862F, Loveland, Colorado
Hindustan Aeronautics Ltd. 748					
2/224	506	VT-DUO	03/05/84	Indian Airlines	Hyderabad-Begumpet, India
2/224	511	VT-DXF	08/18/81	Indian Airlines	Mangalore, India
2/224	512	VT-DXG	12/09/71	Indian Airlines	Chinnamanur, Mandurai, India
2/224	514	VT-DXI	06/16/81	Indian Airlines	Tirupatui Airport, India
2/224	541	VT-EAU	03/15/73	Indian Airlines	Hyderabad, India
Lockheed 100 Hercules					
100-30	4225	N14ST	05/23/74	Saturn Airways	Springfield, Illinois
100	4229	N760AL	12/24/68	Interior Airways	Prudhoe Bay, Alaska
100	4234	N102AK	10/27/74	Alaska Int'l Air	north of Fairbanks, Alaska
100-20	4303	S9-NAI	04/08/89	Transafrik	Luena, Angola
100-20	4333	N17ST	08/27/83	Transamerica Airlines	Dundo, Angola
100-20	4361	CF-PWX	11/21/76	Pacific Western Airlines	Kisangani, Zaire
100-20	4364	OB-R-1004	02/19/74	SATCO	Tarapoto, Peru
100-30	4701	HB-ILF	10/14/87	Zimex Aviation Ltd.,	Kuito, Angola
100-20	4830	D2-EAS	05/16/81	TAAG Angola Airlines	shot down by missile Mongua, Angola
100-30	4833	CP-1564	03/16/91	Transafrik	shot down by missile, Angola
100-30	4839	D2-EHD	01/22/93	Compania de Diamantes de Angola	Cachicala-Chiloango, Angola
100-30	5029	ET-AJL	09/17/91	Ethiopian Airlines	location unknown, Djibouti
Lockheed 188 Electra					
188A	1007	RP-C1061	06/04/76	Air Manila Int'l	Agana, Guam
188A	1015	N6101A	02/03/59	American Airlines	East River, La Guardia, New York
188A	1018	HR-SAW	01/08/81	SASHA	Guatemala City, Guatemala
188A	1021	PI-C1060	01/09/72	Air Manilla Int'l	Pasay City, Philippines
188AF	1034	N5523	05/30/84	Zantop	Chalk Hill, Pennsylvania
188A	1044	N357Q	01/09/85	TPI Int'l Airways	Kansas City, Kansas
188A	1052	HC-AZY	09/12/88	TAME Ecuador	Lago Agrio, Ecuador
188C	1057	N121US	03/17/60	Northwest Orient Airlines	Tell City, Indiana
188AF	1059	N401FA	03/12/76	Great Northern Airlines	Lake Udrivik, Alaska
188A	1062	N5533	10/04/60	Eastern Air Lines	Boston, Massachusetts
188AF	1064	N400FA	12/11/74	Fairbanks Air Service	location unknown, Alaska
188AF	1076	N280F	07/06/77	Fleming Int'l Airways	St. Louis, Missouri
188A	1086	OB-R941	12/24/71	LANSA	Puerto Inca, Peru
188A	1087	HK-1976	07/10/75	Aerocondor Columbia	Bogota, Columbia
188A	1089	N283F	04/30/75	Zantop Int'l	Deadhorse, Alaska
188A	1090	N9705C	09/29/59	Braniff Airways	Buffalo, Texas
188A	1099	N9707C	05/03/68	Braniff Airways	Dawson, Texas
188C	1105	N126US	06/30/77	Coopertiva de Montecillos	into sea, Bocas del Toro, Panama
188A	1106	OB-R939	08/09/70	LANSA	Cuzco, Peru
188A	1115	HK-777	08/27/73	Aerocondor Condor	Bogota, Columbia
188A	1117	N6127A	09/14/60	American Airlines	La Guardia, New York.
188A	1121	N6130A	01/21/85	Galaxy Airlines	Reno, Nevada
188A	1127	N403GN	01/05/79	Great Northern Airlines	North Slope, Alaska
188CF	1134	HR-TNL	03/21/90	TAN Airlines	Las Mesitas, Honduras

Type	MSN	Reg.	Date	Airline	Nearest major city
188C	1136	N183H	04/22/66	American Flyers Airlines	Ardmore, Oklahoma
188C	1141	CF-PAB	10/29/74	Pan Artic Oils Ltd.	Rae Point, Melville Island
188C	1142	N137US	09/16/61	Northwest Orient Airlines	Chicago, Illinois
188C	2011	ZK-TEC	03/27/65	Tasman Empire Airways Ltd.	Whenaupai Airport, New Zealand
188CF	2012	N855U	08/24/70	Universal Airlines	Ogden, Utah
188C	2016	N859U	11/18/79	Transamerica Airlines	Granger, Utah
188C	2019	PH-LLM	06/12/61	KLM Royal Dutch Airlines	Cairo, Egypt
188C	2021	PK-GLB	02/16/67	Garuda Indonesian Airways	Menado, Indonesia
NAMC YS-11					
YS-11-111	2023	JA8658	11/13/66	All Nippon Airways	Matsuyama Airport, Japan
YS-11A-211	2059	PP-SMI	04/12/72	VASP	Rio Del Janeiro, Brazil
YS-11A-202	2063	PP-CTG	10/18/72	Curzeiro do Sul del	Congonhas, Brazil
YS-11A-211	2068	PP-SMJ	10/23/73	VASP	Guanabara Bay, Brazil
YS011A-202	2082	N208PA	03/05/74	Pacific Southwest Airlines	Borrego Springs, California
YS-11A-301	2107	RP-C1419	07/17/77	Philippine Airlines	into sea off Mactan Airport, Philippines
YS-11A-219	2110	B-156	08/12/70	China Airlines	Yuan Shan, Taiwan
YS-11A-227	2134	JA8764	07/03/71	Japan Domestic Airlines	Mount Yokotsu-Dake, Hokkaido, Japan
YS-11A-300	2139	N128MP	03/15/89	Phoenix Airlines	Lafayette, Louisana
YS-11A-213	2154	N906TC	01/13/87	Mid-Pacific Airlines	Lafayette, Louisana
YS-11A-220500	2155	SX-BBQ	10/21/72	Olympic Airways	into sea, Athens, Greece
YS-11A-220500	2156	SX-BBR	11/23/76	Olympic Airways	Kozani, Greece
Nord 262					
262E	2	F-BNGB	01/01/71	Rousseau Aviation	into Mediterranean Sea, Algiers, Algeria
262B-11	5	F-BLHT	11/12/73	Rousseau Aviation	Craon, Mayenne
262A-12	11	9Q-CJK	01/27/93	Trans Service Airlift	Kinshasa-Nkolo, Zaire
262A-12	19	7T-VSU	01/24/79	Air Algerie	Bechar-Adrar, Morocco
262A-33	41	N418SA	03/10/79	Swift Aire	into sea, Los Angeles, California
262A-27	47	N7886A	04/09/77	Altair Airlines	midair with Cessna 195 N4377N, Reading, Pa.
262A-36	48	N29824	02/12/79	Mohawk Airlines	Clarksburg, West Virginia
Short SC7					
SC7-2-200	SH.1838	OH-SBB	11/01/89	RV Aviation	into sea off Aaland Islands, Finland
SC7-3-300	SH.1840	VN-PNI	09/01/72	Ansett Airlines of PNG	Mt Siluwe, Mendi, Papua New Guinea
SC7-2-200	SH.1841	N725R	04/14/72	Viking Int'l Air Freight	La Crosse, Wisconsin
SC7-3-200	SH.1850	N4917	08/25/77	Island Airways	Keahole Airort, Hawaii
SC7-3-200	SH.1858	N21CK	07/02/70	Jetco Aviation Int'l	Potomac River, Washington, D.C.
SC7-3-200	SH.1861	N123PA	10/22/70	Pan Alaska Airways	Fairbanks, Alaska
SC7-3-200	SH.1865	A40-SI	11/22/76	Gulf Air	into sea, Das Island, Abu Dhabi
SC7-3-100	SH.1892	G-OVAN	12/28/93	Peterborough Parachute Center	Ampuriabrava, Spain
SC7-3A-200	SH.1918	N20086	07/13/92	Circle Air Service	Bethel, Alaska
SC7-3-100	SH.1961	9M-PID	01/30/93	Pan-Malaysian Air Transport	Medan, Malaysia
SC7-3-100	SH.1963	9M-PIF	02/03/93	Pan-Malaysian Air Transport	Padang Marsirat, Langkawi Island, Malaysia
SC7-3-100	SH.1967	9M-AXM	07/30/93	Hornbill Airways	Miri, Sarawak
SC7-3-100	SH.1975	9M-AZB	09/03/91	Airtech Rajawali Udara	Long Seridan, Sarawak
Short SD-330					
330-200	SH.3083	SX-BGE	08/03/89	Olympic Airways	Samos, Greece
Short SD-360					
360-100	SH.3642	EI-BEM	01/31/86	Aer Lingus Commuter	East Midlands Airport, Derbyshire, England
360-300	SH.3719	EI-BTJ	12/13/87	Philippine Airlines	Mt. Gurain, Mindanao, Philippines
Vickers Vanguard					
950	706	G-APEC	10/02/71	British European Airways	Aarsele, Ghent, Belgium
953	715	F-GEJF	01/29/88	Inter Cargo Service	Toulouse, France
952	730	F-GEJE	02/06/89	Inter Cargo Service	Marseilles, France
952	745	G-AXOP	04/10/73	Invicta Int'l Airlines	Jura Mtns., Hochwald, Switzerland
Vickers Viscount					
701	4	G-ALWE	03/14/57	British European Airways	Wythenshawe, England
708	8	F-BGNK	12/12/56	Air France	Dannemois, France

Type	MSN	Reg.	Date	Airline	Nearest major city
701	25	G-AMOL	07/20/65	Cambrian Airways	Speke Airport, Liverpool, England
701	26	G-AMOM	01/21/56	British European Airways	Blackbushe Airport, Hampshire, England
708	39	F-BGNV	08/12/63	Air Inter	Lyon, France
720	44	VH-TVA	10/31/54	Trans Australia Airlines	Mangalore Aerodrome, Victoria, Australia
720	45	VH-RMQ	12/31/68	MacRobertson Miller Airlines	Port Hedland, Western Australia
720	46	VH-TVC	03/07/60	Ansett-ANA	Botany Bay, Sydney, Australia
724	50	F-BMCH	10/27/72	Air Inter	Mt. Pic du Picon, near Lyons, France
701C	63	G-ANHC	10/22/58	British European Airways	Anzio, Italy, mid-air with Italian Air Force F-86
701C	66	PP-SRR	09/04/64	VASP	Mt. Nova, Caledonia, Brazil
732	74	G-ANRR	12/02/58	Hunting Clan Air Transport	Frimley, Surrey, England
763D	82	YS-09C	03/05/59	TACA Int'l Airlines	Managua, Nicaragua
755D	91	CU-T603	11/01/58	Cubana	Nipe Bay, Cuba
749	94	YV-C-AMV	01/25/71	Linea Aeropostal Venezolana	Merida, Venezuela
749	95	YV-C-AMX	08/14/74	Linea Aeropostal Venezolana	Margarita Island, Venezuela
749	96	YV-C-AMZ	11/01/71	Linea Aeropostal Venezolana	Maracaibo, Venezuela
748D	102	VP-YNE	08/09/58	Central African Airways	Benghazi, Libya
745D	103	N7405	07/09/64	United Air Lines	Newport, Tennessee
745D	108	N7410	05/20/58	Capital Airlines	Brunswick, Maryland, mid-air with U.S. Air Force T-33
745D	128	N7430	11/23/62	United Air Lines	Ellicott City, Baltimore, Maryland
745D	135	N7437	04/06/58	Capital Airlines	Saginaw, Michigan
757	143	CF-TGY	10/03/59	Trans Canada Air Lines	Toronto, Canada
759D	149	TF-ISU	04/14/63	Icelandair	Nesoy Island, Norway
802	150	G-AOJA	10/23/57	British European Airways	Belfast-Nutts Corner, Northern Ireland
802	158	G-AOHI	01/19/73	British European Airways	Ben More, Perth, Australia
803	176	EI-AOF	06/22/67	Aer Lingus, Ashbourne	Dublin, Ireland
803	178	EI-AOM	03/24/68	Aer Lingus	Irish Sea Wexford Coast
764D	183	HC-BEM	12/29/77	Servicios Aereos Nacionales	Cuenca, Ecuador
764D	185	HC-BCL	09/04/77	Servicios Aereos Nacionales	Cuenca, Ecuador
768D	192	VT-DIO	09/11/63	Indian Airlines	Agra, India
745D	212	HK-2382	03/26/82	Aeropesca Columbia	Bogota, Columbia
745D	217	N7462	01/18/60	Capital Airlines	Charles City, Virginia
754D	244	OD-ADE	02/01/63	Middle East Airlines	Ankara, Turkey, mid-air with Turkish Air Force C-47
804	249	SP-LVA	08/20/65	LOT Polish Airlines	St. Trond, Belgium
802	254	G-AORC	04/28/58	British European Airways	Craigie, Scotland
806	260	PK-RVK	01/07/76	Mandala Airlines	Mando, Sulawesi, Indonesia
757	271	CF-THK	04/07/69	Air Canada	Sept-Iles, Quebec, Canada
745D	287	N7463	05/12/59	Capital Airlines	Chase, Maryland
768D	292	VT-DIX	08/09/71	Indian Airlines	Jaipur, India
782D	297	VP-WAS	09/03/78	Air Rhodesia	Whamira Hills near Lake Kariba, Rhodesia
818	317	ZS-CVA	03/13/67	South African Airways	East London, South Africa
785D	328	I-LAKE	03/28/64	Alitalia	Mt. Somma, Naples, Italy
785D	329	HC-AVP	04/23/79	SAETA, Quito	Cuenca, Ecuador
815	336	G-AVJA	03/20/69	British Midland Airways	Manchester, England
815	337	AP-AJE	08/14/59	Pakistan Int'l Airlines	Karachi, Pakistan
814	342	9G-ACL	06/10/78	West African Air Cargo	Sprigga Payne-Monrovia, Liberia
812	353	PK-IVS	08/26/80	Bouraq Indonesia Airlines	Jakarta, Indonesia
812	354	N243V	07/08/62	Continental Airlines	Amarillo, Texas
812	360	G-AVJZ	05/03/67	Channel Airways	Southend, Essex
838	372	SE-FOZ	01/15/77	Skyline Sweden	Kalvesta, Stockholm-Bromma, Sweden
785D	377	HC-ARS	08/15/76	SAETA	Quito-Cuenca, Ecuador
785D	378	I-LIZT	12/21/59	Alitalia	Rome-Ciampino, Italy
785D	379	6O-AAJ	05/06/70	Somali Airlines	Mogadishu, Somalia
785D	380	HK-1058	06/08/74	Aerolineas TAO	Monte San Isidro, Cucuta, Columbia
812	389	PK-RVW	10/07/83	Mandala Airlines	Semarang, Indonesia
798D	392	XA-SCM	02/27/92	Aero Eslava	Mexico City, Mexico
739A	394	G-AFTN	08/09/68	British Eagle Int'l Airlines	Langenbruck, West Germany
804	395	SP-LVB	12/19/62	LOT Polish Airlines	Okecie, near Warsaw, Poland
806	396	XW-TDN	03/00/75	Royal Air Lao	Phnom Penh, Cambodia
827	398	PP-SRD	05/15/73	VASP	Salvador, Brazil
827	399	PP-SRE	09/15/68	VASP	Sao Paulo, Brazil
827	401	PP-SRG	12/22/59	VASP	Rio de Janeiro, Brazil, mid-air with BAF AT-6

Type	MSN	Reg.	Date	Airline	Nearest major city
832	415	PK-RVN	05/01/81	Mandala Airlines	Semarang, Indonesia
832	416	VH-RMI	09/22/66	Ansett, Winton	Queensland, Australia
833	425	4X-AVC	10/26/69	Arkia-Israel Inland Airlines	Tel Aviv, Israel
739B	427	SY-AKW	09/29/60	United Arab Airlines	into sea near Elba
794D	429	TC-SEV	02/17/59	Turk Hava Yollari	Gatwick Airport, London, England
794D	432	TC-SET	02/02/69	Turk Hava Yollari	Ankara, Turkey
816	434	PK-RVU	07/24/92	Mandala Airlines	Liiliboi, Jakarta, Indonesia
837	437	OE-LAF	09/26/60	Austrian Airlines	Moscow-Sheremetyevo, Russia
837	439	B-2029	07/31/75	Far Eastern Air Transport	Taipei, Taiwan
837	442	HK-1347	01/21/72	Lineas Aereas la Urraca	Funza, Columbia
828	444	JA8202	11/19/62	All Nippon Airways	Nagoya, Japan
828	448	PK-MVS	11/10/71	Merpati Nusantara Airlines	Padang, West Sumatra
843	454	PK-IVX	08/26/92	Bouraq Indonesian Airlines	Banjamasin, Indonesia
				Jet Airliners	
Airbus A.300					
B2-320	122	OY-KAA	12/18/83	Malaysian Airline System	Kuala, Lumpur
B2-263	186	EP-IBU	07/03/88	Iran Air	into Persian Gulf, Bandar, Iran
Airbus A.320					
-111	0009	F-GFKC	06/26/88	Air France	Habsheim, France
-111	0015	F-GGED	01/20/92	Air Inter	Strasbourg, France
-231	0079	VT-EPN	02/14/90	Indian Airlines	Bangalore, India
Boeing 707					
707-121B	17586	N708PA	9/17/65	Pan Am	Chances Mtn., Antigua
707-121	17588	N709PA	12/08/63	Pan Am	Elkton, Maryland
707-124	17609	N70773	07/01/65	Continental	Kansas City Intl Airport, Missouri
707-328	17613	F-BHSA	07/27/61	Air France	Hamburg, Germany
707-329	17624	OO-SJB	02/15/61	Sabena	Brussels, Belgium
707-329	17627	OO-SJE	02/15/78	Sabena	Tenerife, Canary Islands
707-123	17629	N7502A	01/28/61	American Airlines	Montauk, New York
707-123	17633	N7506A	03/01/62	American Airlines	Jamaica Bay, New York
707-123	17641	N7514A	8/15/59	American Airlines	Calverton, New York
707-131	17671	N730JP	10/13/76	Lloyd Aero Boliviano	Santa Cruz, Bolivia
707-436	17706	G-APFE	03/05/66	BOAC	Mount Fuji, Japan
707-436	17712	G-APFK	03/17/77	British Airtours	Prestwick, Scotland
707-437	17722	VT-DJI	01/23/71	Air India	Bombay, India
707-437	17723	VT-DJJ	06/22/82	Air India	Bombay, India
707-441	17906	PP-VJB	11/27/62	Varig	Lima, Peru
720-023	18020	OD-AFT	01/01/76	Middle East Airlines	Al Qaysumah, Saudi Arabia
720-022	18044	N37777	04/22/76	US Global of Florida	Barrabquilla, Columbia
707-437	18055	VT-DMN	01/24/66	Air France	Mont Blanc, France
707-030B	18058	D-ABOK	12/04/61	Lufthansa	Ebersheim, Germany
707-328	18247	F-BHST	06/22/62	Air France	Pointe a Pitre, Guadeloupe
720-030B	18249	D-ABOP	07/15/64	Lufthansa	Ansbach, Germany
720-051B	18354	N724US	02/12/63	Northwest Orient	Everglades, Florida
720-040B	18379	AP-AMH	05/20/65	Pakistan Int'l Airlines	Cairo, Egypt
707-328B	18459	F-BHSZ	12/04/69	Air France	Caracas, Venezuela
707-330B	18463	D-ABOT	12/20/73	Lufthansa	New Dehli, India
707-321C	18579	G-BEBP	05/14/77	IAS Cargo Airlines	Lusaka, Zambia
707-351B	18584	CC-CCX	08/03/78	LAN Chile	Buenos-Aires, Argentina
707-373C	18707	HK-2401	12/14/83	TAMPA Columbia	Medellin, Columbia
707-331C	18712	N787TW	07/26/69	Trans World Airlines	Pomona, New Jersey
707-321C	18715	ST-ALX	03/24/92	Golden Star Air Cargo	Mount Hymittus, Greece
707-321C	18824	N799PA	12/26/68	Pan Am	Elmendorf Air Force Base, Alaska
707-321C	18826	CF-PWZ	01/02/73	Pacific Western Airlines	Edmonton, Canada
707-328C	18881	D2-TOV	07/21/88	TAAG Angolan Air Charter	Lagos, Nigeria
707-324C	18887	B-1834	09/11/79	China Airlines	into sea Taipei, Taiwan
707-338C	18955	SA-DJO	03/14/83	United African Airlines	Sheba, Libya
707-321B	18959	N417PA	07/22/73	Pan Am	Papeete, French Polynesia
707-331B	18978	N18701	12/22/75	TWA	Milan-Malpensa, Italy
707-327C	19106	PP-VLJ	06/09/73	Varig	Rio de Janeiro, Brazil
707-327C	19107	OD-AFX	07/23/79	Trans Mediterranean Airlines	Beirut, Lebanon

Type	MSN	Reg.	Date	Airline	Nearest major city
707-351C	19168	5N-AYJ	12/14/88	GAS Air Nigeria	Kom-Omran, near Luxor, Egypt
707-351C	19209	N144SP	04/13/87	Burlington Air Express	Kansas City, Missouri
707-329C	19211	OO-SJK	07/13/68	Sabena	Lagos, Nigeria
707-323C	19235	PP-VLU	01/30/79	Varig	Tokyo, Japan
707-321C	19268	N446PA	04/22/74	Pan Am	Singaraja, Bali
707-321B	19276	HK-2016	01/25/90	Avianca	NE JFK, New York
707-349C	19354	PT-TCS	03/21/89	Transbrazil	Sao Paulo-Guarulho, Brazil
707-321C	19363	HL7429	04/02/78	Korean Air Lines	Murmansk, Russia
707-321C	19368	N459PA	11/03/73	Pan Am	Boston, Massachusetts
707-321C	19371	N461PA	07/25/71	Pan Am	Manila, Philippines
707-321B	19376	N454PA	01/30/74	Pan Am	Pago Pago, Samoa
707-321C	19377	ST-SAC	12/04/90	Sudania Air Cargo	Nairobi, Kenya
720-047B	19439	N3166	03/31/71	Western Air Lines	Ontario, California
707-331B	19572	N7231T	02/08/89	Independent Air Inc.	Santa Maria, Azores
707-338C	19630	5X-UBC	10/17/88	Uganda Airlines	Fiumicino-Rome, Italy
707-321B	19696	N494PA	12/12/68	Pan Am	Caracas, Venezuela
707-344C	19705	ZS-EUW	04/20/68	South African Airways	Windhoek, South West Africa
707-373C	19715	HL-7412	08/02/76	Korean Air Lines	Teheran, Iran
707-328C	19724	F-BLCJ	03/05/68	Air France	Pointe a Pitre, Guadaloupe
707-360C	19736	ET-ACD	11/19/77	Ethiopian Airlines	Rome-Flumicino, Italy
707-379C	19822	PP-VJK	01/03/87	Varig	Point Alepe, Ivory Coast
707-345C	19841	PP-VJZ	07/11/73	Varig	Paris-Orly, France
707-366C	19845	SU-AOW	12/05/72	Egyptair	SE Cairo, Egypt
707-321B	20028	N320MJ	09/20/90	Omega Air	Marana, Arizona
707-331B	20063	N8734	09/08/74	TWA	Aegean Sea, Cephalonia, Greece
707-331C	20068	N15712	09/14/72	TWA	San Francisco Bay, California
707-366C	20342	SU-APE	10/17/82	Egyptair	Contrin Airport, Geneva, Switzerland
707-330C	20395	D-ABUY	07/26/79	Lufthansa	Petropolis, Rio de Janeiro, Brazil
707-340C	20487	AP-AVZ	12/15/71	Pakistan Int'l Airlines	Urumchi, China
707-3D3C	20494	JY-ADO	01/22/73	Alia Royal Jordanian Airlines	Kano, Nigeria
707-3B5C	20522	HL7406	11/29/87	Korean Air Lines	into Andaman Sea, Bangkok, Thailand
707-366C	20763	SU-AXA	12/25/76	Egyptair	Bangkok, Thailand
707-3K1C	21651	YR-ABD	01/10/91	Tarom	Bucharest, Romania
Boeing 727					
727-22	18295	N68650	07/19/67	Piedmont	mid-air with Cessna 310 N31215, Hendersonville, North Carolina
727-22	18322	N7030U	04/07/65	United	Salt Lake City, Utah
727-22	18328	N7036U	08/16/65	United	Lake Michigan
727-81	18822	JA8302	02/04/66	All Nippon Airways	Tokyo Bay, Japan
727-22	18856	TI-LRC	05/23/88	LACSA	San Jose, Costa Rica
727-23	18901	N1996	11/08/65	American Airlines	Covington, Kentucky
727-21	18894	HK-2559	08/04/82	Aerotal Columbia	Simon Bolivar Airport, Columbia
727-21	18995	N317PA	11/15/66	Pan Am	East Berlin, Germany
727-21	18999	HK-1716	03/17/88	Avianca	Cucuta, Columbia
727-21	19035	HK-1803	11/27/89	Avianca	Bogota, Columbia
727-27C	19111	PT-TYS	04/12/80	Transbrasil	24 kms from Florianopolis Airport, Brazil
727-92C	19175	B-1018	02/16/68	Civil Air Transport	Taipei, Taiwan
727-64	19255	XA-SEJ	09/21/69	Mexicana	Lake Texcoco, Mexico City, Mexico
727-64	19256	XA-SEL	06/04/69	Mexicana	Monterey, Mexico
727-46	19279	G-BDAN	04/25/80	Dan-Air	Esperanza Forest, 20 kms S Tenerife Airport
727-193	19304	N2969G	09/04/71	Alaska Airlines	near Teardrop Lake, NE Juneau, Alaska
727-235	19457	N4737	07/09/82	Pan Am	New Orleans, Louisiana
727-224	19514	N88705	10/21/89	TAN Airlines	Tegucigalpa, Honduras
727-24C	19525	HK-1272	09/30/75	Avianca	Barranquilla, Columbia
727-214	19688	N533PS	09/25/78	Pacific Southwest Airlines	mid-air with Cessna 172 N7711G, San Diego, California
727-113C	19690	YA-FAR	01/05/69	Ariana Afghan Airways	London-Gatwick, England
727-116	19812	CC-CAQ	04/28/69	LAN Chile	Colina, Chile
727-86	19817	EP-IRD	01/21/80	Iran Air	Elburz mtns., Teheran, Iran
727-22C	19891	N7434U	01/18/69	United	into sea after take off, Los Angeles, California
727-247	20266	OB-1303	09/11/90	Air Malta	into sea off Newfoundland
727-251	20296	N274US	12/01/74	Northwest Orient Airlines	Bear Mountain Park, Stony Point, New York
727-231	20306	N54328	12/01/74	TWA	Upperville, Virginia

Type	MSN	Reg.	Date	Airline	Nearest major city
727-2E2/281	20436	JA8329	07/30/71	All Nippon Airways	Shizukuishi, Iwate, Japan, mid-air with JASDF F-86
727-225	20443	N8845E	06/24/75	Eastern Air Lines	on approach to JFK, New York, New York
727-232	20750	N473DA	08/31/88	Delta Air Lines	Dallas-Ft. Worth, Texas
727-2D3	20886	JY-ADU	03/14/79	Alia Royal Jordanian Airlines	Doha, Qatar
727-2H9	20930	TC-AKD	02/27/88	Talia Airways	Kyrenia, Turkey
727-2F2	20982	TC-JBH	09/19/76	Turk Hava Yollari	Mount Karatepe, Turkey
727-212	21347	PP-SRK	06/08/82	VASP	Sierra da Pacatuba mtns, Fortaleza, Brazil
727-256	21777	EC-DDU	02/19/85	Iberia	Mount Oiz, Spain
727-264	22414	XA-MEM	03/31/86	Mexicana	into mtns near Maravatio, Mexico
727-225	22556	N819EA	01/01/85	Eastern Air Lines	Mount Illimani, La Paz, Bolivia
Boeing 737					
737-222	19069	N9031U	12/08/72	United Airlines	Chicago, Illinois
737-222	19556	N62AF	01/13/82	Air Florida	Washingtom, D.C.
737-222	19939	B-2603	08/21/81	Far Eastern Air Transport	Miao-Li, Taiwan
737-2A1	20096	PP-SME	01/28/86	VASP	Rio de Janeiro, Brazil
737-247	20131	N4527W	03/31/75	Western Airlines	Casper, Wyoming
737-281	20226	B-1870	02/16/86	China Airlines	into sea near Makung, Taiwan
737-2H6	20585	9M-MBD	12/04/77	Malaysian Airline System	Kuala Lumpur, Malaysia
737-229C	20914	OO-SDH	04/04/78	Sabena	Gosseiles, Belgium
737-241	21006	PP-VMK	09/03/89	Varig	Sao Jose do Xingu, Brazil
737-270C	21183	YI-AGJ	12/26/86	Iraqi Airways	Arar, Saudi Arabia
737-2A1C	21188	PP-SND	06/22/92	VASP	Cruzeiro do Sul, Brazil
737-2P6	21734	A40-BK	09/22/83	Gulf Air	Jebel Ali, Dubai
737-204	22059	HP-1205CMP	06/06/92	Copa Panama	Darien Pass, Tucuti, Panama
737-2P5	22267	HS-TBC	08/31/87	Thai Airways	into sea near Phuket, Thailand
737-2V2	22607	HC-BIG	07/11/83	TAME	Cuenca, Ecuador
737-230	22635	D-ABHD	01/02/88	Condor	Izmir, Turkey
737-2X6C	23121	N670MA	06/02/90	Markair	Unalakleet, Alaska
737-209	23795	B-180	10/26/89	China Airlines	Hualien, Taiwan
737-4YO	23867	G-OBME	01/08/89	British Midland Airways	Kegworth, Derbyshire, England
737-260	23914	ET-AJA	09/15/88	Ethiopian Airlines	Bahar Dar, Ethiopia
Boeing 747					
747-121	19643	N736PA	03/27/77	Pan Am	Tenerife, Canary Islands
747-121SCD	19646	N739PA	12/21/88	Pan Am	Lockerbie, Scotland
747-130	19747	D-ABYB	11/20/74	Lufthansa	Nairobi, Kenya
747-237B	19959	VT-EBD	01/01/78	Air India	Bombay, India
747-206B	20400	PH-BUF	03/27/77	KLM-Royal Dutch Airlines	Tenerife, Canary Island
747-230B	20559	HL7442	09/01/83	Korean Air Lines	into Okhotsk Sea by Soviet missile, near Shakhalin Island
747SR-46	20783	JA8119	08/12/85	Japan Air Lines	NW Tokyo, Japan
747-283B	21381	HK-2910X	11/27/83	Avianca	Madrid, Spain
747-2B5B	21773	HL7445	11/19/80	Korean Air Lines	Seoul, South Korea
747-249F	21828	N807FT	02/19/89	Flying Tiger Line	Kuala Lumpur, Malaysia
Boeing 767					
767-3Z9ER	24628	OE-LAV	05/26/91	Lauda Air	Bangkok, Thailand
BAe-146					
BAe-146	E2027	N350PS	12/07/87	Pacific Southwest Airlines	San Luis Obispo, California
British Aircraft Corp. 1-11					
1-11-200AB	004	G-ASHG	10/22/63	British Aircraft Corp.	Tisbury, Wiltshire, England
1-11-401AK	058	N711ST	02/09/75	Jet Travel	Lake Tahoe, California
1-11-070	070	N1553	08/06/66	Braniff Airways	Falls City, Nebraska
1-11-402AP	092	PI-C1131	09/12/69	Philippine Airlines	Manila, Philippines
1-11-402AP	094	5N-AOW	06/26/91	Okada Air	Sokoto, Nigeria
1-11-204AF	098	N1116J	06/23/67	Mohawk Airlines	Blossburg, Pennsylvania
1-11-424EU	130	YR-BCA	12/07/70	Tarom	Constanta Airport, Romania
1-11-420EL	155	LV-JGY	11/21/77	Austral Lineas Aereas	San Carlos de Bariloche, Argentina
1-11-515FB	207	D-ALAR	09/06/71	Paninternational	Hamburg, Germany
1-11-529FR	212	LV-LOX	05/07/81	Austral Lineas Aereas	Rio de la Plata, Brazil

Type	MSN	Reg.	Date	Airline	Nearest major city
1-11-527FK	248	RP-C1183	08/04/84	Philippine Airlines	Tacloban, Philippines
Convair 880					
880-22-1	22-00-26	N820TW	09/13/65	TWA	Kansas City, Missouri
880-22-1	22-00-27	N821TW	11/21/67	TWA	Cincinnati, Ohio
880-22M-3	22-00-37M	VR-HFX	11/05/67	Cathay Pacific Airlines	Hong Kong
880-22M-3	22-00-45M	JA8030	08/26/66	Japan Domestic Airlines	Tokyo, Japan
880-22M-3	22-00-47M	N48060	08/21/76	Airtrust Singapore	Seletar Airport, Singapore
880-22M-3	22-00-49M	JA8028	06/25/69	Japan Air Lines	Moses Lake, Washington
Convair 990					
990-30A-5	30-10-1	N711NA	04/12/73	NASA	mid-air with Navy P-3, Sunnyvale, California
990-30A-5	30-10-3	PK-GJA	05/28/68	Garuda Indonesian Airways	Bombay, India
990-30A-5	30-10-4	N7876	09/10/73	California Airmotive Corp.	Guam
990-30A-8	30-10-13	N5603	08/08/70	Modern Air Transport	Acapulco, Mexico
990-30A-6	30-10-15	HB-ICD	02/21/70	Swissair	Zurich, Switzerland
990-30A-5	30-10-25	EC-BZR	12/03/72	Spantax	Tenerife, Canary Islands
990-30A-5	30-10-32	EC-BNM		Spantax Arlanda	Stockholm, Sweden
DeHavilland DH.106 Comet					
DH.106-1	06003	G-ALYP	01/10/54	BOAC	Elba, Italy
DH.106-1	06008	G-ALYV	05/02/53	BOAC	Calcutta, India
DH.106-1	06011	G-ALYY	04/08/54	BOAC	into Tyrrhenian Sea, Stromboli, Italy
DH.106-1	06012	G-ALYZ	10/26/52	BOAC	Rome-Ciampino, Italy
DH.106-1A	06014	CF-CUN	03/03/53	Canadian Pacific Airlines	Karachi, Pakistan
DH.106-4	6415	G-APDN	07/03/70	Dan-Air	Monteseny Mtns., Barcelona, Spain
DH.106-4	6430	LV-AHR	11/23/61	Aerolineas Argentinas	Sao Paulo, Brasil
DH.106-4C	6439	SU-ALC	01/02/71	United Arab Airlines	Ben Gashir, Libya
DH.106-4C	6441	SU-ALD	07/28/63	United Arab Airlines	into sea near Bombay, India
DH.106-4C	6444	SU-ALE	02/09/70	United Arab Airlines	Munich, Germany
DH.106-4B	6456	G-ARJM	12/21/61	British European Airways	Ankara, Turkey
DH.106-4C	6475	SU-ANI	01/14/70	United Arab Airlines	Addis Ababa, Ethiopia
Douglas DC-8					
DC-8-32/33	45253	PP-PEA	03/04/67	Varig	Robertsfield, Monrovia
DC-8-33	45273	PP-PDT	08/20/62	Panair do Brasil	into sea near Rio de Janeiro, Brazil
DC-8-31	45277	N4903C	04/28/68	Capitol Int'l Airways	Atlantic City, New Jersey
DC-8-11	45290	N8013U	12/16/60	United Airlines	mid-air with TWA 1049 N6907C
DC-8-51	45409	N802E	03/30/67	Delta Airlines	New Orleans, Louisana
DC-8-21	45428	N8607	02/25/64	Eastern Air Lines	into Lake Pontchartrain, Louisana
DC-8-42/42	45598	OB-R1143	08/01/80	Aeronaves del Peru	Cerro Lilio, Mexico
DC-8-43	45611	CU-T1201	10/06/76	Cubana	into sea, Grantley Adams Int'l Airport, Barbados
DC-8-53	45615	PH-DCL	05/30/61	KLM - Royal Dutch Airlines	into sea en route to Santa Maria, Azores from Lisbon
DC-8-52	45617	EC-ARA	07/06/72	Aviaco	into sea Las Palmas, Canary Islands
DC-8-43	45625	I-DIWB	05/05/72	Alitalia	Mount Lunga, Palermo, Italy
DC-8-43	45631	I-DIWD	07/07/62	Alitalia	Bombay, India
DC-8-51	45633	XA-NUS	12/24/66	Aeronaves de Mexico	Lake Texcoco, Mexico
DC-8-51	45652	XA-PEI	08/13/66	Aeronaves de Mexico	Acapulco, Mexico
DC-8-52	45571	ZK-NZB	07/04/66	Air New Zealand	Auckland, New Zealand
DC-8-55F	45754	HC-BKN	09/18/84	AECA Aeroservicios Ecuatorianos	Quito, Ecuador
DC-8-55F	45818	PH-MBH	12/04/74	Garuda Indonesian Airways	Laxabana Hill, Colombo, Ceylon
DC-8-62	45822	LN-MOO	01/13/69	Scandinavian Airlines System	into sea Los Angeles, California
DC-8-55F	45859	5N-ARH	03/31/88	Arax Airlines	Cairo, Egypt
DC-8-54F	45860	9G-MKB	02/15/92	MK Air Cargo	Kano, Nigeria
DC-8-54F	45880	N8047U	12/18/77	United Airlines	Salt Lake City, Utah
DC-8-61	45889	JA8061	02/09/82	Japan Air Lines	Haneda, Japan
DC-8-63F	45923	N794AL	02/15/92	Burlington Air Express	Toledo Express Airport, Illinois
DC-8-63F	45929	N782AL	02/16/95	Air Transport International	Kansas City, Missouri
DC-8-63CF	45951	N4863T	09/08/70	Trans International Airlines	New York, New York
DC-8-61	45972	N8082U	12/28/78	United Airlines	Portland, Oregon
DC-8-61	45982	C-GMXQ	07/11/91	Nationair	Jeddah, Saudi Arabia
DC-8-63AF	46005	N785FT	07/27/70	Flying Tiger Line	Okinawa, Japan
DC-8-54F	46010	N8053U	01/11/83	United Airlines	Detroit, Michigan
DC-8-63F	46020	TF-FLA	11/15/78	Loftledir	Colombo, Ceylon

Type	MSN	Reg.	Date	Airline	Nearest major city
DC-8-63CF	46050	N8635	03/04/77	Overseas National Airways	Niamey, Nigeria
DC-8-62	46057	JA8040	11/28/72	Japan Air Lines	Moscow, Soviet Union
DC-8-63PF	46058	N950JW	12/12/85	Arrow Air	Gander, Newfoundland
DC-8-63CF	46060	N4909C	11/27/70	Capitol Int'l Airways	Anchorage, Alaska
DC-8-62	46107	N1809E	06/07/89	Surinam Airways	Paramaribo, Surinam
DC-8-63	46114	CF-TIW	07/05/70	Air Canada	Toronto, Canada
DC-8-63CF	46146	N802WA	09/08/73	Mount Dutton	Cold Bay, Alaska
DC-8-62AF	46148	JA8054	01/13/77	Japan Air Lines	Anchorage, Alaska
DC-8-62H	46152	JA8051	09/27/77	Japan Air Lines	Kuala Lumpur, Malaysia
Douglas DC-9					
DC-9-14	45700	N3305L	05/30/72	Delta Airlines	Fort Worth, Texas
DC-9-15	45724	I-TIGI	06/27/80	Itavia	into sea Naples, Italy
DC-9-14	45726	N626X	11/15/87	Continental Airlines	Denver, Colorado
DC-9-14	45771	N8910E	02/09/79	Eastern Air Lines	Dade-Collier Airport, Florida
DC-9-15	45777	N1063T	03/09/67	Trans World Airlines	Urbana, Ohio
DC-9-14	45794	N9101	10/01/66	West Coast Airlines	Portland, Oregon
DC-9-14	45796	N9103	03/17/80	Texas Int'l Airlines	Baton Rouge, Louisana
DC-9-32	47032	N3323L	11/27/73	Delta Airlines	Chattanooga, Tennessee
DC-9-15	47034	N974Z	12/27/68	Ozark Air Lines	Sioux City, Iowa
DC-9-14	47056	YV-C-AVM	12/22/74	Avensa	Maturin, Venezuela
DC-9-31	47075	N975NE	07/31/73	Delta Airlines	into sea near Boston, Massachucetts
DC-9-32	47077	EC-BII	03/05/73	Iberia	Trauche, France
DC-9-15	47100	XA-SOC	06/20/73	Aeronaves de Mexico	Puerto Vallarta, Mexico
DC-9-33F	47192	N931F	03/18/89	Evergreen Int'l Airlines	Saginaw, Texas
DC-9-31	47211	N988VJ	09/09/69	Allegheny Airlines	Shelbyville, Indiana mid-air with PA-28
DC-9-32	47227	I-DIKQ	12/23/78	Alitalia	into sea Palermo, Sicily
DC-9-15F	47240	N565PC	02/17/91	Emery Worldwide Airlines	Cleveland, Ohio
DC-9-31	47245	N97S	11/14/70	Southern Airways	Huntington, West Virginia
DC-9-14	47309	N100ME	09/06/85	Midwest Express	Milwaukee, Wisconsin
DC-9-32	47356	XA-JED	08/31/86	Aeromexico	mid-air with Piper PA-28 Cerritos, California
DC-9-31	47393	N1335U	04/04/77	Southern Airways	New Hope, Georgia
DC-9-31	47400	N8984E	09/11/74	Eastern Airlines	Douglas Airport, North Carolina
DC-9-33F	47407	N935F	05/02/70	ALM-Antillean Airlines	St. Croix, Virgin Islands
DC-9-31	47441	N9345	06/06/71	Hughes Airwest	Duarte, California, mid-air with U.S. Marine Corps F-4 Phantom
DC-9-32	47457	YU-AJO	10/30/75	Inex Adria Airways	Prague, Czechoslovakia
DC-9-32	47482	YU-AHT	01/26/72	Jugoslovenski Aerotransport	Krussne Hory Mountain, Czechoslovakia
DC-9-32	47500	HI-177	02/15/70	Dominicana	into sea off Santo Domingo
DC-9-32	47621	XA-DEN	07/21/81	Aeromexico	Chihuahua, Mexico
DC-9-32	47622	XA-DEO	11/08/81	Aeromexico	Sierra de Guerreo, Mexico
DC-9-32	47641	I-ATHA	11/14/90	Alitalia	Zurich, Switzerland
DC-9-32	47649	YU-AJR	09/10/76	Inex Adria Airways	mid-air with Trident 3B G-AWZT Vrobec Village, Yugoslavia
DC-9-32	47667	I-ATJC	09/14/79	Aero Transporti	Italiani Sarroch, Caliari, Italy
DC-9-32	47720	YV-23C	03/05/91	Linea Aeropostal Venezolana	Torres Mtns, Venezuela
DC-9-32	47741	PK-GNQ	04/04/87	Garuda Indonesian Airways	Polonia, Indonesia
DC-9-82	48047	YU-ANA	12/01/81	Inex Adria Airways	Mont St. Pietro, Ajaccio, Corsica, France
DC-9-81	48050	N1003G	06/12/88	Austral Lineas Aereas	Posadas, Argentina
DC-9-82	48090	-----	08/16/87	Northwest Airlines	Detroit, Michigan
DC-9-81	53003	OY-KHO	12/27/91	Scandinavian Airlines System	Arlanda, Sweden
Douglas DC-10					
DC-10-10	46510	N110AA	05/25/79	American Airlines	Chicago-O'Hare, Illinois
DC-10-10	46704	TC-JAV	03/03/74	Turk Hava Yollari	Senlis, France
DC-10-30	46852	N54629	09/19/89	Union de Transports	Aeriens Niger
DC-10-30	46925	EC-CBN	12/17/73	Iberia	Boston, Massachusetts
DC-10-30F	46960	HL7339	12/23/83	Korean Airlines	mid-air Piper PA-31 N35206 Anchorage, Alaska
DC-10-30	47887	HL7328	07/27/89	Korean Air	Tripoli, Libya
Fokker F.28					
F.28-1000	11011	LN-SUY	12/23/72	Braathens SAFE	Fornebu, Norway
F.28-1000	11015	I-TIDE	01/01/74	Itavia	Turin, Italy
F.28-1000	11039	PK-GVC	09/24/75	Garuda Indonesian Airways	Palembang, Indonesia

Type	MSN	Reg.	Date	Airline	Nearest major city
F.28-1000	11055	PK-GVE	07/11/79	Garuda Indonesian Airways	Mount Sibayak, Indonesia
F.28-1000	11057	TC-JAO	01/26/74	Turk Hava Yollari	Izm, Turkey
F.28-1000	11058	TC-JAP	01/30/75	Turk Hava Yollari	into sea, Istanbul, Turkey
F.28-1000	11059	OB-R1020	10/25/88	Aero Peru	Juliaca, Peru
F.28-1000	11060	C-FONF	03/10/89	Air Ontario	Dryden, Ontario, Canada
F.28-1000	11071	TC-JAT	12/23/79	Turk Hava Yollari	Cucuk Koy, Turkey
F.28-1000	11086	LV-LOB	11/15/75	Aerolineas Argentinas	Concordia, Argentina
F.28-1000	11094	PK-GVP	03/06/79	Garuda Indonesian Airways	Mount Bromo, Probolinggo, East Java
F.28-4000	11141	PH-CHI	10/06/81	NLM Cityhopper	Moerdijk,
F.28-3000	11165	FAC-1140	03/28/85	Satena	San Vicente de Caguan, Columbia
F.28-4000	11223	HL7284	11/25/89	Korean Air	Seoul, South Korea
F.28-4000	11235	N485US	03/22/92	USAir	La Guardia, New York, NY
F.28-1000	11993	5N-ANA	03/02/78	Nigeria Airways	mid-air with MiG-21, Kano, Nigeria
Hawker Siddeley HS121 Trident					
HS.121-1C	2109	G-ARPI	06/18/72	British Airways	Staines, England
HS.121-1C/1E	2118	9K-ACG	06/30/66		Kuwait Int'l Airport, Kuwait
HS.121-1C	2126	G-ARPY	06/03/66	Hawker Siddeley Aviation	Felthorpe, Norfolk, England
HS.121-2E	2170	B-266	04/26/82	Civil Aviation Admin of China	Mt Yangsu, China
HS.121	2172	B-274	03/14/79	Civil Aviation Admin of China	Canton, China
HS.121-	2320	G-AWZT	09/10/76	British Airways	mid-air with DC-9, YU-AJR Vrobec Village, Yugoslavia
Lockheed 1011 TriStar					
1011-1	1011	N310EA	12/29/72	Eastern Airlines	Everglades, Miami, Florida
1011-1	1163	N726DA	08/02/85	Delta Airlines	Dallas-Fort Worth, Texas
Sud Aviation SE.210 Caravelle					
SE.210-1	14	OY-KRB	09/27/61	Scandinavian Airlines System	Ankara, Turkey
SE.210-1	23	OD-AEM	04/17/64	Middle East Airlines	into sea off Dhahran, Saudi Arabia
SE.210-1A	25	HS-TGI	06/29/67	Thai Int'l	into sea off Hong Kong
SE.210-III	32	CN-CCV	04/01/70	Royal Air Maroc	Berrechid, Morocco
SE.210-III	40	HC-BAE	01/18/86	SAETA	Santa Elena, Guatemala
SE.210-III	68	F-BJTB	09/12/61	Air France	Rabat, Morocco
SE.210-VIN	69	OO-SRD	12/22/73	Royal Air Maroc	Mount Mellaline, Morocco
SE.210-III	122	B-1852	11/20/71	China Airlines	into sea off Penghu Island, Taiwan
SE.210-VIN	127	LV-HGY	07/03/63	Aerolineas Argentinas	Cordoba, Argentina
SE.210-10A/VIN	130	VT-DPP	02/15/66	Indian Airlines	New Dehli, India
SE.210-10A/VIN	134	VT-DSB	09/04/66	Indian Airlines	Bombay, India
SE.210-III	147	HB-ICV	09/04/63	Swissair	Duerrenaesch, Switzerland
SE.210-VIN	151	YU-AHD	09/11/73	Jugoslovenski Aerotransport	Titograd, Yugoslavia
SE.210-VIR	163	EC-ATV	01/07/72	Iberia	Atalayasa Mtns, San Jose, Costa Rica
SE.210-VIR	165	HK-1810	12/21/80	TAC Columbia	Riohacha Airport, Columbia
SE.210-10R	200	HB-ICK	12/18/77	SA de Transport Aerien	into sea off Funchal, Portugal
SE.210-10R	202	EC-BDD	11/04/67	Iberia	Black Down, Fernhurst, Sussex, England
SE.210-11R	219	HK-3288X	04/26/89	Aerosucre Columbia	Barranquilla, Columbia
SE.210-10R	225	EC-BIC	08/13/73	Aviaco	Coruna, Alvedro
SE.210-10R	228	EC-BID	03/05/73	Aviaco	Funchal, Portugal
SE.210-III	244	F-BOHB	09/11/68	Air France	into sea off Nice, France
SE.210-10B3	267	OY-STL	03/14/72	Sterling Airways	Dubai, United Arab Emerates
Vickers VC10					
VC10-1101	804	5N-ABD	11/20/69	Nigeria Airways	Lagos, Nigeria

Douglas C-47B-DK NC58121, msn 17086, crashed during a flight from Teterboro, New Jersey to San Juan, Puerto Rico via Miami, Florida. There were four crew members and 19 passengers on board the aircraft, some of whom are seen in this photo. The thought is that the crew fell asleep at the controls, and the autopilot took the aircraft off course. The plane did not have enough fuel to make Nassau and was ditched in the surf at Haines Bay, Bahamas. The aircraft was written off. (Veronico Collection)

Appendix IV

DC-3 Crashes in the United States

The wreckage of United DC-3A N16073, msn 1913, is hauled away after crashing into the San Francisco Bay on Feb. 9, 1937. The crash was caused by the accidental jamming of the elevator controls when a microphone was dropped in the cockpit. The microphone fell under the yoke and jammed the controls in the nose-down position during landing. There was not enough altitude for the crew to dislodge the microphone and recover the aircraft's attitude. (William T. Larkins Collection)

Reg.	Msn	Year	Location	Airline		Date	Rebuilt
N16073	1913	1937	San Francisco CA	United	USA	02/09	
N16070	1910	1937	Cheyenne WY	United	USA	04/27	Yes
N16074	1914	1937	Knight WY	United	USA	10/17	
N18108	1956	1938	Cleveland OH	United	USA	05/24	
N17316	1931	1938	Albuquerque NM	TWA	USA	08/24	Yes
N16066	1906	1938	Point Reyes CA	United	USA	11/29	
N18105	1953	1940	Moline IL	United	USA	01/12	Yes
N21789	2188	1940	Lovettsville VA	Penn Central	USA	08/31	
N16086	1925	1940	Centerville UT	United.	USA	11/04	
N25678	2175	1940	Chicago IL	United	USA	12/04	
N16015	1553	1940	St Louis MO	American	USA	12/11	Yes
N17315	1930	1941	St Louis MO	TWA	USA	01/23	
N28394	3250	1941	Atlanta GA	Eastern	USA	02/26	
N21727	2143	1941	Vero Beach FL	Eastern	USA	04/03	
N16064	1904	1941	Denver, CO	United	USA	06/10	Yes
N1948	3298	1941	Harrisburg PA	TWA	USA	06/16	Yes
N25691	2256	1941	Morgantown WV	Penn Central	USA	10/02	Yes
N21712	2124	1941	Moorehead MN	Northwest	USA	10/30	
N1946	3295	1942	Las Vegas NV	TWA	USA	01/16	
N17322	1918	1942	Little Rock AR	American	USA	02/05	Yes
N18143	2139	1942	La Guardia NY	American	USA	02/17	Yes
N21788	2187	1942	Detroit MI	Penn Central	USA	03/02	
N16064	1904	1942	La Guardia NY	United	USA	04/11	Yes
N18146	1978	1942	Salt Lake UT	United	USA	05/01	
N21714	2129	1942	Miles City MT	Northwest	USA	05/12	
N16018	1556	1942	Little Rock, AR	American	USA	05/21	Yes
N17320	1966	1942	Dayton OH	TWA	USA	06/27	Yes
N21711	2123	1942	Bismark ND	Northwest	USA	08/29	Yes
N16017	1555	1942	Palm Springs CA	American	USA	10/23	

Reg.	Msn	Year	Location	Airline		Date	Rebuilt
N18951	2015	1942	Kansas City KS	TWA	USA	11/04	
N16064	1904	1942	Dayton OH	United	USA	11/18	
N16060	1900	1942	Fairfield UT	Western	USA	12/15	
N16090	1929	1943	Oakland CA	United	USA	01/11	
N16014	1552	1943	Trammel KY	American	USA	07/28	
N33657	4803	1943	Dallas TX	American	USA	09/15	
N16008	1588	1943	Centerville TN	American	USA	10/15	
N19968	3252	1943	New Orleans LA	Eastern	USA	11/19	
N21767	2166	1944	Memphis TN	American	USA	02/10	
N28310	2251	1944	Hanford CA	TWA	USA	11/04	
N17322	1968	1944	Van Nuys CA	TWA	USA	12/01	
N21752	2165	1944	Saline MI	American	USA	12/24	Yes
N25684	2215	1945	Burbank CA	American	USA	01/10	
N18142	2138	1945	Rural Retreat VA	American	USA	02/23	
N25692	2262	1945	Morgantown WV	Penn Central	USA	04/14	
N21914	4965	1945	Lynchburg VA	American	USA	04/28	Yes
N25647	2235	1945	Florence SC	Eastern	USA	07/12	
N33631	4137	1945	Florence SC	Eastern	USA	09/07	
N19939	4992	1945	Western Springs IL	TWA	USA	09/29	Yes
N18123	1999	1945	La Guardia NY	Eastern	USA	12/30	
N21786	4131	1946	Birmingham AL	Penn Central	USA	01/06	
N19970	3254	1946	Cheshire CT	Eastern	USA	01/18	
N25675	2147	1946	Elk Mt WY	United	USA	01/31	
N14941	4468	1946	Newark NJ	Air Cargo Tsp	USA	02/25	Yes
N21799	2203	1946	El Centro CA	American	USA	03/03	
N33621	3286	1946	Hollywood CA	Western	USA	04/24	
N53218	19626	1946	Richmond VA	Viking	USA	05/16	
N28383	4091	1946	Chicago IL	TWA	USA	07/02	
N50040	19980	1946	Lumberton NC	Trans Carib	USA	08/08	
N51878	4542	1946	Moline IL	Trans Luxury	USA	08/21	
N88826	19776	1946	Ashland MS	American	USA	08/25	
N57850	9214	1946	Elko NV	Trans Luxury	USA	09/05	
N38942	12971	1946	Laramie WY	Nat Air Transport	USA	10/17	
N20750	4993	1946	Meridian MS	-----	USA	11/10	
N19947	4873	1946	Cleveland OH	United	USA	11/11	
N18645	11662	1946	Lebec CA	Western	USA	11/13	
N45395	11642	1946	Mt Laguna CA	Western	USA	12/24	
N15577	4805	1946	Michigan City IN	American	USA	12/28	
N88873	13640	1946	Charleston SC	Intercontinental	USA	12/31	
N21746	2104	1947	Jones Beach NY	American	USA	01/05	Yes
N50046	34373	1947	Vineland NJ	Nationwide Air	USA	01/05	
N88872	3274	1947	Galax VA	Eastern	USA	01/12	
N54550	9965	1947	League City TX	Atlantic & Pac	USA	02/14	
N33646	4125	1947	Philadelphia PA	United	USA	02/24	
N88804	9921	1947	Charleston SC	USAir	USA	03/14	
N52710	19095	1947	Lantana FL	Int Air Frt	USA	04/04.	
N49657	9066	1947	Columbus GA	Delta	USA	04/22.	
N53196	19435	1947	Newark NJ	Union Southern	USA	05/04	
N19917	7320	1947	Hartfield, VA	Capital	USA	05/08	Yes
N79024	9887	1947	Melbourne FL	Burke Air	USA	07/13	
N88787	19639	1947	La Guardia NY	American	USA	08/08	
N95486	6065	1947	Yakutat AK	Columbia	USA	11/27	
N60331	12968	1948	Savannah River GA	Coastal	USA	01/07	
N28384	4092	1948	Oxon Hill MD	Eastern	USA	01/13	
N206	4776	1948	Navajo Peak CO	CAA	USA	01/21	
N36480	33598	1948	Coalinga CA	Airline Trnspt	USA	01/28	
N36498	12527	1948	Columbus OH	Bruning Avn	USA	02/25	
N64722	10052	1948	San Jose CA	Eagle Air Frt	USA	03/08	
N79042	9394	1948	Elroy AZ	Eagle Air Frt	USA	06/12	
N17335	1921	1948	Burlington VT	Colonial	USA	09/20	
N66637	11800	1948	Cape Spencer AK	Pacific Alaska	USA	11/04	
N79025	10181	1949	Seattle WA	Seattle Air	USA	01/02	
N53210	13777	1949	Brandywine IN	Coastal Cargo	USA	01/06	
N91006	20208	1949	Homer AK	Alaska	USA	01/20	

Reg.	Msn	Year	Location	Airline		Date	Rebuilt
N17713	4582	1949	Oakland CA	United	USA	01/27	
N16002	1496	1949	off Miami FL	Airborne Trnspt	USA	04/26	
N19963	2260	1949	Chesterfield NJ	Eastern	USA	07/30	
N53594	20193	1949	Teterboro NJ	Meteor Air Trnspt	USA	10/29	Yes
N29086	4304	1949	Akron OH	Harrington's Inc	USA	11/04	
N54337	20136	1949	Detroit MI	Meteor Air Trnspt	USA	11/19	Yes
N60256	9201	1949	Benicia CA	Arrow	USA	12/07	
N25691	2256	1949	Washington DC	Capital	USA	12/12	
N18936	2011	1950	Utica NY	Robinson	USA	09/04	
N19928	7400	1951	Sioux City IA	Mid Cont	USA	03/02	
N63439	20229	1951	Santa Barbara CA	Southwest	USA	04/06	
N16088	1927	1951	Ft. Wayne IN	United	USA	04/28	
N25646	2234	1951	Ocala. FL	Eastern	USA	11/27	Yes
N17109	4999	1951	Denver CO	United	USA	12/04	
N41748	11827	1952	Mt Crillon AK	General	USA	01/12	
N65384	18984	1952	Greenboro NC	Piedmont	USA	10/20	Yes
N21716	2131	1952	Richmond IN	Lake Central	USA	12/15	Yes
N41455	11876	1953	Miles City MT	General	USA	02/15	Yes
N65743	20432	1953	Selleck WA	Miami	USA	04/14	Yes
N28345	2224	1953	Marshall TX	Delta	USA	05/17	
N53596	22433	1953	St Louis MO	Meteor Air Trnspt	USA	05/24	Yes
N15569	4887	1953	Los Angeles CA	Western	USA	06/29	
N19941	6333	1953	Vail WA	Regina	USA	09/01	
N49551	4940	1954	Kansas City MO	Zantop	USA	01/20	
N43V	42958	1954	Bristol, TN	Piedmont	USA	02/26	Yes
N51359	13759	1954	Atlanta GA	Delta	USA	06/15	
N91008	25422	1954	MacGrath, AK	Alaska	USA	08/09	
N61451	4630	1954	Mason City IA	Braniff	USA	08/22	
N17891	11745	1954	Mt Success	Northeast	USA	11/30	
N24320	20197	1954	Pittsburgh PA	Johnson Flt Svc	USA	12/22	Yes
N999B	4255	1955	Covington, KY	Castletown	USA	01/12	
N19942	4872	1955	Lebanon, NH	Northeast	USA	05/31	Yes
N51167	7384	1955	Kansas City KA	TWA	USA	07/12	Yes
N45333	6330	1955	Yakima WA	Northwest	USA	07/15	Yes
N18945	2018	1955	Hobbs NM	Continental	USA	08/29	Yes
N74663	6257	1955	Burbank CA	Curry Air Trans.	USA	09/08	
N62374	12534	1956	Pullman WA	W. Coast Airlines	USA	02/26	
N45V	18984	1956	Shelby NC	Piedmont	USA	06/13	Yes
N33315	4978	1956	Bartlesville OK	Continental	USA	09/09	Yes
N65276	19202	1957	Phoenix AZ	Frontier	USA	04/21	Yes
N88835	19448	1957	Clarksburg MD	Capital	USA	06/22	
N34417	7337	1957	New Bedford MA	Northeast	USA	09/15	
N3947A	9856	1957	Charlottsville VA.	Piedmont	USA	10/02	Yes
N49553	4820	1958	Martinsburg WVA	Capital	USA	06/04	
N64424	4424	1958	Pueblo CO	Frontier	USA	08/23	Yes
N18941	2007	1959	Tri Cities TN	Southeast	USA	01/08	
N17314	1924	1959	Kerrville TX	General	USA	02/01	
N44993	6260	1959	Charleston WV	Capital	USA	08/26	Yes
N67589	19656	1959	Santa Maria CA	Pacific Airlines	USA	10/26	
N55V	20477	1959	Waynesboro VA	Piedmont	USA	10/30	
N38G	4759	1959	Cleveland OH	National Aero	USA	11/05	
N200	20400	1961	Mustang OK	FAA	USA	04/21	
N58731	13532	1962	Big Trees CA	Blatz	USA	01/20	Yes
N3588	20178	1962	Dallas TX	Perdue Aeron	USA	04/18	
N386T	20411	1963	Morgantown WV	Purdue Aeron	USA	11/29	
N65SA	4925	1964	Huntsville AL	Southern	USA	2/12	Yes
N401D	4970	1964.	Chicago IL	Snow Valley	USA	03/09	
N61442	9642	1964	Miles City MT	Frontier	USA	03/12	
N91003	9708	1964	Pueblo CO	Central	USA	07/20	
N61350	4535	1964	Tonopah NV	Hawthorne NV	USA	08/19	
N91016	11853	1965	Nikolski AK	Reeve	USA	05/29	
N123H	12679	1965	Stockton CA	Biffs	USA	07/02	Yes
N485	4848	1965	Salt Lake UT	Edde	USA	11/27	
N17337	1962	1966	Long Beach MS	Aeronaut	USA	06/27	

Reg.	Msn	Year	Location	Airline		Date	Rebuilt
N4994E.	12442	1966	Gallup NM	Frontier	USA	07/27	
N54370	19220	1967	Merced CA	Turkey Farms	USA	03/24	
N65276	19202	1967	Denver CO	Frontier	USA	12/21	
N6898D	20082	1968	Vichy MO	Purdue	USA	06/28	Yes
N15570	6320	1969	Hawthorne NV	Mineral County	USA	02/18	
N142D	1946	1969	N Orleans LA	Avion Inc	USA	03/20	
N154R	6156	1970	McGrath AK	Reeder	USA	07/03	
N47	33155	1970	Anchorage AK	FAA	USA	10/01	
N14273	7366	1971	Shawnee OK	Patterson Lsg	USA	05/14	
N90627	4642	1971	Shelter Cove CA	Greyhound Lsg	USA	06/27	
N44992	11738	1971	Peotone, IL	Unknown	USA	09/06	Yes
N15HC	43080	1974	Houston, TX	Horizon Prop	USA	02/01	
N9BC	9510	1975	Ft Lauderdale FL	Air O'Hare	USA	01/01	
N6	4146	1975	Jefferson PA	FAA	USA	03/27	
N144A	9723	1975	Wakeman, OH	Stoney's	USA	09/11	
N73KW	2252	1977	Miami FL	Air Sunshine	USA	01/15	
N38AP	10217	1977	Newton GA	Hall Mining	USA	06/13	
N51071	4837	1977	Evansville IN	Air Indiana.	USA	12/13	
N45873	12458	1978	Richmond IN	Air Sales	USA	07/09	
N74Z	25953	1978	Ft Walton Bch FL	Evergreen	USA	10/01	
N41447	12987	1978	Des Moines IA	SMB Stage	USA	12/02	
N25656	4845	1978	Lorida FL	Caribe Air	USA	12/06	Yes
N133AC	6260	1978	Port Mayaca FL	Acft Sales	USA	12/11	
N4996E	12141	1978	Belle Glade FL	Rodriguez	USA	12/14	
N9025R	4998	1979	South Bay FL	Waggoner	USA	01/10	
N148Z	20422	1979	Selway River ID	USFS	USA	06/11	
N427W	43073	1979	Ft. Lauderdale, FL	Bradley Avn	USA	06/12	
N21782	2170	1979	Belle Glade FL	M J Supply	USA	07/13	
N59314.	12363	1979	Bettles AK	J L Dodson	USA	07/27	Yes
N99663.	33467	1979	Bettles AK	K.B. Martin	USA	10/30	
N64490	25360	1980	Athol IN	Hackney	USA	04/11	
N709Z	27182	1980	Ft Lauderdale FL	Florida Equity	USA	04/24	
N45864	9304	1980	New Smyrna FL	Rule	USA	08/01	
N3WX	34373	1980	Miami, FL	Air Miami	USA	12/22	Yes
N87652.	25534	1981	Miami FL	S.S Airways	USA	01/17	Yes
N3433P	4346	1981	Laredo TX	Atkins Avn	USA	04/01	Yes
N111ST	4661	1981	Pilot Point AK	Acft Svces	USA	06/01	
N18949	2013	1981	Melbourne FL	Hawthorne Coll	USA	06/24	
N129H	4126	1982	Sandwich, IL	M Borghorst	USA	05/29	Yes
N95C	20139	1982	St Petersburg FL	Fromhagen	USA	06/06	
N38941	6332	1983	Springfield, MO	Crystal Shamrock	USA	03/24	
N95460	20190	1983	Fort Yukon AK	Yukon Air Serv	USA	06/24	Yes
N70003	12938	1984.	Memphis TN	River City	USA	08/11	
N139PB	2239	1984	Naples, FL	P.B.A.	USA	12/27	Yes
N28BA	4583	1985	Charlotte NC	S J Bowman	USA	02/05	Yes
N157U	4132	1985	Perris CA	B Conatser	USA	05/04	
N168Z	20850	1985.	King Salmon AK	Northern Pen	USA	06/30	
N777YA	25634.	1985	Dillingham, AK	L.L. Bingman	USA	12/15	Yes
N711Y	13658	1985	De Kalb TX	Century Equity	USA	12/31	
N25CE	12476	1986	El Paso TX	Atorie Air	USA	04/05	Yes
N3433U	43087	1986	Las Vegas NV	Atorie Air	USA	05/30	Yes
N31MS	11631	1987	Hilliard FL	F.J. Bailey	USA	06/30	Yes
N39DT	4871	1987	Laredo TX	Ferreteria	USA	07/28	
N28889	20520	1989	Summerland FL	Monroe Cty	USA	05/02	
N47E	13456	1989	Waterman IL	Condor Ent	USA	05/22	
N8042X	19041	1989	Scow Bay AK	CA Air Tours	USA	06/26	Yes
N143JR	1995	1989	Columbus IN	Rhoades Int'l	USA	09/15	Yes
N1FN	11685	1990	Caron Bridge WV	K & K Acft	USA	05/19	
N13JA	4082	1991	Apple Creek OH	JAARS	USA	08/24	Yes
N8056	26008	1993	Zepherhills FL	Phoenix Air	USA	04/20	
N3433Y	43089	1994	Spokane WA	Salair	USA	03/18	
N54NA	19475	1995	Whitesville NY	Business Air	USA	07/19	

Appendix V

U.S. Navy Pilot History Cards of Aircraft Accidents

The following Pilot History Cards of Aircraft Accidents are on 16mm microfilm reels. Each roll costs $30, checks payable to the Department of the Navy. They are available from:

Department of the Navy
Naval History and Heritage Command
Naval Aviation History Branch
805 Kidder Breeze Street SE
Washington Navy Yard
Washington, D.C. 20374-5059

The Naval Aviation History Branch will also provide researchers with record cards of a single aircraft at no charge. You must provide them with the aircraft type and Bureau Number (Navy serial number). Additional information can be obtained from the Naval History and Heritage Command's website at: www.history.navy.mil.

NAVY AVIATORS TELL OF EATING SHARK KILLED WITH PENKNIFE. (By the Associated Press)

Pearl Harbor, Hawaii, March 10. A gripping story of beating off sharks with bare fists and of beating hunger and thirst while stark-naked and half-crazed came today from three Navy fliers who survived 34 days in stormy South Seas on a raft smaller than an ordinary bed.

From the time their land plane was forced down on the Pacific until Gene Aldrich, 24 year old radioman of Sikeston, Mo., mouthed through parched lips the startling words, "Chief, I see a field of corn," the three lived a story that would tax the imagination of a fiction writer. The cornfield Aldrich thought he saw was a coconut grove.

"Chief" is Harold Dixon, 42, of LaMesa, Calif., aviation chief machinists mate and pilot of the lost plane. The third of the fliers is Anthony J. Pastula, 24, of Youngstown, O., aviation ordnanceman. They traveled at least 1000 miles on a rubber life raft to a tiny South Sea isle and later were picked up by Navy craft. They now are at Pearl Harbor and virtually recovered. The Navy announced their rescue last month.

Their story is one of quick thinking, resourcefulness and raw courage. Dixon now is partially deaf. When an albatross alighted unexpectedly on the raft, Aldrich fired a pistol too close to Dixon's ear. Dixon jumped into the sea to retrieve the bird and its flesh helped keep the men alive. It was on the night of January 16 that Dixon decided he had better set his plane down on the sea while enough gas remained to keep the plane under control. The plane sank quicker than expected and the men were unable to save the rations, water or instruments. While floundering in the water, they managed to inflate the rubber life raft, its inside dimensions only 28" x 80". In this precarious haven the three crowded for the perilous days ahead.

"We were not concerned much the first night," Dixon said. "We knew searchers would be out and sure enough we saw a plane in the morning; but it did not see us and that was the last we saw of possible help." The raft was not equipped with oars and for some time the trio were just drifting. Later Dixon's shoes were rigged so that they could be used as hand-oars. "Don't say we drifted to the island—we worked," Dixon said. He told of shooting a big leopard shark which came so close he merely held the pistol against the shark's head." He related that still later he struck another shark with his bare fists. The men lost from 20 to 50 pounds each in the long ordeal.

They rigged a sea anchor from a life jacket, using it whenever winds were adverse. They used their own underclothing as sponges when it rained. After the cloth was saturated, they wrung it out to fill a small container with the precious water. At all times they knew where they wanted to go—toward islands to the south. The sea was smooth during the first part of the trip. Later, when they finally sighted land, they were in the middle of one of the worst hurricanes in South Sea history. Time and again they were tossed into the ocean, only to climb back. The last few days they did not have a stitch of clothing and were sunburned so badly it took weeks to heal. Their total food hardly would make more than one good meal, but Dixon insisted coffee and cigarettes were missed more than the food. Aldrich proved the best fisherman, but once his hand was bitten by a shark. They had practically no water the first four days, until they figured out the idea of using their underclothing as a sponge. Neither did they have food. Then Aldrich stabbed a fish with his pocketknife and they chewed the raw flesh. They said it was like chewing rubber. The albatross was next on the menu. After part had been eaten Dixon noted at night that the bird seemed to emit light. He feared it had become poisonous from feeding in phosphorescent waters and heaved the remainder of the carcass overboard.

On the 7th day Aldrich stabbed a 4-foot shark. "We ripped the shark open with pliers," Dixon said. "We had read about vitamins in sharks' livers so ate that first. It was very good. We also ate two sardines found in the shark's stomach with a great deal of relish. And the next day we polished off the shark itself. On the fourteenth day Aldrich caught another fish and I caught a bird by reaching up for it when it landed on the raft. It was some sort of a tern, but to us tasted like fried chicken. We devoured it on the spot. On the 21st day we picked up a coconut. Things looked pretty bad the thirty-third day. We had lost our clothes, all but one shoe, and the pistol long since had corroded into uselessness. We found ourselves periodically in a daze."

"I was lying down as best we could the morning of the 34th day when Gene (Aldrich's nickname) said he saw corn. I didn't pay any attention. I just thought he was gone. [illegible] We tried to paddle all day and finally staggered ashore [illegible] with the hurricane just getting to top force. We decided when we came ashore we would try to march and if the island was Japanese, they would not find us crawling up to them. But we could not straighten up. The next morning, island natives on beach patrol saw us, gave us kernels of coconuts and went for help. They carried us to the governor's house."

Dixon finished his recital with the words: "These boys showed plenty of stuff all the way through." Asked how he liked food in Honolulu, Dixon replied: "Regularly."

Sample Pilot History Card

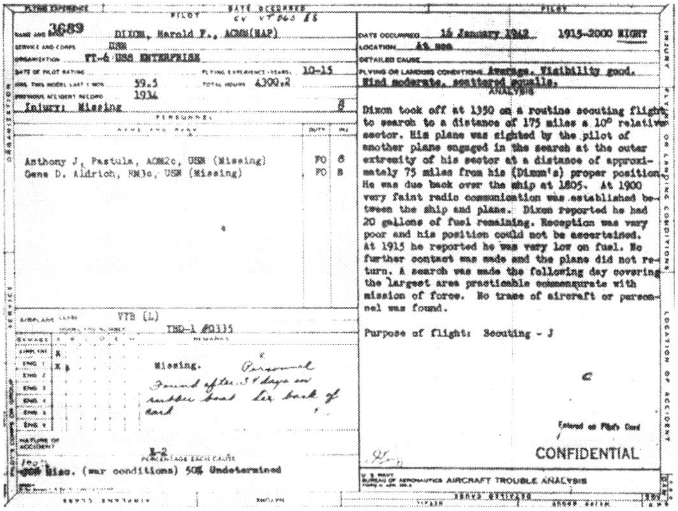

PILOT

CV VT 060 15

NAME AND RATE: 3689 DIXON, Harold F., ACMM(NAP)

SERVICE AND CORPS: USN

ORGANIZATION: VT-6 USS ENTERPRISE

DATE OF PILOT RATING — FLYING EXPERIENCE (YEARS): 10-15

HRS. THIS MODEL LAST 3 MOS.: 59.5 — TOTAL HOURS: 4300.2

PREVIOUS ACCIDENT RECORD: 1934

Injury: Missing

PERSONNEL

NAME AND RANK	DUTY	INJ.
Anthony J. Pastula, ACM2c, USN (Missing)	FO	8
Gene D. Aldrich, RM3c, USN (Missing)	FO	8

AIRPLANE CLASS: VTB (L)

MODEL AND NUMBER: TBD-1 #0335

REMARKS: Missing. Personnel found after 34 days on rubber boat. See back of card

NATURE OF ACCIDENT: X-2

PERCENTAGE EACH CAUSE: 50% Misc. (war conditions) 50% Undetermined

DATE OCCURRED: 16 January 1942 1915-2000 NIGHT

LOCATION: At sea

DETAILED CAUSE

FLYING OR LANDING CONDITIONS: Average. Visibility good. Wind moderate, scattered squalls.

ANALYSIS

Dixon took off at 1330 on a routine scouting flight to search to a distance of 175 miles a 10° relative sector. His plane was sighted by the pilot of another plane engaged in the search at the outer extremity of his sector at a distance of approximately 75 miles from his (Dixon's) proper position. He was due back over the ship at 1805. At 1900 very faint radio communication was established between the ship and plane. Dixon reported he had 20 gallons of fuel remaining. Reception was very poor and his position could not be ascertained. At 1915 he reported he was very low on fuel. No further contact was made and the plane did not return. A search was made the following day covering the largest area practicable commensurate with mission of force. No trace of aircraft or personnel was found.

Purpose of flight: Scouting - J

Entered on Pilot's Card

CONFIDENTIAL

U. S. NAVY BUREAU OF AERONAUTICS AIRCRAFT TROUBLE ANALYSIS

Example of Single Aircraft Record Card

Reel No.	Microdex No.	Model	Crashes Listed By Date	Reel No.	Microdex No.	Model	Crashes Listed By Date
14	3	AD	Apr 1947 thru Dec 1949	13	8	F3F	Jul 1941 thru Jan 1943
14	4	AD	Jan 1950 thru Dec 1950	16	3	F4B	Jan 1941 thru Dec 1942
14	5	AD	Jan 1951 thru Jul 1951	13	9	F4F	Jul 1941 thru Oct 1942
14	6	AD	Aug 1951 thru Dec 1951	13	10	F4F	Nov 1942 thru Dec 1943
14	7	AD	Jan 1952 thru Jun 1952	14	1	F4F	Jan 1944 thru Aug 1945
14	8	AD	Jun 1950 thru Jun 1952	14	2	F5F	Feb 1942 thru Jun 1942
16	1	AE	Jan 1950 thru Dec 1950	9	1	F4U	Aug 1942 thru Dec 1943
23	4	AJ	Jan 1948 thru Dec 1948	9	2	F4U	Jan 1944 thru Mar 1944
23	5	AM	Jan 1947 thru Dec 1947	9	3	F4U	Apr 1944 thru Sep 1944
23	6	AV	Feb 1952 thru Jun 1952	9	4	F4U	Oct 1944 thru Dec 1944
23	7	BD	Jan 1942 thru Dec 1942	9	5	F4U	Jan 1945 thru Mar 1945
16	2	BD-2	Jan 1942 thru Dec 1944	9	6	F4U	Apr 1945 thru May 1945
23	8	BT	Jan 1941 thru Dec 1941	9	7	F4U	Jun 1945
16	2	BTD-1	Jan 1945 thru Dec 1952	9	8	F4U	Jul 1945 thru Dec 1945
16	3	FD-1	Jan 1947 thru Dec 1947	9	9	F4U	Jan 1946 thru Jun 1946
28	2	Fatalities	Sep 1941 thru Jul 1951	10	1	F4U	Jun 1946 thru Dec 1946
23	9	FF	Jan 1942 thru Dec 1942	10	2	F4U	Jan 1947 thru Aug 1947
12	8	FG	Jan 1943 thru Dec 1944	10	3	F4U	Sep 1947 thru Apr 1948
12	9	FG	Jan 1945 thru Mar 1945	10	4	F4U	May 1948 thru Dec 1948
13	1	FG	Apr 1945 thru Jul 1945	10	5	F4U	Jan 1948 thru May 1949
13	2	FG	Aug 1945 thru Aug 1946	10	6	F4U	Jun 1949 thru Sep 1949
13	3	FG	Sep 1946 thru Jul 1947	10	7	F4U	Oct 1949 thru Dec 1949
13	4	FG	Aug 1948 thru Dec 1951	10	8	F4U	Jan 1950 thru Aug 1950
13	5	FG	Jan 1952 thru Jun 1952	10	9	F4U	Sep 1950 thru Dec 1950
24	1	FH	Nov 1947 thru Mar 1952	11	1	F4U	Jan 1951 thru Apr 1951
23	3	FJ	Jan 1947 thru Dec 1947	11	2	F4U	May 1951 thru Jun 1951
15	1	FM	Dec 1942 thru Dec 1943	11	3	F4U	Jul 1951 thru Oct 1951
15	2	FM	Jan 1944 thru Apr 1944	11	4	F4U	Nov 1951 thru Dec 1951
15	3	FM	May 1944 thru Jun 1944	11	5	F4U	Jan 1952 thru Feb 1952
15	4	FM	Jul 1944 thru Aug 1944	11	6	F4U	Mar 1952 thru Jun 1952
15	5	FM	Sep 1944 thru Oct 1944	6	1	F6F	Dec 1942 thru Dec 1943
15	6	FM	Nov 1944 thru Dec 1944	6	2	F6F	Jan 1944 thru Feb 1944
15	7	FM	Jan 1945	6	3	F6F	Mar 1944 thru Apr 1944
15	8	FM	Feb 1945	6	4	F6F	May 1944 thru Jun 1944
15	9	FM	Mar 1945	6	5	F6F	Jul 1944
17	10	FM	Apr 1945 thru Jun 1945	6	6	F6F	Aug 1944
18	1	FM	Jul 1945 thru Nov 1946	6	7	F6F	Sep 1944
16	3	FR	Jan 1944 thru Dec 1949	6	8	F6F	Oct 1944
23	10	FR	Jan 1945 thru Jun 1947	6	9	F6F	Nov 1944
11	7	F2F	Jul 1941 thru Nov 1941	7	1	F6F	Dec 1944
16	3	F2G-1	Jan 1945 thru Dec 1946	7	2	F6F	Jan 1945
13	6	F2H	Jan 1948 thru Dec 1948	7	3	F6F	Feb 1945
16	3	F2L-1	Jan 1946 thru Dec 1946	7	4	F6F	Mar 1945
16	3	F2T	Jan 1945 thru Dec 1946	7	5	F6F	Apr 1945
18	2	F3A	Jul 1941 thru Dec 1941	7	6	F6F	May 1945
18	3	F3A	Jul 1943 thru Oct 1946	7	7	F6F	Jun 1945
13	7	F3D	Dec 1950 thru Apr 1952	7	8	F6F	Jul 1945

Reel No.	Microdex No.	Model	Crashes Listed By Date	Reel No.	Microdex No.	Model	Crashes Listed By Date
7	9	F6F	Aug 1945	28	5	N2S	Sep 1943 thru May 1944
8	1	F6F	Sep 1945 thru Dec 1945	28	6	N2S	Jun1944 thru Jan 1945
8	2	F6F	Jan 1946 thru Jul 1946	28	7	N2S	Feb 1945 thru May 1945
8	3	F6F	Jul 1946 thru Dec 1946	28	8	N2S	Jun 1945 thru Apr 1946
8	4	F6F	Jan 1947 thru Dec 1947	28	9	N2S	May 1946 thru Jun 1952
8	5	F6F	Jan 1948 thru Dec 1948	26	6	N2T	May 1942 thru Aug 1944
8	6	F6F	Jan 1949 thru Dec 1949	26	5	N3N	Jul 1941 thru Jun 1952
8	7	F6F	Jan 1950 thru Dec 1950	17	3	OBM	Jan 1947 thru Jun 1952
8	8	F6F	Jan 1951 thru Dec 1951	27	4	OE	Dec 1951 thru May 1952
8	9	F6F	Jan 1952 thru Jun 1952	27	7	OS2N	Mar 1942 thru Sep 1945
16	3	F6U	Jan 1947 thru Dec 1950	27	5	OS2U	Jul 1941 thru Sep 1947
11	8	F7F	Jan 1944 thru Dec 1944	27	3	OY	Oct 1943 thru Nov 1951
11	9	F7F	Jul 1944 thru Dec 1948	27	6	O3U	Aug 1941 thru Jan 1943
11	10	F7F	Jan 1949 thru Sep 1950	16	6	PB	Jan 1948 thru Dec 1951
12	1	F8F	Mar 1945 thru Jun 1947	25	5	PBJ	Mar 1943 thru Oct 1947
12	2	F8F	Jul 1947 thru Dec 1947	17	1	PBM	Oct 1941 thru Dec 1944
12	3	F8F	Jan 1948 thru Dec 1948	17	2	PBM	Jan 1945 thru Dec 1946
12	4	F8F	Jan 1949 thru Dec 1949	25	4	PBO	Nov 1941 thru Feb 1944
12	5	F8F	Jan 1950 thru Dec 1950	25	6	PBY	Jul 1941 thru Dec 1943
12	6	F8F	Jan 1951 thru Dec 1951	25	8	PB2B	Feb 1945 thru May 1946
12	7	F8F	Jan 1952 thru Jun 1952	28	1	PB2Y	May 1942 thru Jan 1946
23	1	F9F	Oct 1948 thru Apr 1951	25	9	PB4Y	Feb 1943 thru Mar 1945
23	2	F9F	May 1951 thru Jun 1952	25	10	PB4Y	Apr 1945 thru Sep 1945
24	2	GB	Aug 1941 thru Jun 1946	27	8	PV	Oct 1942 thru Aug 1951
24	3	GH	Apr 1942 thru Aug 1946	26	1	P2V	Jun 1945 thru Jun 1952
24	4	Helos	Oct 1943 thru Jun 1952	27	8	P2V	Aug 1951
25	2	JD	Mar 1946 thru May 1952	28	1	P2Y	Nov 1941 thru Feb 1942
16	4	JF	Jan 1941 thru Dec 1943	27	9	P4M	Feb 1950 thru Feb 1952
24	10	JM	Oct 1943 thru Jul 1947	27	10	P4Y-2	Aug 1951 thru Jun 1952
25	1	JRB	Oct 1941 thru Jun 1952	16	7	RB	Jan 1944 thru Dec 1944
16	4	JRC	Jan 1943 thru Dec 1945	16	7	R2D	Jan 1941 thru Dec 1943
24	9	JRF	Jul 1941 thru Sep 1956	17	4	R4D	Jul 1942 thru Jun 1952
24	7	JRM	Aug 1945 thru Aug 1950	17	5	R4Q	Feb 1951 thru Jun 1952
24	8	JRS	Jul 1941 thru Jun 1944	17	7	R5C	Mar 1943 thru Jun 1952
24	6	J2F	Jul 1941 thru Oct 1948	17	6	R5D	Mar 1943 thru Dec 1943
24	5	J4F	Oct 1942 thru Jun 1948	17	8	R5D	Feb 1944 thru Jun 1952
25	3	LTA	Jun 1942 thru Apr 1952	17	9	SBC	Jul 1941 thru Dec 1941
16	10	Misc.	Jan 1941 thru Dec 1952	22	1	SBD	Jul 1941 thru Dec 1942
27	2	NE	Apr 1942 thru Jun 1946	22	2	SBD	Jan 1943 thru Jul 1943
27	1	NH	May 1943 thru Nov 1946	22	3	SBD	Aug 1943 thru Oct 1943
26	9	NJ	Oct 1941 thru Jun 1944	22	4	SBD	Nov 1943 thru Dec 1943
26	10	NP	Dec 1941 thru Jun 1943	22	5	SBD	Jan 1944 thru Feb 1944
16	5	NR	Jan 1942 thru Dec 1944	22	6	SBD	Mar 1944 thru Apr 1944
26	8	NR	Aug 1941 thru May 1943	22	7	SBD	May 1944 thru Jun 1944
26	7	NS	Oct 1941 thru Jan 1943	32	7	SBD	Jul 1944 thru Sep 1944
28	3	N2S	Jul 1941 thru Feb 1943	32	8	SBD	Oct 1944 thru Dec 1944
28	4	N2S	Mar 1943 thru Aug 1943	32	9	SBD	Jan 1945 thru Jul 1945

Reel No.	Microdex No.	Model	Crashes Listed By Date	Reel No.	Microdex No.	Model	Crashes Listed By Date
32	10	SBD	Aug 1945 thru Mar 1946	29	3	SOC	Jul 1941 thru Sep 1946
34	2	SBF	Aug 1944 thru Jan 1946	28	10	SON	Jul 1941 thru Nov 1944
33	10	SBN	Jul 1941 thru Feb 1943	29	1	SU	Aug 1941 thru Mar 1943
34	1	SBU	Jul 1941 thru Jul 1943	29	2	SO3C	May 1942 thru Aug 1945
33	7	SBW	Jan 1944 thru Sep 1946	33	1	TBD	Jul 1941 thru Sep 1943
33	8	SBW	Oct 1946 thru Sep 1948	32	2	TBF	Jul 1943 thru Jun 1944
30	3	SB2A	Feb 1943 thru Aug 1944	33	2	TBF	Jul 1941 thru Aug 1943
29	4	SB2C	Nov 1942 thru May 1944	33	3	TBF	Sep 1943 thru Feb 1944
29	5	SB2C	Jun 1944 thru Aug 1944	33	4	TBF	Mar 1944 thru Sep 1944
29	6	SB2C	Sep 1944 thru Nov 1944	33	5	TBF	Oct 1944 thru May 1945
29	7	SB2C	Dec 1944 thru Mar 1945	33	6	TBF	Jun 1945 thru Dec 1945
29	8	SB2C	Apr 1945 thru Jun 1945	30	4	TBM	Apr 1943 thru Apr 1944
29	9	SB2C	Jul 1945 thru Sep 1945	30	5	TBM	May 1944 thru Sep 1944
29	10	SB2C	Oct 1945 thru Dec 1946	30	6	TBM	Oct 1944 thru Dec 1944
30	1	SB2C	Jan 1947 thru Oct 1947	30	7	TBM	Jan 1945 thru Feb 1945
30	2	SB2C	Nov 1947 thru Oct 1951	30	8	TBM	Mar 1945 thru May 1945
33	9	SB2U	Jul 1941 thru Jul 1943	30	9	TBM	Jun 1945
32	3	SC	Sep 1944 thru Jan 1949	30	10	TBM	Jul 1945
16	8	SF-1	Jan 1942 thru Dec 1942	31	1	TBM	Aug 1945 thru Dec 1945
26	2	SNB	Nov 1942 thru Dec 1945	31	2	TBM	Jan 1946 thru Jan 1947
26	3	SNB	Jan 1946 thru Jun 1950	31	3	TBM	Feb 1947 thru Apr 1948
26	4	SNB	Jul 1950 thru Jun 1952	31	4	TBM	May 1948 thru Jul 1949
32	4	SNC	Aug 1941 thru Sep 1944	31	5	TBM	Aug 1949 thru Dec 1950
19	1	SNJ	Jul 1941 thru Jan 1943	31	6	TBM	Jan 1951 thru Dec 1951
19	2	SNJ	Feb 1943 thru Jul 1943	31	7	TBM	Jan 1952 thru Jun 1952
19	3	SNJ	Aug 1943 thru Dec 1943	16	9	TBY	Jan 1944 thru Dec 1945
19	4	SNJ	Jan 1944 thru Mar 1944	31	8	TBY	Jul 1945 thru Jun 1947
19	5	SNJ	Apr 1944 thru Jul 1944	16	9	TDC	Jan 1943 thru Dec 1944
19	6	SNJ	Aug 1944 thru Oct 1944	16	9	TDN	Jan 1943 thru Dec 1943
19	7	SNJ	Nov 1944 thru Dec 1944	31	9	TD2C	Jul 1944 thru Mar 1950
19	8	SNJ	Jan 1945 thru May 1945	31	10	TO	Oct 1948 thru Mar 1952
19	9	SNJ	Jun 1945 thru Aug 1945	32	1	TV	Mar 1952 thru Jun 1952
20	1	SNJ	Sep 1945 thru Dec 1945				
20	2	SNJ	Jan 1946 thru Jun 1946				
20	3	SNJ	Jul 1946 thru Dec 1946				
20	4	SNJ	Jan 1947 thru May 1947				
20	5	SNJ	Jun 1947 thru Dec 1947				
20	6	SNJ	Jan 1948 thru Apr 1948				
20	7	SNJ	May 1948 thru Sep 1948				
20	8	SNJ	Oct 1948 thru Dec 1948				
20	9	SNJ	Jan 1949 thru Dec 1949				
21	1	SNJ	Jan 1950 thru Dec 1950				
21	2	SNJ	Jan 1951 thru Sep 1951				
21	3	SNJ	Oct 1951 thru Dec 1951				
21	4	SNJ	Jan 1952 thru Jun 1952				
32	5	SNV	Aug 1941 thru May 1944				
32	6	SNV	Jun 1944 thru Oct 1945				

Appendix VI

Obtaining U.S. Air Force Aircraft History Cards

The U.S. Air Force will provide researchers with the individual record card for a certain aircraft at no charge, or you can order an entire reel of aircraft record cards for $20. To order a record card or microfilm reel, contact:

Department of the Air Force
USAF Historical Research Center/HD
Maxwell Air Force Base, Ala. 36112-6678

U.S. Air Force Aircraft Record Cards Available On 16mm Microfilm

ACR-1	216	thru	623	ACR-31	41-20344	thru	41-22467
ACR-2	24-216	thru	26-423	ACR-32	41-22468	thru	41-24808
ACR-3	26-424	thru	28-213	ACR-33	41-24809	thru	41-27325
ACR-4	28-214	thru	29-180	ACR-34	41-27326	thru	41-30049
ACR-5	29-182	thru	30-209	ACR-35	41-30050	thru	41-32171
ACR-6	30-210	thru	31-86	ACR-36	41-32172	thru	41-35037
ACR-7	31-87	thru	31-405	ACR-37	41-35038	thru	41-36952
ACR-8	31-406	thru	32-169	ACR-38	41-36953	thru	41-37199
ACR-9	32-170	thru	33-277	ACR-39	41-37200	thru	41-39600
ACR-10	33-278	thru	08318	ACR-40	42-1	thru	42-2602
ACR-11	08320	thru	KF232	ACR-41	42-2607	thru	42-4641
ACR-12	KF233	thru	Z7499	ACR-42	42-4642	thru	42-6958
ACR-13	36-1	thru	36-446	ACR-43	42-6959	thru	42-9204
ACR-14	37-1	thru	37-520	ACR-44	42-9205	thru	42-12774
ACR-15	37-521	thru	37-679	ACR-45	42-12775	thru	42-15274
ACR-16	38-1	thru	38-513	ACR-46	42-15275	thru	42-17279
ACR-17	38-514	thru	38-610	ACR-47	42-17280	thru	42-19554
ACR-18	39-1	thru	40-818	ACR-48	42-19555	thru	42-23032
ACR-19	40-819	thru	40-1638	ACR-49	42-23033	thru	42-25446
ACR-20	40-1639	thru	40-2731	ACR-50	42-25447	thru	42-28121
ACR-21	40-2732	thru	41-842	ACR-51	42-28122	thru	42-30426
ACR-22	41-843	thru	41-2407	ACR-52	42-30427	thru	42-32912
ACR-23	41-2408	thru	41-6039	ACR-53	42-32913	thru	42-36065
ACR-24	41-6040	thru	41-8100	ACR-54	42-36066	thru	42-38804
ACR-25	41-8101	thru	41-9465	ACR-55	42-38805	thru	42-40811
ACR-26	41-9468	thru	41-11631	ACR-56	42-40812	thru	42-43283
ACR-27	41-11632	thru	41-13472	ACR-57	42-43284	thru	42-46433
ACR-28	41-13473	thru	41-15706	ACR-58	42-46434	thru	42-50040
ACR-29	41-15707	thru	41-17845	ACR-59	42-50041	thru	42-52579
ACR-30	41-17846	thru	41-20343	ACR-60	42-52580	thru	42-55761

U.S. Air Force Aircraft Record Cards Available On 16mm Microfilm (cont'd)

ACR-61	42-55762	thru	42-58763
ACR-62	42-58764	thru	42-64188
ACR-63	42-64189	thru	42-67129
ACR-64	42-67130	thru	42-69620
ACR-65	42-69621	thru	42-72221
ACR-66	42-72222	thru	42-74600
ACR-67	42-74601	thru	42-77622
ACR-68	42-77623	thru	42-79972
ACR-69	42-79973	thru	42-84905
ACR-70	42-84906	thru	42-88654
ACR-71	42-88655	thru	42-92669
ACR-72	42-92670	thru	42-95390
ACR-73	42-95391	thru	42-98074
ACR-74	42-98075	thru	42-100575
ACR-75	42-100576	thru	42-104107
ACR-76	42-104108	thru	42-106379
ACR-77	42-106380	thru	43-356
ACR-78	43-357	thru	43-2321
ACR-79	43-2322	thru	43-4990
ACR-80	43-4991	thru	43-7345
ACR-81	43-7346	thru	43-10059
ACR-82	43-10060	thru	43-13176
ACR-83	43-13177	thru	43-21770
ACR-84	43-21771	thru	43-24170
ACR-85	43-24171	thru	43-26954
ACR-86	43-26955	thru	43-29253
ACR-87	43-29255	thru	43-32464
ACR-88	43-32465	thru	43-36691
ACR-89	43-36692	thru	43-39253
ACR-90	43-39254	thru	43-41627
ACR-91	43-41628	thru	43-45476
ACR-92	43-45477	thru	43-50199
ACR-93	43-50200	thru	43-52437
ACR-94	44-1	thru	44-3969
ACR-95	44-3970	thru	44-7450
ACR-96	44-7451	thru	44-10951
ACR-97	44-10952	thru	44-13309
ACR-98	44-13310	thru	44-17058
ACR-99	44-17059	thru	44-20809
ACR-100	44-20810	thru	44-24925
ACR-101	44-24926	thru	44-26199
ACR-102	44-26200	thru	44-30562
ACR-103	44-30563	thru	44-33272
ACR-104	44-33273	thru	44-40800
ACR-105	44-40801	thru	44-44399
ACR-106	44-44400	thru	44-50636
ACR-107	44-50637	thru	44-63538
ACR-108	44-63539	thru	44-70483
ACR-109	44-70484	thru	44-73698
ACR-110	44-73700	thru	44-77739
ACR-111	44-77740	thru	44-80971
ACR-112	44-80975	thru	44-84873
ACR-113	44-84878	thru	44-88548
ACR-114	44-88550	thru	45-5855
ACR-115	45-5856	thru	45-14629
ACR-116	45-14630	thru	45-58850
ACR-117	45-58851	thru	49-784
ACR-118	49-794	thru	51-600

The following records were out of file at the time the ACR rolls were filmed:

OACR-1	41-32145	thru	50-1639
OACR-2	41-327	thru	42-44668
OACR-3	42-44670	thru	44-35689
OACR-4	44-35705	thru	44-83699
OACR-5	44-83723	thru	45-34995
OACR-6	45-34988	thru	49-2426
OACR-7	49-2427	thru	British planes
OACR-8	41-1143	thru	44-85467
OACR-9	44-85531	thru	51-10909
OACR-10	51-10910	thru	AFF+NGG losses, Navy planes

Appendix VII

Obtaining USGS Topo Maps

The United States Geological Survey (USGS) publishes topographical maps for every inch of the United States. The maps range in cost from $2.50 to as high as $10 and are available at many bookstores, blueprint stores, engineering supply stores, main libraries, and university libraries. Consult your local phone book.

To order USGS maps, you must first obtain the following items for the state in which your wreck is located;

- Catalog of Topographical and Other Published Maps
- Index to Topographic and Other Map Coverage

Both publications are free of charge. To order the above publications, write to:

Map Distribution/Sales
U.S. Geological Survey
Box 25286, Federal Center
Denver, Colo. 80225

The Catalog of Topographical and Other Published Maps will provide you with a list of USGS map dealers in your state. Once you have selected your map, you can order it by mail or visit one of the retailers listed in the map catalog. Be sure to pick up the Guide to Topographic Map Symbols.

Maps must be ordered by map name, state, and series/scale. Payment should be made by check or money order, payable to the Department of the Interior—USGS.

Maps can also be ordered online at: http://store.usgs.gov.

Douglas A-20G-1-DO Havoc 42-53726 over-ran the runway at Nome, Alaska during the war. Was this aircraft returned to service, or was it cannibalized to keep others flying? Many have wondered if the stripped-out fuselage is sitting somewhere on the field. (Library of Congress)

Appendix VIII

Wreckchasing Worksheet

Type

Make/Model ______________________

Registration/Serial ______________ Previous Regs. ______________

MSN __________ Date of Delivery ______________________

Operator ❑ Civilian: __________ ❑ USN ❑ USAAF/USAF

Crash Date ___/___/___

Location ______________________

7.5 Min Quad ______________________

Accident Report ❑ FAA ❑ USN ❑ AAF/USAF Report#/Date ________
date requested (___/___/___)

Aircraft History ❑ FAA ❑ USN ❑ AAF/USAF
date requested (___/___/___)

Newspapers ❑ ______________________

Date ___/___/___ Page ________
Date ___/___/___ Page ________
Date ___/___/___ Page ________
Date ___/___/___ Page ________

❑ ______________________

Date ___/___/___ Page ________
Date ___/___/___ Page ________
Date ___/___/___ Page ________
Date ___/___/___ Page ________

❑ ______________________

Date ___/___/___ Page ________
Date ___/___/___ Page ________
Date ___/___/___ Page ________
Date ___/___/___ Page ________

Witnesses ❑ Mr/Mrs ______________ ❑ Mr/Mrs ______________

❑ Mr/Mrs ______________ ❑ Mr/Mrs ______________

Reported Location (from newspaper descriptions)

____

____

____

On June 18, 1943, Lt. Paul J. Murphy crashed his Bell P-39Q-1-BE Airacobra, 42-19505, into a house in San Bruno, California, shortly after taking off from San Francisco Army Air Field (Mills Field, now San Francisco International Airport). Lucky for Murphy and the residents of the house, there was no post-crash fire. It was reported that Murphy was involved in the write-off of P-39N-0-BE 42-8857 just two days prior, on June 14, 1943.

Appendix IX

Wreckchasing Field Checklist

Although optional, consider including the following items in your day pack:

- Backpack
- Waistpack
- Toilet paper
- Allergy medicine
- Advil
- Matches
- Ziploc bags
- Eye protection
- Compass
- Insect repellant
- Sunscreen
- Knife
- Pliers
- Hacksaw
- Dust mask
- Digging tools
- Sifting screen
- Flashlight & batteries
- Water bottles
- Neck towels
- Camera, memory, batteries
- Pen & paper
- Phone—CB
- Whistle

Clothes

- Long pants
- Long-sleeve shirt
- Two undershirts
- Socks—two pair
- Sturdy shoes
- Hat
- Gloves
- Rain poncho

First Aid Kit

- Band-Aids
- Alcohol wipes
- Ace bandage
- Wide gauze

United Air Lines Boeing 247D NC13323, sits on the rolling hills outside Cheyenne, Wyoming. The plane was on a company test flight and flew into a hill during a storm on Oct. 7, 1935. The aircraft impacted in a flat attitude, regained flight, and came to rest more than 1,000 feet from the original touch-down point. Four perished in the accident. Notice how the plane has been covered with tarps, blankets, and rugs to hide its livery from photographers.

Appendix X

Selected Internet Resources

Below is a list of useful and interesting websites relating to wreckchasing and aviation archaeology. Only sites with dedicated URLs have been included.

Aircraft Wrecks in the Mountains and Deserts of the American West

www.aircraftwrecks.com

Explorer G. Pat Macha's site chronicles the hundreds of sites he's documented and showcases a number of aircraft wreck mysteries he's working to solve. He is currently dedicated to locating missing WASP Gertrude Tompkins Silver, and in the process of looking for her he has located more than 70 other aircraft crash sites in the Santa Monica Bay. Macha is also the host of the History Channel's *Broken Wings*.

Arizona Aviation Archaeology

www.aircraftarchaeology.com

Trey Brandt's excellent site on crash sites in Arizona features visits to a number of interesting wreck sites. Brandt is also the author of *Faded Contrails: Last Flights Over Arizona*, which can be ordered through the site.

Aviation Archaeological Investigation and Research (AAIR)

www.aviationarchaeology.com

Craig Fuller, a classically trained archaeologist, is the driving force behind Aviation Archaeology Investigation and Research, the best Internet site for ordering Army Air Force, Air Force, and Navy crash reports as well as Missing Air Crew Reports (MACRs). You can visit a number of crash sites virtually here as well.

Aviation Archaeology in Maine

www.mewreckchasers.com

Pete Noddin's Internet site is devoted to U.S. and Canadian aircraft crashes in Maine. Noddin reports that between 1919 and 1989 there were 741 military crashes in the state. His site features many of the crash sites in the state that have been investigated.

The Bent Prop Project

www.bentprop.org

Patrick Scannon, MD, Ph.D, has been traveling to the Palau Islands to search for downed aircraft and missing airmen from both sides of the conflict. Follow this outstanding work online.

Colorado Aviation Archaeology

www.coloradoaviationarchaeology.org

A sub-group of the Colorado Aviation Historical Society, this group sponsored the formation of the North American Institute of Aviation Archaeology (NAIAA), which is working to start a national organization to govern and develop standards for aviation archaeology.

Fatal Army Air Forces Aviation Accidents in the United States, 1941-1945

www.warbirdcrash.com

Anthony J. Mireles's site supports his comprehensive listing of more than 7,100 stateside accidents during World War II.

Lost Flights

www.lostflights.org

Author and wreckchaser Michael B. McComb's website features many of the aircraft crash sites he's found in the Southwestern United States. McComb is best known for his explorations of crashes in the Grand Canyon area, and one of his eight galleries is devoted to aircraft accidents in this area.

Oklahoma Wreckchasing

www.okwreckchasing.org

Jeff Wilkinson's Oklahoma Wreckchasing features a great, active message board as well as a virtual tour of many crash sites in Arkansas and Oklahoma.

Pacific Wrecks

www.pacificwrecks.org

Justin Taylan's online database lists aircraft crashes in the battlegrounds of the Pacific. Taylan has also produced a number of DVDs on these crashes, including the *Swamp Ghost* and the B-17 *Black Jack*, as well as his adventures on many of the islands. Also visit Taylan's sister site: www.pacificghosts.com

TIGHAR – The International Group for Historic Aircraft Recovery

www.tighar.org

TIGHAR is searching for a number of high-profile aircraft crashes including Amelia Earhart's, a TBD, and many others.

True Tales From Aviation History

www.donrjordan.com

Don Jordan's site that features stories of many of the aircraft crash sites that he's visited. Jordan is also coauthor, with G. Pat Macha, of the *Aircraft Wrecks in the Mountains and Deserts of Californi*a.

Wreckchasing

www.wreckchasing.com

This site was one of the first of the subject online in 1995 and features a very active message board full of tips, research information, and stories from people interested in the hobby.

X-Hunters Aerospace Archeology Team

www.thexhunters.com

Peter W. Merlin and Tony Moore have been exploring the deserts around Edwards AFB to honor those who perished while expanding the envelope of flight. Their website covers every type of experimental aircraft, from Flying Wings to Blackbirds to all of the downed X-planes. The duo has also written a book on the subject, which lists more than 500 aircraft crash sites in the Mojave Desert area.

Bibliography and Suggested Reading

Alexander, Sigmund Col. *B-47 Aircraft Losses*. Spiral bound and available direct from the author (12110 Los Cerdos St., San Antonio, TX 78233-5953); Newspaper clippings, reports, and photos of all B-47 losses. http://www.b-47.com/SAC%20Accidents.htm

Andrade, John M. U.*S. Military Aircraft Designations and Serials Since 1909*. Hinckley, Leics, Endland. Midland Counties Publications, 1979.

Bailey, Dan E. *World War II Wrecks of the Truk Lagoon*. Redding, California. North Valley Diver Publications. 2000.

_____. *WWII Wrecks of the Kwajalein and Truk Lagoons*. Redding, California. North Valley Diver Publications. 1989.

_____. *World War II Wrecks of Palau*. Redding, California. North Valley Diver Publications. 1991.

Bartelski, Jan. *Disasters in the Air: Mysterious Air Disasters Explained*. London. Airlife Publishing, Ltd. 2001.

Bradley, E. Philip with Richard F. Gaya Sr. *The Crash of Piedmont Flight 349 into Bucks Elbow Mt. as told by the Sole Survivor, E. Philip Bradley*. Available direct from the author: Philip Bradley, P.O. Box 3219, Monroe, NC 28111-3219

Brandt, Trey. *Faded Contrails: Last Flights Over Arizona*. Phoenix, Ariz. Acacia Publishers, 2003.

Cass, William F. *The Last Flight of Liberator 41-1133: The Lives, Times, Training and the Loss of the Bomber Crew Which Crashed on Trail Peak at Philmont Scout Ranch*. West Chester, Pennsylvania. The Winds Aloft Press. 1996.

Cole, Ben. *Four Down on Old Peachtree Road*. Suwanee, Georgia. Crosswind Publications, Ltd. 2007.

Darby, Charles. *Pacific Aircraft Wrecks ... And Where to Find Them*. Melbourne, Australia. Kookaburra Technical Publications Party Ltd., 1979.

Denham, Terry. *World Directory of Airliner Crashes: A Comprehensive Record of more than 10,000 Passenger Aircraft Accidents*. Somerset, England. Patrick Stephens Ltd., 1996.

Field, Andrew J. *Mainliner Denver: The Bombing of Flight 629*. Boulder, Colorado. Johnson Books. 2005.

Hayes, David. *The Lost Squadron: A Fleet of Warplanes Locked in Ice for 50 Years... Can They be Freed to Fly Again?* New York. Hyperion. 1994.

Hoffman, Carl. *Hunting Warbirds: The Obsessive Quest for the Lost Aircraft of World War II*. New York. Ballantine Books. 2001.

Imparato, Edward T. *Into Darkness: A Pilot's Journey Through Headhunter Territory*. Charlottesville, Virginia. Howell Press, Inc. 1995.

Job, Macarthur. *Air Disaster*. Weston Creek, Australia. Aerospace Publications Pty. Ltd. 1994. Volumes One through Four (published in 1995, 1996, 1999, and 2001 respectively).

Kearns, David A. *Where Hell Freezes Over: A Story of Amazing Bravery and Survival*. New York. Thomas Dunne Books (St. Martin's Press). 2005.

Macha, Gary Patric and Don Jordan. *Aircraft Wrecks in the Mountains and Deserts of California* (1909-2002, Third Edition). Lake Forest, CA. InfoNet Publishing, 2002.

Mann, Robert A. *Aircraft Record Cards of the United States Air Force (How to Read the Codes)*. Jefferson, North Carolina. McFarland & Co. Publishers, 2008.

Merlin, Peter W. & Moore, Tony. *X-Plane Crashes: Exploring Experimental, Rocket Plane, and Spycraft Incidents, Accidents and Crash Sites*. North Branch, Minnesota. Specialty Press, 2008.

Mireles, Anthony J. *Fatal Army Air Forces Aviation Accidents in the United States, 1941-1945* (three volumes). Jefferson, North Carolina. McFarland & Co. Publishers, 2006.

Page, Gordon. *Warbird Recovery: The Hunt for a Rare WWII Plane in Siberia, Russia*. New York. iUniverse. 2005.

Panas, Jr., John. *Aircraft Mishap Photography: Documenting the Evidence*. Ames, Iowa. Iowa State University Press. 1996.

Ralph, Barry. *The Crash of Little Eva: The Ultimate World War II Survivor Story*. Gretna, Louisiana. Pelican Publishing Co. 2004.

Serling, Robert J. *The Probable Cause… The Truth About Air Travel Today*. Garden City, New York. Doubleday & Co. 1960.

Sheehan, Susan. *A Missing Plane*. New York. G.P. Putnam's Sons. 1986.

Starks, Richard and Miriam Murcutt. *Lost in Tibet: The Untold Story of Five American Airmen, a Doomed Plane, and the Will to Survive*. Guilford, Connecticut. The Lyons Press. 2004.

Stekel, Peter. *Final Flight: The Mystery of a WWII Plane Crash and the Frozen Airmen in the High Sierra*. Berkeley, California. Wilderness Press. 2010.

Sturkey, Marion. *Mid-Air: Accident Reports and Voice Transcripts from Military and Airline Mid-Air Collisions*. Plum Branch, South Carolina. Heritage Press International. 2008.

Van Waarde, Jan. *US Military Aircraft Mishaps 1950-2004.* Schipol, The Netherlands. Scramble/Dutch Aviation Society. 2005.

Veronico, Nicholas A., et. al. *Wreckchasing: A Guide to Finding Aircraft Crash Sites*, Castro Valley, CA; Pacific Aero Press, 1992.

Veronico, N., Ed Davies, Donald B. McComb Jr., and Michael B. McComb. *Wreckchasing 2: Commercial Aircraft Crashes and Crash Sites*. Miami, FL. World Transport Press, 1996.

Widner, Robert. *Aircraft Accidents in Florida: From Pearl Harbor to Hiroshima*. Lulu.com. 2009.

Young, Cindy Lou. *Out of the Fog: Tragedy on Nantucket*. Alton, New Hampshire. Black Lab Publishing, LLC. 2008.

About the Authors

A. Kevin Grantham

A. Kevin Grantham of Frederick, Maryland is an aviation historian and enthusiast. Having been raised by a career Air Force family, his love for aviation began early. Although he is employed as an engineer by Lockheed-Martin, his second full-time job is researching, documenting, and photographing vintage aircraft. He is known in the aviation history arena as a P-38 expert, partly because of his book, *P-SCREAMERS: The History of the Surviving Lockheed P-38 Lightnings,* which lists the surviving Lockheed P-38 Lightnings along with interesting stories of how each aircraft has come to be where it is today. Grantham is currently working on the research for several other book projects including *The Cleveland National Air Races–The Post-War Years, The Brewster Aeronautical Story,* and a volume on the Fisher P-75 series of aircraft.

Ed Davies

A lifelong aviation enthusiast, Ed Davies became a "wreckchaser" many years ago, when a hiker brought in photograph of a portion of aircraft wing to co-author Nicholas A. Veronico's office. After digging deeper, it turned out to be the BCPA DC-6. From there, Davies was off to the wreck of the *Philippine Clipper* and many others. Davies says the research part of wreckchasing was fun, and the long, sometimes fruitless hikes were a challenge. Davies' new passion is researching the history of Boeing and the airmail. On many days he can be found deep in the archives of the Museum of Flight in Seattle.

Robert A. Kropp

Three decades after visiting his first airplane mishap in Arizona, researcher and historian Robert Kropp still seeks out lost and missing airplanes in his native state with his wife, children, and grandchildren. Retired from the newspaper and communications business, the former writer turned businessman splits his time between residences in Phoenix and Ash Fork, Arizona.

Donald B. McComb Jr.

Donald B. McComb Jr. is a lifelong aviation enthusiast who specializes in the study of commercial aviation accidents. He has been involved in locating, and visited crash sites in Arizona and California. His company, DBM AIRPART, restores aircraft instruments, instrument panels, and airframe components such as doors and fuselage sections for collectors and enthusiasts worldwide. When not working with aircraft parts, he can be found at local rifle and pistol ranges perfecting his shooting skills. Donald can be reached at aircrash@aol.com. He resides in Kendale Lakes, Florida.

Michael B. McComb

Michael B. McComb brings a background in archaeology to his writing, along with a zest for hiking to remote places, and experience as an airline transport pilot and air safety coordinator. A graduate of Embry Riddle Aeronautical University, the Flagstaff, Arizona resident has been involved with aviation archaeology since 1985. He has written feature articles for *Airways* and *Airliners Magazine,* the *Los Angeles Times* and the *Arizona Republic.* He currently works as chief pilot for a large air tour/charter company based at Grand Canyon, Ariz., and is among the very few people in the world who are type-rated and current as a captain in the Ford 5-AT Tri-Motor aircraft. His aviation archaeology website is www.lostflights.org

Thomas Wm. McGarry

The late Thomas Wm. McGarry (1948–2006) was an accomplished writer, aviation enthusiast, and a great friend. After serving with the 101st Airborne Division and the Sixth Special Forces Group in Vietnam, he earned a Scripps-Howard Foundation Scholarship and graduated from the University of Oregon's Allen School of Journalism. Subsequently, as a National Endowment for the Humanities Fellow, he also did postgraduate studies at Yale University. He worked in public relations and marketing in the healthcare industry and was a busy freelance writer contributing to such publications as the *Oakland Tribune, San Jose Mercury News, The Oregonian,* the *San Francisco Chronicle, Rotor & Wing,* Smithsonian *Air & Space, Air Classics, In Flight USA*, and many warbird publications. With R.E. "Bob" Baldwin he coauthored *Last Hope: The Blood Chit Story*, detailing the history of evasion aids used by downed airmen from the days of biplanes through the end of World War II.

Enrico Massagli

Aluminum began running through Enrico Massagli's blood when he first saw giant B-36s from Travis Air Force Base fly over the San Francisco Bay. He joined the Naval Air Reserve at 17 to have a chance to fly, which led to service on-board aircraft carriers during the Vietnam War. He holds a Masters of Science degree from the University of San Francisco and has worked in both the aerospace and telecommunications industries. Massagli was very involved in the *Philippine Clipper* wreck in the late 1980s and early 1990s, and now he is retired and living in New York state.

Nicholas A. Veronico

Nicholas A. Veronico is a science and technology writer who has written or co-authored more than two-dozen books on military, aviation, and local history subjects. He also served as the lead scriptwriter for *Scrapping Aircraft Giants*, a Daurg Productions documentary for the Discovery

Channel on commercial aircraft scrapping. Veronico became interested in aircraft crash sites in the late 1980s, and in 1995 introduced www.wreckchasing.com, one of the Internet's first websites devoted to aircraft crashes and the resources needed to locate them. Many of today's top aviation archaeologists, wreckchasers, researchers, and websites can trace their enthusiasm for the hobby to the books *Wreckchasing: A Guide to Finding Aircraft Crash Sites* and *Wreckchasing 2: Commerical Aircraft Crashes and Crash Sites*, which form the basis for the volume you are currently reading, For information on this other books, visit: www.pacaeropress.com

Walt Wentz

Walt Wentz was born in 1942, when the "Big War" was still going badly for the Allies. In his early youth, magazines, comic books, and cartoons were replete with pictures of wartime aircraft, and he naturally became fixated on such glamorous examples as the P-38, the B-17, and the Mustang. He met Sig Unander in the early 1980s when Unander came to the magazine where he worked, looking for publicity for his wreck searches. Intrigued, Wentz joined a trip to northern Idaho that resulted in an article titled, "Search for the Brown Lady." Later expeditions turned up fragments of an Airacobra in Oregon, another B-17 in the Blue Mountains, and a P-38 in a Washington wheat field.

7604863R0

Made in the USA
Charleston, SC
22 March 2011